THE CINEMA OF RUSSIA

AND THE FORMER SOVIET UNION

First published in Great Britain in 2007 by
Wallflower Press
6a Middleton Place, Langham Street
London W1W 7TE
Copyright © Birgit Beumers 2007

A catalogue record for this book is available from the British Library

ISBN 978-1-904764-98-4 (paperback)
ISBN 978-1-904764-99-1 (hardback)

Printed by Replika Pvt Ltd (India)

THE CINEMA OF
RUSSIA AND THE FORMER SOVIET UNION

EDITED BY

BIRGIT BEUMERS

WALLFLOWER PRESS LONDON & NEW YORK

24 FRAMES is a major new series focusing on national and regional cinemas from around the world. Rather than offering a 'best of' selection, the feature films and documentaries selected in each volume serve to highlight the specific elements of that territory's cinema, elucidating the historical and industrial context of production, the key genres and modes of representation, and foregrounding the work of the most important directors and their exemplary films. In taking an explicitly text-centred approach, the titles in this list offer 24 diverse entry-points into each national and regional cinema, and thus contribute to the appreciation of the rich traditions of global cinema.

Series Editors: Yoram Allon & Ian Haydn Smith

OTHER TITLES IN THE **24 FRAMES** SERIES:

THE CINEMA OF LATIN AMERICA *edited by Alberto Elena & Marina Díaz López*

THE CINEMA OF THE LOW COUNTRIES *edited by Ernest Mathijs*

THE CINEMA OF ITALY *edited by Giorgio Bertellini*

THE CINEMA OF JAPAN & KOREA *edited by Justin Bowyer*

THE CINEMA OF CENTRAL EUROPE *edited by Peter Hames*

THE CINEMA OF SPAIN & PORTUGAL *edited by Alberto Mira*

THE CINEMA OF SCANDINAVIA *edited by Tytti Soila*

THE CINEMA OF BRITAIN & IRELAND *edited by Brian McFarlane*

THE CINEMA OF FRANCE *edited by Phil Powrie*

THE CINEMA OF CANADA *edited by Jerry White*

THE CINEMA OF THE BALKANS *edited by Dina Iordanova*

THE CINEMA OF AUSTRALIA & NEW ZEALAND *edited by Geoff Mayer & Keith Beattie*

THE CINEMA OF NORTH AFRICA & THE MIDDLE EAST *edited by Gönül Dönmez-Colin*

FORTHCOMING TITLES:

THE CINEMA OF INDIA *edited by Lalitha Gopalan*

THE CINEMA OF GERMANY *edited by Joseph Garncarz*

THE CINEMA OF CHINA & SOUTH-EAST ASIA *edited by Ian Haydn Smith*

CONTENTS

INTERNATIONAL EDITORIAL BOARD

NOTES ON CONTRIBUTORS

ANTHONY ANEMONE is Associate Professor of Russian Language and Literature at the College of William and Mary in Williamsburg, Virginia, where he has taught courses in Russian and comparative literature and cinema since 1992. He currently teaches at the New School, New School. Educated at Columbia University and the University of California at Berkeley, he is a specialist in modern Russian literature and culture and the author of essays on a wide range of topics, including the Kunstkamera of Peter the Great in the eighteenth century, Leo Tolstoy, Daniil Kharms, Vladimir Nabokov and the filmmakers Aleksei Balabanov and Aleksei German. He is presently editing a collection of essays on terrorism and Russian culture.

BIRGIT BEUMERS is Reader in the Russian Department at Bristol University. She completed her D.Phil at St Antony's College, Oxford, and moved to Bristol in 1994. She specialises in her research on contemporary Russian culture, especially cinema and theatre. Her publications include *Yury Lyubimov at the Taganka Theatre 1964–1994* (1997), *Burnt by the Sun* (2000), *Nikita Mikhalkov: Between Nostalgia and Nationalism* (2005), *PopCulture: Russia!* (2005), and, as editor, *Russia on Reels: The Russian Idea in Post-Soviet Cinema* (1999). She is also editor of *Kinokultura* and *Studies in Russian and Soviet Cinema*, and is currently working on post-Soviet theatre and drama and on various aspects of contemporary culture in Russia.

PHILIP CAVENDISH is Senior Lecturer in literature and film studies at the School of Slavonic and East European Studies, University College London. His publications include a monograph on the Russian writer Evgenii Zamiatin (2000). He is currently researching the role of camera operators in the development of Soviet cinema. The first fruits of this research, an article entitled 'The Hand that Turns the Handle: Camera Operators and the Poetics of the Camera in Pre-Revolutionary Russian Film', appeared in *The Slavonic and East European Review* (April 2004).

IAN CHRISTIE is Anniversary Professor of Film and Media History at Birkbeck College, University of London, having previously taught at the universities of Oxford (1995–98) and Kent (1997–99), and is a Fellow of the British Academy. At the British Film Institute from 1976–96, he was responsible for directing distribution and exhibition, and launched video publishing. In 1999 he co-founded the new review *Film Studies*, now published by Manchester University Press.

He is the author and editor of many books on Russian, British and American cinema, including *The Film Factory* (1988) and *Eisenstein Rediscovered* (1993) (both with Richard Taylor), *Scorsese on Scorsese* (with David Thompson, 1989), and is Vice President of Europa Cinemas, an EU-funded organisation which supports exhibitors throughout Europe who show European films. He contributed to the BBC Radio 4 series on Russian music, *Playing Stalin's Tune*, has written a column on cinema for the Hermitage magazine and is one of the curators of the 2006 V&A exhibition 'Modernism: Designing a New World'.

DAVID GILLESPIE is Professor of Russian at the University of Bath, where he has taught Russian language, literature and film since 1985. His doctoral thesis on Soviet Russian village prose was completed at the University of Leeds, with much time spent at the Universities of Moscow and Leningrad. He has written books on the work of the Soviet writers Valentin Rasputin and Iurii Trifonov, and articles on Boris Mozhaev, Evgenii Popov and Vladimir Sorokin. He is the author of *Early Soviet Cinema: Innovation, Ideology and Propaganda* (2000) and *Russian Cinema* (2003). He is currently working on concepts of masculinity in Russian film, and the use of landscape in post-Soviet film.

STEPHEN HUTCHINGS is Professor of Russian at the University of Manchester. He is the author of monographs on Leonid Andreev (1990), *Russian Modernist Prose* (1997) and *Russian Literary Culture in the Camera Age: The Word as Image* (2004). He is also the co-editor, with Anat Vernitski, of *Russian and Soviet Film Adaptations of Literature, 1900–2001: Screening the Word* (2005), and has published numerous articles on Russian film, literature and culture. He currently holds an AHRC Research Grant to support a project investigating post-Soviet television culture. He was formerly Associate Professor of Russian at the University of Rochester, New York.

MARCIA LANDY is Distinguished Service Professor of English and Film Studies at the University of Pittsburgh and holds a secondary appointment in the French and Italian Department. She teaches courses in critical studies, film theory, history and film, and national cinemas (British and Italian). Her publications include *Fascism in Film: The Italian Commercial Cinema 1930–1943* (1986), *British Genres, 1930–1960* (1991), *Imitations of Life: A Reader on Film and Television Melodrama* (1991), *Film, Politics, and Gramsci* (1994), *Queen Christina* (with Amy Villarejo, 1995), *Cinematic Uses of the Past* (1996), *The Folklore of Consensus: Theatricality in*

Italian Cinema, 1930–1943 (1998), *Italian Film* (2000), *The Historical Film: History and Memory in Media* (2000), *Stars: The Reader* (with Lucy Fischer, 2003), and *Monty Python's Flying Circus* (2005). She is currently at work on a book-length study on Italian stars.

SUSAN LARSEN teaches courses on Russian literature, language and cultural history in the Department of German and Russian at Pomona College. Her previous publications include articles on Soviet theatre, contemporary Russian cinema and gender issues in Russian culture. She is presently completing a book on girls' culture entitled *Reading and Writing Girlhood in Russia, 1764–1917*.

DAVID MacFADYEN is Professor of Russian Language and Literature at the University of California, Los Angeles. He is the author of several books on Russian culture, including *Joseph Brodsky and the Baroque* (1998), *Joseph Brodsky and the Soviet Muse* (2000), *Red Stars* (2001), *Estrada?!* (2002), *Songs for Fat People* (2003), *The Sad Comedy of El'dar Riazanov* (2003), *Yellow Crocodiles and Blue Oranges* (2005) and *Russian Culture in Uzbekistan: One Language in the Middle of Nowhere* (2006). Currently he is finishing a book of essays on Anna Akhmatova for the National Library of Russia and an overview of Russian television series since the 1998 'default'.

RACHEL MORLEY is completing a PhD thesis at the School of Slavonic and East European Studies, University College London, on the representation of female performers in early twentieth-century Russian film and literature. She has published on gender relations in Evgenii Bauer's films and her article on Bauer's use of nineteenth-century Russian literary sources in his 1914 melodrama *Child of the Big City* appeared in *Russian and Soviet Film Adaptations of Literature, 1900–2001: Screening the Word* (2005).

KARLA OELER is Assistant Professor of Film Studies at Emory University. Her teaching and research focus on film theory and aesthetics, their history, and their intersection with philosophy, and literary theory. She is completing a book called entitled *A Grammar of Murder: Violent Scenes and Film Form*.

MIKE O'MAHONY is Lecturer in the History of Art department at the University of Bristol. He completed his PhD in 1998 at the Courtauld Institute of Art in London and specialises in visual culture in the Soviet Union, especially during the early Soviet and Stalinist eras. He has particular interests in cinema, painting, sculpture and the decorative arts, and has published articles on the Moscow metro and on the works of Aleksandr Deineka. He is the author of *Sport in the USSR: Physical Culture – Visual Culture* (2006) and the editor of the online journal *Art on the Line*.

ANDREI PLAKHOV graduated as a film critic at the Film Institute, VGIK. In 1978 he completed his dissertation on the role of history and myth in Visconti's films. He now works as a journalist for *Kommersant Daily*, but regularly contributes also to the film journals *Iskusstvo kino (Film Art)* and *Seans (Seance)*. From 1986 to 1990 he was secretary to the Filmmakers' Union and chairman of the 'conflict commission' that was in charge of un-shelving censored films. He is the author of several books on cinema and is an official selector for several international festivals. Since 2005 he has been president of the International Film Critics' Association (FIPRESCI).

ALEXANDER PROKHOROV teaches Russian culture and film at the College of William and Mary, Williamsburg, Virginia. He received his doctorate in Slavic Studies and PhD Certificate in Film Studies at the University of Pittsburgh. He has taught at Stetson University, as well as in Russia at Moscow State University. His publications include articles and reviews on Russian literature, cinema, visual culture and intellectual history in *Slavic Review, Slavic and East European Journal, KinoKultura, Dictionary of Literary Biography* and *The Routledge Encyclopedia of Contemporary Russian Culture* (2006).

ELENA PROKHOROVA is Visiting Assistant Professor at the College of William and Mary, Williamsburg, Virginia. She specialises in late Soviet and post-Soviet culture, film and the media. Her recent publications include articles in the *Slavic and East European Journal* and *Slavic Review* on serial television and national identity. Among her current projects is a study of Sergei Mikhalkov's poetry and plays for children.

NATASHA SYNESSIOS is a freelance writer and translator and specialist on the work of Andrei Tarkovskii. She is one of the translators of Tarkovskii's Collected Screenplays and the author of a 'KinoFile Film Companion' on the film *Mirror* (2001).

RICHARD TAYLOR is Emeritus Professor of Politics at Swansea University in Wales. He is the author of numerous articles and books on Soviet cinema, including *The Politics of the Soviet Cinema, 1917-1929* (1979), *Film Propaganda: Soviet Russia & Nazi Germany* (1998) and studies of

Eisenstein's films, *The Battleship Potemkin* (2000) and *October* (2002). He is also co-editor, with Ian Christie, of *The Film Factory: Russian & Soviet Cinema in Documents, 1896–1939* (1988, 1994), *Inside the Film Factory: New Approaches to Russian & Soviet Cinema* (1991, 1994) and *Eisenstein Rediscovered* (1993), and, with Derek Spring, of *Stalinism and Soviet Cinema* (1993). He has also edited and part-translated the five-volume British Film Institute edition of Eisenstein's writings in English and is General Editor of the KINO series of studies of Russian and Soviet Cinema for I.B. Tauris.

JOSEPHINE WOLL teaches Russian literature and film at Howard University in Washington DC and has written extensively on Soviet culture. Her most recent publications include 'The Russian Connection: Soviet Cinema and the Cinema of Francophone Africa', in *Focus on African Films* (2004), *The Cranes are Flying* (2003) and *Real Images: Soviet Cinema and the Thaw* (2000).

ACKNOWLEDGEMENTS

All photos are courtesy of *Iskusstvo Kino* archive, except those for *A Life for a Life* (British Film Institute), *Russian Ark* (Artificial Eye), *Brother* (CTB) and *House of Fools* (Venice Film Festival).

A note on transliteration: this follows the US Library of Congress system throughout the text and the bibliography in order to avoid confusion between 'academic' and 'user-friendly' transliterations systems.

The editor would like to thank Julian Graffy, who kindly and patiently discussed the possible inclusions and exclusions to the '24 Frames' included here, but is missed greatly as contributor to this volume; Richard Taylor for his support; Sergei Bodruv Sr for time to offer the preface during a busy shooting schedule; and Yoram Allon, editorial director of Wallflower Press, for venturing on the former Soviet territory with the series.

PREFACE

The role of Russian cinema today and the need for a volume of this kind on the history of Russian and Soviet cinema is not a simple or straightforward question. Sometimes I feel that film history is no longer important, because right now everything is starting all over again: there is a completely new cinema, and the old films and their history are vanishing from the horizon; and yet I also believe that real art never disappears and will always play an important role, even if only indirectly. The young generation knows neither the classics of cinema nor Soviet or Russian cinema history, and yet they get by without it. However, when you watch the works of young directors, you can see that they have a sound foundation; their work is not created in an empty space. Nothing can, in my view, grow on a dry spot or on rubbish: the soil must be fertile.

Soviet cinema was influenced strongly by those films of world cinema which filmmakers managed to see in the Soviet era, when access to foreign films was restricted. On the one hand, there were 'stolen' black-and-white prints; on the other, cultural exchange programmes facilitated the viewing of foreign films. Moreover, the influence of Russian and Soviet cinema in other countries should not be underestimated. The works of Sergei Eisenstein, Lev Kuleshov and Dziga Vertov definitely made a great impact. I think – and not just because I am an optimist – that we need film histories for film students and filmmakers alike, as well as those interested in other cultures.

Nowadays Russian cinema, not unlike American cinema, is less concerned with the national idea than, say, was the case for the work of Vasilii Shukshin in the 1970s. His films were sensational, because they were released in the deepest stagnation, set against the backdrop of propaganda cinema. People often tend to forget about these times when everything went against the official ethos. The state called for official propaganda films, and subjected cinema to censorship that was very harsh, much more rigid than in theatre or literature. After all, the scope of cinema was so much larger, because it had the potential to reach the masses, as Lenin had said: 'the most important of all arts is the cinema'. Therefore cinema was controlled very carefully. Nevertheless, many films were first completed and then shelved, such as those by the great filmmakers Larisa Shepit'ko and Elem Klimov. In literature, many writers managed to express their ideas between the lines; in cinema directors also found a way of expressing themselves in a manner to which the officials could hardly object. Audiences understood the irony right from the first film by El'dar Riazanov, *Beregis' avtomobilia* (*Beware of the Car*, 1966), but the censors had no ground for a challenge. The same also happened in literature, where a range of ironic texts were written. Serious writers had only two options: either they found a language that allowed them to hide their ideas in the text, using Aesopian language, or else they published in the West.

Censorship had a devastating effect. I am always stunned by comments that a real artist has to suffer, and that the more he suffers the better his work becomes. Take, for example, Marc Chagall: he suffered in Russia but not in France. Yet he remained Chagall. The lives of many filmmakers and painters were broken. If we compare Kazimir Malevich's 'The Black Square' with his paintings of the 1930s, we see that the later Malevich is a crippled artist, whose works bear hardly any resemblance to the earlier paintings. The great Andrei Tarkovskii had a number of film projects that remained unrealised, even if this is often forgotten. Ideological control is much more terrifying than commercial control. Commercial control can be comprehended: if you want to make expensive films, then you have to think about the audience that will have to pay for the tickets. Normally, you can ask for financial support or find sponsors. Under ideological constraints you are forced to make films to praise the Party, and that is really strange. The Soviet Union of the 1960s and 1970s sold cheap tickets to a large numbers of spectators for screenings in outdated cinemas; films were even shown to peasants in the fields with mobile projectors. The Soviet state spent money on film in order to reach the masses, but then that mechanism broke down, because nobody was interested in profit. The filmmaker would get a small bonus only if his film had over 60 million spectators, whereas theatre playwrights received royalties on the basis of the number of tickets sold. In cinema, the director got nothing and the money went back to the state.

With the 1990s came the illusion of freedom. A freedom granted to the people, not a freedom people had fought for. A freedom largely driven by economic considerations in the collapsing planned economy. For Mikhail Gorbachev it was easier to give people the right to speak, with glasnost, than to reorganise the economy. Nevertheless, people were impressed. For the first two years it was as though a radio station has been seized and everybody was shouting non-stop, worried they might be kicked out any minute. Then things turned really weird, when it transpired that you have to pay for that radio station. Freedom is expensive. First it cost nothing, and then things had a price in the market. In a free market nobody is obliged to give you money for films. You might borrow money, but the loan has to be repaid, and practically nobody was prepared for that situation.

Russian cinema in the 1990s went through a difficult period as it almost had to re-invent itself as an industry. None of the great Soviet masters of cinema has made a single successful film in the post-Soviet era. But Russia is a huge country, and talented people often emerge against all odds. A young generation of filmmakers came to the fore, including Sergei Selianov, Aleksandr Rogozhkin, Aleksei German Sr and Aleksandr Sokurov. The film *Brat* (*Brother*, 1997), produced by Selianov, is a landmark in film history, even if it is not quite my kind of film. I find it impressive partly for personal reasons, because I saw my son in a different light in this film: a hero who impressed millions of viewers. *Brother* also develops a new approach to cinema, despite the faults it may have. Sokurov is one of the most prolific filmmakers of Russian art-house cinema, although he could probably not have made his most recent films without the support from Germany, Japan and France. Unfortunately, Russian critics label his films as 'made for the West', but filmmakers really wish to tell a universal story, which is of interest not only for Russian audiences. Only commercial cinema can be made on special demand; art films cannot be created with the intent to please the West. No genuine artist can make such a claim. However, the label 'festival cinema' is frequently applied, since a festival is important for promotion and distribution of independent cinema especially, which always has a hard time whether it is made in America, Europe or Russia.

This volume covers the history of Soviet cinema. As a Russian proverb says, you cannot delete a line from the song. The honest propaganda cinema of Eisenstein, Pudovkin or the Vasil'ev Brothers was abandoned after the 1930s when films were made on the state's demand. Then there were the comedies of Riazanov and Leonid Gaidai, which made audiences laugh and became very popular, but were received warily by critics and officials. Laughter was not what the State wanted. Gaidai's films were not shown at festivals, and he never received a State Prize, but he was an honest artist loved by the people. At present, the hopes rest with the new generation that is only just surfacing and could not yet be represented in this volume: Andrei Zviagintsev with his debut *Vozvrashchenie* (*The Return*, 2003), Il'ia Khrzhanovskii with *4* (2004), and Boris Khlebnikov and Aleksei Popogrebskii with their debut film *Koktebel'* (*Roads to Koktebel*, 2003). Moreover, a new commercial trend is developing, represented by Fedor Bondarchuk's *Deviataia rota* (*Company 9*, 2005), or the films of Egor Konchalovskii which are essentially fine remakes of American action movies. Audiences like this new Russian cinema: *Nochnoi dozor* (*Night Watch*, 2004) and *Dnevnoi dozor* (*Day Watch*, 2006) are extremely interesting, because they represent a new genre for Russian cinema. It is quite appropriate that Timur Bekmambetov should now go to work in the United States.

Overall, Russia appears to be more of an Asian country than a European one. The major part of the population lives in Asia, the larger part of the territory is in Asia, together with the oil. Human psychology is more oriented towards Asia, which sometimes makes it difficult to comprehend. Kyrgyz and Kazakh cinema have always had a rich history, especially the Kazakh New Wave of the 1980s, those filmmakers who studied in Moscow and made a different kind of cinema when they returned to Kazakhstan. The film *Shizo* (2004), directed by Gulshat Omarova, which I produced, is an example of a new generation emerging in Kazakh film, a country with a stable economy. The film concerns themes that transgress national issues, because genuinely good cinema crosses borders. That, I think, is the main task of cinema.

Sergei Bodrov Sr
Moscow
January 2007

INTRODUCTION

Whenever scholars have written about Russian cinema, they have treated it as a cradle of cinematic art and experiment – even though the art itself was invented in France in 1896. Starting with the silent era, Russian cinematographers were at the forefront of discoveries in cinema, from Wladyslaw Starewicz and his experiments in animation, to Evgenii Bauer with his melodramas, from Sergei Eisenstein's montage theories to the 'Kuleshov' effect (Lev Kuleshov), from the eccentric dramas of the Leningrad FEKS (Factory of the Eccentric Actor, founded by Grigorii Kozintsev and Leonid Trauberg) to Dziga Vertov's documentaries. After the Revolution many filmmakers emigrated, influencing significantly both the cinema industry and film aesthetics in Europe and the US – a history that left its obvious traces on the names of the film studios of the time, such as the Ermolieff Studios in Paris, founded by Iosif Ermol'ev who had first worked for Pathé in Russia before emigrating to France to establish the studio that would later become Albatros Film, where legendary films starring Russian émigré actor Ivan Mozzhukhin were produced. Similarly, one could mention the fate of Fedor Otsep, co-writer of Iakov Protazanov's *Aelita* (1924), who worked in Germany and France before emigrating to North America in the 1930s. Indeed, Protazanov himself had also left Soviet Russia after the Revolution and made several films in Berlin and Paris before returning to the USSR.

In the 1920s, experiments in film art continued. While some directors returned from abroad, others (largely the former avant-garde) were eager to put their art and their skills at the service of the Revolution. The Soviet avant-garde was not only important in political terms in its own country, but also in aesthetic terms for world cinema. Its influence lay not only in practical matters, but also in the theories that were formulated by its chief exponents: Eisenstein's theories of montage and on the use of colour, Kuleshov's writings on acting techniques, Vertov's manifestoes on the function of the camera and the lens, or Grigorii Aleksandrov's ideas on the role of sound. Many of these documents are contained in the collection entitled *The Film Factory*, edited by Richard Taylor and Ian Christie in a pioneering move to make key texts available to non-Russian speakers.

If in the 1920s Western movies enjoyed great popularity among Soviet viewers, reflecting the intense interaction between European and Soviet artists and filmmakers, then in the

1930s, under Stalin, Soviet cinema was severed from Western developments. Nevertheless the Soviet musical tradition of Aleksandrov and Ivan Pyr'ev in the 1930s and 1940s, and El'dar Riazanov in the 1950s, stands in no way behind that of the Hollywood-produced musicals, albeit that these musicals remained largely hidden from the Western eye, even up to the present day (only few of the classical Soviet comedies and musicals are available with English subtitles, and 'popular' films have become the subject of scholarship only very recently). The Soviet musical was deemed to be a perfect tool for reaching the masses and wrapping an ideological message in an entertaining plot. Boris Shumiatskii, in charge of film production in the 1930s, stipulated the mass appeal the cinema should have ('cinema for the masses'), which destroyed with one stroke the eclecticism of artistic developments that had been possible under Lenin and had lasted until the late 1920s. At the same time, the constraints of Socialist Realism required filmmakers to varnish reality: to show reality in a positive light that would allow people to trace the path to the bright (communist) future – and they could hardly show the Soviet reality with its purges, collectivisation and famine.

After World War Two and the Cold War came the first the international success of Soviet cinema. War films, such as Mikhail Kalatozov's *Letiat zhuravli* (*The Cranes are Flying*, 1957), screened at the Cannes Film Festival in 1958, and it was followed by Grigorii Chukhrai's *Ballada o soldate* (*Ballad of a Soldier*, 1959) which screened at Cannes in 1960. The 'great' auteurs of Soviet cinema, albeit forbidden, censored and banned in their own country, made a name for themselves internationally: Andrei Tarkovskii, Kira Muratova and later Aleksandr Sokurov and Aleksei German Sr. The Socialist Realist hero, who represented entirely positive qualities and found himself on a path from good to perfect, was modified: the hero was endowed with human features and became an individual. Domestic settings took over from the public and political spaces that had dominated earlier films.

In this period, the film industries in the Soviet republics also blossomed, influenced by the great avant-garde filmmakers who had worked in cities such as Alma-Ata and Frunze, during the war's evacuation. The post-war period brought to the forefront the most talented and innovative directors: Tolomush Okeev and Bolat Shamshiev in Kyrgyzstan, Bolat Mansurov in Turkmenistan, Ali Khamraev and Shukhrat Abbasov in Uzbekistan, Shaken Aimanov in Kazakhstan, Tengiz Abuladze and Otar Ioseliani in Georgia and Sergo Parajanov in Georgia/Armenia. Many of the national film studios began to develop their own style, to tell their own (hi)stories ranging from epic to 'the Red western'. Russian and Soviet cinema ranked once again highly on the festivals circuit, and the Soviet art-house style was often associated with dissident voices because of the use of visual metaphors and an Aesopian language instead of simple and plain narratives. Soviet cinema became part of numerous film studies programmes all over the (not only English-speaking) world and assumed a solid position in written film histories.

The period of Stagnation of the 1970s was dominated by more commercial films, ranging from *Voina i mir* (*War and Peace*, 1965–67) to the epic depiction of contemporary life in *Moskva slezam ne verit* (*Moscow does not Believe in Tears*, 1979), and including mass entertainment such as Leonid Gaidai's comedies and television serials, such as the well-known spy thriller *Sem'nadtsat' mgnovenii vesny* (*Seventeen Moments of Spring*, 1971).

During the Gorbachev era of glasnost and perestroika, the international interest towards Soviet cinema was unprecedented: numerous films were shown on European television channels, from forbidden and unshelved films such as Tengiz Abuladze's *Monanieba* (*Repentance*, 1986), shedding a new light onto the horror of Stalin's purges, to new films by young directors, such as Rashid Nugmanov's *Igla* (*The Needle*, 1988) or Vasilii Pichul's *Malen'kaia Vera* (*Little Vera*, 1988), depicting the bleakness and hopelessness of modern life.

After the 'Soviet Spring' the interest in Russian cinema plummeted. If we consider the international releases of Russian films in the 1990s, it is obvious that only a few films entered the distribution network, and few of them represented new trends in Russian cinema. Sergei Bodrov Sr's *Kavkazskii plennik* (*The Prisoner of the Mountains*, 1996), Nikita Mikhalkov's *Utomlennye solntsem* (*Burnt by the Sun*, 1996), Pavel Chukhrai's *Vor* (*The Thief*, 1997), as well as all of Aleksandr Sokurov's films have been released internationally. Mikhalkov's *Sibirskii tsiriul'nik* (*The Barber of Siberia*, 1998) was released in the UK. Aleksei Balabanov's films *Brat* (*Brother*, 1997), *Pro urodov i liudei* (*Of Freaks and Men*, 1998) and *Brat-2* (*Brother 2*, 2000) had an international release. From the former Soviet republics, Darejan Omirbaev's *Killer* (*Tueur à gages*, 1998), co-produced with France, and his earlier films *Kairat* (1992) and *Kardiogramma* (*Cardiogram*, 1995) were released in France, and were followed by *Jol* (*The Road*, 2001). Serik Aprymov's *Konechnaia ostanovka* (*Terminus*, 1989) created furore in Rotterdam, and his subsequent *Tri brata* (*Three Brothers*, 2000) and *Okhotnik* (*The Hunter*, 2004) were picked up by small international distributors, while Aprymov himself found a co-producer in Japan. The Kyrgyz director Aktan Abdykalykov made his films *Beshkempir* (*The Adopted Son*, 1998) and *Maimil* (*The Chimp*, 2001) with French support. The Uzbek director and head of the country's studio Yusup Razykov's films were shown at small international festivals, as was the Kazakh film by Nariman Turebaev *Maneken pil* (*Malen'kie liudi/Little People*, 2003). From a politically-rocked Georgia, hardly any films entered the international festival circuit of distribution market, while Armenian films such as Albert Mkrtchian's *Urakh avtobus* (*The Merry Bus*, 2001) and Harutiun Khachatrian's *Vaveragrogh* (*The Documentarist*, 2003) have recently attracted the attention of festival selectors. A few Russian directors have been involved in co-productions: Sergei Bodrov Sr acquired experience in the US film industry before returning to work in Russia, and he has since collaborated on Regis Wargnier's *East West* (1999). His feature *The Quickie* (2001) was produced entirely in the US, while *The Bear's Kiss* (2002) was a European co-production; Bodrov is currently working on a project which is produced by the US, Germany and Russia, entitled *The Mongol*. Aleksandr Sokurov has worked for several years with a German producer and is frequently funded by Japanese sources. Kira Muratova works in Ukraine and enjoys support from the Ukrainian Culture Ministry.

After the collapse of the Soviet Union, Russian cinema has been the subject of many discussions and post-mortems. In the early 1990s, Russian cinema suffered from an artificial rise in production as a result of money-laundering, and while the number of completed films rose steadily, audiences disappeared completely from the crumbling movie theatres with poor projection facilities. Few new directors appeared on the billboards of festivals, not to mention film courses. Cinema art suffered from a lack of experimentation. But there was also another reason for the waning interest in Russia in general – Boris Yeltsin's Russia was, after all, a country in chaos and crisis – and Russian cinema in particular: for many years Western scholarship had focused on the 'auteurs' of Russian cinema, ignoring almost entirely the 'popular' strand of cinema, beginning with the musicals of the Stalin era that were rediscovered only in the last decade – and largely in Slavic, not film scholarship. In a new economy where cinema had turned into a branch of the industry that had to at least endeavour to stand on its own feet, Russian filmmakers were trying to find a connection with the audience – an audience that had deserted the auditoria with the result that many cinemas were closed. Filmmakers tried to develop an art-house language in a society that had neither time nor money for such an experiment, where cinema was becoming an industry rather than an art form, and which allowed only some established art-house directors to continue their searches and experiments with the medium. It is for this reason that names like Aleksei German Sr, Kira Muratova, Aleksandr Sokurov, Andrei Konchalovskii or Nikita Mikhalkov have remained at the forefront of festival attention, while only a few new directors have been able to launch their films on a large, international scale, and even these were mostly one-off appearances or, as in recent years, debut filmmakers (such as, for example, Andrei Zviagintsev or Il'ia Khrzhanovskii). Only independent studios like CTB, producing the works of Sergei Bodrov Sr and Aleksei Balabanov, can afford to finance more experimental films with the profits made on commercial projects, while other debuts are supported by the Federal Agency for Cinematography and Culture. In the mid-1990s, the number of films produced had plummeted to an all-time low. Cinemas were closed and Russian features could be viewed only at the 'Kinotavr' Open Russian Film Festival in Sochi, which became a showcase for the national film scene.

The Russian film industry landed back on its feet after 2000, when the film market had restructured itself. It now has a proper distribution and theatre network with numerous distributor-owned multiplexes across the larger cities, such as Moscow, St Petersburg and Ekaterinburg. In January 2004 *Screen Daily* published figures that inspired confidence: after an increase in box office grossing of $112 million in 2002 the Russian film market had seen an increase of 70 per cent to $190 million for 2003. The prediction for 2004 at this point was an estimated $250 million. Russia is thus set to become the sixth-highest grossing cinema market in 2007, with an estimated $400 million, whilst ticket prices reached $11 (compared to the average ticket price in the US of $2.6). These figures make the Russian film market a considerable player in world cinema distribution, a fact that is assisted by the steady growth of the number of cinemas and multiplexes in cities. A nine-screen multiplex ('Formula Kino') opened in central Moscow in 2002, after prolonged building work in front of Kursk railway station, while 'Kino Star De Luxe' opened in September 2003, offering 3,100 seats in eleven cinemas. The nine-screen multiplex 'Cinema Park' opened in January 2004 with 1,186 seats, and the multiplex 'October' on New Arbat opened after more than ten years of reconstruction in September 2005. Russian cinema has become an industry that functions well within its own country, and that is able to attract audiences at home. Slowly but steadily it also ventures onto the European, and even world, market. The number of Russian films with international release is rising: In the autumn of 2005 alone three Russian films were released in the UK: Il'ia Khrzhanovskii's *4*, Aleksandr Sokurov's *Solntse* (*The Sun*) and Timur Bekmambetov's blockbuster *Nochnoi dozor* (*Night Watch*).

By 2005 the Russian film market had not only turned into a serious player in the distribution network for American and foreign films, but has also revived its own film industry, capable of producing blockbusters with a box office that ranks them in the top twenty of world box office grossing according to *Screen International*; this has been the case for blockbusters like *Night Watch* or *Turetskii gambit* (*Turkish Gambit*, 2005). The film industries in Kazakhstan, Kyrgyzstan and Uzbekistan also dispose of an excellent infrastructure and of a competitive national film industry. However, the Caucasus republics, which boasted in the Soviet days of a thriving film industry and created a highly poetic cinematic language, are struggling to survive. Hay-Film, the Armenian studio in Erevan, is ill-equipped for film production and instead recently closed down. The Baltic states, on the other side, have integrated extremely well into European structures and are able to benefit from European funding initiatives.

Russian cinema has shifted across its hundred-year history from French imports to émigré cinema, from isolation to withdrawal and dissidence, from stagnation and commercialisation to a political and economic tool, down to a proper industry where commercial and art house film co-exist. The selection of films in this volume attempts to reflect these movements of Russian cinema, between commerce and art, and from conservative support to rebellious challenge of the status quo. While many other volumes in the *24 Frames* series begin by defining their regional focus, the region of this volume is, in many ways, historically pre-determined. The Soviet Republics were 'cinefied' only in the 1930s, and the first national films were made largely after the war. The Kyrgyz studio was used in the 1940s for chronicles and produced the first feature in 1955; the Kazakh studio was established in 1925 and completed its first feature in 1954; Uzbekfilm was founded in 1924 and the first Uzbek films appeared as early as the 1930s; the Tajik and Turkmen studios were set up in the late 1920s and early 1930s, and immediately started producing their own feature films. All the regional film production fell neatly into the Soviet era.

It is for this reason that the volume follows the chronology of cinematic history. Considering regional structures of the post-communist world, the Baltic states are not covered in this volume because their cinematographies were not strong under Soviet rule, while today they clearly form part of European tradition. The cinemas of Central Asia, on the other hand, have always had strong links with Soviet culture and history, and although they may occasionally reveal a greater affinity with the poetic cinema of Iran or Turkey than with European-oriented Russian films, they are an integral part of Soviet cinema. Moreover, the special role that the Caucasus played is represented through two films in this volume. Ukraine is also represented through its most significant director, Aleksandr Dovzhenko. I have selected here those films that had an impact on Soviet or world cinema.

In the selection of films, I have tried to cover the former Soviet republics – if not all of the fifteen republics, then at least those with a significant film industry – and the most important directors. However, instead of choosing the best-known films, many of which have been written about extensively in journals and separate book-length companions, I have selected lesser-known films. Thus, I have chosen Eisenstein's *Stachka* (*The Strike*, 1924) instead of the 'usual suspects', such as *Bronenosets Potemkin* (*The Battleship Potemkin*, 1925), *Oktiabr'* (*October*, 1928) or *Ivan Groznii* (*Ivan the Terrible I* (1944) and *II* (1946, released in 1958)); for Tarkovskii his first feature film *Ivanovo detstvo* (*Ivan's Childhood*, 1962) is included here rather than the better-known *Andrei Rubliov* (*Andrei Rublev*, 1966) or *Zerkalo* (*Mirror*, 1975). At the same time I have tried to include both internationally well-known directors and films as well as national cult figures and features, such as Grigorii Aleksandrov's *Veselye rebiata* (*The Happy Guys*, 1934), El'dar Riazanov's *Karnaval'naia noch'* (*Carnival Night*, 1956) or Leonid Gaidai's *Brilliantovaia ruka* (*The Diamond Arm*, 1969). The national cinemas are representated through Dovzhenko's *Zemlia* (*Earth*, 1930) a classic film that is extremely important for the development of cinema language in Soviet Russia at the time; through Sergo Parajanov's *Nran guyne* (*The Colour of Pomegranates*, 1969) and Otar Ioseliani's *Iko shashvi mgalobeli* (*Zhil pevchii drozd*/*Lived Once a Song-Thrush*, 1970), which are both easily available and represent the early work of both directors; through one of Kira Muratova's early films made at Odessa film studios; and through Rashid Nugmanov's *Igla* (*The Needle*, 1988), a cult film for the 'new wave' of Kazakh cinema that emerged in the late 1980s. I have included an international co-production by Andrei Konchalovskii, which is not only a good example of his work, but moreover offers a deep insight into the conflict in Chechnya that also lies at the heart of Bodrov's anti-war film, *The Prisoner of the Mountains*. Silent cinema and musical comedy, art-house experiments and popular cinema have been explored here, as well as animation, which is represented by Iurii Norshtein's *Skazka skazok* (*Tale of Tales*, 1980). No documentary is included in this volume, however: the obvious film would have been Dziga Vertov's *Chelovek s kino-apparatom* (*Man with a Movie Camera*, 1929) which has been the subject of a number of book-length studies. Instead *Aelita* has been selected here to represent the close collaboration between various artistic disciplines, characteristic of the 1920s avant-garde.

The selection is also representative of the social and political developments of the twentieth century. In the following I offer a narrative that aims to link the chapters of this collection to form a (hi)story of Soviet and Russian cinema.

Zhizn' za zhizn' (*A Life for a Life*, 1916) is a film of the pre-Revolutionary era and Evgenii Bauer one of the key directors of this period. The film deals with the theme of social conventions that cripple man, a theme that ties in well with the Revolutionary movement. Kuleshov's *Neobychainye prikliucheniia Mistera Vesta v strane bol'shevikov* (*The Extraordinary Adventures of Mr West in the Land of the Bolsheviks*, 1924) offers a view of Russia as seen by the West, mocking the prejudices of the visitor vis-à-vis a socialist country. In this sense, it taps into the propagandist mode of the early 1920s. *Aelita* represents the avant-garde and the merger of artistic disciplines for the creation of a visually stunning sci-fi world. And finally, *The Strike* was commissioned by the state. It is the clearest example from this period of film putting itself at the service of the Revolution and its power to manipulate history. These first four films trace the Revolutionary movement and reveal filmmakers' sensitivity and suscep-tibility to social injustice, which ultimately made them put their art at the service of political ideals.

The Stalinist era (1930s–1953) is represented in the volume through *Earth*, a film that dwells upon the poeticism of the cinematic image and is set in the countryside, foreboding the concern with provincial life in the 1960s. *Chapaev* (1934) is a classic propaganda film, which operates extremely well within the parameters of Socialist Realism: it shows the simple man's potential to become a socialist hero. *The Happy Guys*, with its musical reference to the Soviet Union being superior to the West, also echoes the increasing isolation of Soviet cinema. The film is also characteristic of its epoch in emphasising the central role of Moscow, a feature that dominated in Stalinist geopolitics. The 1940s are not directly covered in this volume, although any film by Grigorii Aleksandrov or Ivan Pyr'ev could have been chosen to represent the war years, making same points as the musical comedy *The Happy Guys*. There are also no films that glorify Stalin and justify his role as political dictator (such as *Ivan the Terrible*), but once again, there are two separate studies written just on this film.

The Thaw (1956–1964) made films such as *Carnival Night* possible. It is another musical, prolonging the tradition of mass entertainment begun in the 1930s, but has a romantic plot that juxtaposes the bureaucrat and the individual, the political and the private. Ultimately, the private side wins: the emphasis is shifted from state and society to the individual. A similar pattern can be discerned in *The Cranes are Flying*, where the loss of happiness for Boris and Veronika weighs more than the victory in the war. Likewise, in *Ballad of a Soldier* the loss of the son overrides the fact that Alesha is a hero who has knocked out four tanks single-handedly. And in *Ivan's Childhood*, too, the individual and his loss are the dominant theme. The Thaw has turned the hero back to an individual human being, placing humanist values before ideological concerns.

During the Stagnation (1964–82) under the regime of Leonid Brezhnev many films were banned (especially in the late 1960s), among them several showing village life in a negative light (such as *Asino schast'e* (*Asya's Happiness*, 1967) by Andrei Konchalovskii). However, Vasilii Shukshin's *Kalina Krasnaia* (*Red Guelderbush*, 1973), based on a village prose text and showing the isolation of the countryside, was released in this time and enjoyed popularity. Muratova's *Korotkie vstrechi* (*Brief Encounters*, 1967) is also set in the provinces, dealing with the personal life of a vagrant geologist and a city bureaucrat, whose relationship suffers from her predicament to play a strong and decisive role in Soviet society, which proves incompatible with the role of a submissive and caring housewife. Muratova's experiment with flashbacks to restructure the temporal flow of the film is also indicative of the period that suffers from a fragmentation of time, sensing the disruption of a continuous historical development through revolutions and wars.

The Colour of Pomegranates and *Lived Once a Song-Thrush* are examples of Georgian cinema that reached the peak of its popularity among dissident and intellectual audiences in the 1960s, especially because of the metaphors it employed to hide dissident views (the use of the so-called Aesopian language). The gangster comedy *The Diamond Arm*, on the other hand, was a blockbuster with 76 million viewers. Nikita Mikhalkov's directorial debut *Svoi sredi chuzhikh, chuzhoi sredi svoikh* (*At Home Among Strangers, A Stranger at Home*, 1974) is a Soviet western ('Red western', or 'eastern'), a genre that also enjoyed huge popularity at the time, if we think only of Vladimir Motyl's hit *Beloe solntse pustiny* (*White Sun of the Desert*, 1969). Vladimir Men'shov's *Moscow Doesn't Believe in Tears* was not only a blockbuster at home but also internationally, winning the Academy Award for Best Foreign-Language Film in 1980. The epic tale of three women in post-war Soviet Russia breaks with Socialist Realist convention in its honest portrayal of the problems of the modern world (alcoholism, single motherhood, complacency), but it also remains safely within the conventions, making happiness a reward for a positive social contribution.

Animation played an important role in the Soviet film industry, and was centralised through the studio Soiuzmul'tfil'm (established in 1936). The studio produced numerous animated films for children, using both puppet and drawn animation. This volume covers the masterpiece of animation by Iurii Norshtein, which was voted the 'best animation of all time' by a critics' poll. It is unconventional in the story it tells and pioneering in the techniques it uses.

The Gorbachev era (1985–1991) was characterised on the one hand by the release of films that had previously been banned and by encouraging films to be made that told the 'truth' about the (Stalinist) past. *Moi drug Ivan Lapshin* (*My Friend Ivan Lapshin*) is an example of this. Made in 1984 and released only under Gorbachev, Aleksei German Sr's film reassesses the Stalinist era and the period (1934) that represented the last hope that the Revolution could keep its promises, before that hope was annihilated by the purges. On the other hand, a number of new, young filmmakers appeared who broke with the positive portrayal of reality and showed the despair, meaninglessness and bleakness of life in Russia. *Little Vera* was one such film, another is the Kazakh feature *The Needle* (which represents also the Kazakh 'new wave') that spoke of the disheartened youth who seeks to escape from a society that cripples their aspirations: the time for change has come.

The post-Soviet period is represented by four films which were made by directors of different backgrounds, but dealing with similar themes. Bodrov Sr is a director who had gained his experience as scriptwriter in Kazakhstan and as director in the US and Europe before making *The Prisoner of the Mountains*, a film dealing with the Chechen war. The same theme is also explored in Andrei Konchalovskii's *Dom durakov* (*House of Fools*, 2002) made after the director's return from his emigration to America in the 1980s. It seems that both directors are shocked by the war they find raging in their own country after a period of absence, a war against an ethnic group that was once part of the Soviet empire. *Brother* is made by a young director, representative of a new generation, who creates a new hero. This protagonist too suffers from disorientation, both physically and morally. Aleksandr Sokurov's work had been suppressed in the 1980s, but in post-Soviet Russia he became one of the most articulate and prolific filmmakers. In *Russkii kovcheg* (*Russian Ark*, 2002) he reassesses Russian history, condensing entire centuries into a 90-minute single-track shot captured on digital media. The camera races through the Hermitage Museum, catching sight of historical figures and paintings in search for Russia's national identity that lies somewhere between Europe and Asia. All these four films ponder upon the issue of Russia's identity and seek an answer to the question: who is Russia? And what was the Soviet Union? At least 24 different answers to this question are contained in this volume.

Birgit Beumers

ZHIZN' ZA ZHIZN' A LIFE FOR A LIFE

EVGENII BAUER, RUSSIA, 1916

Since the rediscovery of his films at the Eighth Festival of Silent Cinema in Pordenone, Italy, in 1989, the pre-Revolutionary Russian director Evgenii Bauer (1867–1917) has come to be seen not only as the major filmmaker of his era but also as a figure of fundamental importance in the history and development of Russian and Soviet film and world cinema. A student of the Moscow College of Painting, Sculpture and Architecture, Bauer had worked as a portrait photographer and was already well-known as a theatre set designer when he entered cinema in 1912, as scenic director on Drankov and Taldykin's *Trekhsotletie tsarstvovaniia doma Romanovykh* (*The Tercentenary of the Rule of the House of Romanov*, 1913). Bauer worked as a director both for them and for Pathé before joining Aleksandr Khanzhonkov's company at the end of 1913, where he remained until his untimely death in 1917. Bauer quickly rose to become Khanzhonkov's leading director and was, reputedly, the most highly-paid in Russia. Despite the brevity of his cinematic career, Bauer's output was prodigious. He directed at least 82 films, of which 26 are known to be extant, including his debut for Khanzhonkov, *Sumerki zhenskoi dushi* (*Twilight of a Woman's Soul*, 1913) and *Korol' Parizha* (*The King of Paris*, 1917), the film on which he was working at the time of his death. The number and range of Bauer's surviving films make it possible for the modern viewer both to acquire a sense of the recurrent features of style and theme that make a 'Bauer film' instantly recognisable and to trace the development of his artistic and thematic concerns.

Released on 10 May 1916 and also known as *Za kazhduiu slezu po kaple krovi* (*A Tear for Every Drop of Blood*) and *Sestry-sopernitsy* (*The Rival Sisters*), *Zhizn' za zhizn'* (*A Life for a Life*) is a key late Bauer film. It was conceived with definite and ambitious aims, both commercial and artistic. Envious of the popular and critical success enjoyed by the rival film company Ermol'ev, Khanzhonkov instructed Bauer to create a masterpiece which would, as he recalled in a 1937 interview, 'stagger the cinema world' and enhance the reputation of his company. From the scenarios offered to him, Bauer chose an adaptation of *Serge Panine* (1881), a bestselling but critically denigrated novel by the popular French writer Georges Ohnet (1848–1918). No expense was spared in the making of the film and Bauer made full use of Khanzhonkov's technological and material resources, even insisting that one of his studios – already the largest in Moscow – be extended to accommodate his ambitious set designs. He also selected an all-star cast: Vera Kholodnaia (1893–1919), 'Queen' of the pre-Revolutionary screen and the only major star of this period to begin her acting career in the cinema, in Bauer's *Pesn' torzhestvuiushschei liubvi* (*Song of Triumphant Love*, 1915, not preserved); Lidiia Koreneva (1885–1982), a respected actress from the Moscow Art Theatre; Vitol'd Polonskii (1879–1919), a 'King' of the screen whose 'aquiline nose' and 'regular features' embodied the epitome of male beauty of that era; Ivan Perestiani (1870–1959), the future Soviet actor, director and lecturer in film; and Ol'ga Rakhmanova (?–1943), a revered actress who turned to directing after Bauer's death, completing for him *The King of Paris*.

A Life for a Life tells the story of two young women, Musia (Koreneva) and Nata (Kholodnaia). Although they are brought up as sisters by Khromova (Rakhmanova), a millionaire factory owner and businesswoman, only Musia is Khromova's natural daughter; Nata is adopted. Both young women fall in love with the same man - the handsome Prince Bartinskii (Polonskii), to whom Zhurov (Perestiani), a rich merchant friend of Khromova, introduces them – but it is Nata who catches Bartinskii's eye. Zhurov, himself besotted with the beautiful Nata, dissuades Bartinskii from marrying her: Nata has no dowry, but Musia is worth millions. Beset by gambling debts, Bartinskii asks for Musia's hand. When Khromova sees how Musia adores Bartinskii, she accepts his proposal, against her better judgement. The devastated Nata agrees to become Zhurov's wife out of spite and the sisters are married in an extravagant double ceremony. After the wedding Nata confides in Khromova, confessing her affair with Bartinskii and revealing that he has married Musia for her money. Reminding Nata of how much she owes her, Khromova instructs her to forget Bartinskii and to do nothing to destroy Musia's happiness.

Months pass. Bartinskii does not modify his bachelor lifestyle. Neglecting his new wife, he spends his time gambling away her dowry, returning home late and impatiently dismissing Musia's tears. When the family gathers to celebrate Khromova's birthday Nata and Bartinskii resume their affair, with a passionate kiss that is witnessed by Musia. Too proud to confront her husband and sister, Musia suffers in silence.

In an unexpected twist to the plot, Zhurov discovers that Bartinskii has forged his signature on some promissory notes. When he subsequently learns from Khromova of his affair with Nata, Zhurov threatens murder but he proves unable to carry out his threat and instead reports Bartinskii's fraud to the police, demanding his arrest. His resolve again weakens, however, when Nata, at Musia's request, asks him to drop the charges. At this point, when it seems Bartinskii may escape without punishment, Khromova steps in. Anxious to protect her daughter, her fortune and her family name, she urges Bartinskii to do the honourable thing and kill himself. Bartinskii merely laughs at her suggestion; in this he underestimates Khromova's resolve and strength of feeling, for she takes his gun and shoots him herself, placing the gun in his hand so his death looks like suicide.

In *A Life for a Life*, Bauer embraces the well-worn sensationalism and emotionalism of the popular melodrama, with its villains and victims, high passion, unrequited love, life-threatening despair, adultery, jealousy, fury, revenge, murder and – most important in the Russian context – a tragic ending; Russian audiences' liking for tragic endings was so pronounced that they became known as 'Russian endings'. Not surprisingly, the film proved enormously popular with contemporary audiences – it was shown at a Khar'kov cinema for twelve consecutive days, at that time the longest ever uninterrupted run. It also found almost universal favour with reviewers: *Teatral'naia gazeta* (*Theatre Gazette*) proclaimed it 'a monumental picture'; *Kine-zhurnal* (*Cine-Journal*) declared it 'an undoubted artistic treasure' and praised the intelligent directing; Valentin Turkin, writing in *Pegas* (*Pegasus*), judged it Bauer's best film; even Khanzhonkov's rival, Ermol'ev, praised *A Life for a Life* in his journal *Proektor* (*Projector*), pronouncing it 'a film that deserves a place alongside the best foreign productions'. Bauer had realised Khanzhonkov's hopes.

Although Bauer's genius was recognised by his contemporaries, his films fell from favour after the 1917 Revolution, for both ideological and aesthetic reasons. Not until the Thaw did Soviet film historians attempt a reappraisal of Bauer's films. Although they admired his artistic and technical skill, however, they were critical of Bauer's choice of themes and scenarios, including that of *A Life for a Life*.

Since the recent retrospective, Bauer has received critical attention from various quarters, with *A Life for a Life* regularly singled out for particular comment. The film is frequently cited as the quintessential example of Bauer's consummate technical and artistic expertise: commentators draw attention to the enormous scale and opulence of the set designs, to the atmospheric lighting, to Bauer's innovative use of montage, crosscutting, parallel editing and tracking shots. The film has also been discussed as a vehicle for Vera Kholodnaia.

The early 1990s also saw the publication of several Western feminist responses to the films shown at the retrospective, including those by Mary Ann Doane, Miriam Hansen, Heide Schlüpmann and Jane Gaines. While they all discuss Bauer, only Gaines focuses on

A Life for a Life, considering Bauer's apparent reluctance to approach the actions of his female protagonists, and especially of Khromova, from a moral perspective. More recently, several American socio-cultural historians with an interest in the popular culture of early twentieth-century Russia have written about Bauer, approaching his films first and foremost as 'cultural documentation' that can shed new light on the dominant ideologies – political, cultural and social – of the time. Denise Youngblood provides a synopsis of *A Life for a Life* on the grounds that it is representative of the typical 'murder and mayhem' plots enjoyed by pre-Revolutionary audiences. She also analyses it from a thematic perspective, considering what it says about class conflict at this time. Louise McReynolds focuses on Bauer's presentation of gender relations and considers how, through its exaggerated/melodramatic but still recognisably contemporary presentation of the male and female protagonists' 'struggles' with each other, this film might have affected and influenced the sense of self of the ordinary members of the audience. A discussion of the theme of gender relations in sixteen films by Bauer, including *A Life for a Life*, has also recently been published; its focus is Bauer's use of specifically cinematic means in his exploration of his theme, but it also considers the films in the context of the contemporary social, artistic and cultural landscape.

The following analysis of *A Life for a Life* will similarly pay particular attention to the film's cinematic language, in order to convey a sense of Bauer's distinctive directorial style, which is highly visual and heavily reliant on the expressive properties of all aspects of *mise-en-scène*. Concerned to overcome the flatness of the cinema screen, Bauer enhanced the depth and stereoscopic quality of his sets by using carefully-placed columns, furniture, curtains, partition walls or plants to divide the space into different planes. His sets are so distinctive that the Soviet avant-garde director Lev Kuleshov, who in 1917 worked as art director on several Bauer films, talks of 'the Bauer method' of set building. Although no doubt partly intended as impressive backdrop, Bauer's sets and the objects he places within them are always more than mere ornament and function to highlight aspects of character and theme. Bauer's actors, too, are deliberately costumed and carefully positioned, in relation both to the camera and to each other. Bauer also experiments with lighting, camera angle, types of shot and ingenious ways of making his camera mobile. Again, however, technical innovation is never simply to impress, but always contributes to mood, characterisation and theme. The starting point for this reading of *A Life for a Life* therefore sees Bauer's *mise-en-scène* – the 'look' of the film – as functioning to provide the viewer with an important interpretative key.

A Life for a Life is, in many respects, firmly anchored in early twentieth-century Russian life. Bauer's themes are topical. The villain of the piece – Prince Bartinskii – is a member of the nobility. Explicitly introduced as 'a carouser and a spendthrift', Bartinskii is shown to lead an idle life of self-indulgence. On one level, he is contrasted negatively with two hard-working and sober merchants: Zhurov and Khromova who, an intertitle informs us, 'spends a great deal of time in her office'. This comparison expresses in miniature the shift that was taking place in Russian society at this time, with the falling aristocracy losing its place in society to the industrious mercantile class. Moreover, with their grandiose columns and high ceilings, the characters' spacious Moscow houses reflect the contemporary taste for the newly-revived neo-classical style of 'big' architecture made popular in Russia in the 1910s by the architect Fedor Shekhtel' (1859–1926), with whom Bauer had studied. Their homes are also filled with the accoutrements of modern urban life – telephones, newspapers, clocks, electric lamps – while Musia and Bartinskii leave for their honeymoon by train and Nata, anticipating the heroines of *film noir*, travels to her adulterous assignations with the Prince in a motor car.

Bauer's set designs are neither as naturalistic nor as contemporary as they first appear, however, for in them the salient features of the neo-classical architectural style are exaggerated. Indeed, a contemporary reviewer was amused by Bauer's 'excessive love' of columns, observing wryly: 'Columns, columns and more columns … Columns in the drawing-room, by the fire in the office, columns here, there and everywhere.' Moreover, other details of Bauer's opulent sets situate the characters in a very different era, for they are also surrounded by artefacts which belong more to the classical age than to early twentieth-century Moscow. In Khromova's drawing room, on either side of each door, stand busts on marble pillars; ornate candlesticks abound; the hothouse garden is filled with statues and on one wall is a shining mosaic of a Greek youth; the telephone shares the office desk with miniature urns and classical figurines. The life-size statues that line Zhurov's entrance hall are similar to the miniatures on Khromova's desk and he has what appears to be a large model of a Greek temple next to his desk. Even Bartinskii's more sparsely furnished home contains a frieze depicting classical scenes of olive trees, toga-clad youths, urns and griffin-like creatures. Moreover, Bartinskii gambles away Musia's dowry at harness races, a modern-day equivalent of the chariot races that entertained the ancient Greeks and Romans.

This classical context is given additional reality during the sequence in which Nata first visits Bartinskii. His clichéd 'chat up line' – 'Do you believe in reincarnation? It seems to me that we loved each other many centuries ago' – is followed by an extravagant enactment of this fantasy about their previous affair that transports them back in time to the classical world. Here Bartinskii, like the youths in his frieze, is dressed in a toga and he watches as Nata, wearing long robes, drapes herself languorously over an exedra in a bower decorated with marble columns and urns. In all its details this scene recalls the contemporary paintings of Sir Lawrence Alma-Tadema (1836–1912), famous for depicting 'Victorians in togas'.

These details of *mise-en-scène* are neither superfluous nor gratuitous. Through the clash of cultures, the collision of contemporary and classical that is embodied concretely in the *mise-en-scène*, Bauer gives visual expression to the clash between the temperaments and sensibilities of his male and female protagonists. One of Bauer's main themes – here and in other films – is relationships between men and women and, specifically, their different approaches to love. Bauer suggests that the male protagonists see love, or at least marriage, in practical terms, as a financial arrangement to be brokered between men, rather than an emotional union that recognises equally the wishes of both partners. When Zhurov and Bartinskii meet to discuss their marriage plans, Bartinskii decides not to marry Nata, whom he appears to love, because, as Zhurov reminds him, 'She's adopted and has no money.' Musia is a much better match, as '[she] can net you a million'. For both men a wife is a commodity that can be bargained over and bought. Thus, Zhurov promises to help Bartinskii secure Musia's hand on the condition that the Prince help him to secure Nata's, and the two men then shake hands three times, as if concluding a business transaction. Both young women accept unquestioningly the men's materialistic approach. When Nata attempts to dissuade Bartinskii from marrying Musia, she does so by insisting 'I do have money'; unfortunately, as Bartinskii informs her, she does not have enough. Likewise, Musia, distraught at her husband's growing indifference, attempts to win his affection by granting him unrestricted access to her money, thus relinquishing one of the few rights married women had in early twentieth-century Russia, that of retaining control over the property they owned before marriage.

In contrast to this calculating and materialistic male attitude, the young women are shown to experience love as an all-consuming passion, stronger than logic or reason. The love-struck Musia declares that, if Bartinskii were to stop loving her, she would die. Indeed, this prediction seems destined to be fulfilled, for on learning of her husband's unfaithfulness, Musia falls ill. Her love is stronger than her sense of dignity and she kneels before Nata, begging her to persuade Zhurov not to press charges against her husband. Nata's passions are similarly visceral. Her attempts to overcome her passion for Bartinskii prove unsuccessful and, unable to forget him, she attempts to convert her love into hatred, another extreme emotion; when this also fails, she yields to her feelings and resumes her affair. As a somewhat superfluous intertitle informs us towards the end, 'Under the influence of love, a woman forgets everything.'

One sequence in particular makes this clash of sensibilities explicit: believing Zhurov to be away on business, Nata prepares for a clandestine liaison with Bartinskii, dressing to please in a long white gown that recalls the robes she wore during the 'reincarnation' sequence. When Bartinskii arrives, dressed, as ever, in a fashionable suit, the effect is that of classical heroine meeting modern man about town. While Nata believes in Bartinskii's fantasy of them as classical lovers, for him it is clearly an empty blandishment, intended merely to seduce. Moreover, when Zhurov enters he is dressed in the same style as Bartinskii. Thus, if a social analysis of *A Life for a Life* contrasts Prince Bartinskii negatively with the merchant Zhurov, a reading of the film that focuses on its gender analysis shows that it places them side by side and finds them both lacking. As in most Bauer films, gender is shown to be a greater dividing line than class; his 1914 film *Nemye svideteli* (*Silent Witnesses*) is the exception that proves this rule.

Bauer's examination of love is not restricted, however, to erotic love between men and women. *A Life for a Life* also examines maternal love, a new theme for Bauer and one he would return to in *Za schast'em* (*In Pursuit of Happiness*, 1917, also known by the English title *For Luck*). Indeed, the film's central character is, arguably, Khromova, as Bauer suggests visually, during the 'double wedding' sequence. The camera tracks in past the guests to the head table, as Khromova proposes a toast. She stands in the middle of the group; on her immediate right and left stand Musia and Nata, with their new husbands next to them. As she speaks, Khromova embraces both young women, pulling them more closely towards her and away from the men, who can only stand and look on. The composition of this frame and the inward movement of the camera marginalise the men at the extreme edges of the frame and draw attention to Khromova's position at the centre of the group, between her daughters. The viewer's expectations are overturned by this privileging of maternal love in the traditional context of conjugal love. Khromova is thus involved in 'love triangles' in the same way as the men and women. Consider the triangular relationship between Khromova, Nata and Musia and that between Khromova, Bartinskii and Musia.

Furthermore, Khromova's love for her biological daughter is shown to be as passionate, all-consuming, uncompromising and blind as the young women's love for Bartinskii. The depth of Khromova's love is emphasised in intertitles, such as her afore-mentioned request/

threat to Nata to forget her love for Bartinskii, and her warning to Bartinskii: 'I have only one concern in life – that my daughter be happy. If you are not good to her, then remember you will answer to me for it.' Typically, Bauer also uses visual means to emphasise Khromova's love for Musia, notably in his positioning of the actors. Consider the film's opening sequence in which the young women are dressing for a ball. Khromova enters the room and immediately walks to Musia and starts fussing with her outfit. After a cursory glance at Nata's dress, Khromova turns her back on her adopted daughter, moving with Musia to a dressing table positioned in the foreground of the frame, while Nata moves away from them and the camera, to the back of the room, with a maid. The camera then excludes Nata completely, moving to a (relative) close-up of Khromova helping Musia with a necklace, thus emphasising the exclusive intimacy of mother and (natural) daughter. This technique – which also, of course, emphasises Nata's inferior social status – recurs throughout the film, most notably in the final sequence where Nata is forcibly excluded from the centre of the frame when Khromova pushes her behind a column, away from Bartinskii and Musia. The film's dramatic dénouement also shows how far Khromova is prepared to go to protect Musia and avenge her suffering at Bartinskii's hands.

The strength of the women's passions makes them into strong – if misguided – characters and in contrast the men appear weak. Zhurov fails to carry out his threat to kill the faithless lovers; although he picks up a candlestick – one of the classical accoutrements that decorates Nata's bedroom – with which to strike Bartinskii; he is unable to commit such a physical, spontaneous and passionate act of revenge and staggers away from his wife and her lover, head hung in shame, later admitting that he did not have the 'spirit' to kill them. Instead, he will rely on the law to punish Bartinskii. He is too weak, however, to see through even this second threat and makes an almost pathetic telephone call to the police, informing them: 'I made a mistake. Those promissory notes were not forged. They were signed by me.' Khromova despises both men for their weakness, but it is her interpretation of what it means to be strong that is most interesting. When she confronts Bartinskii at the end of the film she challenges him to 'Be a man, at least once in your life' and hands him his gun. For her, courage is associated with a willingness to kill himself. Her response to Zhurov's decision to report Bartinskii to the police is similar: 'I prefer to see him dead than in prison.'

The men are thus shown to have typically 'modern', practical sensibilities and to belong to the contemporary world; their pragmatic, business-like approach to marriage is one manifestation of this, as are their fashionable suits and their faith in the institution of the law.

Zhurov is confident that the law will punish Bartinskii, while the Prince believes he will escape punishment because there is no legal proof of his forgery; he has no sense of shame about his treatment of his wife and his friend. The female protagonists are not, however, restricted by contemporary institutions. Their sensibilities are closer to those of the protagonists of classical drama and Khromova in particular is shown to adhere to an older morality based on codes of honour and shame. Their actions and impulses are driven by their passions and there is an inevitability about the way they act. From the moment Khromova warns Bartinskii that he must answer to her if he hurts Musia, his death at her hands becomes inevitable. Khromova takes it upon herself to administer justice and, for her, the punishment should fit the crime. The film's title and subtitle encapsulate her philosophy: 'A life for a life. A tear for every drop of blood.'

The willingness to kill for the sake of love, be it maternal or erotic, was a prerequisite of classical drama, just as a tragic ending was, at this time, a prerequisite of Russian melodrama. *A Life for a Life* is thus as much classical drama as it is modern social melodrama. Even its plot fits the classical mould. Khromova has a 'fatal flaw': her extreme love for Musia. This love clouds her judgement and blinds her to the reality that Bartinskii is not a good match for her. Bauer leaves the viewer in no doubt that Khromova is fully aware of Bartinskii's faults by conveying her astute assessment of him in an intertitle: 'The Prince is a carouser and a spendthrift. He is not the sort of person who could run our business.' However, Khromova's initial rejection of Bartinskii's proposal leaves Musia in floods of angry tears; she turns her back on her mother and refuses to be comforted by her. This is the film's most dramatic sequence, even though all the drama takes place in Khromova's mind, and in this respect it exemplifies the so-called pre-Revolutionary 'Russian style' of acting, which emphasised psychology over action. Khromova's face expresses her pain at witnessing the sorrow she has caused her daughter. She hesitates; her indecision is clear. Then she makes her fatal mistake: she runs to Musia and when, several shots later, we see Musia smiling and embracing her mother the viewer understands that the marriage will go ahead. The drama of the sequence is also heightened by montage. Bauer cuts between this scene and one in which Nata and Bartinskii are also discussing the Prince's proposal. Bartinskii reassures Nata that, even after his marriage, they will love each other just as they do now, thereby underlining Khromova's error. Everything that subsequently happens springs from this one act of folly.

When *A Life for a Life* is read through its *mise-en-scène*, the originality of Bauer's treatment of the traditionally melodramatic plot becomes clear. Bauer uses all aspects of *mise-en-*

scène expressively and, by identifying his male and female protagonists with the contemporary and the classical respectively, suggests fundamental differences in their temperaments and sensibilities. In this way, Bauer portrays the men and women as being 'out of joint' with each other. *A Life for a Life* can therefore be read as a specific depiction of the gender anxieties that unsettled Russian society at this time, as men and women alike struggled to adapt to the changes in their social roles ushered in by modernity. The classical associations accumulate, however; they overshadow the contemporary and situate the film in a broader context than that of early twentieth-century social melodrama. That Bauer, as early as 1916, conveys the film's many and varied meanings primarily in cinematic language, through his exploitation of the visual and technological properties of film, is evidence of his precocious affinity for this new artistic medium. It also illustrates why Evgenii Bauer has, deservedly, come to be seen as the outstanding *auteur* of pre-Revolutionary Russian film.

Rachel Morley

REFERENCES

Cherchi Usai, P., L. Codelli, C. Montanaro and D. Robinson (eds) (1989) *Silent Witnesses. Russian Films, 1908–1919*. London: British Film Institute.

Doane, M. A. (1990) 'Melodrama, Temporality, Recognition: American and Russian Silent Cinema', *East-West Film Journal*, 4, 2, 69–89.

Gaines, J. (1995) 'Revolutionary Theory/Pre-revolutionary Melodrama', *Discourse*, 17, 3, 101–18.

Hansen, M. (1992) 'Deadly Scenarios: Narrative Perspective and Sexual Politics in Pre-Revolutionary Russian Film', *Cinefocus*, 2, 2, 10–19.

McReynolds, L. (2000) 'The Silent Movie Melodrama: Evgenii Bauer Fashions the Heroine's Self', in L. Engelstein and S. Sandler (eds) *Self and Story in Russian History*. Ithaca and London: Cornell University Press, 120–40.

Morley, R. (2003) 'Gender Relations in the Films of Evgenii Bauer', *Slavonic and East European Review*, 81, 1, 32–69.

Schlüpmann, H. (1992) 'From Patriarchal Violence to the Aesthetics of Death: Russian Cinema 1900–1919', *Cinefocus*, 2, 2, 2–9.

Youngblood, D. (1999) *The Magic Mirror: Moviemaking in Russia, 1908–1918*. Madison, WI and London: University of Wisconsin Press.

NEOBYCHAINYE PRIKLIUCHENIIA MISTERA VESTA V STRANE BOL'SHEVIKOV THE EXTRAORDINARY ADVENTURES OF MR WEST IN THE LAND OF THE BOLSHEVIKS

LEV KULESHOV, USSR, 1924

Neobychainye prikliucheniia Mistera Vesta v strane bol'shevikov (*The Extraordinary Adventures of Mr West in the Land of the Bolsheviks*, 1924) offers something highly unusual, if not unique, in the history of cinema – quite apart from the record length of its title. Made to demonstrate the value of an aesthetic thesis and a new experimental working method, it became an immediate commercial and critical success, and remains highly entertaining today. However, it is also little known, since it does not seem to correspond to the typical subject matter of Soviet cinema of the 1920s. Without striking workers, brutal police and Revolutionary leaders – how can it be a true exemplar of the Soviet cinema that provoked official panic while inspiring radicals throughout the world?

The simple answer is that *The Extraordinary Adventures of Mr West...* appeared before these became the defining elements of a Soviet cinema that would prove more successful internationally than at home. When it was released domestically in the spring of 1924, with a deliberately satirical title, it seemed to confirm a long-awaited revival in Russian production. Ivan Perestiani's comedy adventure *Krasnye diavoloiata* (*Red Imps*, 1923) had already scored an immediate success with audiences starved of attractive Russian-made films. Later in 1924 would come *Aelita*, the first Soviet super-production complete with stars and eye-catching spectacle; Dziga Vertov's (1896–1954) radical feature documentary *Kino-glaz* (*Cine-Eye*); and an equally contemporary comedy by the Leningrad FEKS collective, *Pokhozhdeniia Oktiabriny* (*The Adventures of Oktyabrina*). Taken together, these provided clear evidence that the domestic film industry was at last beginning to recover from the virtual collapse which followed the Bolshevik seizure of power in 1917. But they also pointed toward a choice of strategies which would continue to be hotly debated throughout the 1920s: provocative low-cost production in the style of FEKS and Vertov, or full-scale adventure and drama, but with 'Soviet' values?

The 1924 films shared a somewhat irreverent pop-culture attitude towards the Revolution. The teenage hero and heroine of *Red Imps* are avid readers of adventure stories who find themselves living such a story when they become scouts for the Red cavalry fighting the Whites, while 'Oktyabrina' is a serial-queen revolutionary let loose on Soviet Russia's foreign enemies and *Aelita* contrasts a fantasy revolution on Mars with everyday Soviet reality. *The Extraordinary Adventures of Mr West...* fits this pattern by showing a fantastic distortion of the same reality, deliberately created by a gang of crooks intent on swindling a gullible American visitor. Ingeniously, it offers both a critique of the scandal-mongering which was common among opponents of the Soviet regime and many of the pleasures associated with capitalist entertainment cinema.

Russian audiences responded enthusiastically to all of these, savouring their irreverent humour after the solemn exhortations which had been a feature of the previous five years of sporadic production. The demand for *The Extraordinary Adventures of Mr West...* was so great that 32 prints were made, quite exceptional in Russia at a time when raw film stock was still in desperately short supply. Aleksandra Khokhlova (1897–1954), who plays one of the gang, 'the Countess', and was Kuleshov's partner off-screen, later recalled how kids would call out to her in the street, 'Hey it's the Countess', because they had all seen the film several times.

After an intertitle, 'a yankee's curiosity is punished and rewarded', Mr West (Porfirii Podobed (1886–1965)) is introduced as the president of the American YMCA who wants to go to Russia to see for himself if the stories he reads in American papers about Bolshevik barbarity are true. Fearing for his safety, his wife persuades him to take Cowboy Jeddy (Boris Barnet (1907–1965)) as a bodyguard; but Jeddy proves unable to prevent his briefcase being stolen almost immediately on arrival in Moscow. Armed with the briefcase and its contents, an unscrupulous con-man, Zhdan (Vsevolod Pudovkin (1893–1953)), is able to lure Mr West into a trap, after convincing him that he is in danger from real-life versions of the beastly Bolsheviks pictured in America. These have been hired by Zhdan and his accomplices, known as the Countess (Khokhlova) and the Dandy (Leonid Obolenskii (1902–1991)), with a sinister 'One-Eyed Man' (Sergei Komarov (1891–1957)) making up the quartet. Meanwhile, after an exciting chase in which police on motorcycles pursue Jeddy, who is driving a hijacked horse-drawn sledge in pursuit of what he mistakenly thinks is Mr West's car, Jeddy meets Elly (Valentina Lopatina), an American girl living in Moscow, who takes him to the police to seek their help. Zhdan now has his gang pretend to capture both Mr West and the Countess, and condemn them to death, as a prelude to extorting as much as possible of the American's money in return for their 'rescue'. Just when the scam seems to have worked, and the Dandy is trying to extract Mr West's last dollars as compensation for having insulted his 'wife', the Countess, the police arrive with Jeddy and Elly and capture them all. The OGPU (State Policital Directorate) officer in charge then treats Mr West to a tour of the 'real' Moscow and shows him 'real' Bolsheviks – prompting him to send a radio message to his wife that she should burn all the misleading American papers and hang a portrait of Lenin in the study.

In spite of its domestic box office and critical success, the film was not offered for foreign sale or even for special screenings – in the way that Vertov's *Cine-Eye* and Sergei Eisenstein's *Stachka* (*The Strike*) were shown at the Paris Exposition des Arts Decoratifs in 1925. *The Extraordinary Adventures of Mr West...* remained unknown to the first foreign critics who wrote excitedly about the new Soviet cinema. For these, Soviet cinema began with Eisenstein's *Bronenosets Potemkin* (*The Battleship Potemkin*, 1925) and with Kuleshov's next film, *Po zakonu* (*By the Law*, 1926), both of which were widely seen and admired abroad. As a result, the once-popular *Extraordinary Adventures of Mr West...* is oddly absent from critical accounts of Russian cinema before Jay Leyda's landmark book, *Kino*, published in 1960; and was not actually seen in Western Europe or America until the late 1960s, when Kuleshov's reputation began to be reassessed, beyond his dutiful inclusion in the pantheon of Soviet pioneers.

Some knowledge of Kuleshov's career before 1924 is vital to understanding the film and its unusual combination of qualities. Born in 1899, Lev Kuleshov grew up in the provincial Russian town of Tambov, the second son of an impoverished landowner's son and a school-teacher. A typical child of the era, Kuleshov saw the French comedies of Max Linder (1883–1925) and Danish melodramas starring Asta Nielsen (1881–1972) in the town's cinemas. After his father's early death, the family moved to Moscow to join his older brother, and Kuleshov prepared to enter the School of Painting, Sculpture and Architecture. To support himself, he drew fashion sketches for a women's magazine and painted stage scenery before finding work at the Khanzhonkov film studios in 1916. Here, he was fortunate to learn quickly about the special requirement of cinema set design from one of the outstanding directors of the period, Evgenii Bauer.

Before Bauer's premature death in 1917, Kuleshov clearly learned much from his unusually integrated approach to filmmaking. Bauer would take responsibility for lighting, photography, direction and editing, producing films of remarkable quality within the popular genres of the early Russian industry. This idea of integration, of relating all aspects of the film's design and realisation, would stay with Kuleshov, even when the massive upheaval of Revolution in 1917 pushed him to repudiate the aesthetic world that Bauer represented. Having started professional work in cinema at the early age of 17, Kuleshov began his parallel career as a theoretician by publishing articles about film aesthetics in the following year. He also conceived and directed his first film in this same year, *Proekt inzhenera Praita* (*Engineer Prite's Project*, 1917), drawing on his brother Boris's profession as an electrical engineer – and having him write the script and star in the film, for good measure.

Kuleshov drew several important conclusions from making *Engineer Prite's Project* that would have a bearing on *The Extraordinary Adventures of Mr West...* six years later. One was the need for post-Revolutionary cinema to embrace 'modern' subjects, rather than the society melodramas which dominated Russian cinema before 1917: the drama in *Engineer Prite's Project* is about competition between rival power plants. Another was the value of dynamic events and situations, such as abounded in American cinema. So, according to Kuleshov, *Engineer Prite's Project* 'contained fights, car and motor-bike chases, accidents, a hunt', as well as the obligatory 'simple love story with a happy end' (how successfully is hard to judge, since the film only partly survives). A further conclusion he drew was that this kind of modern cinema actually benefited from using non-professional actors, even though sheer economy had made this necessary for a novice director.

Kuleshov's work situation, after the collapse of the commercial cinema during 1918, became precarious. Yet it offered him a significant range of new experiences that would shape both his theory and his later productions. First, there was the obligation to shoot newsreel during the Civil War which dominated the early years of Soviet power. Kuleshov filmed on various fronts and also worked briefly on re-editing imported films, to make them ideologically suitable for release in the new political climate. All of these experiences culminated in his film *Na krasnom fronte* (*On the Red Front*, 1920), which combined documentary footage of cavalry operations with an acted story about the capture of a Polish spy. This is what was known as an '*agitka*', or agitational film, intended as topical propaganda to arouse popular sentiment against the new regime's enemies and enthusiasm for the Red Army.

In the same year, Kuleshov composed his first 'Revolutionary' manifesto, *The Banner of Cinematography*, proclaiming a new aesthetic of cinema. The theme is similar to that of the essays he had published in 1917 – how can cinema become a true art? – but now Kuleshov had a bolder answer. The 'essence of film art', he declared, is montage, or the assembly of shots, and the principles which govern the efficient use of montage can best be learned by studying American films. Noting that American suspense stories appealed most to Russian audiences, he described the typical reaction in a cinema: 'When the hero makes a good move, when there is a wild chase or a fearless fight, people in the cheap sets howl, whoop and whistle, and jump to their feet to see better.' This 'Americanitis' used to be deplored by 'superficial critics' and 'wise old officials', who linked it with the 'loose morals' supposed to be promoted by American films. But Kuleshov insists on a sharp distinction between the plot, which may be trivial or even immoral, and the method, which he describes as truly 'cinematic', by virtue of its economy in making every shot count towards a 'maximum intensity'.

Kuleshov's justification for the study and imitation of American films is deliberately 'scientific', as if to ward off accusations of pandering to capitalism; and it may have been influenced by Ivan Pavlov's (1849–1936) and Vladimir Bekhterev's (1857–1927) experimental study of physiological stimulus and response. Indeed Bekhterev had coined the term 'reflexology' in 1917 to describe the objective investigation of behaviour and environment, which may have had some bearing on the shift in Kuleshov's terminology. Later, one of Kuleshov's pupils and the leading villain of *The Extraordinary Adventures of Mr West...*, Pudovkin, would make an educational film about Pavlov's work, *Mekhanika golovnogo mozga* (*Mechanics of the Brain*, 1926) and link the theory of montage with Pavlov's work on reflexes. Meanwhile, inspired by what he felt was a breakthrough in theorising film, Kuleshov assembled a number of experimental sequences taken from old films to demonstrate what has since become famous as 'the Kuleshov effect'. According to one of his accounts, this involved parts of a shot of the most popular pre-Revolutionary Russian star, Ivan Mozzhukhin (1890–1939), intercut with images such as a half-naked woman and a child's coffin. The point being made was that spectators tended to interpret Mozzhukhin's expression according to the emotional significance of what he was shown 'looking at'. Thus, apparently, what was in truth the *same* expression might be considered joyful, sad or whatever – proving that 'in the cinema the expression of an emotion by the actor does not depend on the [psychological] cause of that emotion'. Rather, it depends on the context created by editing.

Many consequences followed from Kuleshov's realisation of the power of montage, which he would explore during the following three years, before gathering them together in *The Extraordinary Adventures of Mr West....* One immediate deduction cannot really be considered Kuleshov's discovery, even if 'magic geography' is often attributed to him. This involves editing together images taken in widely different locations, so that they are assumed by the film spectator to be spatially linked. Kuleshov recalled how he had previously filmed electricity pylons separately from the characters who are shown pointing at them in *Engineer*

Prite's Project. In fact, such shots would be called 'inserts' (or later 'cutaways') and were already in wide use in filmmaking by 1918, precisely for reasons of economy and impact. In *The Extraordinary Adventures of Mr West...*, however, such 'magic geography' is used for satirical and narrative effect. Zhban takes advantage of Mr West's ignorance and gullibility to show him how the 'barbarian' Bolsheviks have destroyed both Moscow University and the Imperial Bolshoi Theatre, and forced him to move from his former palace to a hovel. The respective insert shots of rubble and of a palace are of course seen by the film's spectators as entertainingly 'false' – the visual equivalent of a tall story – and the still-standing university and Bolshoi are duly shown to Mr West after his rescue by the same means.

The other, perhaps indirect, consequence of Kuleshov's montage doctrine had to do with acting. Starting from the principle of efficiency, he argued that the film actor did not need to be a theatrical actor – indeed would be better raw material for the filmmaker if he were simply a 'model', trained to execute whatever movements are required. Behind this radical approach lay Kuleshov's impulse to distance himself from the star 'kings and queens of the screen' with whom he had worked before 1918; and also to distinguish cinema more sharply from theatre – especially the psychological tradition of the Moscow Art Theatre, with its emphasis on motivation and intuition. Instead, Kuleshov's group worked with the idea of 'rhythm', seeking to correlate the actor's physical movement to the film frame and tempo of editing – as Pudovkin, Khokhlova and Obolenskii do in their exaggerated poses and gestures in *The Extraordinary Adventures of Mr West....*

The opportunity to put these ideas into practice came when he started teaching at the new state film school in 1920. With no film stock available for students' exercises, Kuleshov developed the idea of 'films without film', in which his workshop would rehearse and perform as if for the camera. Rejecting 'Russian psychological drama' in favour of 'American detective thrillers and stunts', Kuleshov's group became an important element in Moscow's explosion of avant-garde performance, including the Central Proletkult theatre, soon to stage Eisenstein's daring productions, and the latest incarnation of the veteran producer Vsevolod Meyerhold (1874–1940), staging boldly avant-garde work suffused with Revolutionary fervour.

Kuleshov's regime of training for his students, emphasising sport, circus and vaudeville skills and everyday movement, has often been compared with Meyerhold's concept of 'bio-mechanics', a supposedly scientific form of training, aimed at replacing 'inner' preparation with an externalised new mode of performance felt to more in keeping with Soviet values. In fact, it seems quite possible that Meyerhold was influenced by Kuleshov's group work, which began somewhat earlier; and in any case, highly stylised performance was in vogue among many of this period's experimental companies. Kuleshov later described some of the *études* in his memoirs adn writings edited by Ronald Levaco. One, entitled 'At No. 147 St Joseph Street', began with a young female dancer coming home after a show and going to bed, only to be awakened by an attempted kidnapping, with the action 'conveyed only be a flickering pinpoint of light'. We might see this as the basis for the flashback episode in *The Extraordinary Adventures of Mr West...* when an American girl who befriends Mr West's bodyguard Jeddy tells the militia how she was once attacked at night and only saved by Jeddy's intervention. Here the stark street-light makes what could have been a banal scene visually dramatic, especially when combined with highly acrobatic performances.

By 1923, Kuleshov's workshop group had perfected their 'rehearsal method', and were performing *études* lasting up to forty minutes with as many as 24 scenes – effectively films that lacked only celluloid to record them. The key members included the angular *jolie-laide* Aleksandra Khokhlova, the future directors Pudovkin, Barnet and Komarov, the actors Obolenskii and Vladimir Fogel', and others with diverse backgrounds, such as Podobed – Mr West in the film – who had been a naval officer in the World War One, and somehow combined being a manager at the Moscow Art Theatre with belonging to the Kuleshov workshop. Then, unexpectedly, came the chance to put their theory and preparation into practice.

State film production had just been re-organised, and the new studio, Goskino, was keen to show it could produce a popular success. Cinema was also fashionable among leading writers and artists, and the poet Nikolai Aseev (1889–1963), an associate of Vladimir Maiakovskii's (1893–1930) and member of the LEF (Left Front of Art) group, had written an experimental scenario. This was offered to Kuleshov in the hope that he and his group could film it quickly and successfully, despite continuing shortages of all kinds. Kuleshov was unimpressed by the scenario, which apparently revolved around a young Moscow cigarette-seller, but rather than lose the commission he swiftly reworked it with his pupils as a vehicle to demonstrate their collective abilities.

Nowhere are these more apparent than in the film's climax, when the gang's plan to blackmail Mr West is finally sprung. Once he is alone with the Countess in a bare dilapidated room, she briskly sets about seducing him, pulling him towards her in a parody of the conventional screen love scene. The gang has assembled outside, and are seen in a celebrated shot as a vertical row of faces peering through the partly open door, creating a striking stylisation of imminent ambush. The Dandy bursts in first to accuse Mr West of kissing his wife.

True to the workshop's acrobatic style, he mimes an exaggerated response, using the business of tearing off his coat to justify an exaggerated gesture in what is, after all, a performance, as the rest of the gang pretend to restrain him. Yet there is another appearance at the door, rhyming with the earlier shot of the gang: a gloved hand in close-up is followed by a gun and then a grim face as the film toys with 'real' suspense. Mr West cowers, offering his remaining dollars in desperation, until his look towards the door cues a wide shot of the leather-clad 'real' Bolshevik who leads the rescue.

The gang have meanwhile frozen and further demonstrate their physical skills by turning slowly towards the intrusion in an acted version of the filmic device of slow motion, broken only by the One-Eyed Man's insect-like scuttling on crutches. The Bolshevik's entry is signalled by the gang's eyes following him off-screen, until he appears dramatically as a looming silhouette in a deft reversal of the normal adventure stereotype of a menacing shadow. Jeddy and Elly burst in to explain, leading to the intertitle that cues the theme of the film's conclusion – 'look at a real Bolshevik'. The leather-suited saviour smiles, showing his human side, before resuming a vigilant watch on the gang; and in a further rhyme on the 'door' image, the four swindlers are seen one after another behind prison bars in a series of vertical panning shots. Now Jeddy and Elly are free to enjoy a true romance; and Mr West will see the 'real Moscow' and thousands of 'real Bolsheviks'. Underpinning the sequence is Kuleshov's demonstration that the devices of American cinema can not only be used to entertain the audience 'efficiently', but can also be renovated by being deployed in unusual ways, thus fulfilling two of the 'Formalist' critical concepts: that of 'laying bare the artistic device' and also of refreshing dulled perception through such devices. In a trope that recalls the familiar scenes of 'release' from a spell in classic literature, such as Shakespeare or Cervantes, Mr West learns to see the 'real' land of the Bolsheviks through a re-working of the narrative devices of anti-Bolshevik cinema.

Perhaps surprisingly, the leading Formalist literary critic of the period, Viktor Shklovskii (1893–1984), was initially unimpressed. Why introduce, implausibly, an American cowboy into a Russian film, he asked, unless this was a shameless bid to make an 'exportable' film? Why not stay close, as Aseev had in his original scenario, to 'our reality'? Although Kuleshov's materialist 'art of film' seems close to the Formalists' and the Constructivist artists' de-mystifying technical view of art, Shklovskii also believed strongly in the need to create a new Russian popular culture; hence his hostility to the exotic elements in *The Extraordinary Adventures of Mr West...*, despite an admiration for the skills of Kuleshov's group. Moving closer to cinema, Shklovskii would in fact become the scenarist of the group's next film, *By the Law*, adapted from a story by the American author Jack London, but successfully universalised.

Kuleshov himself summed up *The Extraordinary Adventures of Mr West...* as 'a light-hearted film which was distinctly a comedy and a political satire', noting that while it had 'faults in composition' it nonetheless proved that 'Soviet films could be made professionally' at a time when this was widely doubted. Granted this sense of a job well done, and a vindication of the Workshop's long years of preparation, the film remains significant for other reasons. One is the relish with which it creates a Bohemian shadow world on the margins of Soviet society – a feature shared with Eisenstein's *The Strike* and the FEKS Group's *Chertovo koleso* (*The Devil's Wheel*, 1926), both possibly influenced by the anarchic energy and dandy elegance of Zhban's gang. Such raffish figures both kept alive the older Russian tradition of the bandit story and illustrated the carnivalesque style that was typical of the Revolutionary theatre of the period. They would disappear in the future brave new world of heroic Socialist Realism, where narrative was seriously weakened by the suppression of strong and colourful antagonists.

Another pioneering aspect of the film gives it continuing relevance in the study of cinematic narrative. Like Buster Keaton's comedy of the same year, *Sherlock Junior*, in which a sleeping projectionist imagines himself involved in a screen melodrama, *The Extraordinary Adventures of Mr West...* explicitly plays with different levels of filmic reality. When Zhban sets the scam in motion by going to see Mr West and 'tells' him a false version of how he came to find it in a flashback, this begins a series of interpolated episodes which includes Elly's account of being saved from attackers by Jeddy, and Jeddy's subjective image of how he imagines barbarous Russians behave, roasting a girl over a fire. Together with the comic counterfactual shots of the demolished university and Bolshoi Theatre, these link the film with the cluster of reflexive works that defined modernism in the early 1920s, notably Luigi Pirandello's *Six Characters in Search of an Author* (1921) and James Joyce's *Ulysses* (1922), but also Maiakovskii's poetry, Bertolt Brecht's re-writing of earlier popular culture and Dada's exuberant irreverence. Unburdened by any sense of its own importance – Kuleshov was as proud of his troupe's ability to stage fight scenes as anything else – *The Extraordinary Adventures of Mr West...* offered a template for a new cinema that could successfully parody the existing styles of American thrillers and German expressionism, while ending on a note of pride by showing 'the real Moscow' in documentary form. Here, the film gestures towards the 'Left' artists' case for 'factography', a utilitarian art based upon reality. And it leaves us with the intriguing question of what international image Soviet cinema might have had if *The*

Extraordinary Adventures of Mr West... and the films of Kuleshov's young pupil and natural successor Boris Barnet had been exported, instead of those of his older pupils, Pudovkin and Eisenstein.

Ian Christie

REFERENCES

Kuleshov, L. (1988 [1924]) 'Mr West', in R. Taylor and I. Christie (eds) *The Film Factory: Russian and Soviet Cinema in Documents 1896–1939*, London: Routledge.

Levaco, R. (ed.) *Kuleshov on Film: Writings of Lev Kuleshov*. Berkeley: University of California Press.

Leyda, J. (1960) *Kino: A History of the Russian and Soviet Film*. London: Allen & Unwin.

AELITA

IAKOV PROTAZANOV, USSR, 1924

In late September 1924, huge crowds gathered outside the Ars Cinema in Moscow to see the premiere of the blockbuster production of the season. The movie screening was a science fiction extravaganza entitled *Aelita*. To celebrate this event the exterior of the cinema was adorned with giant figures illustrating two of the principal characters, Martians dressed in strikingly outlandish costumes, whilst inside a full orchestra performed an accompany-ing score specially commissioned for the event. Ticket touts had a particularly successful evening and, somewhat ironically, the director of the movie, Iakov Protazanov (1881–1945), was reportedly prevented from attending the premiere by the sheer size of the crowds. *Aelita* was Protazanov's first movie since his return to the Soviet Union the previous year.

Though less well-known today than many of his contemporaries (film directors such as Sergei Eisenstein and Dziga Vertov), Protazanov was a household name in his own life-time. Born in Moscow to a comfortable merchant family, he had developed an early interest in the theatre. It was not until he was in his twenties, however, whilst visiting the Pathé studio in Paris, that he chose to enter the still relatively new film industry. On his return to Moscow Protazanov initially found employment as an interpreter for the Italian 'Gloria' film studio before moving on to the German firm of Thiemann and Reinhardt. Here he worked in several capacities before being given his first directorial opportunity with *Pesn' katorzhanina* (*A Convict's Song*, 1911). From this point onwards, Protazanov never looked back and soon established a reputation as one of Russia's most active and pre-eminent directors. Between 1911 and 1917 he directed over sixty movies including *Kliuchi schastia* (*The Keys to Happiness*, 1913), reputedly the biggest box-office success of pre-Revolutionary Russian cinema. The outbreak of World War One barely interrupted Protazanov's output and he continued to produce highly popular and successful movies including *Voina i mir* (*War and Peace*, 1915) and *Pikovaia dama* (*The Queen of Spades*, 1916). By now working for the Ermol'ev studio, he also made one of his most infamous movies, *Satana likuiushchii* (*Satan Triumphant*, 1917), a dark and sombre melodrama highlighting death and destruction released just days before the cataclysmic events of the October Revolution. The changed conditions brought about by the Revolution inevitably impacted upon Protazanov's output, although his highly successful adaptation of Lev Tolstoi's *Otets Sergii* (*Father Sergius*, 1911), completed before the Bolsheviks came to power, was released in the summer of 1918. By the winter of that year, however, with conditions in Moscow becoming ever more desperate, Protazanov, together with the entire Ermol'ev studio, left for the southern resort of Yalta. By 1920 he had abandoned his native Russia for self-imposed exile in Paris. Even here Protazanov was not inactive for long. Indeed he was to direct five more movies before moving to Berlin where he directed one film for UFA (Universal Film). It was towards the end of 1923, however, that Protazanov was persuaded to return to his native Moscow, doubtless as part of the wider campaign to lure exiles back to the Soviet Union launched that year by the Commissar for Enlightenment and sometime film script-writer Anatolii Lunacharskii (1875–1933). Whilst it remains unclear precisely what Protazanov's motives were for returning to the Soviet Union, the promise of significant financial support for his cinematic projects must certainly have played a part.

Notably, funds were in no short supply for *Aelita*. The production stage extended to over a year, in contrast to Protazanov's own pre-Revolutionary average of completing ten movies during the same period. Further, vast quantities of film stock were used (reported as 22,000m in the programme accompanying the premiere) at a time of relative shortage of this imported material and a huge cast and crew were employed. All of this served to distinguish *Aelita* from any other movie made at this time. Moreover, in advance of the first night a promotional campaign was launched in the press. *Pravda*, for example, published a cryptic message – ANTA … ODELI … UTA – accompanied by no further explanation starting from 19 September 1924. Shortly afterwards this phrase was reprinted in *Kino-gazeta* (23 September 1924) with a claim that these words constituted a signal that had been picked up by radio stations across the world. 'What do they mean?' the journal asked. 'You will find out on 30 September at the Ars Cinema.' The campaign was a glowing success and *Aelita* proved to be a box office smash. Film critics, however, were less generous and despite this popular success the film was roundly condemned in the press: Denise Youngblood cites various comments that describe the film as 'ideologically unprincipled', 'alien to the working class' and 'too Western'. Negative attitudes towards *Aelita* have continued to haunt its reputation and to this day the film is generally regarded as one of the director's failures. However, one key aspect of the movie has helped to prevent it from drifting into obscurity: the spectacular and fantastical costumes designed specifically for the scenes on Mars by the celebrated Soviet Constructivist artist Aleksandra Ekster (1882–1949).

Significantly, these designs are best known through the numerous drawings and still photographs that illustrate texts on the early Soviet avant-garde. As Ian Christie has pointed out, this fact has tended to obscure the wider significance of *Aelita* the movie. In his article 'Down to Earth', Christie posed a simple but rather telling question: 'Has anyone actually seen *Aelita*?', thus highlighting the fact that much work referring to the movie was heavily dependent upon these stills and frequently paid little or no attention to the context of the movie itself. Christie states that 'a self-perpetuating tradition has developed which effectively substitutes the paradigmatic quality of the stills for the implied failure of the film'. However, as he continues, 'to screen *Aelita* is to discover something rather different'.

Many commentators, especially those operating within the art historical tradition, have tended to over-emphasise the innovative formal qualities of Ekster's costumes at the expense of the plot. To take one example: John Bowlt wrote of *Aelita* that 'the nature of the film medium enabled Exter [sic] to experiment with contrived spatial situations undergoing constant change. Into such fluid space Exter integrated bizarre costumes that emphasised geometric asymmetry, harsh black-and-white contrast, and innovative juxtapositions of such machine-cult media as aluminium, metal-foil, glass and perspex.' Steven Nash, in a more recent essay published in the catalogue accompanying the 1992 *Theatre in Revolution* exhibition held in San Francisco, shares this predominant interest in the geometrical formalism of Ekster's designs, although concerning himself more with tracing specific influences back to European developments. Thus for Nash, 'here we may see a distant memory, in her transparent faceted and strutted constructions, of Balla's "plastic complexes" of 1914–15'. These are, doubtless, reasonable enough claims from a formalist perspective. However, it is noteworthy that neither author is concerned with how such a vocabulary might operate within the context of the movie itself. To what ends these specific forms have been deployed remains largely unexplored. Christina Lodder's groundbreaking book *Russian Constructivism*, first published in 1983, is far more successful in its attempt to place the development of a Constructivist vocabulary into a broader historical and socio-political context. Nonetheless, Lodder too excludes the context of the movie from her interpretation. Instead, she criticises Ekster's costumes as merely 'decorative fripperies', which she contrasts with a superior 'utilitarian' Constructivism as epitomised in Liubov Popova's production clothing, or *prozodezhda*, designs for Meyerhold's production of *The Magnanimous Cuckold*. Yet in neither case does Lodder consider the implications of these costumes in terms of their significance for the performances for which they were designed. Rather she concludes that Ekster's costume designs come up short because 'geometrical ornament completely dominates all other concerns'. However, Ekster's costume designs for *Aelita* can be read as far more than isolated examples of Constructivist engagements with the cinema. Indeed, they constitute a vital component within Protazanov's complex and subtle plot, and can be regarded as key signifiers of socio-political concerns central to the period in which *Aelita* was made. In an attempt to explore the wider socio-political questions raised by the movie, as well as to offer a further consideration of the specific role that costume plays here, I want to offer a brief synopsis of the plot in *Aelita*.

The movie commences with radio stations all over the world receiving strange signals that cannot be deciphered. They read, as indicated in the advertising campaign, ANTA ... ODELI ... UTA. Los, the principal character within the movie, works at the Moscow Radio station and becomes convinced that these signals are coming from Mars. At night, he works on his private plans to build a spaceship to travel to the red planet and, gradually, his fantasies about this exotic journey take over his whole worldview. Yet, despite the obvious science fiction fantasy element central to this plot, Protazanov is far more directly concerned with the more mundane realities of life in Moscow in the winter of 1922–23, shortly after the launch of the New Economic Policy (NEP, 1921–24). To explore this issue, Protazanov presents his audience with an assortment of character types. For example, one of the principal anxieties of the NEP period was the re-emergence of an unreformed bourgeoisie. This is suggested through the character of Erlikh. Presented as a potential saboteur of the Revolution, Erlikh fulfils all the clichés of decadence, corruption and exploitation. He uses fraudulent documentation to expropriate food supplies for himself, encourages his wife to seduce another man for material gain and, significantly in terms of the way costume is deployed within the movie, stages a secret society ball in honour of former times. Perhaps not surprisingly the film concludes with Erlikh having been placed under arrest by Kravtsov, a comic character spoofing the Hollywood detective genre and played by the famous Russian actor Igor' Il'inskii (1901–1987), popularly regarded as the Soviet Charlie Chaplin. A second major concern of the NEP period was for the necessary readjustment from War Communism to economic stability. Protazanov addressed this issue through the character of Gusev, a Red Army soldier whose practical and emotional difficulties in adapting to peace and reconstruction are epitomised in his insatiable appetite for adventure. Once again the significance of costume for Protazanov is revealed in a scene in which Gusev's new young wife, in an attempt to prevent him from setting off in search of adventure, hides his clothes, thus forcing Gusev to escape by climbing out of a window wearing his wife's dress. The main character of the film, however, is Los the engineer and it is through him that Protazanov expresses the main message of the movie; namely, the need to put aside utopian dreams and concentrate upon practical endeavours. Los operates as a rather unconventional hero. He is presented as an assiduous and valuable worker committed to the Revolution, yet is still 'infected' by idealism and romanticism; he is fascinated with the idea of space flight. At night, in his own private sphere, he fantasises about a journey to Mars in a spacecraft of his own design. Increasingly driven by his own ill-founded jealousy concerning his wife Natasha and Erlikh, Los's fantasy begins to take over his life. In a dream he travels to Mars, accompanied by Gusev, for whom this trip offers the adventure he so desperately seeks, and Kravtsov, whose incompetent detection results in his boarding the spaceship immediately prior to take-off. Once on Mars, Los falls in love with Queen Aelita, the monarchical leader of the planet. Aelita's power, however, is held in sway by the elders, and in particular Tuskub who holds the true political reins. Los, together with Gusev, is hunted as an alien invader but escapes with the help of Aelita. The three then conspire to instigate a revolution amongst the oppressed Martian workers but when victory looks assured Aelita, whose ultimate goal is to gain power for herself, turns on the insurgents, ordering her guards to massacre the workers. Los, still in his dream of course, murders Aelita, whom he simultaneously perceives as his own wife, before waking up and realising that the whole Martian episode has been a figment of his vivid imagination.

The first point to make here is that the scenes from Mars actually constitute less than a quarter of the total screen time, the rest of which is set in Moscow during the early days of the NEP, and represent a dream rather than reality. Notably this is a significant departure from the literary source for the movie, Aleksei Tolstoi's 1922 novel also entitled *Aelita*. Both Tolstoi's novel, in which Los and Gusev actually travel to Mars and back again, and Protazanov's movie can be read, on one level, as a product of the craze for science fiction that characterised early twentieth-century popular literature in Russia. As early as 1908 Aleksandr Bogdanov, later known for his involvement with the Proletkult movement, had published a Martian adventure entitled *The Red Star*, later followed in 1913 by *Engineer Menni*. These novels drew upon the science fiction adventure stories of Jules Verne and H. G. Wells, many of which were early translated into Russian. In the early post-Revolutionary era, science fiction continued to capture the imagination of many Russian and Soviet readers and by the early 1920s a new generation of Soviet science fiction writers had emerged, including Aleksandr Grin (1880–1932), Aleksandr Chaianov (1888–1937) and Evgenii Zamiatin (1884–1937). Yet, despite this emerging pedigree, Protazanov's *Aelita* sits rather uncomfortably within the science fiction genre, operating as much as melodrama, comedy and detective story. Ultimately, the significance of the Martian scenes to the overall ideological message of the movie is essentially metaphorical; the main objective of the movie being to chart the social problems generated by the NEP. With this in mind, it is possible to offer some alternative readings of the significance of the costume designs for the Martian scenes in *Aelita*. To take one example, Lodder criticises Ekster's costumes as being more decorative than functional. Yet this fails to acknowledge that this is precisely the point. In Protazanov's movie Mars represents a pre-Revolutionary monarchical society and the Martian characters presented to us clearly inhabit the upper echelons of this world. The over elaboration of the Martian costumes is thus a direct comment upon aristocratic or bourgeois modes of dress and how their impracticality for labour practices is a purposeful means to distinguish them socially from the working classes. Protazanov further elaborates this point in the scene in which Erlikh organises a secret society ball. Here we see the guests arrive covered from head to foot in hats, overcoats and boots, not just because of the cold, but also to disguise the fact that underneath they are wearing evening clothes, a now socially unacceptable practice. As the scene unfolds, the outer garments, indistinguishable from those worn by the masses, are gradually discarded to reveal the silks, satins and jewels beneath this outer mask. Natasha is clearly drawn in by this dazzling array. However, in a moment of dawning realisation she stares at the elaborate and decorative footwear of three female guests and simultaneously recalls, by means of a spliced edit, the bast shoes of the peasant women recently arrived at the Kursk station checkpoint of which she is in charge. Racked by guilt she determines to leave the party, and thus the old world, behind forever. Protazanov here emphasises how the wearing of impractical aesthetic costumes becomes an important aspect of pre-Revolutionary social rituals, an expression of elitism; and here, of course, we should not overlook the use of the term *elita* (elite) as part of the name of the Martian queen and title of the movie, *Aelita*. In subsequently highlighting the elaborateness of the Martian costumes Protazanov is clearly identifying class parallels between social groups on Mars and in Moscow. Lodder's criticism of Ekster's costume designs ignores this analogy. In condemning the design of the trousers worn by Ihoshka, Aelita's maid, as having no practical function and impeding rather than facilitating movement, Lodder does highlight a significant factor in Ekster's aestheticisation of a Constructivist vocabulary. Yet far from being a weakness, this becomes a critical component of the costume design.

A second important cultural significance can also be explored in light of the plot of *Aelita* the movie; that the Martian costumes hold a clear resonance for a notional 'orientalism'. The most striking element here is in Aelita's costume, and particularly the headdress with its overt references to Japanese woodcut designs. Nor was this the first time that Ekster had engaged with *japonisme*. The previous year, whilst both submitting articles and designs for the new Soviet fashion journal *Atel'e* (*Studio*), she designed an overdress based extensively on a traditional Japanese costume. A further suggestion of these 'orientalist' interests can be traced in the similarities of Ekster's costumes to those designed by Aleksandr Vesnin (1883–1959) for the Kamerny Theatre production of Racine's *Phèdre*, staged in Moscow in early 1922 and later toured in Paris in 1923. Ekster and Vesnin had both worked in Tairov's company at this time and there was clearly an open exchange of ideas. For the critics, these costumes operated polyphonically, evoking simultaneously antiquity and, notably, the east. Ekster's costume for *Aelita* drew extensively from Vesnin's designs for *Phèdre*.

But it is clearly not just a visual reference that is here being made. The question reverts to what political significance could the deployment of such an 'oriental' reference carry in the context of the movie. In 1923–24, whilst Protazanov was working on *Aelita*, Soviet-Japanese relations were still at a low ebb. Since Russia's defeat in the 1903–5 war with Japan, territorial disputes between the two territories were an everyday occurrence, most notably over the oil rich island of Sakhalin which, under Tsarist Russia, had been turned into a penal colony. Japan had held the south of the island since 1905 and, following 1917, with the new Soviet state preoccupied with civil war, Japan took the opportunity to extend its influence not just here but on the Russian mainland too. With British, French and American support Japan invaded Vladivostok on the east coast and extended its influence over the trans-Siberian railway as far west as the trans-Baikal district. Even after the release of Protazanov's *Aelita*, Japanese troops were still holed up in Northern Sakhalin, not finally leaving until 1925. It might be added here that in Russia, fears of invasion from the east carried historical resonances that dated back to Genghis Khan and earlier. Moreover, in the last days of the Russian Empire, expansion eastwards was still justified by some writers in terms of racial superiority. Pre-Revolutionary paranoia concerning what was termed 'the yellow peril' (*zhëltaia ugroza*) seemed to be somewhat assuaged by the internationalist concerns of the new Bolshevik state. Yet here, also, a new form of colonialist attitude can be detected. For example, the decision of the Soviet Union to focus its energies on supporting the workers of east and central Asia notably post-dated their initial concerns for European revolution, whilst the Soviet perception of such nations was clearly generically 'under-developed' rather than culturally distinct. An example of how seemingly sympathetic voices raised in praise of internationalism could still be tinged with a fundamentally racist ideology can be traced in a 1923 diatribe against European values launched by the poet Sergei Esenin (1895–1925). Whilst praising the notionally less socially corrupt existence of the east Esenin still drew upon a stereotypical vision of a barbaric 'oriental' society: 'Let us be Asians', cries Esenin, 'let us stink, let us scratch our buttocks shamelessly in sight of everyone. Even so we don't have such a putrid smell as they have inside … Only an invasion of barbarians like us can save and reshape [Europe].'

It is within this context, then, that Queen Aelita is presented very much as an exotic other, not just in appearance, but in behaviour too. In one scene she is shown voyeuristically, almost luridly, watching a human kiss and subsequently expresses a fascinated desire to experience this earthly practice. Her revealing dress adds an obvious frisson of eroticism to this aspect of her character, not least of all in its suggestion that this represented 'other' (be she Martian or 'Oriental') has three breasts. Such overt female sexuality, within cinematic melodrama, is conventionally linked to depravity and Aelita is inevitably presented as the embodiment of monarchical evil. Having gained Los's trust she turns on him and is willing to sacrifice countless lives in the pursuit of power. Ultimately, this representation of an erotic *femme fatale* in eastern garb buys in to a conventional European notion of the 'oriental', both in its enticements and its threats. To reinforce the message of danger in the east, the movie concludes with Gusev, the Red Army soldier, back in military uniform and notably setting out to defend the Eastern Front.

But Aelita's costume carries one more, crucial significance in the context of 1924; namely the fact that the very Constructivist vocabulary that Ekster employed was utilised to stand for the utopianism that the movie explicitly opposed on ideological grounds. At the conclusion of the movie Los gives up his Martian dream by burning his plans for the building of a spaceship. Instead he now turns to more practical and direct labour, helping in the rebuilding of the new socialist state. Clearly this invokes the broader political rejection of world revolution to concentrate on the most immediate needs of the state, and thus suggests the revised policy of building socialism in one country. Therefore, by implication, the Constructivist vocabulary utilised by Ekster for the Martian costumes in *Aelita* becomes representative of this very rejected utopianism. It is important to recognise that the Martian scenes in *Aelita* are purely imaginary and that, as such, they become symbolic of the confusions that Los experiences on his journey from self-obsessed romantic individual to fully-rounded Soviet New Man. The German movie *Das Kabinett des Dr Caligari* (*The Cabinet of Dr. Caligari*, 1919) has frequently been invoked as a significant influence in the making of *Aelita*. Ian Christie, has interestingly linked the use of German Expressionism and Russian Constructivism in these two movies as both being devices to express 'the thoughts of a distracted mind', thus highlighting how specifically modern artistic developments were used conventionally in cinematography to assist a reading of alienation and disruption. As such, the Martian costumes in *Aelita* can be seen as highly topical in addressing contemporary debates concerning the future role of visual culture in the Soviet Union. The ultimate destruction of Queen Aelita is at Los's own hands, a murder metaphorically expressing his rejection of romantic utopianism. Thus, in a final twist, Protazanov's movie implies support for a cultural policy of reconstruction that ultimately rejects the very avant-garde artists, such as Ekster, whose innovative costume designs gave his movie such visual force.

In the final analysis, *Aelita* is a complex, confusing and sometimes contradictory movie whose message is rich, yet sometimes vague and inconsistent. However, this should not necessarily be regarded as a weakness. Rather it is perhaps this ambiguity, this very uncertainty, within its overall message, that makes Protazanov's movie such a revealing and compelling document of the times in which it was produced.

Mike O'Mahony

REFERENCES

Bowlt, J. (1980) 'Catalogue entry on Aleksandra Ekster', in S. Barren and M. Tuchman, *The Avant-Garde in Russia 1910–1930: New Perspectives*, exhibition catalogue, Los Angeles.

Christie, I. (1991) 'Down to Earth: *Aelita* Relocated', in R. Taylor and I. Christie (eds) *Inside the Film Factory: New Approaches to Russian and Soviet Cinema*. London and New York: Routledge, 80–102.

Lodder, C. (1983) *Russian Constructivism*. New Haven and London: Yale University Press.

Nash, S. (1991–92) 'East Meets West: Russian Stage Design and the European Avant-Garde', in *Theatre in Revolution: Russian Avant-Garde Stage Design 1913–35*, exhibition catalogue, San Francisco.

Youngblood, D. (1991) 'The Return of the Native: Yakov Protazanov and Soviet Cinema', in R. Taylor and I. Christie (eds) *Inside the Film Factory: New Approaches to Russian and Soviet Cinema*. London and New York: Routledge, 103–23.

STACHKA THE STRIKE

SERGEI EISENSTEIN, USSR, 1925

Stachka (*The Strike*, 1925) was the first feature-length film to be made by the leading Soviet avant-garde filmmaker of the 1920s and principal advocate of the centrality of montage, Sergei Mikhailovich Eisenstein (1898–1948).

Eisenstein had begun his creative career on stage and screen as a sapper in the Red Army during the post-Revolutionary Civil War of 1918–21, when he had designed stage sets and costumes for amateur dramatic performances for political propaganda purposes. As the Civil War drew to an end, he became involved with the Moscow Proletkult (Proletarian Culture) and staged a number of radical productions for them, culminating in a performance of Sergei Tretiakov's *Protivogazy* (*Gas Masks*) in the Moscow gas works in 1924. The stage realism of this production was undermined, rather than reinforced, by the setting. As Eisenstein himself put it in his essay, 'Through Theatre to Cinema': 'Theatre accessories in the midst of real factory plastics appeared ridiculous. The element of "play" was incompatible with the acrid smell of gas. The pitiful platform kept getting lost among the real platforms of labour activity. In short, the production was a failure.' As a consequence, 'the cart dropped to pieces, and its driver dropped into the cinema'.

The film was not Eisenstein's first experience of filmmaking. He had already worked with the documentary filmmaker Esfir Shub (1894–1959) on a re-edited one-part version of Fritz Lang's two-part *Dr Mabuse der Spieler* (*Dr Mabuse the Gambler*, 1921–22) to make it ideologically suitable for a Soviet release in 1923 as *Pozolochennaia gnil'* (*Gilded Putrefaction*). *The Strike* was also not Eisenstein's first film. In 1923 he had also made a short comic film sketch for his stage production of *Mudrets* (*The Wise Man*), his radically re-worked version of Aleksandr Ostrovskii's *Na vsiakogo mudretsa dovol'no prostoty* (*Enough Simplicity for Every Wise Man*, 1868), in which he parodied the methods used by the avant-garde documentary filmmaker Dziga Vertov (1896–1954) and his Cine-Eye (Kino-glaz) group.

The Strike was not a bolt from the blue, but it did mark a significant moment in Eisenstein's career; although he retained an interest in theatre, both theoretical and practical, for the rest of his life, his subsequent career, and indeed the international reputation that it created, were dominated almost entirely by his work in cinema. A dispute over the authorial rights to the script for *The Strike* also led to his final acrimonious break with Proletkult and eventually propelled him into the role of 'Master' in his own right. Although Eisenstein almost immediately claimed sole authorship of the film, the opening credits attribute the script to 'Proletkult under the general editorship of Valerian Pletnev', while the film is 'performed by the collective of the First Workers' Theatre [of Proletkult]'. Individual credits are given only to Eisenstein as director, Eduard Tisse (1897–1961) as cameraman and Vasilii Rakhals (1890–1942) as set designer.

The Strike, like Eisenstein's second and more famous feature film, *Bronenosets Potemkin* (*The Battleship Potemkin*, 1925), was made for the First Goskino Studio in Moscow and originally envisaged as one episode in a cycle of revolutionary films; in this instance the cycle of seven films for Proletkult was intended to cover the history of the workers' movement in the Russian Empire under the title *K diktature* (*Towards the Dictatorship*; that is, of the Proletariat). As with *The Battleship Potemkin*, once filming had begun, the fifth episode (which ultimately became *The Strike*) took on a life of its own and became a free-standing feature-length film in its own right, the rest of the cycle being abandoned, although it is still referred to in the opening title which describes the film as the 'first issue' ('vypusk pervyi').

Although there is some evidence that Eisenstein had one particular strike in mind, the film's depiction of 'the strike' is a generalised one, as befits its original purpose in the proposed film cycle. The film is divided into six sections, which follow the sequence of events of a typical strike in pre-Revolutionary Russia. Between the opening credits and the first part there is an epigraph written by Vladimir Il'ich Lenin in 1907 emphasising the importance of organisation to the workers' movement in Russia: 'The strength of the working class is organisation. Without the organisation of the masses, the proletariat is nothing. Organised, it is everything. Being organised means unity of action, unity of practical activity.'

The first part of the film is entitled 'All is calm at the factory' ('Na zavode vse spokoino'). It opens with the image of smoking chimneys and drifting clouds. A close-up of a stereotypical smiling capitalist is intercut with overhead shots of a busy office corridor and the factory's shop floor. The title of this opening part of the film is repeated in larger and bolder capitals – the last two letters of the Russian 'spokoino' – *no*, meaning 'but' – are repeated and then distorted to make a visual transition to what at first looks like the end of a gun barrel but then turns out to be a wheel spinning on one of the machines. This is the first of the many experimental visual transitions that characterise the work of Eisenstein and Tisse in *The*

Strike. In silhouette two workers exchange a message: 'There is trouble brewing.' A reflection in an outside pool shows the inverted figure of a worker and then a reverse-shot of a group of workers plotting. The 'inverted' worker is a spy, working for the factory management.

Already the two opposing sides in the drama that is about to unfold have been established and characterised. The capitalist and his spy are isolated and alone: the workers act as a collective. We see the workers clambering over the rooftops while the spies report through the factory hierarchy, finally reaching the manager. An obese man, he sits behind an enormous desk, wearing a top hat and overcoat – the first of many caricatures of the typical bureaucrat to appear in an Eisenstein film. He repeats what has been reported to him to the factory owner, who in turn phones a friend in the police, who contacts the secret police: another visual link is established through the use of the telephone.

The secret police officer looks through the files on the factory gathered by his agents and through an album of their photographs. They have been given names like the Monkey, the Bulldog, the Fox and the Owl. Their pictures come to life on the page and two of them appear in the policeman's office to be recruited for a renewed bout of espionage. In scenes reminiscent of the later piece by Bertolt Brecht and Kurt Weill, *Die Dreigroschenoper* (*The Threepenny Opera*, Berlin stage premiere 1928, film version directed by G. W. Pabst and released in 1931), the spies are kitted out with their disguises. In grotesque indoor caricatures they are shown with the attributes of the animals or birds from which they take their names. Outdoors the workers meet to discuss a strike. For security reasons preparations continue with a group of workers swimming out to a ship's anchor suspended in mid-air. The Owl, who is spying on them, becomes entangled in some ropes and is discovered. In a homoerotic scene that presages the hammock sequence in *The Battleship Potemkin*, the workers dive into the water and swim ashore. Their next meeting takes place in the factory toilets but even there they discover they are being spied on.

On a wooded hillside workers sing and dance to the accordion. In the factory yard one spy is deliberately knocked down by workers driving a crane. Shots of a printing press and of printed text remind us of the Bolsheviks' strike calls. Workers distribute leaflets; by clear implication it is the Bolsheviks who are the organising force referred to in the epigraph. The final shot of this part of the film returns to the shop floor, this time being showered with these leaflets.

The second part is called 'A reason to strike' ('Povod k stachke'). The section begins with an *agent provocateur* stealing a micrometer from a worker's locker. When the worker

– Iakov Strongin, the only named character in the whole film – goes to report the theft he is branded as a thief and, unable to prove his innocence, hangs himself from 'his' machinery. This provides the catalyst to rally the workers to strike. Not all are willing and there is some fighting, particularly over access to the factory hooter. Once this is in the control of the workers it is used as a repeated clarion call in this section of the film.

The liberating organisational strength of the workers is represented by a large locomotive moving sideways across the factory floor, a device used again in the reverse sense in *Oktiabr'* (*October*, 1928), with a descending artillery piece embodying the oppression of the proletariat. The weakness of the capitalist class is underlined by their resort to the telephone and to the authorities, ordering that the gates be locked, just as the police chief in *October* will telephone to order that the bridges of Petrograd be raised to cut off the workers' districts. Nonetheless the workers emerge victorious and at the end of this section they unceremoniously ferry both the manager and the foreman out of the factory in a wheelbarrow, dumping them down a slope and into the river. The manager's hat floats in the muddy river, a potent symbol of the impotence of the ruling class, and an early example of Eisenstein's principle of *pars pro toto* or synecdoche.

The third section of the film, 'The plant stood still' ('Zavod zamer'), begins with scenes of a new dawn, an idyll of family life, with man at one with nature – as opposed to slaving away in the factory – as represented by ducklings, piglets, a kitten and children. This idyll contrasts with the life of the director, alone in his villa on the hill overlooking both the city and the factory: orders pile up and he cannot fulfil them. The contrast with the shareholders who pull the strings is even greater. Rejecting the workers' demands, the chief shareholder opens up a table concealing a drinks cabinet and symbolically squeezes a lemon, as the police arrive to break up the workers' meeting in the woods. The paper listing the demands is characteristically used to wipe a lemon slice from a shareholder's shoe. The caricatures of the capitalists in this sequence owes much to the tradition of the satirical Russian woodcut, the *lubok*, and its grotesque style had been deployed in posters and ROSTA windows of the Civil War by Maiakovskii, Malevich and others, and would therefore have been familiar to contemporary audiences. The workers dispersed, the leaves of a birch tree rustle in the breeze as a waiter clears up the debris from the shareholders' drinks.

In the fourth section, 'The strike drags on' ('Stachka zatiagivaetsia'), the grocer's shop is 'closed for repairs' and the children are starving as money runs out – the kitten too is now emaciated. The family idyll deteriorates into domestic strife. In the streets workers are followed by a spy – here Eisenstein makes good use of the human eye to link the narrative development.

The Owl uses a spy camera to photograph one worker tearing down the management's rejection of the workers' terms. The film is developed and the worker identified. In a rather confusing nocturnal downpour sequence the worker is arrested and beaten up. The police are urged on first by a bourgeois woman and then by criminals already incarcerated. A day passes and the following night arrives: the scene is an exclusive restaurant, a dwarf couple dance on one of the tables for the amusement of the other guests. The secret policeman is 'entertaining' the worker, threatening him with hard labour if he does not turn traitor to the working class. He hesitates but takes the proffered bank note: as he does so, the dwarf woman 'surrenders' to her male companion in an ironic commentary on the main action. By the following morning the worker 'has been brought round' and is identifying the ringleader of the strike. Eisenstein uses the same technique here of still photographs coming alive that he had used to introduce the various agents used by the secret police in an earlier sequence. The action cuts to a cemetery, where the workers decide to continue the strike action. In the final scene of this section of the film we see an arrest warrant being signed.

The fifth part of *The Strike* is entitled 'A provocation to disaster' ('Provokatsiia na razgrom') and it opens with some striking images of one of the agents walking past a scaffold on which dead cats are hanging. A dwarf takes him to meet the 'King' of the underworld. His milieu and apparel both again foreshadow *The Threepenny Opera*. Following a grotesquely conducted and acted 'shady deal', the 'King' claims that, 'My realms are limitless'. In the Kadushkino cemetery he literally whistles up a whole host of criminals, who, again literally, emerged from the underground, where they have been concealed in submerged barrels. A team of ruthless crooks is recruited from these grotesque caricatures. Meanwhile the Owl follows two workers through the back alleys and streets of Moscow: here Eisenstein makes very effective use of chiaroscuro (as he would later do in the unfinished *Que viva Mexico!* and in *Ivan the Terrible*, 1944–46).

As the workers return *en masse* from a meeting, the band of crooks sets light to a vodka warehouse, encouraging some errant workers to loot the stocks as the building collapses. The workers' leader realises that this is a deliberate provocation and asks for the firemen to be summoned, but the fire alarm is guarded by policemen to prevent it being used. One woman worker outwits them and calls for help. Prompt action by the workers' leaders has foiled the plot and the workers begin to disperse as the fire brigade arrive. But, instead of turning their hoses on the burning building, they turn them on the workers' backs. It is not too fanciful to imagine this sequence as a nightmarish extension of the early Lumière brothers' film *L'Arroseur arrosé* (*The Sprinkler Sprinkled*, 1895). What begins as an almost purifying experience rapidly degenerates into something much more sinister as some workers are caught in a dead end. The workers are routed, the ringleaders literally flushed out.

The final shot of workers trapped under the pressure of the hoses leads into the title that introduces the sixth and final section of the film, 'Liquidation' ('Likvidatsiia'). This section begins with an official statement justifying the presence of troops in the area. The cavalry descend on the factory ordering the workers to disperse. A small boy plays under one of the horses and his mother goes to retrieve him. One of the mounted soldiers lashes her with his whip and she appeals to her comrades for assistance. They rush forward and drag the soldier from his horse. But the soldiers gain the upper hand and the workers escape back to their living quarters, hotly pursued by the troops who burst through the barricades and brutalise men, women and children, behaving 'like wild animals' and tossing one little girl to her death. Back in his office a police chief shows the turncoat worker a map of his district. When the worker bangs the table in defiance he upsets bottles of ink that spill their contents over the map like the blood that is being shed.

As the worker is led back to his cell the final debacle unfolds with the intertitle 'Carnage'. In this very famous sequence Eisenstein intercuts shots of a butcher slaughtering a cow with a series of images showing the workers being driven down a hillside. As the cow's throat is slit, infantrymen open fire on the strikers. The soldiers drive the workers to the river. The title 'Defeat' precedes the death agonies of the cow and a shot of workers' corpses strewn across a field. The camera pans left across the field as the infantrymen retreat. The film cuts to a close-up of a worker's eyes and the intertitle, 'And like bloody unforgettable scars on the body of the proletariat lay the scars of Lena, Talka, Zlatoust, Yaroslavl, Tsarisyn and Kostroma', which generalises the experience of this particular strike into its broader historical context. The final shot is an extreme close-up of the same eyes, followed by two titles: 'Remember ... Proletarians'. Thus the political message of the film is rammed home while the audience is still reeling from the shock of the on-screen slaughter.

Eisenstein analysed this most famous sequence in the film in his October 1924 article 'The Montage of Film Attractions':

> The method of the montage of attractions is the comparison of subjects for thematic effect. I shall refer to the original version of the montage resolution in the finale of my film *The Strike*: the mass shooting where I employed the associational comparison with the slaughterhouse. I did this, on the one hand, to avoid overacting among the extras

from the labour exchange 'in the business of dying' but mainly to excise from such a serious scene the falseness that the screen will not tolerate but that is unavoidable in even the most brilliant death scene and, on the other and, to extract the maximum effect of bloody horror. The shooting is shown only in 'establishing' long and medium shots of 1,800 workers falling over a precipice, the crowd fleeing, gunfire etc, and all the close-ups are provided by a demonstration of the real horror of the slaughterhouse where cattle are slaughtered and skinned. One version of the montage was composed roughly as follows:

1   The head of a bull. The butcher's knife takes aim and moves upwards beyond the frame.

2   Close-up. The hand holding the knife strikes downwards below the frame.

3   Long shot: 1,500 people roll down a slope. (Profile shot.)

4   Fifty people get up off the ground, their arms outstretched.

5   The face of a soldier taking aim.

6   Medium shot. Gunfire.

7   The bull's body (the head is outside the frame) jerks and rolls over.

8   Close-up. The bull's legs convulse. A hoof beats in a pool of blood.

9   Close-ups. The bolts of the rifles.

10   The bull's head is tied with rope to a bench.

11   A thousand people rush past.

12   A line of soldiers emerges from behind a clump of bushes.

13   Close-up. The bull's head as it dies beneath unseen blows (the eyes glaze over).

14   Gunfire, in longer shot, seen from behind the soldiers' backs.

15   Medium shot. The bull's legs are bound together 'according to Jewish custom' (the method of slaughtering cattle lying down).

16   Close shot. People falling over a precipice.

17   The bull's throat is cut. Blood gushes out.

18   Medium close-up. People rise into the frame with their arms outstretched.

19   The butcher advances towards the (panning) camera holding the blood-stained rope.

20   The crowd rushes to a fence, breaks it down but is met by an ambush (two or three shots).

21   Arms fall into the frame.

22   The head of the bull is severed from the trunk.

23   Gunfire.

24   The crowd rolls down the precipice into the water.

25   Gunfire.

26   Close-up. Teeth are knocked out by the shooting.

27   The soldiers' feet move away.

28   Blood flows into the water, colouring it.

29   Close-up. Blood gushes from the bull's throat.

30   Hands pour blood from a basin into a bucket.

31   Dissolve from a platform with buckets of blood on it … in motion towards a processing plant.

32   The dead bull's tongue is pulled through the slit throat (one of the devices used in a slaughterhouse, probably so that the teeth will not do any damage during the convulsions).

33   The soldiers' feet move away. (Longer shot.)

34   The head is skinned.

35   1,800 dead bodies at the foot of the precipice.

36   Two dead skinned bulls' heads.

37   A human hand in a pool of blood.

38   Close-up. Filling the whole screen. The dead bull's eye. Final title.

The final montage was slightly different and included the final close-up of a worker's eyes with the last intertitles urging 'Remember … Proletarians'. This is probably just as well, as there is at least anecdotal evidence that contemporary audiences, especially the workers at whom the film was supposedly aimed, found the visual metaphor too difficult to fathom. Ironically, one film director whose ideology Eisenstein found abhorrent did realise the powerful impact that this scene might have. Dr Fritz Hippler used a similar sequence to conclude his virulently anti-Semitic Nazi propaganda film *Der ewige Jude* (*The Eternal Jew*, 1940).

As an experiment designed to realise the 'montage of film attractions' in practice, *The Strike* was ahead of its time: it was too avant-garde and was in any case rapidly overshadowed by Eisenstein's second feature, *The Battleship Potemkin*, the film that cemented his reputation both within and outside the Soviet Union. Although *The Strike* was awarded the gold medal at the 1925 Paris Exhibition of Decorative Arts, to a mass audience it lacked a plot and the density of shots (379 per reel, as opposed to the usual 40–60 at that time) made it too difficult to follow. The reviewer for the Moscow evening paper wrote that 'The furious montage often makes a hash of the action; episode piles upon episode; the fundamental thread is lost. It's not always clear what is going on on the screen.' The film was not a commercial success, a fact that still mattered under the New Economic Policy (NEP, 1921–24). Nonetheless in Kirill Shutko, a high-ranking Bolshevik and member of the Party Central Committee's Agitprop Department, Eisenstein had an influential patron. Shutko helped to arrange the subsequent commission for *The Battleship Potemkin* and it was his wife, Nina Agadzhanova-Shutko, who helped Eisenstein to devise the script treatment for the film.

As Yon Barna has observed, '*The Strike* contained in embryo – and sometimes in much more developed form – the momentous artistic innovations that came later … Nearly every aspect of Eisenstein's montage method can be traced back to *The Strike*.' Eclipsed by *The Battleship Potemkin*, and later by Eisenstein's historical sound epics, *The Strike* was restored and rediscovered in the 1960s. Now that we are more familiar with early filmmakers, especially those in Russia and the Soviet Union, we can detect the clear influence of Lev Kuleshov on both the acting style and the montage, and the footprints not only of D. W. Griffith, but also of Fritz Lang in such devices as the use of the dissolve. We can also see the influence of traditional Russian culture, from the *lubok* style of caricature to the repeated use of the all-seeing eye as both symbol and linking device. What is most gratifying, however, is that of all Eisenstein's seven completed feature films, this first experiment in the genre remains the freshest, the most innovative and the most exciting.

Richard Taylor

REFERENCES

Barna, Y. (1973) *Eisenstein*. London: Secker & Warburg.

Eisenstein, S. (1949 [1934]) 'Through Theatre to Cinema', in *Film Form: Essays in Film Theory*, ed. & trans. J. Leyda. New York & London: Harcourt Brace Jovanovich, 16.

_____ (1998 [1924]) 'The Montage of Film Attractions', in *The Eisenstein Reader*, ed. R. Taylor. London: British Film Institute, 38–9.

ZEMLIA EARTH

ALEKSANDR DOVZHENKO [OLEKSANDR DOVZHENKA], USSR, 1930

Aleksandr Dovzhenko (1894–1956) was famously sceptical about the durability of cinema's impact on the national or individual consciousness. In the speech to the All-Union Creative Meeting of Cinematographers in 1935 he spoke about film's 'illusory state of imprintedness', and argued that, while an individual work might reach a mass audience within a quicker space of time when compared with other art forms (he was thinking primarily about litera-ture), such works quickly became museum pieces, their power to move and influence relent-lessly eroded by the passage of time.

First released in 1930, *Zemlia* (*Earth*) is the fortunate repudiation of this gloomy prog-nosis. Despite the loss of the negative due to the German bombing of Kiev during World War Two – a tragedy that cannot be overemphasised in view of the extraordinary lyrical intensity of the cinematography – Dovzhenko's film has become a classic of world cinema, taking its place among a number of iconoclastic works associated with the Soviet avant-garde of the 1920s and early 1930s. He is regarded as a pioneer of cinematic modernism, a poetic visionary who eschewed conventional narrative forms and genres, and sought radically to reshape cinema as a means of expressive communication. The influence of *Earth* on successive gener-ations of Soviet directors, in particular the 'new wave' of the 1960s, some of whose pioneers were taught by Dovzhenko at the State Institute of Cinematography (VGIK) prior to his death in 1956, is universally acknowledged. Unlike his avant-garde contemporaries, however, Dovzhenko's poetic sensibilities were moulded in large part by the history, folk-religious culture, and rural landscape of his native Ukraine. This was also the case, incidentally, for his camera operator, Danylo Demutskii (1893–1954), with whom he enjoyed an extremely close relationship, and whose creative contribution to the originality of *Earth* (barely acknowl-edged by writers on the subject hitherto) was vital. The 'rediscovery' of Dovzhenko as a nationalist as well as Soviet artist, pioneered in large part by émigrés, has gained momentum since the emergence of an independent Ukraine in the 1990s. This has prompted renewed investigation into the circumstances of his life, and the specifically Ukrainian political and cultural contexts which manifest themselves in his films, as is evident from recent studies by Vance Kepley Jr and George O. Liber.

Dovzhenko was born in 1894 in Sosnytsa, a village near the town of Chernihiv, about 100km north of Kiev. His parents were relatively poor peasants, descendants of Cossacks, and he was one of fourteen children, only two of whom survived into adulthood. At the age of sixteen he went to train as a teacher, graduating in 1914, whereupon he taught at a secondary mixed elementary school in Zhytomyr. He managed to avoid military conscription during World War One on medical grounds, but his activities during the complex period of 1917–19, when different political groups were vying for power after the collapse of the monarchy, are shrouded in mystery. Liber claims that, contrary to the version of events given in his autobiographical statements, Dovzhenko's nationalist sympathies at this time brought him into direct conflict with the Bolshevik movement; and that, as a member of the Ukrainian Socialist-Revolutionary Party, which was agitating for an autonomous republic within a wider federal system, he fought against the Red Army, joining the Communist Party only in April 1920 after his capture, arrest and incarceration. Whatever the truth of these allegations, the early 1920s witnessed him working in an official capacity as a diplomatic representative for the Soviet Ukrainian Government, firstly in Warsaw, and then in Berlin, where he formally studied art and moved among artists associated with the German Expressionist movement. After his recall in 1923, he worked as a political cartoonist and illustrator in Kharkiv, but three years later, frustrated and depressed, he decided to try and move into film. His first works as director at VUFKU's Odessa Studios – *Iahidka kokhannia* (*Iagodka liubvi/Love's Berry*, 1926) and *Portfel' dypkuriera* (*The Diplomatic Pouch*, 1927) – are essentially apprenticeship works. They exploit the popular genres of (Harold Lloyd-style) comedy and international espionage thriller (*The Diplomatic Pouch* draws upon the real-life assassination of Theodore Nette by Russian émigrés), and reveal a young artist in the process of acquiring the rudiments of his craft. At this stage Dovzhenko was forced to work within the constraints of a studio system which at the time was geared very much towards foreign (mainly Hollywood) competition.

Zvenyhora (*Zvenigora*, 1927), was an astonishing debut. It was an eclectic epic that blended a contemporaneous account of the October Revolution, Civil War and early Soviet period in the Ukraine with myths and legends ostensibly drawn from peasant folklore, and spanning a whole millennium of history. The structure of the film was highly experimental for its time. The interweaving of time-frames and *dramatis personae* (the main protagonist is a symbolic archetype who features in all the different historical episodes) creates a complex and at times confusing tapestry. To a certain extent the film is a barely-concealed political allegory: the treasure buried in the hills of Zvenyhora, the unifying motif which holds the various episodic strands together, functions as a metaphor for Ukrainian national identity over the centuries (in other words, as a legitimising modern myth) rather than an authentic product of the folk-religious imagination (the 'founding myth' of the pagan princess Roksana and the Varangian invaders, along with the legend of the treasure itself, has yet to receive independent ethnographic confirmation). The treatment of the 'mythological' Varangian invasion is dazzlingly original: a theatrical-style interlude consisting of double and triple exposures, each photographed in soft-focus and in slow motion. If such scenes seem surprisingly static for the avant-garde of the 1920s, they are contrasted elsewhere with powerful montage sequences – some of them only a few frames in length – and Constructivist-style industrial landscapes, executed by hand-held camera, and equally stunning.

Dovzhenko's next film, *Arsenal* (1928), was envisaged as a sequel to *Zvenyhora*. Narrower in scope, this work was commissioned for the tenth anniversary of the Revolution and tells the story of the violent storming of the Bolshevik-controlled munitions plant in Kiev (the 'arsenal') by nationalist forces after the declaration of a republic in January 1918. Like Eisenstein's *Stachka* (*The Strike*, 1925) and *Bronenosets Potemkin* (*The Battleship Potemkin*, 1925), the plot belongs essentially to the history of early utopian-communist martyrology: the combatants die violent deaths at the hands of their reactionary 'bourgeois' oppressors, but their ideological struggle lives on and, as the contemporary spectator knows, eventually culminates in victory. In its treatment of its revolutionary subject, however, Dovzhenko's second film is a great deal less programmatic and intellectual than these precursor works by Eisenstein. Dovzhenko's vision emphasises lack of shape and the fragmentation of experience: a sense of confusion reigns, and it is not obvious, despite the coda, in which direction events are moving or indeed why eventual triumph might be expected. The overwhelming impression is one of turbulence, chaos and impending catastrophe.

Bearing in mind the recriminations (regarding the film as an apology for collectivisation and famines) which have been levelled at *Earth* from the political point of view (both at the time of its release and subsequently), it is important to recognise that its conception and realisation (the autumn and early winter of 1929) occurred during the brief and so-called 'voluntary' phase of collectivisation: this mostly preceded the brutal policy of 'dekulakisation', which was declared in December 1929, when Dovzhenko was already cutting and editing his film. *Earth* tells the story of a young rural Komsomol activist, Vasyl, who is enthusiastic about the policy of collectivisation and the potential for modern technology to transform the agriculture of his small peasant community. In the face of resistance on the part of a wealthy peasant family (the Bilokins), he nevertheless endeavours to assert the primacy of collective ownership over private property by ploughing through the boundaries of their land. The family responds violently: the son, Khoma, having drunk heavily, shoots Vasyl in cold blood in the middle of the night while the latter is dancing down the village road, an ecstatic, triumphant, life-affirming dance which celebrates both the successful gathering of the harvest with the aid of a tractor (newly introduced into the community) and the love he feels for his fiancée, Natalka. Vasyl's funeral becomes the occasion for public grieving and acceptance of the need to embrace the modern (symbolically represented by the Bolshevik aeroplane which is evoked in one of the speeches at the funeral). In response to this collective solidarity, Khoma confesses his guilt – thus condemning himself and his class to ignomy and historical anonymity.

Despite its setting in post-Revolutionary times, the plot of *Earth* belongs also to the genre of utopian-communist martyrology: Vasyl's murder is the symbolic equivalent of a ritual sacrifice, one which is necessary to ensure the forward march of progress. At the same time, however, in common with Pudovkin's *Mat'* (*Mother*, 1926) and *Konets Sankt-Peterburga* (*The End of St Petersburg*, 1927), Dovzhenko's film also exploits a prototypical 'coming to consciousness' paradigm, one which subsequently came to dictate the 'master-plot' of the socialist-realist works (literary and cinematic) of the 1930s. The relationship between Vasyl and his father, Opanas, is crucial here: this is the vehicle by means of which the director explores the cultural differences between the two generations. The father, strongly attached to tradition, and thus conservative and cautious, is sceptical in relation to the modernising zeal of his son (his laborious ploughing of the earth with three oxen is dramatically juxtaposed with the rapid work of the tractor). The shift in ideological position, the event that brings the required enlightenment, takes place directly as a result of Vasyl's murder. Opanas's angry rejection of religion, and his advocacy of a new form of burial without the mysticism and rituals of the Orthodox Church, marks the end of the God-fearing world of the past and the embrace of a new secular spirit which is still, nevertheless, strongly wedded to the land.

In an eerie anticipation of Dovzhenko's views about cinema's impermanence – it is possible that his remarks were in fact prompted by his experiences with *Earth* – the political furore which greeted the release of his film was partly a reflection of the fact that it had been overtaken by events. These had simply moved too swiftly for the director to adapt (unlike Eisenstein, who had somehow managed to re-edit and re-title *Staroe i novoe* (*The Old and the New*; originally entitled *General'naia liniia* (*The General Line*), 1926–29) in order to keep abreast of shifting party policy on agriculture). The permanence of *Earth* as a work of art, however, has been secured less on the foundations of its political message than on its radical formal experimentation and grand philosophical vision. First and foremost, *Earth* is a cinematic poem. It adopts the rhythms and structures of a poem, the rhythms understood both in terms of the lengths of individual sequences in relation to one another, and the movements of human figures and objects within the frame. Furthermore, its meanings reside less in the movement of narrative than in the symbolic associations which emerge as a result of the visual imagery; as such, Dovzhenko's work supplies the experimental template for the 'new wave' films of the 1960s which eschewed narrative dynamic in favour of visual poetry, the most celebrated examples being the early films of Andrei Tarkovskii, Larisa Shepit'ko and Sergo Parajanov.

The linear momentum of *Earth*, which is not strong and contains some breathtaking ellipses (these have given rise in some quarters to the accusation of narrative incoherence) disguises its essentially episodic (one might even say stanzaic) structure. Gilberto Perez has argued that the film has an overarching structure which consists essentially of two central movements. Each movement begins with a serene, tranquil and static series of images, and ends with a burst of rapid-fire montage. The first movement consists of the opening sequences (the lyrical scenes of the countryside and the death of grandfather Symon in the family orchard) and ends with the frenetic activity of the harvest by means of modern technology (the tractor and threshing machines, leading eventually to the machinery used for mass bread-making). The second movement consists of the tableaux of the young couples standing shoulder to shoulder motionlessly in the moonlight after the harvest and ends with the sequences which accompany Vasyl's funeral. We are presented here with a veritable kaleidoscope of parallel activities. Tracking shots of the funeral procession (the determined faces of the marchers) are intercut with scenes depicting Natalka's anguished reaction to her fiancé's death (she is naked), the desperate confessions of Khoma, the wrathful denunciations of the 'paganistic' funeral by the local priest, and the scenes of Vasyl's mother Odarka giving birth to another child. One might add that these two movements culminate in an epilogue which returns the viewer to the static images which launched the beginnings of the first and second movements respectively: the vision of ripe apples (some fallen, some still clinging to their branches) gently caressed by rain (first movement); and the scene of Natalka and her new lover, staring into each other's eyes, much in the manner of the moonlit couples (second movement).

While one may question the validity of Perez's structuring division, it is clear nevertheless that the juxtaposition of movement and stasis, in particular in relation to the human body, is a key element in *Earth*. These produce a pulsating rhythm within each of the film's episodes, and offer multiple points of comparison and contrast.

Among the images of staticity, for example, one might include the scenes of the grandfather lying in the orchard, the body of Vasyl lying on his catafalque, his mother lying in post-natal contentment, the couple glimpsed briefly asleep, lying next to one another during the moonlit sequence, and the various bodies and faces pictured in statuesque poses – the opening image of Vasyl's sister, played by Iuliia Solntseva (1901–1989), pictured next to a giant sunflower, the faces of the male and female members of the Trubenko family as they stand around the grandfather in the orchard, the faces of the villagers as they expectantly await the delivery of the tractor, and the faces of the moonlit couples. These are images of serenity, tranquillity, and (according to Perez) durability.

By contrast, we are also presented with various kinds of bodily movement. These range from the choreographed and semi-ritualistic (Vasyl's dance, Khoma's drunken, clumsy anticipation of this dance, and his subsequent re-enactment or parody of the dance during his confession) to what might best be termed the spontaneous, frenetic or hysterical: the dramatic response of the Bilokin family on learning of their denunciation in the newspaper, the various movements of bodies (sliding off roofs, running along roads) which accompany the arrival of the tractor, Khoma's extraordinary attempt to 'burrow' into the earth during his confession, and Natalka's violent movements from one side of her bedroom to the other, and her symbolic smashing of an icon. In this general category also belongs the harvesting sequence which juxtaposes the natural rhythms of the peasants with the mechanical movements of the machines. The violent movements of animals, for example the head of the horse which jerks sharply upwards in response to the 'sound' of the gunshot that kills Vasyl, and the horses which charge chaotically (and for no apparent reason) across the screen during the funeral sequence, should also be considered here. Finally, the impression of movement arises as a result of the tracking shots employed at several junctures in the film. These accompany individual figures or groups of figures moving slowly (and axially) in relation to the camera while it retreats with equal speed. This technical device appears on three separate occasions: during Vasyl's dance (the initial stages); when his father advances to confront Khoma the very day after his murder; and at several moments during the funeral procession. Accompanying tracks with the figure running occur on two occasions: Khoma's manic sprint across the fields to make his declaration of guilt; and the man who runs excitedly behind the tractor during the harvesting sequence. Although it is true that Soviet versions of the American dolly had only just begun to appear at around this time, the novelty of this device lay less in the technical domain than in the impact of the perceived unity of movement (man and machine moving at the same pace, with a shared rhythm).

Dovzhenko's interest in the human body as a means of expression partly reflects the poetics of silent film, with their emphasis, in the absence of the spoken word, on mime and gesture, but also the theories of plasticity which were becoming increasingly fashionable during the 1920s as a means of defining cinema as a medium. The focus on expressive movement within the theatrical avant-garde had already been well established by this time. It is significant that Dovzhenko's actors since *Zvenyhora* had emerged from Les Kurbas's experimental Berezil Theatre in Kiev; and that Demutskii himself, while working as a stills photographer for the very same theatre in the mid-1920s, had demonstrated a fashionable interest in the 'fixing' of moving human figures on celluloid.

These facts notwithstanding, the idea of dance as an expression of emotion in the context of *Earth* is essentially a product of folk culture. Vasyl's dance is the keystone of the film, and the point at which its specifically Ukrainian flavour and antique cultural influences are felt most strongly. In contrast to the screenplay, which was published more than twenty years after the film was released, this is not strictly speaking the *hopak*, a traditional Cossack dance, although it would seem to incorporate elements from it. This is made clear in the account of the preparations for the scene given by the actor Symon Svashenko. He records that the dance consisted of a series of improvised movements devised on the basis of conversations with elderly (male) villagers in the area where the film was shot (Iareska, Poltava region) and guidance supplied by Dovzhenko. These villagers boasted about the way in which their feet would stamp so hard on the ground that the 'whole earth shook', but Dovzhenko rejected some of the movements which formed part of the traditional repertoire and desired something that was, in his own words, 'simple, clear and maximally precise'. Svashenko himself interpreted these instructions to mean that he should emphasise the ideas of triumph and transformation. Encouraged by the director to keep a piece of music in mind when he came to perform, Svashenko opted for a song in a minor key, 'Kozachok', which had been composed by Reingol'd Glier for a 'romantic' production of Taras Shevchenko's *Haidamaky* in the Berezil Theatre (the title, which literally means 'little Cossack', refers to a traditional song with few words – in the stage adaptation of Shevchenko's narrative poem it is performed by Zaporozhian Cossacks before going into battle). Vasyl's dance is launched by slow, gliding movements which become more and more rapid, culminating in powerful stamping and violent, jerking movements of the body: we witness here a display of masculine prowess and at the same time ecstatic, soulful celebration. The idea of contact with and flight from the earth is crucial here. In his 1835 article on 'Little Russian' music, the writer Nikolai Gogol' referred to the notes of Cossack songs 'detaching themselves suddenly from the earth so as to strike the ground even more powerfully with shining boots before lifting off again into the ether'. The decision to emphasise visually the stamping of the feet – Vasyl's traditional, festive boots produce little clouds of dust which rise up from the ground and are caught by the light – dictated that the scene be photographed in the early morning rather than late evening (despite the indications in the scenario that the scene takes place at night). The essence of Cossack being – strength, vitality, joy and a sense of boundless freedom – is palpable here.

If there is something dream-like in this sequence, a sense of time unfolding and losing its anchor in reality, it is largely due to the decision to shoot the entire scene in soft-focus. This strongly emphasises the air of mystery about the dance, and undermines the arguments of those, like Perez, who identify the essence of Dovzhenko's image-making in its clarity and tangibility, rather than elusiveness and intangibility. The recourse to soft-focus photography in *Earth* is neither random nor haphazard; on the contrary, it is a general aesthetic principle, and characterises a number of important sequences – the opening scenes in the apple orchard, the tableaux of the moonlit couples, Natalka's distress after the murder, the closing images of the fruit caressed by rain, and the sequence of Natalka and her new lover. Furthermore, it is undeniably controversial in the context of the Soviet Union of the 1930s because it associates the film explicitly with the Pictorialist tradition in American and European photo-graphy, a supposedly 'bourgeois' tradition increasingly under attack as orthodox Marxist critics and Party hacks began to flex their repressive muscles towards the end of the 1920s. The use of softening or diffusing techniques – either through innovative printing procedures or specially designed soft-focus or uncorrected lenses (for example, the monocle lens) – was an aesthetic which essentially sought to emulate the discoveries of the French Impressionists.

Soft-focus cinematography can be encountered widely in the silent films of the 1920s, both in America and Europe: at best, it is an attempt to produce aesthetically pleasing images; at worst, an extension of fashion photography. In *Earth*, by contrast, it is fundamental to the vision of nature which Dovzhenko seeks to express in his film. In the moonlit tableaux scenes, for example, the images of the human figures and the natural landscape are simultaneously atmospheric and poetic. As the director himself indicates in his scenario, their primary purpose is to convey the quiet enchantment of a summer's evening in the Ukrainian countryside. At the same time, by virtue of the diffusing effect, and the statuesque posing of the individual couples (the placing of masculine hands on feminine breasts, for example, and the curiously unblinking expressions on their faces), these scenes border on the surreal. On the one hand they seek to defamiliarise the landscape – Dovzhenko referred to the images having been 'transformed … into poetry full of new and exciting meanings'; and on the other they express a philosophical attitude towards the natural world which emphasises beauty, tranquillity and harmony. As part of this vision, the human figure is fused almost indistinguishably with the landscape. Because of the monocle lens, the outlines of the human body lose their sharpness, and the elements in the foreground and background blend into a seemingly indissoluable whole (the monocle, because it is uncorrected, denies the possibility of differential focusing). Furthermore, unlike other softening techniques (such as the placing of gauze across the front of the camera lens, or the smearing of vaseline around it), the monocle causes a distinctive blurring of natural light which gives rise to the perception of a special luminosity or 'aura', in particular around the face. Oleg Aronson has commented on the way in which the faces in *Earth* seem to be illuminated 'from within', rather than externally – a phenomenon which he links to the tradition of icon-painting. This hypothesis is suspect in view of the adoption of soft-focus. Nevertheless, there is a sense in which these sequences verge on a vision of natural harmony which is at the very least semi-mystical.

Earth is concerned fundamentally with the cyclical movement of death and re-birth. It is essentially a vision of renewal, one strongly allied to a folkloric perspective. From its opening images of death – grandfather Symon – to its closing images of birth – Vasyl's mother – the viewer is presented with the idea of continuity. The images of circularity and fecundity which abound in these sequences are primarily folkloric in origin. The symbolic occasion of the harvest is relevant here. The situating of the grandfather in an orchard of fallen apples, and the images of his reclining body juxtaposed briefly with the field of swaying corn, imply a symbolic analogy. Death is lyrical but not tragic – it is accepted as part of the endless cycle of renewal, the presence of the four generations of the family gathered around him testament to the replenishing potential of the natural world. This is a neo-paganistic rather than a pantheistic vision. It is further evidenced in Dovzhenko's de-eroticised and somewhat perfunctory treatment of the naked body and its natural functions. Although deemed provocative at the time (the censors insisted that they be cut from the released version), the scenes of Natalka's anguished movements while naked and the images of the male peasants urinating into the tractor's radiator so that the engine can be kept cool are essentially naturalistic rather than carnivalesque.

Although in private Dovzhenko lamented the passing of Ukrainian folk culture, *Earth* offers a vision of continuity within the context of transformation. His art is an attempt to reconcile the old and the new, and as such restates the Dionysian myth of creativity born of violence. The final images of fruit caressed by rain – for all their blatant artifice (rain is combined in the foreground with glorious sunshine in the background) – suggest the possibility of catharthis (if not, rather more baldly, re-fertilisation and thus regeneration). That this vision of peaceful reconciliation and regeneration proved so disastrously premature and inappropriate in the context of the 1930s collectivisation campaign in no way lessens the mythopoetic power and universal dimensions of Dovzhenko's film.

Phil Cavendish

REFERENCES

Aronson, O. (1994) 'Kinoantropologiia *Zemli*', *Kinovedcheskie zapiski*, 23, 141–8.

Dovzhenko, Aleksandr [1935] Speech at the All-Union Creative Meeting of Cinematographers, cited in A. S. Troshin (1994) '*Zemlia* i my: priglashenie k razgovoru', *Kinovedcheskie zapiski*, 23, 103–7.

Gogol', Nikolai [1835] 'About Little Russian Songs' ['O malorusskikh pesniakh'], first published in *Arabeski*, reprinted in N. V. Gogol' (1978) *Sobranie sochinenii* 6. Moscow: Khudozhestvennaia literatura, 102–9.

Kepley Jr, V. (1986) *In the Service of the State: The Cinema of Alexander Dovzhenko*. Madison WI: University of Wisconsin Press.

Liber, G. O. (2002) *Alexander Dovzhenko: A Life in Soviet Film*. London: British Film Institute.

Perez, G. (1975) 'All in the Foreground: A Study of Dovzhenko's *Earth*', *Hudson Review*, 28, 1, 68–86.

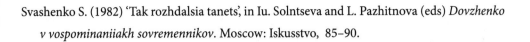

Svashenko S. (1982) 'Tak rozhdalsia tanets', in Iu. Solntseva and L. Pazhitnova (eds) *Dovzhenko v vospominaniiakh sovremennikov*. Moscow: Iskusstvo, 85–90.

CHAPAEV

GEORGII AND SERGEI VASIL'EV, USSR, 1934

Chapaev (1934) was directed by Georgii and Sergei Vasil'ev (1899–1946 and 1900–1959 respectively), who styled themselves the 'Vasil'ev brothers'. They had earlier been involved as editors on a number of competent but unremarkable silent films, including the documentary film *Ledokol Krassin* (*Ice-breaker Krassin*, 1928) whose success enabled them to realise their ambition to direct, *Spiashchaia krasavitsa* (*Sleeping Beauty*, 1930) and *Lichnoe delo* (*A Personal Matter*, 1932). They never achieved the same level of success after *Chapaev*, which was awarded the Silver Cup at the 1935 International Film Festival in Moscow, and received the Grand Prix at the 1937 Paris Exhibition.

 Chapaev, is perhaps the most famous, and certainly one of the most influential, films of the Soviet period. Like its hero – whose reputation owes much to the film – it achieved a cult status soon after it was released that it has never really lost. Images from the film such as Chapaev on his white horse, and Chapaev demonstrating battle tactic using potatoes, are now imprinted in Russian cultural memory. Generations of Soviet children played at 'Chapaev' just as American children played at 'Cowboys and Indians'. Released for the anniversary of the October Revolution on 7 November 1934 in the year that Socialist Realism, the doctrine which was to dominate the Soviet arts to the very end, was officially inaugurated, it was hailed as a model for the realisation of that doctrine in Soviet cinema. Indeed, most critical work on *Chapaev* has treated it as an exemplar of Socialist Realist art. Both Stephen Crofts and Mark Ferro adopt a Marxist-influenced approach to the film, examining how Socialist Realist ideology influences the form of the film and placing it in the political and historical context surrounding the emergence of the dogma. Ferro, for example, highlights the Vasil'ev brothers' use of parallel structures – pairs of characters such as Chapaev and Furmanov and Pet'ka and Anka – to confer ideational coherence on what is otherwise a somewhat fragmentary and disjointed plot. Jan Leyda, who provides an excellent account of the story behind the making of the film, points out that heads of Government and the Army had endorsed it at earlier screenings in the Kremlin. Neya Zorkaya sets *Chapaev* within Soviet film history and establishes some important links between the Vasil'ev brothers and the avant-garde cinema of

Eisenstein and Dovzhenko with whom they are frequently contrasted, a line also developed by Leyda. More recently, Jeremy Hicks has discussed *Chapaev* in relation to its literary source and in the context of the debate over the status of documentary in relation to film that raged during the 1920s in the USSR.

The fact that the period in which *Chapaev* was made coincided with the birth of Soviet sound film is significant, since the technological innovation made the accommodation of the film medium to Socialist Realism's ideological dictates much easier than was the case with silent film. *Chapaev* was in fact one of the first Soviet sound films. Its soundtrack was, in common with all early sound films, recorded in a studio and superimposed on the external visual narrative. This accounts for the hollow echo apparent in the characters' speech. In fact, like the literary work of which it is an adaptation (also listed as a canonic Socialist Realist text), *Chapaev* is far from a straightforward piece of propaganda, obedient to the ideological principles that it purports to illustrate. Indeed, it is the ways in which the film subverts the ideological template according to which it was made that form the main focus of this chapter.

Chapaev is based on Dmitrii Furmanov's (1891–1926) autobiographical novel, set in the period of the Civil War which raged in Russia between 1919 and 1921. Furmanov draws heavily on the diary that he kept whilst serving as a political commissar for the Communist Party, amongst relatively undisciplined, peasant-led elements of the Red Army. Furmanov gives himself the name Fedor Klychkov to signal the pseudo-documentary status of his text, but Chapaev himself, who actually existed and whose historical role was not dissimilar to that attributed to him by Furmanov, appears under his own name. As one might expect of a text based on diary entries, Furmanov's novel is highly episodic in nature, lacks a clear plot line and is punctuated with extracts from factual documents. The plot, such as it is, tells of Klychkov's initial awe and fascination before the legendary ataman and his gradual assertion of party authority and values over the recalcitrant Chapaev, whose outbursts of spontaneous voluntarism (*stikhiinost'*) diminish as the novel wears on. Klychkov's enchantment decreases as his function as a literate observer, consciously organising what he sees, increases. The narrative degenerates into a series of sketches, ever more reliant on the use of hindsight – the enwrapping of Chapaev's image as a figure from the past in the light of his significance for the post-Civil War present.

The shift of emphasis from representation as visual embodiment to representation as a verbal (and temporal) 'putting in place' can be traced to Klychkov's first battle experience, in which he agonises over his cowardice. In the next scene we find Klychkov, in recompense, enacting his role as the tool of party discipline, joining Chapaev in punishing his men for looting from defeated White villagers. Henceforth, Klychkov is in control, just as Furmanov asserts his organising presence over the recalcitrant image of his subject. By the end, Chapaev has been largely (though not entirely) re-educated by Klychkov, only to meet a tragic and untimely death at the hands of the White Army as he is fleeing across the Ural river with his orderly, Pet'ka.

Klychkov's account is punctuated throughout with reflections on why a figure like Chapaev should achieve mythical acclaim precisely during the Civil War period, why the consciousness of such a leader and his contributions to the Party cause are limited, and how such untramelled spontaneity and voluntarism should be controlled and re-channelled. At the end, the narrator even expresses doubts about the very existence of the heroic feats attributed by the people to him: 'Where is the heroism of Chapaev? Where are his great feats? Do they exist at all?'

The novel is not without contradictions and it is often this complexity, acknowledged in a highly reflexive, meta-textual manner, which renders it interesting. For example, it becomes evident that Chapaev's petulance, his fits of anger and stubborn refusal to acknowledge facts, those attributes which prevent him from attaining the level of consciousness possessed by the Commissar, are the very same qualities which, in differentiating him from the abstract concept he is called upon to embody (peasant *stikhiinost'*), lend his figure the visual originality (*samobytnost'*) which Klychkov/Furmanov recognises is required to make the embodiment gel into something tangibly real. The episode, just before he dies, when Chapaev is treated to some frontline theatre performances organised by Anna Nikitichna (Zoia Pavlovna in the novel), Furmanov's future wife, is also contradictory in an artistically self-conscious way. Klychkov enthuses in response to the performances: 'The artist, the agitator and the commissar – all this merged together in one concept: the warrior.' This ideal concept is, however, undermined by Nikitichna's condescending perception that the soldiers needed 'simple, comprehensible pieces', which re-establishes the very gap between observing subject and observed object, art and action, required by Furmanov in order to structure his fiction. It was, appropriately, the popularising Anna Nikitichna who, following her husband's death, collaborated with the Vasil'ev brothers in the making of *Chapaev*.

In 1924 Furmanov had submitted a film scenario based on his novel to the Leningrad film studio, but it was lost and forgotten. In 1932, Furmanov's widow submitted her own version to the studio and it was passed on to the Vasil'ev brothers, who agreed to take it on, working hard to adapt the script for the cinema. Apart from the ideologically motivated omission of references to Klychkov's initial cowardice, and attempts to bolster his authority (he is, incidentally, called Furmanov rather than Klychkov in the film), the obvious differences between the novel and the film (which starred Boris Babochkin (1904–1975) in the lead role) are: (i) the added subplot depicting the love of Pet'ka, Chapaev's loyal orderly (played by Leonid Kmit (1908–1982)), for Anka, a female machine gunner (Varvara Miasnikova (1906–1978)), whom he instructs and 'educates' in the art of warfare just as Furmanov instructs Chapaev in the principles of Party discipline; (ii) insights into enemy behaviour including a memorable scene of the peasant polishing the floor to the sound of Beethoven's 'Moonlight Sonata' played by the 'cultured' White Colonel Borozdin who has ordered his brother to be flogged (in a marked deviation from the book, the peasant later switches allegiances to Chapaev after Pet'ka, who initially incurs Chapaev's wrath, then releases him from capture when he learns that his brother is now dying from the beating); (iii) episodes depicting Chapaev's native wit, as when he demonstrates battle tactics with potatoes, or when, at the beginning of the film he fools Furmanov into thinking that the soldiers he has dispatched to the river to retrieve their rifles are merely bathing because it is too hot.

In general, humour is emphasised in the film, both (as in the previous example) in Chapaev's favour and at his expense; there are several comic exchanges between Furmanov (played by Boris Blinov (1909–1943)) and Chapaev in which the latter demonstrates his misplaced arrogance and lack of education (he stubbornly insists at one point on defending the use of local horse surgeons to treat human sickness, maintaining that they know more than any 'intellectual' doctor from the city, until Furmanov dissuades him of his illusions). Pet'ka's clumsy attempts to woo Anka also provide light relief (an early scene in which they appear revolves around a suggestive pun on the name for a machine gun part that Pet'ka is instructing Anka how to polish and which coincides with the Russian word for 'cheeks').

The film traces a more definitive path than the novel from Chapaev as unenlightened, impulsive peasant leader to Chapaev as disciplined Bolshevik commander and by the end of the film the Vasil'evs portray the peasant commander more or less uncritically as an (albeit still unsophisticated) hero of mythic proportions – precisely the attitude that Furmanov set out to question. In a scene depicting Chapaev's intervention into the heart of a mutiny against his leadership, his incisive, disciplined reprimand to his troops is contrasted with the hyperbolic gesticulations of the leader of the mutineers. And in the battle scenes (which are strongly reminiscent of the westerns by which the Vasil'evs were invariably influenced)

Chapaev is an awe-inspiring, righteous figure, striking terror into the hearts of his enemy. At the end of the film, after the death of Chapaev and Pet'ka following a desperate attempt to swim across the Ural river in flight from the Whites who have routed Chapaev's men with a sudden night-time raid, the Vasil'evs close with shots of the Red Army, Anka at its heart, launching a ferocious counter-attack, thus replacing Furmanov's measured, and less-than-wholly-uncritical, assessment of Chapaev's role in Civil War history with an undiluted optimism about his legacy.

Many of these changes are explained by the apocryphal oral legends of the 1920s which, with their inflated versions of Chapaev's prowess, mediated his migration from screen to page. In conjunction with structural changes imposed by the transfer from page to screen, the plot differences can be aligned with ideological issues arising from a comparison of the two works. Draft scenarios open with Furmanov waking from a dream of Chapaev looking commandingly down from his steed, to the sound of the real Chapaev entering the room. In the definitive scenario, the first frames represent Chapaev riding into camera. The abandonment of the dream (and of the build up to Chapaev's appearance) result from cinema's lack of a distinctive narrative consciousness. Positioned at the site of the camera, the viewer replaces Furmanov as the perceiving subject of the unfolding events. But with no distinct reality to wake up to, viewers remain in dreamlike thrall to the fantasy figure. This effect is reinforced by the inclusion at a later point in the film of the 'Chapaev on horseback' shot within a pseudo-objective battle scene. Because film's perceiving subject migrates with the camera from character to character, a visually embodied holder of party values is liable to become the object of other, less reliable visions, as in scenes where the viewer shares Chapaev's jokes at the Commissar's expense. Thus, the Vasil'ev brothers inadvertently undermine their own efforts to correct Furmanov's ideological waverings and bring the text into line with Socialist Realist axioms.

Even cinematic flashbacks cannot emulate the verbal, past-tense narration of Furmanov's original, as the film's depiction of Chapaev's death indicates. The directors translate the temporal omniscience accorded Furmanov's readers who know Chapaev is to die into a spatial montage juxtaposing shots of the White assault with shots of Chapaev relaxing. We experience the impending threat to Chapaev, but not the inevitability of his death, whose meaning is crowded out by our vicarious desire to forestall the hero's fate. When the film was first shown, some of the same mature socialist workers praised by the film's reviewers went from cinema to cinema hoping to find a true version in which their hero lives on!

Whilst Furmanov's novel is compressed into sketch-like summaries illustrated by individual episodes framed by an iterative 'he would', since film lacks an imperfect tense, the film barely differentiates the central from the marginal, constructing each episode as a singular event to be integrated with the main plot. It thus underscores its capacity to invoke in its viewer pure, authentic presence. Even Boris Shumiatskii, Stalin's film czar, acknowledged in *Pravda* that the film's effect on 'today's masses' relies on its ability to unite them in co-presence with the individual heroism of yesterday, unwittingly recalling the very '*stikhii-nost*' Furmanov aimed to expose and eradicate. The audience senses its collective belonging through its identification with visually striking images of singular individuals. Thus, in a scene in which Anka is about to be engulfed by the Whites, she suddenly rejoices at Chapaev's appearance. The camera oscillates between mirror-like close-ups of Anka's ecstatic face, and long shots of the massing Red Army, instigating a three-way identification between viewer, heroine and heroic masses. The Vasil'evs' use of such montage editing bears the influence of the earlier cinematic avant-garde, demonstrating that its lessons had now been absorbed into mainstream Stalinist film. Eisenstein, who had advised the brothers earlier in their career, lavished praise on *Chapaev*, suggesting that it represented the start of a 'third period' in Soviet cinema. Indeed, the famous 'psychic attack' sequence in the film (in which vast columns of White soldiers are shown marching to the beat of drums straight at the heart of the Chapaev division) is often compared with the 'Odessa steps' sequence in Eisenstein's *Bronenosets Potemkin* (*The Battleship Potemkin*, 1925).

In reinforcing the Party's role (the film's task is not just to adapt Furmanov's novel, but to 'adopt' it into the socialist realist canon), the Vasil'ev brothers depict Furmanov (Klychkov) rather than Chapaev solving the looting crisis. This sequence is emblematic of the ideological work carried out by the film as a whole and repays closer attention. It begins with shots of a bemused peasant who, having been robbed of his livestock by marauding Chapaev soldiers, complains that the Reds and the Whites are all the same. The leader of the looters (one of Chapaev's most trusted men) is subsequently arrested by a suitably stern and authoritative Furmanov, who orders the looted goods to be returned. When he learns of the arrest of his trusted lieutenant, Chapaev explodes with anger, accusing Furmanov of being a bureaucratic Party paper-pusher, to which Furmanov retorts by reminding Chapaev that he, too, is a servant of the Party. Chapaev remains stubbornly resistant to the notion of Party discipline and to acknowledging the impropriety of his mens' actions until a small group of peasants come to him and mistakenly thank him instead of Furmanov for righting the wrong done to them. At this point Chapaev undergoes a radical and permanent transformation conveyed dramatically through a facial close-up highlighting his 'moment of truth'. (This is in stark contrast with the novel which, with its predominantly imperfective narration, does not accommodate such transformations and in which Chapaev remains in essence unreformed.) Chapaev immediately calls all his men to a meeting and gives his admonitory speech (lifted word for word from the novel), in which he describes the looters as 'a disgrace to the Red Army'. He is shot admiringly from below, with Furmanov sitting silently and inconspicuously in the audience, rather than actively interpreting the event through his verbal narration. Visual gesture becomes the outer manifestation of the inner Party truth, which remains unseen, silent, but forever present. Rather than contradicting inner truth, visual surface, with all its excesses, becomes that truth's ideal expression.

This filmic desire for a coincidence of inner truth and outer gesture is apparent also in the rendition of Furmanov's depiction of the peasantry's long 'coming to knowledge', compressed here into sudden revelations. The decision of the White servant to switch allegiance is identified with the precise moment when he realises that the General bears responsibility for his brother's fate. The camera once again focuses on the peasant's face to capture the moment of inner truth made available for public scrutiny. The very impulsiveness critiqued by Furmanov in his novel provides the mechanism by which its cinematic representation is achieved.

In another transformative gesture with ideological consequences, the novelistic hindsight framing Chapaev's death is translated into a musical soundtrack dominated by the mournful tones of the 'Black Raven' folksong. The enwrapping of emotive image by rational word is replaced by a mystic fusion of word and image in which Chapaev becomes a fated, mythic figure. Far from undermining the Party's underlying truth, Chapaev's folksy eccentricities confirm that truth and, contrary to the novel's intention, remove him from time. The 'Black Raven' theme also confirms that the film is an embodiment of the official folklore that accumulated around Chapaev following the publication of Furmanov's novel, assimilating novel to legend and allowing the portrayal of Furmanov besides the fictionalised figures of Pet'ka and Anka. The Vasil'ev brothers' adaptation is thus not merely one of text to screen, but also one of a literary text that still displays the vestiges of the Leninist avant-garde, to an officially sanctioned culture bearing a deeply conservative populism grafted onto a preexisting rural folklore.

No discussion of *Chapaev* can be left without reference to the enduring fate of its intrepid hero beyond the year of its release. The film served initially to cement and augment the hero's cult status. Buildings, streets, battleships and even small towns were renamed after Chapaev. He became an object of reverence within the artificially manufactured Stalinist folklore documented by Frank Miller. World War Two even saw the release of a short film sequel: *Chapaev s nami* (*Chapaev is with Us*, 1941), directed by Vladimir Petrov, in which Chapaev makes it to the other side of the Ural river and returns to aid the Soviet war effort. But it was, ironically, the very public visibility and mythic abstraction of the hero dominating the 1934 film which generated the hero's subversive, post-Stalinist hypostasis. This subversion was the price to be paid by Stalinist ideology for the constructing of such inflated abstractions. Much of the cinematic Chapaev's humour is directed against the lack of practical know-how characteristic of the much-derided bureaucratic intellectual. In the context of Stalinist efforts to undermine the status of the *intelligent*, the presence of such humour in the Vasil'ev brothers' film is understandable. (The fact that it sits uneasily with their counter emphasis on the principles of Party-mindedness is one of many tensions with which viewers must engage.) In the political jokes (*anekdoty*) which circulated in the 1960s and 1970s, the humour is inverted since the addressee of the typical Chapaev joke is precisely the knowing intellectual (by now replete with dissident tendencies) who mocks the naïve beliefs and impossible feats of the unwitting socialist hero. In a post-Soviet twist to the Chapaev story, and to his peregrinations from text to oral culture to film and back, the anecdotes provided the basis for Viktor Pelevin's novel *Chapaev i Pustota* (*Chapaev and Pustota*, 1996) in which the characters of the anecdotes find themselves entangled in a web of absurd plot lines involving post-Soviet businessmen, Eastern mystics, Western popular icons, as well as the heroes of the 1934 version of *Chapaev*.

The seeds of the inversion that Chapaev suffered under Stalin's successors were present in the original film which itself echoed tensions inhabiting Furmanov's original text. For Furmanov, the problem is one of self-justification: how can a text railing against the ideological pitfalls of individualistic spontaneity establish as its centre of narrative interest the enigma of a spontaneous individual? Through its tortuous ideological ratiocinations, Furmanov's text foregrounds this contradiction, but in the 1934 film, the tension is superseded by an all-too-convenient elision of inner (verbal) abstraction and outer (visual) surface in which the latter supports the emphasis on reason and discipline propagated by the former. Yet the shift from text to film, and the accompanying change in political function (that of marking the emergent official consensus around the dogma of Socialist Realism with whose launch the film's release coincided), means that the film must initiate viewers into its ideology of abstract Party Truth precisely through spontaneous celebrations of visual surface. It is only logical that a revanchist, post-Stalinist intelligentsia with distinctly unofficial allegiances should later turn the tables on the Vasil'ev brothers by replacing the cinematic Chapaev's witty vitality with a puffed-up Socialist Realist abstraction ripe for puncturing by its own subversive brand of witty vitality. It was left to Pelevin to complete the circle by re-appropriating Chapaev for the new post-Soviet literary avant-garde.

Chapaev lives on, too, thanks to the nostalgic Soviet 'retro-culture' which has insinuated itself into post-Soviet society at a number of levels; newly published books of Chapaev jokes coexist with websites devoted to (sometimes scatalogically, sometimes affectionately) humorous visual and verbal caricatures of the legendary hero and his two eternal sidekicks, Pet'ka and An'ka. And there now even exists a web-based computer game based around the comic exploits of the Chapaev and Pet'ka of the anecdote genre: 'Petka and VICH Save the Galaxy'. Chapaev, it would seem, is as much a man for all media as he is a man for all seasons.

Stephen Hutchings

REFERENCES

Crofts, S. (1977) 'Ideology and Form: Soviet Socialist Realism and *Chapayev*', *Essays in Poetics*, 2, 1, 43–57.

Ferro, M. (1976) 'The Fiction Film and Historical Analysis', in P. Smith (ed.) *The Historian and Film*, Cambridge: Cambridge University Press, 80–95.

Furmanov, D. (1966) *Chapaev*. Moscow: Detskaia literatura.

Hicks, J. (2005) 'Educating Chapaev: From Document to Myth', in S. Hutchings and A. Vernitski (eds) *Russian and Soviet Film Adaptations of Literature, 1900–2001: Screening the Word*, London: RoutledgeCurzon, 43–58.

Leyda, J. (1960) *Kino: A History of the Russian and Soviet Film*. Princeton: Princeton University Press.

Shumiatskii, B. (1988 [1935]) 'A Cinema for the Millions (extracts)', in R. Taylor and I. Christie (eds) *Inside The Film Factory: Russian and Soviet Cinema in Documents 1896–1939*. London and New York: Routledge, 358–69.

Zorkaya, N. (1991) *The Illustrated History of the Soviet Cinema*, New York: Hippocrene Books.

VESELYE REBIATA THE HAPPY GUYS

GRIGORII ALEKSANDROV, USSR, 1934

Veselye rebiata (*The Happy Guys*, 1934; also known as *Jolly Fellows, Jazz Comedy, Moscow Laughs, The World is Laughing, Happy-Go-Lucky Guys*) was the first feature-length film made by Sergei Eisenstein's former assistant Grigorii V. Aleksandrov (né Mormonenko, 1903–83). It marked a significant break from Eisenstein's film theory and practice and inaugurated a series of Soviet 'musical comedies' which held audiences in thrall during the Great Terror of the 1930s and the Great Patriotic War of 1941–45.

Like the Hollywood musicals that were their inspiration, Soviet musical comedies 'varnished reality'. Their ideological task was to divert the mass audience of workers and peasants from their difficulties and offer them the hope that the future would be better and that present sacrifices were not in vain. As Richard Taylor has demonstrated, for Boris Shumiatskii, who was in charge of the Soviet cinema industry from 1930 until his execution in 1938, musical comedies were the lynchpin of the 'cinema for the millions' he hoped to create and the centre-piece of his 'Soviet Hollywood'.

Aleksandrov's previous career had been as principal assistant to Eisenstein in both his stage and film work, appearing in *Dnevnik Glumova* (*Glumov's Diary*, 1923) and working (sometimes as actor, sometimes as scriptwriter) on all Eisenstein's silent features from *Stachka* (*The Strike*, 1925) to *General'naia liniia* (*The General Line*, released as *Staroe i novoe* (*The Old and the New*) in 1929). He accompanied Eisenstein and his cameraman, Eduard Tisse, on their foreign travels from 1929 to 1932 and it was Aleksandrov who was left behind in New York to try and sort out the mess surrounding Eisenstein's unfinished Mexican film, *Que viva Mexico! The Happy Guys* was not, however, Aleksandrov's first film; in Paris in 1930 he had made a short film to earn some money by promoting the career of the singer Mara Gris. Some historians have attributed this film to Eisenstein himself but it clearly bears the stylistic hallmarks of Aleksandrov's work and the direction was probably attributed to Eisenstein purely for marketing purposes. Aleksandrov had also directed two documentaries: *Giftgas* (*Poison Gas*, 1928) and *Internatsional* (*The Internationale*, 1933), so he came to *The Happy Guys* with broad experience not only of filmmaking but also of what was happening in cinema world-wide. He had evidently been particularly impressed with the choreography of Busby Berkeley in American stage and screen musicals.

The Happy Guys was Aleksandrov's first collaboration with other members of what was to become a remarkably successful filmmaking team. From his work with Eisenstein and his documentary The Internationale, Aleksandrov brought with him the cameraman Vladimir Nil'sen (1905–1938), who introduced a variety of Western film techniques, including composite shots and back projection, into Soviet cinema and died shortly afterwards in the purges. They were joined by the singer and classically-trained actress Liubov' Orlova (1902–1975), the composer Isaak Dunaevskii (1900–1955), the lyricist Vasilii Lebedev-Kumach (1898–1949) and the satirist and scriptwriter Nikolai Erdman (1900–1970). It was also Aleksandrov's only collaboration with the leading figure in Soviet jazz, Leonid Utesov (né Vaisbain, 1895–1982); their egos proving to be a hindrance to any positive professional relationship. At the other extreme, Liubov' Orlova, who had already appeared on both stage and screen, soon became Aleksandrov's wife. Most of the team went on to make Tsirk (The Circus, 1936; Nil'sen was arrested during the shooting), Volga-Volga (1938, reputedly Stalin's favourite film), Svetlyi put' (The Radiant Path, 1940), with some of them also involved in Vesna (Springtime, 1947) and Vstrecha na El'be (Meeting on the Elbe, 1949), although these last two films could by no stretch of the imagination be classified as musical comedies.

The Happy Guys began life as a script called 'Dzhaz-komediia' ('Jazz Comedy') and even at that stage proved controversial. Jazz had an ambiguous and highly insecure position in Soviet culture, with many critics regarding it as both alien and bourgeois, while its popularity among members of the Soviet elite gave it some protection. Comedy was in an equally ambiguous and insecure position, given its essentially subversive nature. But as Aleksandrov has noted the 'social command' of the early 1930s was to make films that were 'accessible' and 'intelligible to the millions' and the viewers were demanding Soviet sound-film comedies. Eisenstein and Aleksandr Dovzhenko were among the directors recruited to the cause of film comedy, although their projects did not come to fruition. According to the film historian Ivan Frolov, it was Shumiatskii himself who suggested a film version of Dunaevskii's Muzykal'nyi magazin (Music Shop), staged at the Leningrad Music-Hall (where he was director) and performed by Utesov and his 'Thea-Jazz' (an attempt to combine the traditions of both theatre and jazz) ensemble and they all contributed to the script for 'Jazz Comedy'.

It was the custom in those days for a developing film project to be discussed both professionally and politically at every stage of its production. 'Jazz Comedy' was no exception. The organ of the Communist Youth, *Komsomolskaia Pravda* (26 March 1933), welcomed the film as 'the first swallow of the comic "film spring"' and praised the speed – two-and-a-half months – with which the script had been produced. The newspaper was to be a constant pillar of support throughout the controversies that raged around the film. A long and acrimonious discussi

on took place at Moscow's House of Scholars in April 1933. Frodov cites Esfir Shub, the documentary filmmaker, as stating: 'Substitute English names and you have a real American comedy. The film is nothing to do with us. It's a sort of demonstration of skills, done in a very interesting and entertaining way. But nothing to do with us. It comes from America, from revue.'

Frodov also cites Iulii Raizman as comparing the script to a Harold Lloyd comedy: 'The only difference is that a Lloyd comedy is inseparable from its background in everyday life ... and society in America. *Jazz Comedy* has no such background and no basis.' The trade paper *Kino* commented on 16 April 1933: 'Those who were arguing about its social significance were essentially knocking on an open door. The author has from the very outset openly declared that he actually wanted to produce a script with weak ideological content. *Jazz Comedy* makes no pretence at a problematic.'

Aleksandrov's response was swift and pithy: 'Soviet comedy has too many problematics and it has ceased to be funny.' When the script was re-worked, any ideological issues were removed. Cited in Frolov's volume, Aleksandrov argued that 'Our basic task is to resolve the problem of laughter. And that is all! So there is no idea in the film. The author himself makes this confession to both his supporters and his adversaries.' This confession apparently unnerved the Party cell at the Moscow studios at Potylikha, although the concentration of resources on this film at the expense of other current projects may also have provoked their wrath. According to *Kino* on 28 May 1933, the cell members declared: 'The well-tried tenets of bourgeois comedy and comic film and the experience of Chaplin and Buster Keaton are mirrored with no critical assimilation in the script for *Jazz Comedy* ... We consider that the script is unsuitable for both production and release.'

In the same edition of *Kino*, they argued that the script's approval 'must be seen as a political mistake' by those responsible. But those responsible were also in charge of the film press and their response was swift and sharp: 'The statement about *Jazz Comedy* by the [Party] cell reflects the most backward attitudes of those hacks and aesthete-filmmakers who cannot or will not make the films that the millions of workers and peasants in the audience need.'

The shock effect of the film begins with the opening titles, which are animated in both senses of the term. Caricatures of Charlie Chaplin, Harold Lloyd and Buster Keaton appear, for the audience to be told that they do not appear in the film. Here Aleksandrov is throwing down the gauntlet to his critics, defiantly asserting that *The Happy Guys* is emphatically not an American film. This is followed by caricatures of those who *do* appear in the film: Leonid Utesov, Liubov' Orlova, Mariia Strelkova and the mysterious Mariia Ivanovna, a common Russian woman's name and patronymic that appropriately turns into a question mark and then a cartoon cow, running across the screen, dipping its tail into a bucket of paint and writing out the title of the film. The restored version then shows the full film credits unfolding against a jazzy moving background of wavy lines, stars and stripes, conveying the impression of action and excitement, and all accompanied by a jazz-based tune from Dunaevskii.

The film proper opens with a shot of the sign over the entrance to the 'Limpid Springs' collective farm: the name is painted against a rising sun. It is morning and a new day dawns. We hear a trumpet fanfare and, as the gates open, we see a shepherd (Kostia Potekhin, played by Utesov) wearing a floppy hat. He plays the first notes of the 'March of the Happy Guys' on his whistle. Like the Pied Piper, he is joined by a band of followers, each playing a different instrument and together they march forward, to the sound of the animals in the background, through the village. This scene is cleverly designed to appear as a continuous panning shot from right to left, but is in fact carefully edited in a veritable 'montage of attractions'. The camera is in constant motion, moving with the protagonists from left to right and up and down: this makes the viewer feel that s/he is walking alongside. The rhythm of the screen movement is matched by the rhythm of Dunaevskii's march. This is hardly surprising as Aleksandrov and Dunaevskii worked out in advance a 'phonogram' for each scene, a precise record of how image and sound should relate to each other. There is a general air of festivity and flag-waving and various characters wave and smile in the background. The whole atmosphere is upbeat and optimistic, and this too is echoed by the music and the lyrics:

Merry singing fills the heart with joy, it will never let you be sad.
The countryside and villages love singing, and big cities love singing too.

The song, given in full in the volume edited by James von Geldern and Richard Stites, brings everyone together, man and nature in unison. Singing is central to life, as the refrain implies:

A song helps us building and living, like a friend it calls and leads us forth.
And whoever goes through life singing, will never ever fall behind.

Kostia is filmed in low-angle shots against the sky, increasing the sense of unity with nature and his surroundings. As he crosses a wooden bridge, he 'tap-dances' on the logs. Passing some iron railings, he plays on them like a xylophone. Crossing the veranda of a wooden hut, he wakes the man sleeping in a hammock with a cheery 'Guten Morgen, Karl Ivanovich!' Pots upturned on a wattle fence also serve as musical instruments. Tap-dancing on another wooden bridge, he crosses and meets a servant-girl (Aniuta, played by Orlova), who is captivated. She spills the milk from her urns, drops them and runs after him. As he passes a fence, she leans against it and it collapses. He marches on without noticing her, past the village smithy and out of the village. Wielding his whip above his head, we see him in low-angle shot as he calls to his cattle by their human names. This opening sequence is crucially important, as Aleksandrov uses it to engage his audience completely through his combination of imagery and music. We are, in the space of less than five minutes, completely immersed in the fantasy world of *The Happy Guys*.

Kostia reads out the roll-call of his animals, starting with Chamberlain the bull, whom we shall encounter later. The animals respond as if they are human. One of them is a cow, the mysterious Maria Ivanovna of the opening titles. The sound of the march returns as Kostia goes to meet his music teacher, a good German, the Karl Ivanovich we have already briefly encountered (played by Robert Erdman, Nikolai's father). He is so appalled at his pupil's playing (and at his choice of music) that he gives him a violin and tells him to play the music on a stave marked out by the birds sitting on the telegraph wires. The last bird hovers and flies away and the music follows suit. Kostia then plays a seriously romantic piece of music and the film cuts to the beach scene.

The Happy Guys now shows us the first of a series of grotesque caricatures of the unhappy guys, the remnants of the old bourgeoisie who have survived the 1920s under the New Economic Policy. A band plays a waltz in the background. The women in particular evoke the caricatures of the bourgeoisie in Eisenstein's *Oktiabr'* (*October*, 1927), even down to the parasols. They are getting excited at the prospect of the arrival of the foreign conductor Costa Frasquini. Their gestures, clothing and speech are all exaggeratedly 'refined'. Chief amongst them are Lena (Mariia Strelkova) and her mother (Elena Tiapkina (1900–1984)). Frasquini is indeed on the beach 'in foreign dress'. Meanwhile Kostia is finishing his violin piece, with Aniuta listening in admiration. He disrobes and jumps into the sea, allowing the first of a series of mistaken identities to move the plot forward.

The camera tracks to the right across the beach: a special narrow-gauge railway was built to facilitate this manoeuvre. As Lena saunters along to Frasquini's pitch, we are treated to a host of caricatures of the bourgeoisie at play. As she approaches, Frasquini also disrobes and swims into the sea. Lena settles down on the pebbles and mistakes the approaching Kostia for the departing foreigner. In the conversation that follows she invites Kostia to a reception to meet her mother. The mistaken identity is reinforced by the dialogue.

Lena and her mother are staying in the former 'Black Swan', now a 'pension for non-organised tourists'. This description marks them out as bourgeois individualists, since by the mid-1930s all tourism within the USSR was organised in groups. They are unorganised and will shortly also be *dis*organised by their encounter with Kostia and his carnival of the animals. The reception is full of caricatures: the only real character in the household is the maid, Aniuta, who sings as she does the housework. Here she plays the same kind of Cinderella role as she was later to play in *The Radiant Path*. She can sing, whereas Lena merely has pretensions in that direction. Overhearing Aniuta sing, Kostia thinks it is Lena. His animals have followed him and, once he starts playing his flute, they follow him inside, consuming all the food and drink that has been laid out for the guests. It is an orgy of destruction in which the animals undermine the pretensions of the bourgeoisie. The scene is packed with gags and the descent into anarchy that they signpost is reminiscent more of the Marx Brothers than of Chaplin, Lloyd or Keaton. In places the humour is even distinctly surreal. By the end of the evening, Kostia's true identity has been unmasked and he is asked to leave. Apparently alone in the moonlight he sings for the first time of the problems of love and a broken heart in the song with a tango rhythm, 'Kak mnogo devushek khoroshikh...' ('How many fine girls...'), which became a popular hit. He has Lena in mind, but it is Aniuta who has been listening.

A cartoon intertitle tells us that several hours have passed. Lena has left by steamer and Kostia is downcast. Aniuta, rejected, sings to a waltz rhythm, 'The Heart'. The love interest has now been clearly established. Another animated intertitle tells us that a month has passed. The action moves to Moscow, and specifically to the music-hall, where Frasquini is eagerly awaited to conduct an orchestral revue, with banks of *white* grand pianos, double basses and harps and lots of flashing lights. The foreigner is late and another case of mistaken identity leads Kostia to usurp his costume and his position and conduct an 'original treatment' of Liszt's 'Hungarian Rhapsody' in a scene where the orchestra takes his spontaneous physical gestures as movements of the conductor's baton. As he descends the onstage stairs, the music descends the scale, and so on. In the audience Lena and her mother think they have made a mistake and that Kostia *was* the foreigner after all. Frasquini eventually arrives and, after a series of gags and chase scenes, Kostia is once more unmasked and chased from the stage. His escape is aided by a group of lads who turn out to form a band, and he agrees to join them.

Another animated intertitle tells us that several months have passed. The lads are rehearsing but disagreements soon descend into fighting, in which the various instruments are used as weapons. According to Frolov, this scene is 150 metres, or four minutes, long and consists of 250 different shots. Dunaevskii remarked that this was the most complicated music scene he ever wrote. Once more the film descends into anarchy, although according to Mark Kushnirov this is reputed to have been Stalin's favourite scene, driving him into a state of 'childish delight'. By contrast, in a brief interlude, Lena's ambition to sing at the Bolshoi is undermined when she is outsung by Aniuta, who has also been mysteriously translated to Moscow. Evicted from their rehearsal room, the lads get their music practice in a funeral procession (a scene apparently inspired by René Clair), dancing and playing in the street, at least when the policeman is not looking. The funeral procession is caught in the rain and, as the hearse rushes to get the band to the Bolshoi on time, Aniuta is run over and Kostia extracts her from beneath the horses' hooves.

In the closing scene, the band arrive at the Bolshoi, soaked to the skin. The hearse-driver holds Aniuta hostage for the fare. On stage, battered and bruised, the lads cannot play their instruments because they are filled with water. They improvise by humming the sound their instruments would have made. The hearse driver gets drunk on vodka and leads a somewhat inebriated Aniuta to join the lads on stage as they reprise the march that opened the film. In a Cinderella-turned-princess transformation that was to become her hallmark, she reprises in a duet with Utesov the film's most popular songs and a new comic love song, 'Tiukh, tiukh…'. The pace becomes more hectic and the music less jazz-like and more folk-like (Cossack dancing included) as the curtain falls. Kostia tries to declare his love for Aniuta but is repeatedly interrupted by the hearse-driver. To popular acclaim the band reappears onstage in a final rendition of the march that opened the film. As Orlova and Utesov reprise the refrain for the last time, the camera draws back though the theatre in a device worthy of the Hollywood stage musical. On this triumphant note *The Happy Guys* ends.

The completed film caused – in the words of Aleksandrov, Frolov and Kushnirov – a *bol'shoi skandal*: a big scandal. *The Happy Guys* was undoubtedly the most controversial film in Soviet cinema history. Support came, once again, from the *Komsomolskaia Pravda*, whilst *Literaturnaia gazeta*, the official organ of the Soviet Writers' Union, led the attack. One critic accused Dunaevskii of having plagiarised 'The March of the Happy Guys' from Jack Conway's Hollywood film *Viva Villa!* (1934), which had been shown at the first Moscow International Film Festival that summer. A special commission was set up to investigate and found the composer not guilty. Crucially, the attack was supported by the People's Commissar for Enlightenment, Andrei Bubnov (1884–1938), to whom Shumiatskii was ultimately responsible. Bubnov banned the film and said that it would only be released 'over his dead body'. Shumiatskii, who still supported the film, had to outwit his superior. He suggested to Aleksandrov that they show the completed film to the writer Maxim Gor'kii, who had previously been critical of jazz. This proved to be a very shrewd move. Gor'kii rejected the charges of 'Americanism' and, as cited by Frolov, remarked: 'The Americans would never have dared to do anything like this … Here I see real Russian bravery on a grand scale.'

Gor'kii and Shumiatskii then organised a special showing for the Politburo, including Stalin. Shumiatskii showed them the first two reels, while Aleksandrov waited in the wings on the pretence that it was not yet finished. This was an even shrewder move because it left them demanding more. Frolov cites Stalin as stating: 'It's a very happy film. I feel as though I have been on holiday for a month. It will be useful to show it to all our workers and collective farmers. But take the film away from the director. He will only spoil it.'

Aleksandrov's film was eventually released on 25 December 1934 and proved to be one of the most popular films in Soviet cinema history. At the 1934 Venice Film Festival it was selected as one of the six best films. Critics have argued ever since over whether it is an Aleksandrov, an Orlova or a Dunaevskii film, but, whatever audiences decide for themselves, it is Dunaevskii's unforgettable music that will come back to haunt them.

Richard Taylor

REFERENCES

Aleksandrov, G. (1976) *Epokha i kino*. Moscow: Izdatel'stvo politicheskoi literatury.
Frolov, I. (1976) *Grigorii Aleksandrov*. Moscow: Iskusstvo.
Kushnirov, M. (1998) *Svetlyi put', ili Charli i Spenser*. Moscow: Terra-Knizhnyi klub.

Taylor, R. (1991) 'Ideology as Mass Entertainment: Boris Shumyatsky and Soviet Cinema in the 1930s', in R. Taylor and I. Christie (eds) *Inside the Film Factory. New Approaches to Russian and Soviet Cinema*. London and New York: Routledge, 193–216.

Von Geldern, J. and R. Stites (eds) (1995) *Mass Culture in Soviet Russia: Tales, Poems, Songs, Movies, Plays and Folklore, 1917–1953*, Bloomington, IN: Indiana University Press.

VESELYE REBIATA

KARNAVAL'NAIA NOCH' CARNIVAL NIGHT

EL'DAR RIAZANOV, USSR, 1956

Karnaval'naia noch' (*Carnival Night*, 1956) is the movie that began the career of Russia's most popular comedy director, El'dar Riazanov. The name of this film alone hints at magical festivity, at how the (usually) impossible can briefly become possible, just as it does during carnivals all the way from Moscow to Rio de Janeiro or Venice. As one might imagine, those types of disrespectful, if not 'subversive', intimations might have unnerved the Soviet film industry. The film's plot revolves around some students' plans for a chaotic celebration on New Year's Eve. While their jokes and musical numbers are practiced for the forthcoming entertainment, two of the students, Grisha Kol'tsov and his sweetheart Lena Krylova, are constantly interrupted by the club's meddlesome director, Comrade Serafim Ogurtsov. He objects to the students' understanding of festive humour and declares a lot of their planned performances 'offensive'.

He soon becomes so irritating and unhelpful that there remains only one solution if the evening's games are to go ahead: he must be kidnapped and hidden somewhere in the club until the evening is over! As soon as Ogurtsov is absent, all his miserable suggestions for 'entertainment' are dropped from the playbill and light-hearted humour makes a most welcome return. The 'reliable' aged members of a small orchestra tear off their false beards to reveal a youthful jazz ensemble. The dancing begins and Ogurtsov's role as compère is now handed over to a new generation, to Grisha. In this unexpected responsibility as 'director', he gains confidence and is able (for the first time) to tell Lena that he loves her.

Despite this risky role-playing, the names of our student sweethearts seem from the very outset to work in their favour: Kol'tsov comes from the word for '(wedding) ring' and Krylova hints at the plural noun 'wings'. Even Ogurtsov's first name is angelic (though his surname is less romantically translatable into English as 'Pickleson'). It is this air of heart-warming inevitability that makes the film so popular today. Every year it plays on several channels as the New Year approaches. Because the Soviets replaced Christmas with New Year as the major state-approved family festival of the calendar, 'Carnival Night' has become as important for holiday television programming as, say, *It's a Wonderful Life* (1946) in the

United States, or *A Christmas Carol* (1984) in Great Britain. The closing song of the film, 'Piat' minut' ('Five Minutes'), defines these holiday hopes and dreams best of all; it celebrates both an impending inevitable happiness at midnight and the fact that a mere five minutes can change what seems inevitable!

So why is little known about this man and his work in the West? Despite making more than twenty films, all of which enjoyed nationwide success, Riazanov has not been blessed by critical attention in the English language. This is because the usual figures emphasised in Western studies of Russian cinema tend to be those of a more 'serious' inclination, in particular Andrei Tarkovskii. Yet Russian viewers have always preferred good entertainment to intellectual cinema. This fact is borne out in a 1991 survey conducted in the journal *Ekran* that declared Riazanov 'The Union's All-Time Favorite Director'. The result left Tarkovskii in second place, receiving no more than a third of the votes allotted to his cheerful adversary.

The accolades were nothing new; Riazanov had already been held in very high regard for decades. In August 1983, when readers of *Izvestiia* were asked to choose the one figure (actor or otherwise) for whom they felt the greatest sympathy, Riazanov again came top. Indeed this pattern can be traced back further still, to the first few years after the release of *Carnival Night*. One of his earliest features, *Devushka bez adresa* (*Girl Without an Address*), appeared in 1957 and although Riazanov was at this stage still very much a fledgling director, entertainment bureaus in the capital had to abandon the idea of screening the feature in movie theatres alone, since the eager crowds could not be housed in traditional venues. As a result, one Moscow sports stadium was equipped with an enormous temporary screen and the seats usually occupied by screaming sports fans were soon filled by 8,000 visitors for each showing.

As suggested by the mockery of Ogurtsov, similar noisy passion from a film director's fans was tied to new dreams of democracy after Stalin's death. Nikita Khrushchev's 'Secret Speech' in 1956, so damning of his predecessor, had brought to an end both the Cult of Personality and the grand art thereof, but it remained unclear what types of kinder, more accepting arts were now expected. Despite the logical usefulness of wit and satire in any period of liberal reform, the state's definition of appropriate comedy films remained vague. How funny or disrespectful could a comedy director afford to be? The Soviet critic Rostislav Iurenev considered this matter in his 1961 study of Soviet cinematic comedy; even here, four years after Riazanov's debut, it appears that the complicated debate over acceptable humour continued:

The Communist Party of the Soviet Union has placed a new task before Soviet culture with several proclamations pertaining to the relationship between life and enlightenment. They reveal a new age in the evolution of cinematic comedy … Nonetheless the Soviet people's high expectations of this genre still allow us to conclude that all is far from well in our nationally cherished, happy art form. We produce a great deal of comedies today, but not enough of them are successful! Fear of being satirical has not yet disappeared. Clichés are still widespread, together with other repetitious, hackneyed images and subjects. Feeblemindedness and bad taste have still not been eradicated.

Post-Stalinist humour was still expected to play an educational role, much as it had done in the 1930s, but beyond that films should also reflect upon moral and existential choice. They should explore family relationships: humorous films would therefore spell out the workings of small social networks, together with the role of free will therein. Funny storytelling would start all over again and clarify the proper way to interact (without recourse to grandeur). El'dar Riazanov's first feature film introduced this new concept of Soviet comedy by focusing on the individual, that is on a few lovers rather than teeming hordes. In doing so, his musical comedy *Carnival Night* managed to show respect for the Stalinist variety traditions of Grigorii Aleksandrov's and Ivan Pyr'ev's comedies of the 1930s, whilst mapping out potential directions for future fun and games on the silver screen after the death of Stalin.

Iuren'ev was able to remark with greater freedom by 1964 that the importance of *Carnival Night* lay in its ability to conclude the erstwhile miserable tendency to 'over-insure' oneself against the dangers of ignoring or overstepping dogma; in the past this was done by 'varnishing' over any negative aspects of contemporary life that did not fit simple ideologised rubrics. This seems a heavy legacy to place upon the shoulders of a throwaway comedy, but after *Carnival Night*, more serious films also investigated small-scale micropolitical interaction with greater honesty in a political country. Riazanov's film introduced a relativity of values that found expression in subsequent dramas. The small but telling domains soon scrutinised elsewhere included the difficulties of marriage (Mikhail Shveitser's *Chuzhaia rodnia* (*Someone Else's Family*, 1955)), love between teacher and adult pupil (Feliks Mironer and Marlen Khutsiev's *Vesna na Zarechnoi ulitse* (*Spring on Zarechnaia Street*, 1956)) or ways in which people tried to work together in the cramped quarters of urban lodging (Lev Kulidzhanov's *Dom, v kotorom ia zhivu* (*The House I Live In*, 1957)). And so began the employment of unique characters and unique experience in a way that prior Stalinist decades would undoubtedly have dismissed as 'subjective idealism'.

Conflict between some young people and an aging bureaucrat hardly seems like material for a dazzling farce, but newspapers of the late 1950s help us understand the movie's success. Laughing at people like Ogurtsov and all the Stalinist misery he represented was a moral enterprise. On 24 June 1959, the leading paper *Izvestiia* declared: 'The positive heroes of this comedy are agreeable primarily because they use laughter as a weapon in the moral battle with Ogurtsov. Being inclined to lectures and sloganeering, he cuts short every instance of creative initiative. These young people struggle against Ogurtsov, a real figure, seen in real life and hyperbolised here in the character of a bureaucrat. This is the secret of the film's popularity, its social meaning.'

That meaning comes not only on the wings of purportedly 'subversive' humour but invisibly, too. Love starts to change the world. Imperceptible sensations enter a stately system and change reality. They alter a realist art form with a comedy that although fundamentally acceptable to that same state also uses giggles and tears to evade the tedious terminology of somebody important. Private emotion starts doing a better job than somebody else's political posturing. Two philosophies are involved here and neither of them is inherently bad; one of them just deserves a little pity. Both are principally emotional (as public pathos or private passion) and are anticipations (not celebrated realisations) of something yet to come. Both are concerned with and directed towards the future.

The hopeful happy future of several youngsters' private outlook is established by muddling two styles (rant and romance), whilst simultaneously underscoring the fact that they can coexist. This is done through evident disrespect for 'generic purity'. Over the course of his career, Riazanov deliberately jumbled various cinematic genres, producing as a result what he would later call comedy-tracts, tragicomedies, satirical comedies or lyrical dramas. They would, conversely, be unified by repeated and shared emphases upon love among his heroes, all as defence against any 'standardisation of feelings'. Iurii Dmitriev, writing in *Moskovskii komsomolets* in January 1957, may have declared that this film showed the 'logic of Soviet society' but we can see already how such logic, when examined closely between two people (not two million) confounds standardisation.

As a wonderful example of how this story and outlook were applicable to the outside, real world, Evgenii Gromov cites how even the film's heroine, Liudmila Gurchenko (b. 1935), claimed she was infected by the jollity on set. She ran around, saying to herself: 'I want everything; I can do everything, I love everybody and like everything!' We therefore have a story of change, of youthful metamorphoses both behind and in front of the cameras. Alterations of various kinds would often find expression in Riazanov's oeuvre, in particular his films set before or on New Year's Day, a time offering hope for 'unbelievable' metamorphoses. The emotional and social changes of *Carnival Night* are likewise reflected in a movement back and forth between songs and skits that recalls an old, if not pre-Revolutionary art form: the cabaret or estrada vaudeville. A narrative centred on the small stage with multiple funny performers and genres served as the perfect vehicle for an affirmative but unpredictable venture. Riazanov uses an old-fashioned well-loved jumble of songs also reminiscent – as he said – of a Broadway musical to express pity for Ogurtsov, whilst outpacing him with the kind of emotional and social changes that leave bureaucrats in a cloud of dust. This sentimental sedition might have unnerved some pencil-pushers at the state film studio of Mosfil'm, but at the movie's debut Riazanov saw one bureaucratic viewer fall from his chair, another chortle loudly, a third smile broadly and a fourth wipe tears of glee from his eyes This was not an angry critical practice but an interface of two philosophies.

The screenplay offers us many examples of this interface, beginning with the definition of Ogurtsov as walking talking hindrance. He does not like to joke and will give nobody else the opportunity to do so. Ogurtsov decides that the students' party could benefit from a lengthy educational lecture; the narrator sympathises with this admirable intent but moans under his breath: 'Happiness was so close!' Movement towards misery increases when Ogurtsov and his 'childish curiosity' at rehearsals become 'concern and suspicion' at everything unfamiliar. He complains to his superiors that the students' physical pranks might cause the audience injury, thus hurting the 'frontline workers of industry', even though the youngsters' vivacious 'danger' had already prompted amusement from the adult audience.

Ogurtsov will 'organise the event in a way that nobody can say anything about it'. He truly wishes to arrange a fine party beyond all reprimand (in terms of 'proper' leisure), yet in actual fact he fears the reactions of his superiors and thus risks a party so tedious and abstract that people would be unable to define what it is. By attempting to be clear, ideology is vague; by attempting to be serious it is funny. This tendency of political language to include its (often frightening) inverse as a result of a non-affirmative stance (law is law and that's all there is to say) sometimes results in an interesting paradox. A universalised category can no longer be an isolated, exclusive or exclusionary category; it is everywhere and everything. Total employment of *all* an ideology applies to will by implication touch upon its opposite too. The more constructive Ogurtsov tries to be with his well-intentioned ubiquitous politics, the more destruction he causes. We might be inclined to think the students' laughter would turn his bossiness upside down with a roar of 'revolutionary' laughter, but we should never lose sight of love's importance in this film. Here the students' carnival is not a Bakhtinian inversion of hierarchies (a time when *everything* is made relative), but almost the opposite: a simple attempt to fashion a reasonable and enduring philosophy alongside a series of grumpy negations about which 'nobody can say anything'.

That continuing philosophy, as one of Gurchenko's songs tells us, 'will never leave you'. It needs no more than a 'good mood' ('khoroshee nastroenie'). Since the mood itself is social, and one is already a member of a social(ist) collective, shyness over entering society is in fact a more pressing concern than privacy. *Carnival Night* is not concerned with social exclusion but with the possibility for inviting one and all. The private love interest between Lena and Grisha is therefore very significant and very much at the forefront of the screenplay. It is between these two people that we see the difficulties caused by bashfulness: Grisha's talk of possible love starts occasionally to sound like that of a man scared. He wavers on the edge of love as Ogurtsov wavers on the edge of another social group. Both are potential outsiders and Lena indeed upbraids Grisha on a regular basis for both 'bashfulness and equivocation'. He announces his love only when out of sight, in disguise or over an intercom. He does so anonymously and in such a staid awkward way that Ogurtsov thinks (wrongly) these amplified speeches are quotes from the world of histrionic English drama, from Shakespeare's tragedies.

Love is proposed as a fixative, albeit as kindly as possible; in Riazanov's films it always harbours the potential to alter big collectives from their smallest social core. Ideology and shy boyfriends may disagree over the nature of a better culture, and Ogurtsov may indeed disavow this 'mess' of an emotional affective public, but he will not leave it. The students' love is both within and ultimately respectful of Ogurtsov's 'other' collective, hence the prevalence in this tale of bashfulness and blushing cheeks, not the reddened faces of irate satire. The victory and safety of a compassionate society, overseen by love, allow Grisha to overcome his timidity only at the film's close, as shown in the following scene, quoted by Boris Laskin.

Lena [*without confidence*]: Grisha – maybe we could have a dance?
Grisha: Why 'maybe'?
Lena: What about it?

Grisha: What's all this shyness and indecision? We will dance. Right now.

    [*And so they waltz away.*]

Grisha: Here we are … dancing. Happy New Year! [*He kisses her.*]

Lena: What are you doing? Everybody here is watching. Aren't you ashamed!

Grisha: Happy New Year!

    [*Having summoned his nerve once and for all, he wants to kiss her again.*]

Lena [*reproachfully*]:   Oh, Grisha… [*Lena sees from the way that Grisha is looking at her that she'll have to give in.*] Oh, all right … close your eyes…

Grisha: You won't deceive me?

    [*Lena shakes her head.*]

Lena: Go on then, close them. You won't peek? Honest? Yes? … Happy New Year.

    [*She kisses him.*]

Grisha: Will it be a happy one?

    [*They keep dancing; Lena answers him with the kind of smile that takes the place of any words. The camera moves off and the entire frame is filled with the happy whirling movements of a waltz.*]

The concrete confident word to assure happiness in this slow departure from Stalinism has not yet been (or cannot be) uttered. Acquiescence to a social multitude does exist, but it is very much within a re-semanticised status quo. Later films would speak more assertively and with greater clarity. This early film does no more than offer happy hope.

If language is maybe outplayed by sentiment, charity and cheerfulness in *Carnival Night*, a word or two should be said about their visual representation. The film's opening establishing shot is a key scene in these processes of snowballing cheerful assertion. It amplifies our heroine's enthusiasm for life with some audacious, if not radically angled framing; the camera looks up at Gurchenko as she descends swiftly down a slide towards us. Then, with no time for rest, we follow her on a long dolly shot (with few words) through a crowd of many acquaintances, none of whom we yet know. She moves through and among these people by pushing the camera constantly backwards. We feel spatially the speed of her forcefulness because we give in to it. This eventful multidirectional technique of presentation is as far as possible from how Riazanov presents the bureaucrats on screen. They are shown to us less often, yet they fill each of their frames more, due to 'self-important' close-ups. The initial scenes of confrontation between Lena's happiness and a visually imposing severity take place almost in real time; the world does not yet belong to our swift youngsters. Little by little they will accelerate the proceedings.

The small domains through which Gurchenko and her male friends pass are made more private by the absence of non-diegetic sound. Although it controls the speed of life, the public context impinges very little upon the private. What, however, is underscored (as in several of Riazanov's other later movies) is the empty realm in which selfhood must realise itself. The depth of field in this film is often overwhelming, even though it was shot entirely indoors. Fleeting groups of youthful enthusiastic acquaintances try to map out and manage the vacuous parqueted realms of Stalinist dancehalls and corridors. The students' modest project must try and fill spaces built for grand, self-assured and 'adult' public functions.

This burgeoning activity within the student groups is emphasised by the visual presentation of their members' speech; the editing of their scenes accelerates as they discuss how to alter the status quo. The resultant crosscutting back and forth between people who are starting to interact passionately is in marked distinction to the long, leisurely shots of monotone bureaucrats. Lighting also plays a related role and helps to emphasise the initial differences between generations. The illumination cast upon Lena's face when she is inspired is softer, often from an unclear source.

The influence of Ogurtsov and his slower modus operandi find special, awkward expression during the songs; frame angles soon undermine that slowness, though, and begin to alter more and more often as the musical cabaret creates an active, infectious significance in multiple (shown) members of the adult crowd. Ogurtsov is thus slowly distanced from the camera more and more; as new, accepting and sentimental significances are created, the depth of field also lessens. Little by little something positive begins to fill the Stalinist emptiness – and thus make it a great deal smaller. The spectator, too, is offered a chance to enter these lively, moving spaces of song as the camera descends to the busy guests sitting at small tables near the stage. When observation becomes participation, the spotlights on stage become those of the film set. The spectator is at – and in – the event.

Gurchenko's face in the concluding number of 'Five Minutes' is shown in close-up; she has taken the place of Ogurtsov. He is now off-screen, under lock and key, very much an ignored voice. A voice pushed to the edges of our sentimental busy frames now becomes even non-diegetic; nobody hears it, nor do they care to! Grisha, inspired by this new atmosphere, invites Lena onto the dance floor; suddenly, in the tiny playing field of a visually compact deixis, we float across the floor with her. She spins around Stalinist opulence faster with Grisha than she did along corridors (without him); goal-directed movement has now involved another caring individual and become extremely ornate. A final, retreating crane shot pulls back to make public a venue now brimming with ballroom dances and balloons.

Just as a boyfriend and girlfriend changed an entire ballroom, the film went on to infect its audience with goodness and (almost improper) glee! *Carnival Night* slipped naturally into the hearts of a wide-ranging audience; one police officer told the newspaper *Sovetskaia kul'tura* in January 1957 he would like to see more movies in the same spirit, 'educating today's youth in the spirit of collectivism!' Despite the fact that Ogurtsov is sometimes pilloried, therefore, it seems once again unreasonable to call this film a satire, even if we ask the audience and ignore the academics. It was awarded several major prizes around the USSR.

Riazanov was not a huge fan of satire because in his view it pays more attention to the nasty, not the nice. After perestroika it certainly seemed to die a natural death and indeed, said the director, was bound to pass away with its context. Good satire, as Riazanov understands it, tries to improve its object both emotionally and (therefore) in a permanently valid manner. The director also, in a related philosophical stance, held that earnest self-critique is the foundation of any genuinely progressive society; shunning bureaucratic notions of proud progress in favour of self-deprecation and sentiment would always help to make Soviet society truly 'advanced'. Those same sentiments would steer satire towards an ethical, social benefit. To aid that movement, Riazanov sometimes quoted Marx's helpful dictum with regard to a people 'happily' abandoning their (faulty) past; *Carnival Night* happily abandons the progressive, linear outlook that even allows for the creation of a past. It advocates a caring point of view 'constantly based on love'.

David MacFadyen

REFERENCES

Gromov, E. (1989) *Komedii i ne tol'ko komedii*. Moscow: Kinotsentr.

Iuren'ev, R. (1961) *Sovetskaia kinokomediia*. Moscow: Institut istorii iskusstv.

_____ (1964) *Sovetskaia kinokomediia* (revised edition). Moscow: Nauka.

Laskin, B. (1990) *Izbrannoe*. Moscow: Sovetskii pisatel'.

BALLADA O SOLDATE BALLAD OF A SOLDIER

09

GRIGORII CHUKHRAI, USSR, 1959

Late in 1959, *Ballada o soldate* (*Ballad of a Soldier*) opened in Soviet cinemas, and soon there-after received international distribution; one of the first post-war Soviet films to reach Western audiences. At home and abroad, audiences and critics responded warmly to the film's straight-forward honesty, its organic simplicity, its compelling combination of innocence and pathos. *Ballad of a Soldier* quickly became, and has remained ever since, a classic of both Soviet and world cinema. Its stars, the appealing Vladimir Ivashov (1939–1995) and Zhanna Prokhorenko (b. 1940), continued to work on screen; one of its script-writers, Valentin Ezhov (1921–2004), authored or co-authored scripts for many films, including Vladimir Motyl"s smash hit *Beloe solntse pustyni* (*White Sun of the Desert*, 1969); its director, Grigorii Chukhrai (1921–2001), went on to make other well-regarded films, particularly *Chistoe nebo* (*Clear Skies*, 1961) and *Zhili-byli starik so starukhoi* (*There Once Lived an Old Man and an Old Woman*, 1965). But they never again found the magical combination of elements that produced *Ballad of a Soldier*.

The film begins as it ends, with a voice-over narration accompanying the image of a country road. A very young couple, a swaddled infant in the woman's arms, walk in one direction, and watch sadly as a middle-aged woman wearing a dark headscarf walks the other way, before stopping and gazing down the road. The narrator informs us that the woman's son left the village by this road and did not come back. Until her son went off to be a soldier, the narrator comments, his mother knew everything about him; the narrator knows the rest of the story...

That story begins with her son, 19-year-old Alesha Skvortsov, at the front. Confronting enemy tanks, Alesha, a radio signalman, tries to make contact with headquarters and then runs from the tanks as they advance on him like giant predators. Echoing a world gone mad, the camera spins upside-down as Alesha flees, sliding into a trench and ducking from what he assumes will be his inevitable death. He fires at one tank, more from desperation than any serious calculation: when the tank, mortally wounded, rears up in smoke before shuddering to stillness, no one is more surprised than he.

Though modestly disclaiming his bravery, Alesha receives a medal for disabling two tanks. He diffidently requests 24 hours' leave to go home – his unit is due for a break – so that he can fix a leaky roof, and see the mother he did not have time to kiss goodbye when he left for war. Alesha's village, Sosnovka, would normally be no more than a few hours' away. But as the paternal general understands, life is hardly normal. He authorises two days home, two days back, and two more 'to fix the roof'. As it turns out, his generous dispensation barely suffices for the kiss, let alone the roof.

The remainder of *Ballad of a Soldier*, Alesha's journey to his mother/motherland and home/homeland, consists of many small episodes and encounters with soldiers and civilians. Beads on the narrative chain of the film, one episode leads to another, linked visually by Alesha's transportation, mainly trains but also trucks and, at one point, a raft. Thematically the episodes confirm one another in presenting the literal and metaphoric dislocation of Soviet life wrought by war. One victim of that dislocation, a lovely girl called Shura, sneaks into the train-car where Alesha has stowed away, and after initial comical antagonism, they fall innocently, chastely, whole-heartedly in love before separating – a separation, as we know from the initial voice-over, that will last forever. Alesha's quietly heroic behaviour finds its echo in the undemonstrative steady heroism displayed by civilians: the exhausted woman who gives him a lift in a rattletrap truck; the stoical father who wants to hide his illness from his son at the front; the old men, women and children who stop digging long enough to listen to the latest war news – German advances, Soviet retreats – over the station loudspeaker before bending over their shovels once more.

Nearly every episode tests Alesha's mettle, forming as well as revealing his character, and redefining the nature of heroism. Forced time after time to choose between performing an act of goodness, kindness or generosity, and pursuing his goal of getting home, Alesha consistently makes the selfless choice. Frequently his generous impulse involves little or no initial cost: he cheerfully offers to carry a suitcase for a soldier on crutches; he blithely promises to deliver soap to a soldier's wife *en route*. Inevitably, however, those impulses end by costing him precious time, so that each one becomes a genuine choice. As Maia Turovskaia has commented, like the journeys of other epic travellers, Alesha's 'road to his native village becomes his road to himself'. Finally he reaches Sosnovka with time enough only to embrace tightly his mother – a woman who lost her husband to one war – before leaving once more for his unit. The narrator concludes with words at once grieving and valedictory: that Alesha, a boy of infinite potential, remains a soldier, remembered as such forever.

The phenomenon known as the Thaw, the decade of liberalisation following Stalin's death in 1953, enabled filmmakers to rediscover and re-examine cinematically the national trauma of World War Two. The war cast a long shadow over Soviet society, widowing millions of women and orphaning millions of children. So many men disappeared, dying at the front or vanishing into the labour camps of the Gulag upon their return, that the resulting gender imbalance endured for two generations. Yet post-war films about the war rarely showed with any verisimilitude the experiences of either civilians or soldiers, preferring victories to losses, HQ officers and Kremlin leaders to rank-and-file soldiers, the front to the rear, while films dealing with contemporary life ignored it altogether. Thus, for instance, *Vesna na Zarechnoi ulitse* (*Spring on Zarechnaia Street*, 1956) and set in the mid-1950s, shows no trace of the war, although the twentysomething characters, if too young to have fought themselves, are certainly of an age to have lost fathers or brothers in the conflict.

Nikita Khrushchev, in his 'Secret Speech' of 1956, acknowledged that strategic errors at the top, specifically decisions made by Stalin, cost many lives during the war. A wave of memoirs by soldiers, partisans and former prisoners of war resulted, along with autobiographical fiction by writers who had fought at the front. On screen, the war offered a ready-made context for depictions of the kinds of heroism accessible to – indeed, demonstrated by – millions of Soviet viewers. From Zakhar Agranenko's *Bessmertnyi garnizon* (*Immortal Garrison*, 1956), one of the first Thaw films to depict the war, to Andrei Tarkovskii's *Ivanovo detstvo* (*Ivan's Childhood*, 1962) and Larisa Shepit'ko's *Kryl'ia* (*Wings*, 1966), the 'War of the Fatherland' and its aftermath became central concern of Soviet cinema. Two of the best movies of 1957, *Letiat zhuravli* (*The Cranes are Flying*) and *Dom, v kotorom ia zhivu* (*The House I Live In*), and others like them revised the history of the war, ascribing the defeat of Nazi Germany not to the Kremlin leadership but to the Soviet people. They expanded the definition of conflict far beyond military engagement, shifting focus from the front to the rear, from firearms to the picks and shovels needed to dig out from under bombed rubble, from generals to privates, from resolutely upbeat mothers and irreproachably faithful wives to lonely, despondent women who did not always wait for their men.

The Thaw introduced a panoply of soldier-heroes: heartbroken but indomitable (*Sud'ba cheloveka* (*The Fate of a Man*, 1959), *Otets soldata* (*A Soldier's Father*, 1964)); shell-shocked into muteness (*Mir vkhodiashchemu* (*Peace to Him Who Enters*, 1961)); ferocious and permanently damaged (*Ivan's Childhood*); valiant but permanently damaged (*Wings*). Several films feature disingenuous, inexperienced protagonists. Inept Ivan Brovkin, in *Soldat Ivan*

Brovkin (*Soldier Ivan Brovkin*, 1955), has girlishly lovely blond curls, plays the accordion, and screws up his assignments with slapstick energy before the army licks him into shape. Big Fedor, a demobbed soldier played by Vasilii Shukshin in Marlen Khutsiev's *Dva Fedora* (*Two Fedors*, 1958), is patently more naïve than the orphaned child he adopts, Little Fedor. The war has damaged both of them, but the child is more mature, in practical terms, than the adult, who relied on the army for structure and support. The child knows how to push past a line of people waiting to buy food and he makes sure to train an unblinking gaze on the salesgirl weighing out his ration. The child knows how important ration cards are; Big Fedor does not. The child slurps ice-cream with delight but reflects that the money would be better spent on potatoes, and he makes sure Big Fedor gets his vitamins via a stolen bunch of carrots.

It is to this company that artless and unsophisticated Alesha Skvortsov belongs, in a film the very title of which implies both the folkloric quality of the tale about to be told, and the universalising identification of the soldier-hero. Yet although the war is hardly peripheral to Alesha's maturation, or to the film, battlefield heroics are. Alesha's heroism derives not from his military actions against the enemy, however admirable they may be, but from his behaviour as an individual toward other individuals. Director Grigorii Chukhrai utilises both sound and image to emphasise the mythic and epic qualities of Alesha's coming-of-age, his journey from innocence to experience, from rawness to maturity.

Chukhrai knew war first-hand. Born 23 May 1921, he was twice wounded and decorated before enrolling in the premier film school of the USSR, the State Institute of Cinematography (VGIK). He graduated in 1953, and was just starting work in the Kiev Studio when he criticised a script commemorating the 300th anniversary of Ukraine's union with Russia. The studio fired him, and he was fixing radios to support his family when director Mikhail Romm (1901–1971), one of Chukhrai's teachers at VGIK, rescued him: Romm supported Chukhrai's criticism of the script under discussion, and he arranged to have Chukhrai invited back to Moscow to work at Mosfil'm, the USSR's biggest studio.

For his first solo directorial effort Chukhrai proposed a remake of a Soviet classic, Iakov Protozanov's 1927 Civil War drama *Sorok pervyi* (*The Forty-First*), and was given the assignment, over studio objections and mainly thanks to the backing of Mosfil'm director Ivan Pyr'ev. *The Forty-First* – the title refers to a Red Army sniper's forty-first victim – justified Pyr'ev's faith, earning 'best film' designation by the studio itself in 1956, the year of its release, and prizes at the Cannes and Edinburgh film festivals a year later.

Chukhrai told a Belgian interviewer that he had no ideology in mind when he made *The Forty-First* except the desire to create art. Together with the brilliant cameraman Sergei Urusevskii (1908–1974), Chukhrai succeeded in turning a pat conflict between Revolutionary faith and passionate love into a credible, lyrical and visually beautiful drama. Chukhrai breached conventional Soviet film presentations of love as constancy (in, for instance, *The Bol'shaia sem'ia* (*Big Family*, 1954)) and love as friendship (in, for instance, *Neokonchennaia povest'* (*The Unfinished Tale*, 1955)). The Red Army sniper Mariutka and her White Army officer and captive, Govorukha-Otrok, share an autonomous and elemental love when they are stranded on a desert island. However, love rules unchallenged only in the primal world of nature. The human world, when it impinges in the form of a boatload of Whites, destroys the idyll. The film's title shadows the entire picture, implying its conclusion from the start. Chukhrai devised a variant of that circularity in *Ballad of a Soldier*, by announcing Alesha's fate in the opening frames of the film.

Unlike the Civil War following the 1917 Revolution, World War Two precluded political or ideological divisions: Alesha and Shura (and everyone else in *Ballad of a Soldier*) are united against an enemy, the consequences of whose inimical ideology are plain to see. Yet once again, as he did in *The Forty-First*, Chukhrai creates an island of innocence amid a sea of chaos. Hidden in the hay-packed train-car, Alesha has no control over his progress. Nothing he can do will get him home faster. So in the middle of the constant motion toward his goal, Alesha paradoxically enjoys a timeless interlude, an 'Eternal Present' in the words of Peter Barta and Stephen Hutchings, with Shura, escaping not only the all too physical realities of bombed homes and uprooted families but also the unheard but ever-present clock ticking away Alesha's precious leave.

Alesha begins the film as an innocent, with his beardless face and gawky motions. Turning sharply about-face to exit the general's dugout, he bangs his head on the low lintel, much to the amusement of the watching officers. In actuality, plenty of 19-year-olds fought in the Soviet Army during World War Two. Chukhrai, however, shows us hardly any of them, other than Alesha. Instead we mostly see weathered, unshaven men old enough to be his father or, in the case of Vasia, the one-legged soldier memorably played by Evgenii Urbanskii (1932–1965), his elder brother. Sexually innocent as well as emotionally pure, Alesha laughs uncomprehendingly at one soldier's coarse jokes and readily accepts Shura's transparent self-protective fiction that she is on her way to care for her wounded fiancé. Lighting visually enhances the chaste love he and Shura come to share, especially in the extreme close-ups when they gaze at each other on the jammed train, brimming with feelings but without the words to express it. Alesha remains a virgin in what is, despite the war, a pre-lapserian world.

His inability to hide his feelings suggests his emotional candour. We see this immediately, when his fear – the opposite of combat-bravery – impels him to run like hell away from the pursuing tanks. The accidental nature of Alesha's heroic feat, and the astonishment on his face when he hits the tank, subvert the notion that heroes perform exploits, *podvigi*, a notion common to conventional Stalin-era war movies. The general's praise embarrasses him; so does the good-natured ribbing he gets from other men travelling on the first leg of his journey, who cannot believe this fresh-faced kid has earned a decoration for heroism. In both scenes Alesha sets the record straight: he resolutely admits to the general that he had been scared, and – with a kind of guileless boastfulness – he shows his train-mates the picture of him in the army paper as proof that he genuinely earned his leave.

Alesha, almost as naïve as Candide if rarely so funny, expects people to live up to his own moral standards. That is, he expects them to be truthful and honorable and selfless; he does not anticipate lies and deceit. His own integrity assumes honesty in others; his own simplicity ill-prepares him for the complexity of others, especially the convoluted human emotions connected with love. Alesha accepts Shura's 'wounded fiancé' story instantly, backing away from his own growing desire for her and commending her loyalty. With the venal if comical corporal who guards the train, Alesha begins by appealing to his fellow-feeling as a soldier; he resorts to offering a can of meat only after the sentry clearly evinces both his greed and his lack of any such fellow-feeling. Not coincidentally, the sentry's appearance underscores his moral ugliness: short and squat, his boorishness and theatrically exaggerated gestures contrast with Alesha's slim grace and natural postures. The corporal plays a role; Alesha is himself.

Just as the sentry's venality highlights Alesha's honesty, Vasia's emotional turmoil and the complexity of his emotions set off Alesha's inexperience. Alesha here acts as an observer, shrewd enough to know that he cannot begin to understand Vasia's fear that his wife will reject him because of his disability, his hope that she will still love him despite his disability. Alesha can only sympathise, not empathise, when Vasia's potent emotional cocktail nearly derails him from going home at all. But if he cannot quite identify with Vasia – for the demons of sexual jealousy and fear of inadequacy must be alien to the virginal boy – he can and does learn, as he learns from every encounter on his journey. Vasia's mini-story culminates in the belated arrival of his wife on the platform, her cry of his name punctuating the sudden if – in real terms – wholly implausible silence. It is a resolution that accords with Alesha's notion of love, encompassing as it does steadfastness, fidelity and support.

As he travels Alesha grows from observer to judge. The second time he has to bribe the sentry, when the latter discovers Shura hiding in the train-car, Alesha's face eloquently expresses his contempt as he pulls out more cans of meat. Thanks in part to what he has learned from the episode with Vasia, Alesha becomes more than an observer in the later episode with the unfaithful wife Liza. Her husband Pavlov – more, his entire army unit, demonstrating stereotypically Russian open-handedness – had entrusted Alesha with two bars of soap, a precious and rationed commodity, to give Liza. Taking Shura with him, Alesha uses up more of his valuable time to deliver it, first to number 7 Chekhov Street, which turns out to be rubble, then to the apartment to which Liza has moved. Despite the evidence of another man in Liza's life – his uniform jacket on the chair, his voice from the bedroom off-screen – Alesha pulls the soap out of his rucksack before leaving, his disgust visible but unspoken. Then, as a watching child's soap-bubble descends in mute disillusion, Alesha wordlessly turns, ascends the stairs, bangs on the door, demonstratively replaces the soap in his pack, and proceeds to deliver it to Pavlov's bedridden father. Moral knowledge thus requires commensurate action, and Alesha rises to the occasion. Again he sacrifices his time, spending moments he can ill spare to praise the son to the father.

Chukhrai and Ezhov's script employs contrast as the primary structural device to establish Alesha's naiveté and his growing maturity. In addition to the binaries of youth versus age, sexual inexperience versus adult sexuality, and honesty versus corruption, the present tense (as it were) of the body of the film contrasts with the omniscient retrospective voice of narrator, who melds past and future. The six days, at once timeless and inexorably disappearing, depict what may not be Alesha's last week of life on earth, but certainly represent his final opportunity to experience what life – as opposed to war – can offer: knowledge, friendship, romantic love, familial intimacy. Characters appear and disappear, but the journey goes on, transporting Alesha 'between the realms of public duty and private emotion', as Barta and Hutchings claim. The journey gives *Ballad of a Soldier* its rhythm and unity, while the narrative frame bracketing that journey creates the sense of temporality, of past and future, that forms and informs our response to the body of the film.

In Alesha Chukhrai creates a hero who may ultimately be martyred, but who neither believes himself to be nor behaves as a victim. In fact, *Ballad of a Soldier* represents virtually all its characters, physically deprived and psychologically stressed though they are by the war, as agents of their own lives. (Even Shura's comically misplaced suspicion of Alesha denotes agency: foolishly ready to jump off the train, she at least tries to controls what happens to her.) The single scene depicting people who are merely victims – the evacuating Ukrainians whose train is hit by a German bomb – rings false, because it violates the tone of the rest of the film.

At the front, Alesha is neither the iconic fearless warrior nor the soldier who triumphs in spite of his fear, such as Andrei Sokolov, in *The Fate of a Man*. He disables the tanks precisely *because* of his fear. Furthermore, the remainder of the film challenges the notion that a single action, however brilliant, constitutes heroism. Instead, it defines heroism as a mosaic of ordinary, even trivial actions. The most profitable Soviet film of 1959, *Ch.P.: Chrezvychainoe proizshestvie* (*Ch.P.: An Extraordinary Event*), based on the Kuomintang capture of a Soviet tanker in 1954 and the interrogation *cum* torture of its crew, asserted precisely the opposite: that the essence of a human being emerges in the context of an extraordinary occurrence. The meaning and impact of Alesha's choices occur more in our minds than on screen, but the rhythmic repetition of the theme penetrates our minds with the power of what Sergei Eisenstein called 'shamanic incantation'. Behaviour we would judge as admirable but relatively commonplace becomes much more significant, because we know it is the last week of such behaviour. Alesha's entire life becomes the 'heroic feat'.

Most Soviet 'thaw' films, and not only those portraying World War Two, depict characters trapped by history. For much of *The Cranes are Flying*, Veronika remains the passive object of tragedy before she finally retakes control of her life and fate. In *The Fate of a Man*, Andrei Sokolov responds with valour to a sequence of horrifying events – but he responds reactively rather than proactively. One of the most heralded 'anniversary' films celebrating the Revolution, *Kommunist* (*The Communist*, 1958), showcases a hero who sacrifices his life, less out of revolutionary zeal than for what Vitalii Troianovskii calls 'Thaw altruism'. These characters make choices that have decisive consequences, but they cannot change the inexorable movement of historical circumstances where ultimate meaning resides. Chukhrai shifts the whole domain of meaning so that historical circumstances become, in a sense, irrelevant. What matters is the individual. In the moral logic of *Ballad of a Soldier*, good proceeds from within the individual when he acts, and it engenders good; generosity engenders generosity. As critic Neya Zorkaya has written, 'while the dividing line between the rear and the front is fluid, the border between good and bad is marked very distinctly'. Alesha Skvortsov does not have to make one fateful choice on which his future depends; he has to make many small choices, none of them decisive, most of them inconsequential – but choices they indubitably are, and he consistently opts for kindness, honesty, integrity.

When *Ballad of a Soldier* appeared at Cannes in 1960, as Lev Anninskii notes, critics found it a 'calming note in a discordant symphony', an appealing alternative to the themes of alienation, corruption and cruelty characteristic of its Western European competitors – Federico Fellini's *La Dolce Vita*, Michelangelo Antonioni's *L'Avventura* and Ingmar Bergman's *Virgin Spring*. Chukhrai's film offered viewers then a persuasive moving salute to kindness, honesty, and the possibility of meaningful love in a context of upheaval and tragedy. It still does.

Josephine Woll

REFERENCES

Anninskii, L. (1991) *Shestidesiatniki i my*. Moscow: Soiuz kinematografistov SSSR.

Barta, P. and S. Hutchings (2002) 'The Train as Word-Image Intertext in the Films *Ballad of a Soldier* and *Thief*, *Intertexts*, 6, 2, 127–44.

Troianovskii, V. (1996) *Kinematograf ottepeli: kniga pervaia*. Moscow: Materik.

Turovskaia, M. (1961) '*Ballada o soldate*', *Novyi mir*, 4, 246–52.

Zorkaya, N. (1991) *The Illustrated History of Soviet Film*. New York: Hippocrene.

IVANOVO DETSTVO IVAN'S CHILDHOOD

ANDREI TARKOVSKII, USSR, 1962

Ivanovo detstvo (*Ivan's Childhood*), Andrei Tarkovskii's first feature film, brought him international recognition when it won the prestigious Golden Lion award at the Venice Film Festival in 1962. It was a fitting start to the career of one of the most promising young directors of the 'thaw' generation, that unique and all-too-brief moment in Soviet history in which the breath of freedom and new possibility swept through the arts.

The project came Tarkovskii's way when the Mosfil'm studio decided to shut down production of a film based on Soviet writer Vladimir Bogomolov's popular story 'Ivan' (1957) due to the poor quality of the material that had been filmed. The studio looked for someone to take over and veteran film director Mikhail Romm, who was Tarkovskii's teacher at the State Institute of Cinematography (VGIK), suggested him. Tarkovskii read the story and, though he was not drawn to its laconic style and the detailed descriptions of army life the author concentrated on, he was impressed by the essential plotlessness of the narrative, and the absence of heroic battle scenes and the 'happy ending' that was typical of Socialist Realism. The story, narrated by Senior Lieutenant Gal'tsev, recounts the interval between two reconnaissance missions by the young scout Ivan. At the end Gal'tsev finds out quite by chance that Ivan has been captured and shot. Tarkovskii was also moved by the character of Ivan, whom he saw as someone who had been utterly destroyed by the war, an event that had created a dramatic, heightened quality in him.

Tarkovskii agreed to make the film on one condition: that he be allowed to introduce Ivan's dreams into the script. He also – rather boldly for a young, untested director – wanted to rewrite the script from scratch. The original story had been adapted by veteran scriptwriter Mikhail Papava (1906–1975), who changed the title to 'A Second Life' and resurrected Ivan, having Gal'tsev chance upon him and his pregnant wife, on a train, many years later. Bogomolov had disapproved of this change and was relieved when Tarkovskii restored the original ending. However, the relationship between author and director was not an easy one; Bogomolov, a war veteran, wanted the minutiae of army life depicted on screen, and did not approve of the love angle between Captain Kholin and nurse Masha, which does not exist in the story. He found the script too wordy, and disliked the way Tarkovskii depicted Gal'tsev – too inexperienced and diffident for someone in his position. Tarkovskii's defiant response was, 'We have as much right to our creative individuality as you have to yours, but you deny us this.'

Tarkovskii rewrote the script, published in *Collected Screenplays*, in two-and-a-half weeks, with his friend and fellow-student, the film-director Andrei Konchalovskii (with whom he had co-authored his diploma film, *Katok i skripka* (*The Steamroller and the Violin*, 1960) and would co-author *Andrei Rubliov* (*Andrei Rublev*, 1966)), though both remain uncredited. They changed the title to *Ivan's Childhood*, thus mapping out, in the simplest way, the emotional and formal territory the film explores. The very first version of the script already contained the four dreams, or memories, almost in their final form. Tarkovskii later wrote that the first dream was one of his earliest childhood memories. The film took eight months to complete and came in under budget, all of which impressed the studio. Interestingly, it is the only Tarkovskii film to be so faithful to the shooting script.

Ivan's Childhood begins and ends with images of peacetime – Ivan's dreams. They frame the main action, which takes place in a time span of 24 hours, between Ivan's two reconnaissance missions. Ivan arrives at Lieutenant Gal'tsev's military outpost, where Captain Kholin comes to take him to Lieutenant-Colonel Griaznov's headquarters. When Ivan finds out they want to send him to a military academy, he tries to run away. During his flight, he comes across an old man who has gone mad from losing his wife and home to the Germans. Ivan is picked up and returned to the post, where Gal'tsev is reprimanding Masha, the nurse, for slackness. Kholin is attracted to her and later flirts with her in a birch forest, where Gal'tsev goes to look for her, worried to leave her alone with Kholin. Back at Gal'tsev's post, Ivan plays at war, while Galt'sev, Kholin and an old scout, Katasonych, go in search of a boat to take Ivan on his next mission. We later learn that Katasonych has been killed while returning from the boat. Gal'tsev and Kholin see Ivan off and return to the post. We see newsreel footage of the Soviet army in Berlin, the bodies of Goebbels and his daughters, the signing of the surrender agreement and more dead Nazis and their families. At the Reichstag, Gal'tsev comes across a file, which reveals that Ivan was captured and shot. The film ends with another dream of peacetime.

Tarkovskii moulded this otherwise unexceptional material into something quite unique. The subject matter – World War Two, childhood, orphanhood – had been popular themes in Soviet films and, during the thaw period, had been depicted in all their complexity and ambivalence. Films like *Letiat zhuravli* (*The Cranes are Flying*, 1957), *Ballada o soldate* (*Ballad of a Soldier*, 1959), *Sud'ba cheloveka* (*The Fate of a Man*, 1959), *Serezha* (1960), *Dva Fedora* (*Two Fedors*, 1960), to name a few, eschewed heroism, grand battle scenes and two-dimensional characters. They focused, instead, on the personal worlds of their protagonists, exploring the darker and more controversial aspects of war, childhood and love. Most significantly, they refused to pass moral judgement. Aesthetic innovation (of which *The Cranes are Flying* is the supreme example) excelled during this period – the perpetual motion of hand-held cameras, sharp camera angles, the play of light and shadow, fantasy sequences, use of documentary footage, all contributed to a new cinematic language. In this sense, Tarkovskii's film is entirely in and of its time. But Tarkovskii pushed the revised themes and aesthetics to extremes and subjected them to his inimitable vision creating, in the process, something entirely new. Tarkovskii, at the time, called *Ivan's Childhood* his 'qualifying examination'. In later years, he dismissed the film as 'a typical VGIK film, dreamed up in a student hall of residence'. Though it is a very 'Soviet' film in many aspects, it also contains, in embryonic form, the cinematic language and sensibility that characterise the Tarkovskii oeuvre.

After the film had been completed, Tarkovskii advocated the importance of poetic links in the cinema, as opposed to linear sequentiality, and revealed his interest in editing film material in such a way as to 'lay open the logic of a person's thought', which was closer to poetic reasoning. Later, he rejected the term 'poetic cinema', speaking only of directors who recreated the world as it was and those who created their own world. He felt that this heightened emotion and made the spectator a participant in the events unfolding on screen. His most significant innovation in this respect in *Ivan's Childhood* are the four dreams, although to call them dreams is to limit their significance; while two take place when Ivan has gone to sleep, the other two do not, and it is quite clear that Tarkovskii's own consciousness is present in these 'digressions', which appear more as memories and reveries than dreams. They are remarkable not merely as a stylistic device, but also in the way they have been executed: in their content, their tactile quality, their extraordinary use of space and texture and the way they fit inside the fabric of Ivan's consciousness and of the film. They are singular examples of Tarkovskii's facility with the deeper folds of consciousness, memory and longing.

The film's opening sequence maps out the two distinct realities Ivan moves between. Ivan walks through a sun-drenched landscape, accompanied by highly lyrical music, which is both intoxicating and plaintive. This is an Eden-like place brimming with life, beauty and innocence. The frames are filled with the textures and marvels of nature and Ivan responds with joy to everything he sees – the play of light, the flight of a butterfly, a dew-embroidered spider's web, the glistening river-water. As if from happiness and excitement – but because this is also a dream and everything is possible – he slowly begins to rise up, through the trees, and above the earth where he continues his ecstatic journey (the flight motif is present in all of Tarkovskii's films). An aerial shot, from his point of view, reveals the river and his mother – an integral part of this space – carrying a pail of water, the life-giving element, which he drinks from. The camera becomes Ivan's eyes, his perception; its movements communicate, almost viscerally, his sense of excitement and intoxication, his state of harmony and communion with all things. This is true of all four dream/memory sequences – never again does Vadim Iusov's (b. 1929) camera (he went on to shoot Tarkovskii's *Andrei Rublev* and *Soliaris* (*Solaris*, 1972)) achieve this immediate, unfettered quality. But the idyll ends when Ivan's mother looks up and begins to wipe her forehead. Over the sound of machine-gun fire we cut to a dark interior to watch Ivan, dirty, dishevelled, apprehensive, sit up and look around him, accompanied by an ominous soundtrack. He emerges from what turns out to be a windmill into a desolate, dark landscape, filled with smoke, debris and devastation. He runs through this harsh place, dwarfed by the ruin of a huge agricultural machine. We watch him wade through a dead birch forest, submerged in swampy water. The living, shimmering river of the previous sequence, is now deadly, heavy and still, hindering his movement towards the Russian side and safety. The river has become the Styx, the passageway to Hades. As Ivan floats out on a log, into the wide river and towards the Russian side, we hear a sombre orchestration of the music for the first dream, reminding us of what was lost.

Tarkovskii looked for a long time for the place that would become Ivan's crossing from the enemy camp to the Russian one. The dead birch forest is an ideal image of Ivan's inner state. In this film, as in all of Tarkovskii's subsequent films, nature is not merely a backdrop, but one of the protagonists, resonating and reflecting a state of mind. The dreams/reveries of peacetime – Ivan's *childhood* – always take place on the water's edge, in the shimmering light. But the landscape in the rest of the film is pitiless and desolate. The river is a swamp, there is mud everywhere, debris, ruins (Gal'tsev's military dugout is in the basement of a ruined church whose former contents – frescoes, a cross, a bell – are often in frame), desolate chimneys, and remnants of a downed German plane. Nature has been ravaged by war just as surely as Ivan has. The only exception is the dense birch forest, where Kholin and Masha meet. It is a beautiful place, but it feels oppressive and eerily white. Love cannot flourish there. Although this sequence has always been interpreted as another example of the effect of war on human life, it has more to do with Tarkovskii's own sensibility. Erotic love never flourishes in Tarkovskii's world. In his films, the notion of love is primarily familial; men and women are always in dissonance. Kholin is cruel towards Masha, he uses her innocence and timidity, and taunts her. She is clearly attracted to him but cannot react. When he embraces and kisses her over a trench (Tarkovskii called this a 'death kiss'), her body feels limp and her legs dangle lifelessly. Yet later, when she waltzes alone amongst the birches, it is clear she is in love.

Tarkovskii paid great attention to *mise-en-scène*, which he marshalled to communicate the protagonist's – and author's – world of emotions and ideas. Nothing enters the frame by chance – everything works to impart a mood, a feeling, and an association – to achieve a state before thought and word. The second dream, which follows the first sequence in Galtsev's post, is a superb example of Tarkovskii's ease at subverting familiar places and objects in order to capture the abstract space of dreams. In the dugout, Ivan sleeps. Water drips from his hand into a basin, then the camera pans upwards, revealing the shaft of the well, which is made of thick wooden logs, rendering its weight and texture almost tangible. We realise that Ivan has been lying at the bottom of the empty well, but he is simultaneously at the top of the well with his mother. This spatial dislocation during a dream/memory sequence became a hallmark of Tarkovskii's cinematic language; a person is often found simultaneously in several different points in a space (there is a version of this in the third dream, where the little girl comes into the frame three times from the same direction). The space itself is made strange by certain elements within it. Ivan drops a feather into the well and comments that it is deep. A series of reverse-angle shots show him either at the top of the well with his mother, or at the bottom. The camera films from above and below, at one point even filming Ivan and his mother through the water, which ripples across their faces. This constant shifting of perspectives and angles creates a sense of disorientation and suspense and draws the viewer into the action. The sequence concludes dramatically: the pail is drawn upwards by Ivan's mother while German voices speak offscreen. Ivan looks up and shouts 'mama', as a shot is fired and the pail comes crashing down, towards Ivan and us. We cut to an angular shot of the pail, dominating the foreground, while Ivan's mother lies face down on the ground. Water is thrown across her limp body, like a whip. This is a breathtaking sequence, which communicates the strange disorientation and foreboding dreams contain. It also speaks eloquently, but without violence, of Ivan's tragedy – the loss of his mother.

Ivan, too, is a child unlike any other in the cinema of the thaw, because he is irredeemable. The war has destroyed all hope and love – taking away his family, especially his mother

– leaving in its place only hatred and revenge. Katasonych, who may have adopted him after the war, dies (the theme of adoption was very popular in Soviet films of that time). Kholin, whom he clearly loves (the moment he sees him again is the only one in the film, apart from the dreams, where he allows himself to be a joyful child) will die too, as we learn at the end. Ivan himself will die, there is no other way out for him as there is no future inside him, only his overwhelming hatred and desolation, which compel him to court death on a daily basis. Throughout the film, the grown-ups try to convince him to give up his missions and go to a military academy. But he lives for danger and revenge and remains defiant, arguing with them fiercely, warning them that he will simply run away, as he has done in the past. 'I have no one', he says, and 'I am my own master'. When Gal'tsev tries to distract him by showing him a book of Albrecht Dürer's etchings, Ivan can only see the present in the images, remarking that Germans have always trampled people and have no writers since they burn books. The message scratched out in Gal'tsev's dugout, 'There are eight of us, none older than 19. In an hour from now, they are going to execute us. Avenge us', embodies everything Ivan has experienced and everything he lives for.

Ivan's deep trauma and vulnerability is best expressed in the sequence where he plays at war, included in the original story. It is ironic and terrifying that this broken boy, who lives the war down to his sinews, still needs to play at it. The sequence is shot mostly with a hand-held camera, in half-shadow and with expressionistic lighting, and the soundtrack includes German speech and the sobbing of children. Ivan borrows a knife from Gal'tsev and, while the men are out choosing a boat to take him on his next mission, he hangs up a bell which has been lying on the ground and then puts out the candle. He pretends to stalk imaginary Germans, shining his torch around the dark dugout. His mother appears twice during the sequence, fleetingly glimpsed in the shadows, suggesting that the action unfolds as much in an internal as in an external realm. Ivan rings the bell frantically, as if to alert people to an imminent threat. In the end, when he finally captures his imaginary foe he is unable to kill him, breaking down into sobs. An offensive begins outside soon after, but Ivan now lies calmly on the ground, chewing a reed. When Gal'tsev runs in, asking him not to be afraid, his defiant and chilling response is, 'But I'm not'. Yet Tarkovskii's bold choice of documentary footage at the end suggests that it is not just the Russian Ivan (or indeed the two slightly older scouts, Liakhov and Moroz, whose dead bodies we see several times throughout the film) whose childhood was blighted by war. Josef Goebbels' dead daughters are innocents too, victims of overwhelming human vanity, cruelty and destruction.

Tarkovskii counterpoints this horror by reminding us of the elevated, inspired side of humanity, expressed in artistic endeavour. These are brief glimpses – the Dürer album, the painter Vasilii Surikov (1848–1916) and the writers Aleksei Tolstoi and Kornei Chukovskii, which Masha and Kholin mention during their walk in the forest, the broken frescoes in the ruined church. And, most powerfully, it is Fedor Chaliapin's (1973–1938) soaring, melancholy voice (courtesy of Katasonych, who brings Gal'tsev the record and fixes the gramophone) which has a profound effect on the protagonists – even Ivan stops in his tracks – for in this inopportune place and time it brings a memory of the other life, which to many will be lost forever. Chaliapin sings, 'Masha will not cross the river', that is to say, she cannot marry, echoing the aborted love scene in the birch forest and Masha's unrequited love. But all three times we begin to hear the song are interrupted, as if to underline the absurdity of music like this in such a dissonant time.

'Remember this name: Andrei Tarkovskii.' This is how Romm introduced the first screening of *Ivan's Childhood* at the House of Cinema (Dom Kino) in the early spring of 1962. The film was received as a prime example of the evolving language of contemporary cinema. It was discussed at length in the press, mostly favourably, although some critics were left confused by its complexity, its pessimism and what they perceived as its anti-war ethos. Two young critics, Maia Turovskaia and Neia Zorkaia (who have continued to write on Tarkovskii), wrote articles in respected journals. The former regarded the film as a prime example of poetic cinema, and both wrote extensively on Tarkovskii's treatment of landscape and interiors, and especially on the dreams, which they considered his most notable innovation. They also pointed out the unusualness of Ivan – such 'dark', irredeemable children had never before appeared in Soviet films. But the most famous apologist for *Ivan's Childhood* is Jean-Paul Sartre, who wrote an open letter to the editor of the Italian communist newspaper, *Unità,* after several articles were published accusing Tarkovskii of being 'petit-bourgeois' and of recklessly borrowing outdated stylistic devices from Western cinema. Sartre sees Ivan as a child who has been turned into a madman and monster by the horrors he has witnessed, and which crowd his days and nights; reality and hallucination are contiguous in him. He suggests that war kills its participants, even when they remain alive, and that Ivan is a product of history, exposing the duplicity of heroism. Sartre echoes other critics in believing that Tarkovskii also spoke for his own generation in the film, whose childhood was smashed to pieces by the war and its consequences. The critic Lev Anninskii, writing in the early 1990s on the thaw generation, does not believe that Tarkovskii wanted to depict the war through

Ivan's eyes – a common interpretation among critics; rather, that he wanted to show 'Ivan's distorted soul through the eyes of a man for whom the war remained a universal catastrophe, which overthrew the system of values'.

In an interview Tarkovskii gave in 1973, which was published almost twenty years later in *Kinovedcheskie Zapiski*, he said that the most important thing for Ivan was to defend his mother, despite the fact that she was already dead (he was making *Zerkalo* (*Mirror*, 1975) at the time, and the notion of the mother was foremost in his mind). Some Russian critics picked up on this comment in the 1990s and wrote articles weaving in the idea of the absent father (who should have been the mother's defender) and the notion of self-sacrifice for the salvation of the world. This fits in perfectly with Tarkovskii's increasingly apocalyptic and messianic vision, which permeates his later films. Contemporary critics see *Ivan's Childhood* as the cornerstone of the films that followed – and rightly so, for Tarkovskii was utterly constant in his preoccupations. It is now almost impossible to extricate *Ivan's Childhood* from the totality of Tarkovskii's work and vision, and the film does, indeed, contain the kernels of the Tarkovskian universe and the beginnings of his particular cinematic language. Ivan is the first in a long line of Tarkovskian heroes – people who are possessed of an idea, who burn with it, live for it, and stretch it to extremes. Most importantly, the inner world, the world of dream, memory and metaphysical longing – Tarkovskii's most unique contribution to cinema – appears here, for the first time, in all its spontaneity and immediacy. There are, of course, clumsy, laboured moments in *Ivan's Childhood* (Tarkovskii considered the sequence with the old man one of them). The music (by Viacheslav Ovchinnikov (b. 1936), who had written music for *The Steamroller and the Violin* and would do so again on *Andrei Rublev*) is often too illustrative; certain images are too obvious, the acting overdone in places. But the dreams are breathtaking in their beauty and heartbreaking in their tragic dénouement, none more so than the final dream, which comes after we have learnt of Ivan's death. It begins with the same shot of his mother wiping her forehead that the first dream ends with. But the moment is uninterrupted by tragedy and she continues to smile at Ivan, who looks up at her from the pail of water he is drinking from. We witness Ivan's life as it could have been; his mother is alive and he is on the water's edge, playing hide and seek with other children; the river flows and shimmers, the day is sun-drenched. But the black silhouette of the dead tree in the midst of this joyful innocence is a precursor of the impending tragedy. Ivan chases the little girl from the previous dream, catches up with her and runs past her, into the water, the music urging him gently on his way. But a menacing note appears on the soundtrack, and

Ivan stretches out his arm and runs straight at the tree, whose darkness swallows the frame. The brutal finality of this concluding sequence is unprecedented in Tarkovskii's work, for whom endings are the places where harmony is restored – in the world and in the hero's/author's, psyche. But this film does not end with the ravishing images on the river's edge. It must end in darkness.

Ivan's Childhood can seem overstated, even dated, to contemporary audiences who have reached a high level of sophistication – and cynicism – from exposure to the constantly evolving language of cinema and whose boundaries are pushed ever further through experiment and constant technological innovation. Yet this 'typical VGIK film' is a precious breath of freedom and spontaneity in an often formal and portentous oeuvre. It is the young Tarkovskii, flexing his muscles, preparing for the great leap that was *Andrei Rublev*. It is also a mirror of its time and generation, capturing its boldness and excitement, but instinctively expressing the tragedy that would soon envelop it, and its maker.

Natasha Synessios

REFERENCES

Anninskii, L. (1991) *Shestidesiatniki i my*. Moscow: Soiuz kinematografistov SSSR.

Sartre, J.-P. (1991) 'Po povodu *Ivanova Detstva*', in *Mir i fil'my Andreia Tarkovskogo*. Moscow: Iskusstvo, 11–21.

Tarkovskii, Andrei (1964) 'Ivanovo detstvo', in Anon. *Kogda fil'm okonchen. Govoriat rezhissery 'Mosfil'ma'*. Moscow: Iskusstvo, 136–71.

_____ (1992) 'Tarkovskii v besede s Germanom Kherlingkhauzom', *Kinovedcheskie Zapiski*, 14, 34–48.

_____ (1999) *Collected Screenplays*. London: Faber, 55–126.

Turovskaia, M. (1989) *Tarkovsky: Cinema as Poetry*, London: Faber.

Zorkaia, N. (1991) 'Nachalo', in *Mir i film'y Andreia Tarkovskogo*. Moscow: Iskusstvo, 22–36.

KOROTKIE VSTRECHI BRIEF ENCOUNTERS

11

KIRA MURATOVA, USSR, 1967

Korotkie vstrechi (*Brief Encounters*, 1967) was the first solo feature film shot by Kira Muratova (b. 1934), one of the most critically acclaimed contemporary Russian filmmakers. Interpretations of the film have been determined from the outset by the troubled circumstances of its production and initial release. Censored and revised at each step from script to screen, the film was released in only five copies, shown primarily in film clubs and then removed from official distribution altogether in 1971, together with Muratova's second feature, *Dolgie provody* (*Long Farewells*), which was banned, apparently for its violations of the aesthetic norms of Socialist Realism. Between 1971 and 1986 Muratova made only two films, both with great difficulty. Once removed from the unofficial but effective blacklist in July 1986 through the efforts of the newly-formed Conflict Commission on Creative Issues of the Soviet Filmmakers' Union, Muratova began the second, infinitely more prolific phase of her career. Between 1987 and 2005, she released eight feature-length and two short films and was awarded many national and international prizes.

The dramatic circumstances of Muratova's career – political persecution, dramatic rehabilitation and international critical acclaim – have overwhelmed most discussions of her earliest film and obscured its aesthetic achievements and stylistic innovations. Most critical discussions of the film to date have focused on the aspects of the film that may have been politically offensive to Soviet censors and film industry bureaucrats when the film was first released. Re-released in 1987 after almost two decades 'on the shelf', *Brief Encounters* was quickly eclipsed in critics' attention by the release of Muratova's *Peremena uchesti* (*Change of Fate*, 1987) and *Astenicheskii sindrom* (*The Aesthenic Syndrome*, 1989), both of which addressed issues that seemed of more immediate concern to Russian viewers in the *glasnost'* era than did *Brief Encounters*, which reflects the formal and thematic concerns of Soviet filmmakers at the end of the 'Thaw' era. Popular reception of the film was also shaped by the celebrity of its male star, Vladimir Vysotskii (1938–1980), a beloved actor and singer-songwriter who won tremendous popularity with songs that were never released on record in his lifetime, owing to their irreverent and often passionate critique of everyday life in the

USSR. Vysotskii's celebrity as film actor – still in its early stages at the time *Brief Encounters* was made – shaped later viewers' reception of the film.

Assigned the generic label of 'provincial melodrama', *Brief Encounters* is ostensibly the story of a love triangle – two women in love with the same man – yet what distinguishes it are its narrative innovations and deliberate attempt to convey in visual terms a distinctively female subjectivity. The film begins and ends with two shots of the same moment in time – the five or ten minutes preceding the arrival of Nadia (Nina Ruslanova (b. 1945), in her film debut), a young girl from the provinces, on the doorstep of Valentina Ivanovna Sviridova (Muratova), a mid-level bureaucrat in charge of housing in a provincial city. The film's opening is shot from Valentina's point of view within her apartment, but the closing adopts Nadia's point of view as she approaches Valentina's building for the first time. The story framed by these two scenes unfolds in a series of brief encounters, many of which are presented as flashbacks to moments in two separate narrative threads – Valentina and Nadia's respective romances with the same man, Maksim (Vysotskii).

Both romances begin and end before the moment when the two women first meet and their paths briefly intertwine in yet a third narrative thread, the story of Valentina and Nadia's relationship with each other. This story is the only one of the three narrative threads that the film presents in chronological order, and its storyline frames a series of flashbacks – all but one explicitly marked as the recollection of either Nadia or Valentina – that present events from each woman's romance with Maksim in a sequence motivated by psychology, not chronology. The structural complexity of the film is compounded by the fact that it interweaves the subjective and fragmentary recollections of two separate characters into its framing narrative. The film presents the middles, beginnings and ends of each romance not in linear order, but in the order that the film's two heroines recall them. As a result, many of Nadia's gestures and comments make sense only in retrospect – her stunned echo of the word 'husband' in an off-hand comment by Valentina when they first meet, for example, or her slow tracing of Valentina's ringless wedding finger with her own hand as she gets up for the first time from the kitchen table.

A reconstructed timeline of the events portrayed in the film would read as follows: Valentina and Maksim, a peripatetic geologist, meet and begin a romance. Valentina wants Maksim to give up fieldwork and take a desk job in the city; he wants her to quit her post in charge of city housing and join him in the field. After a quarrel, Valentina orders Maksim to leave, which he does, taking his razor and toothbrush, but leaving his guitar behind. Subsequently, Maksim meets Nadia, a young girl from the countryside who has taken a job working in a rural road-side café. Several cryptic scenes suggest that Nadia has fallen into what most provincial melo-dramas would label 'love' with Maksim and indicate at least one potentially sexual encounter between the two. When Maksim heads out on yet another expedition, he gives Nadia his address. When she goes to look for him, a neighbour directs her to Maksim's other, city address, Valentina's apartment. This is the chronological point at which the film begins.

Valentina assumes that Nadia is the domestic servant she has been expecting and invites her in, never giving the stunned, silent Nadia a chance to explain her presence. Nadia falls into the role assigned her and lives with Valentina for several months, during the course of which she accompanies Valentina on several tours of an apartment building that is under construction and for the satisfactory completion of which Valentina is responsible. Brief encounters with other city residents and visitors from Nadia's rural hometown add historical and cultural resonance to the story of the country girl's encounter with the urban bureaucrat. An unexpected phone call from Maksim reveals that he is ready to reconcile with Valentina and will return to see her in a few days. She, however, will be out of town when he arrives, attending a conference where she has been assigned against her will to deliver a formulaic speech about the importance of renewed efforts to improve Soviet agriculture. As a result, Nadia remains alone in Valentina's apartment to meet Maksim, but this potentially climactic encounter does not take place. The film ends as Nadia slowly sets a festive table for two and walks out the door, avoiding a meeting that might have renewed her romance with Maksim or revealed her brief role in his life to Valentina.

As recounted above, this is a simple story. As revealed on screen, however, it is extraor-dinarily complex. Only at the end of the film does the viewer realise how completely Valentina has misunderstood Nadia and the extent of Nadia's complicity in that misunderstanding.

The production history of *Brief Encounters* was long and complicated. Muratova's orig-inal idea for the film originated in her discovery on a trip to Odessa in 1952 that it was 'a city living without water' as a result of defects in the city's water supply system. In an interview with the critic Dmitrii Bykov, Muratova stated: 'So I wanted to make a story about a young decisive woman who is in charge of all the water in the city, and yet there is never any water. And absolutely nothing in her life is going right: a man comes and goes … and he also has his own life. And there's a girl who's in love with him, and nothing works out for any of them.' The young woman's story was all Muratova's invention, but the story of Nadia and Maksim was inspired in large part by Leonid Zhukhovitskii's short story 'The House in the Steppe'

('Dom v stepi', 1959). Zhukhovitskii co-authored the script with Muratova, and almost all of the scenes between Nadia and Maksim are drawn directly from 'The House on the Steppe'.

Zhukhovitskii's story makes it clear that the relationship between Nadia and Maksim was sexual, but by 1967 it was no longer possible to put on film scenes that were acceptable in print in 1959. At the top of the list of cuts in the script that the State Committee for Cinematography (Goskino) demanded in 1966 were all 'scenes indicating physical intimacy between Maksim and Nadia'. These scenes – all of which occur in Zhukhovitskii's story – seem tame by contemporary standards: a kiss by a bonfire, for example, was declared impermissible. The memo listing the necessary cuts (and published in Valerii Fomin's study on film censorship) concluded with some regret that 'it was impossible to remove the theme of Nadia and Maksim's romance entirely since in that case the film, which raises a moral problem, would cease to exist'.

In addition to concerns about the film's potential immorality, both the national Committee for Cinematography and the Editors' Collegium of the Odessa Film Studio, which produced the film, were worried about the many conversations in the original script that might seem critical of life on collective farms, allude to corruption within Soviet bureaucracy, or refer to the 'period of the cult' (a euphemism for the Stalin era).

Although Muratova made the changes demanded in the film's literary script in order to receive permission to make the film, she then restored many of the cut scenes to the shooting script. When this was discovered, the film's financing was halted until a suitably altered version of the shooting script was submitted to the studio. Nevertheless, she went ahead and shot some of the forbidden scenes portraying 'physical intimacy' between Nadia and Maksim. Protesting the 'blatant vulgarity' of those scenes, the studio demanded at least two more rounds of cuts to the completed film before approving its release, as is revealed by a letter from Odessa Studio published in Fomin's collection.

The film seems to have been reviewed in only one national publication after its release, and that article, which appeared in the leading Soviet cinema journal, *Iskusstvo kino*, was both detailed and highly critical. Indicating that some audiences of *Brief Encounters* 'are ready to defend the picture and to argue about it for hours', the eminent critic and scriptwriter Nikolai Kovarskii systematically refutes the positive interpretations of Valentina's character he has heard from viewers who are 'benevolently inclined' towards the film and calls Maksim 'just a character with a guitar singing some forgettable little songs'. Acknowledging the apparent influence of Anton Chekhov's plays on the film's use of overlapping, apparently inconsequential monologues and of director Sergei Gerasimov (1906–1985) (Muratova's film school mentor) on its actors' 'quiet, everyday' performances, the review rejects any positive comparison of Muratova's film with the works of these two classic figures. Contending that the inner world of Muratova's characters is 'impoverished, limited and empty', Kovarskii's review denounces the film for its failure to portray the connection between 'the individual and the historical process' and brands it 'an insignificant story of the personal relationship between the hero and heroine'. Kovarskii concedes that Muratova is a talented actress and director, praises the work of cameraman Gennadii Kariuk (b. 1937), and commends the film's presentation of Nadia's 'love for her native village' as a theme that, in contrast to the rest of the film, is both 'serious and significant', but concludes that these 'partial successes are no compensation for the principal error in the film, which masks the enormous truth of life with a flat verisimilitude'.

Kovarskii repeatedly identifies the flaws in *Brief Encounters* with those of other contemporary films, and it is clear that he is polemicising not only with Muratova's work but with that of the entire generation of filmmakers who came of age in the brief cultural and political thaw that began after Stalin's death in 1953 and was already coming to a close in 1966, when Muratova began work on *Brief Encounters*. Like many other films made during the Thaw, *Brief Encounters* borrows the aesthetic style of documentary films to portray the everyday lives of seemingly insignificant individuals in an attempt to achieve the sort of emotional authenticity that was markedly absent in films of the Stalin era. The film's violations of conventional narrative form and its revelations of contemporary social problems – bureaucratic corruption, workers' incompetence, the housing shortage and rural flight – are traits common to many other films from this period. Muratova attended film school and began her career at a time when it seemed as if Soviet cinema was making a dramatic break from the Stalinist past, finally able to explore new subjects, new styles and new freedoms. But *Brief Encounters* appeared just as those new freedoms were being revoked.

The significance of *Brief Encounters* for Soviet film history, however, transcends the historical circumstances of its production at the end of the Thaw, its dramatic return to Soviet screens in the glasnost era, and the star power of its male lead. These are important issues, but they have over-determined critical responses to the film and forestalled analysis of the film's most distinctive features: its unusual narrative structure and idiosyncratic attempts to articulate a sense of specifically female subjectivity on screen. In her influential 1975 article, 'Visual Pleasure and Narrative Cinema', Laura Mulvey argues that cinema presents 'the image of woman as (passive) raw material for the (active) gaze of man' and 'builds the way [woman] is to be looked at into the spectacle itself'. Well before the appearance of Mulvey's article, and decades before the emergence of anything resembling feminist thought in the former Soviet Union, Muratova structured *Brief Encounters* in ways that disrupt the viewer's ability to identify with the male gaze at every level of the film's structure, which repeatedly locates the origin of the on-screen gaze within the memories of her two female characters. Within these memories, the look becomes the central metaphor for the women's troubled relationship with Maksim. The film's first subjective leap into the past is triggered by Nadia's vision of Maksim's guitar hanging on Valentina's wall. As she touches it the film cuts to a shot of Nadia covering her eyes with her hand, foregrounding the question of vision and Nadia's resistance to the gaze of camera, viewer, lover. The film jumps back and forth five more times in the next four minutes between Valentina's apartment and the café where Nadia is watching Maksim. On the third leap into the past Maksim demands of Nadia, 'Why are you looking at me like that? Don't look at me', suggesting in words what the rapid cuts from silent memory to silent present have already indicated: looking is a problem.

The problem of the look is developed in Valentina's first flashback to her time with Maksim. As he lies in her lap, the camera repeatedly fixes on her face looking down at him, occasionally cutting to his face as he looks away with half-closed eyes, never meeting her gaze. The dialogue in this scene, too, underscores the disjunction between looking and knowing. The film cuts to a shot of Maksim's face in Valentina's lap, as she tells him, 'In essence, I don't know you at all. You lie here, you lie here, I see you … I see your eyes, your cheeks, your lips … I know all this. But you, I don't know you at all.' Later in this same scene, throughout which the gaze of the two lovers never meets, Valentina tells Maksim that when he is gone, she 'invents' him in her thoughts. In this carelessly delivered dialogue the film spells out the point that its frequent dissolves and jump cuts to and from the remembered past make visible: the role of the look in fabricating fictions of both self and other. A later scene between Maksim and Valentina films them as they are reflected in a large mirror, a frame within the larger frame of the shot that suggests the narcissistic impulse that shapes even the lover's look at another. In this episode, too, Maksim rebels against Valentina's look, telling her that he does not want to be examined 'under a microscope', and advises her to live, as he does, 'with half-closed eyes … If you love me, you should look at me with loving eyes, blind eyes'. In these arguments over Valentina's 'look' at him, the film is explicitly exploring the power relations implicit in the on-screen gaze. Maksim repeatedly accompanies his protest against

Valentina's scrutiny with declarations that she wants to 'tame' him and 'put a ring' through his nose like a wild beast, or that she is acting as if she were his boss.

Although Maksim is nominally at the centre of the love triangle, the film consistently portrays him as the object of the two women's gaze. Maksim appears on screen only within the context of the two women's memories, a figure summoned only in recollection. He enters the framing narrative of Nadia's life with Valentina only as a disembodied voice on the telephone and on a tape that he records and sends to Valentina with an enormous reel-to-reel tape player as a birthday gift. Maksim's presence within the film, in other words, is always mediated, never immediate. His own vision of the women is constantly undermined, marginalised and called into question.

The ways in which cultural forces shape the looking and power relations among the three characters is exemplified in a pair of scenes that reveal the role of mass culture in commodifying the female image and fabricating romantic fictions. Each scene might seem at first glance to be peripheral to the film's central drama, but the structural and thematic parallels between the two and their position within the film's narrative indicate their importance. In the first, Maksim and his fellow geologists examine a creased page torn from a Western magazine. An ad for Hennessy cognac, the page portrays a smiling woman whom they examine through a magnifying glass that, at one point, throws an enlarged image of a single eye up at the camera. The men's gaze is directed at the photo, of which the camera never reveals more than a partial, fragmentary glimpse. The men prop the photo up against a bottle on the table and speculate about the story that it tells, concluding that the woman is waiting for a boyfriend with whom she will 'toss back a few' when he arrives. The viewer sees only the back of the photo as the camera shows the men contemplating the image and slowly intoning the names of a series of alcoholic beverages. In the background Nadia watches them looking at the – literally – foreign image. The examination concludes with a call for a bottle of vodka and Maksim's demand for a comb, which he begins to play, announcing that he left his guitar behind 'in a certain house'. Nadia, who is meeting Maksim for the first time in this scene, brings him a guitar left in the café by another traveller and he begins to sing, but makes Nadia stop looking at him, since he cannot play if she is going to make him laugh. The camera shows Nadia peering at him from behind a row of bottles on the counter, hiding her gaze, but not her fascination with the singer. Like the girl in the photograph, Nadia also – literally – provides the men with liquor and she gives Maksim the instrument that represents his masculinity. As a result of this gift the geologists ask Nadia her name and invite her to join them at the table. Maksim begins singing, addressing Nadia by name and gazing at her directly – and seductively – for the first and most extended period of time in the entire film.

This scene in the café is intercut with a scene in which an acquaintance of Valentina is telling Nadia's fortune, and it directly precedes the most unusual flashback in the film, the episode portraying Maksim's first meeting with Valentina. This flashback is unusual both because it reveals the chronological starting point of all the film's events, but also, more importantly, because it is the only one in the film that is not clearly anchored in either Nadia's or Valentina's point of view. Rather than cutting or dissolving from Valentina's point of view, the film cuts from Maksim's face as he performs one of Vysotskii's trademark songs, 'Akh, eshche raz, eshche mnogo, mnogo raz' ('One more time'), to his entrance into Valentina's life. That sequence, which ends with Maksim literally sweeping Valentina off her feet and carrying her away into the shadows, is followed with a cut back to Valentina's apartment and the scene in which she articulates the film's implicit criticism of the ways in which popular culture usually represents everyday life. This speech, which Kovarskii singled out in the beginning of his review as articulating an aesthetic viewpoint that could only be deplored, formulates in very precise terms the film's organising narrative principle: 'You watch some film or read some book. And everyone there is so handsome and beautiful, and the feelings and actions are considered and definite. Even when they suffer, it's still somehow all logical and correct. The causes are clear, and also the consequences. There's a beginning, a middle, an end. And here everything is all so indefinite and formless ... but that's enough, this is all lyricism.'

This speech follows the juxtaposition of two scenes – both of which occur almost exactly in the middle of the film – which portray the beginning of Maksim's romance with each woman, creating an effect of simultaneity at the same time that it suggests his relationship with Nadia begins as a reaction to the end of his romance with Valentina. The odd, apparently inconsequential discussion of the Hennessy girl – the only scene set in the café that does not originate in Zhukhovitskii's story – thus serves as a prologue to the film's portrait of these two beginnings, while Valentina's speech serves as a sort of epilogue. The men can only imagine a single story for the Hennessy girl, a minimalist narrative of a girl waiting for a man to arrive. Initially, this is Nadia's story, too, but when she leaves before Maksim's arrival at the end of the film – carefully positioning two bottles on the table before she goes – she steps out of that neatly defined narrative and enters the world of women for whom beginnings, middles and ends are never clear or definite.

The power of commercial images of feminine beauty to shape women's own experiences of themselves – the ways in which they accept the Hennessy' girl's story as their own – is made apparent in a scene that is a structural and thematic twin of the scene with the men in the café. When Valentina learns that Maksim is planning to return, she goes to have her hair done in the local beauty salon, a public space that is as exclusively female as the café – with the exception of Nadia – is male. The scene begins with a slow pan across a row of seven large photos of smiling women with model coiffures to a mirror that reflects Valentina having her hair cut and set in preparation for Maksim's anticipated arrival. Valentina says not a word in this scene, which is packed with the visual detail of women having their hands and nails done, a process that the camera shows in a series of tracking shots that elides the women in the salon with their reflections in the mirrors that line its walls. All the dialogue in the scene is spoken by the salon workers as they ignore their clients and discuss husbands and sons. As Valentina leaves, the camera tracks back along the row of smiling female images, then records an exchange in which the hairstylist rejects the cashier's reproaches for having spoken so freely in front of an important city official like Valentina. 'So what, she's a woman isn't she? An ordinary broad.' The influence of mass-reproduced images of feminine beauty on women of all sorts is revealed on Valentina's return home, where she discovers that Nadia has had her own hair done in a similar style. The photographs on the wall of the beauty salon are analogous to the image of the Hennessy girl: they market a pre-packaged notion of feminine beauty that is an integral part of a cultural norm that renders all women, even the 'special ones', like Valentina, 'ordinary broads' where men are concerned.

The film's revelation of the way this cultural system compels women to sit and wait for men, to relinquish their own 'I' and appearance in order to please men, thus embeds its resistance to the male gaze in a broader critique of a social system that values women as images, rather than individuals.

Susan Larsen

REFERENCES

Bykov, D. (1997) 'Prem'era', *Profil'*, 9, 11 March, 31.

Fomin, V. (1996) *Kino i vlast': Sovestkoe kino 1965–1985 gody*. Moscow: Materik.

Kovarskii, N. (1967) 'Chelovek i vremia', *Iskusstvo kino*, 10, 57.

Mulvey, L. (1988) 'Visual Pleasure and Narrative Cinema', *Screen*, 16, 3, 6–18.

BRILLIANTOVAIA RUKA THE DIAMOND ARM

LEONID GAIDAI, USSR, 1969

When Leonid Gaidai's *Brilliantovaia ruka* (*The Diamond Arm*) was released in 1969, it became a box office leader and drew almost 77 million viewers. Since then the film has acquired cult status and is screened several times a year on Russian television. The film's enduring success among Soviet and post-Soviet spectators alike has puzzled many critics. The reasons for the film's success are, on the one hand, the themes of paranoia and ubiquitous fear of persecution, and, on the other, its emphasis on physical humour. In the Soviet Union viewers could easily identify with a protagonist obsessed with fear, while physical humour and slapstick provided a breath of fresh air in the ideologically repressive culture.

Gaidai (1923–1993) is one of the few Soviet directors whose films outlived his time and remained popular after the end of the Soviet Union. In the 1960s he made slapstick comedies that Russian viewers had not seen since the 1920s experiments of Lev Kuleshov. The short film *Pes Barbos i neobychnyi kross* (*Dog Barbos and the Unusual Race*, 1960), had launched the director's popularity overnight: it introduced the Soviet version of the Three Stooges – Georgii Vitsin, Iurii Nikulin and Evgenii Morgunov (in short, ViNiMor) – who captured Soviet mass audiences for decades. They were known by their telling nicknames: Vitsin as *Trus* ('Coward'), Nikulin as *Balbes* ('Dumb Ass') and Morgunov as *Byvalyi* ('the Experienced One'). Gaidai's subsequent comedies with ViNiMor, *Operatsiia Y i drugie prikliucheniia Shurika* (*Operation Y and Other Adventures of Shurik*) and *Kavkazskaia plennitsa, ili novye prikliucheniia Shurika* (*Kidnapping Caucasian Style, or New Adventures of Shurik*), were the biggest box office successes of 1965 and 1966 respectively. After the dizzying triumph of *The Diamond Arm*, Gaidai shot several films at Mosfil'm's Experimental Film Unit, which had been created by Grigorii Chukhrai and Vladimir Pozner Sr in order to set economic incentives within the ideology-driven film industry. The Unit became so profitable and successful that the Soviet authorities closed it in 1976, because the financial results of the rest of the film industry looked pathetic in comparison with the profits of the Experimental Unit. While working at the Unit Gaidai made three screen adaptations based on the satirical works of Il'ia Il'f and Evgenii Petrov, Mikhail Bulgakov, and Mikhail Zoshchenko: *Dvenadtsat' stul'ev*

(*Twelve Chairs*, 1971), *Ivan Vasil'evich meniaet professiiu* (*Ivan Vasil'evich Changes Profession*, 1973), and *Ne mozhet byt'!* (*It Can't Be!*, 1975). Although the films were well received, they were less popular than Gaidai's comedies of the 1960s. Like Gaidai's idol Charlie Chaplin, who could never adjust to the advent of sound, Gaidai never adjusted to the narrative constraints of the genre of screen adaptation.

The Diamond Arm starts with the modest Soviet clerk Semen Semenovich Gorbunkov going on vacation abroad. In a country like the USSR of the 1960s – behind the Iron Curtain – a story about a trip abroad sufficed to make the film a blockbuster. Nevertheless, Gaidai complicated the travel story with the elements of a comedy of errors: when Semen arrives to Istanbul, he is mistaken for a diamond smuggler. The local accomplices of the smugglers take Semen for their Russian connection and put a fake cast on his arm, in which they hide diamonds to be brought into the Soviet Union. Intimidated by the foreign environment, Semen does not resist the medical procedure but reports the incident to the proper Soviet authorities. For the rest of the film, the Russian smugglers try to remove surreptitiously the cast from Semen's arm. In order to do this, they try to knock him out by hitting him on the head, by making him drunk, and by seducing him with a prostitute, but each time they fail to accomplish their goal. The attempt to remove the valuable cast turns, again and again, into a cascade of slapstick scenes.

By choosing physical comedy, Gaidai inadvertently made body politics central to his films. In Stalinist culture, the body controlled by the individual had virtually disappeared from the screen: the human body was important either as a synecdoche for the ideological message, or as a fragment of the communal, machine-like body. Human bodies participated in ritualistic reenactments of the utopian project, such as parades and organised rallies accompanied by mass songs. Gaidai's comedy reinvented the individual human body in his slapstick routines. In his films he created a zone for the physical joke, where the body stopped being a representation of Soviet ideology and became a comic body *par excellence*. This comic body was anarchic and profane, thus defying the collective discipline of Soviet ideology.

While Semen's body contributes to many slapstick scenes, Gaidai also allows Semen's plaster cast arm to act independently as a comic hero. In a dream sequence, the plaster cast fights with the smuggler 'Count' (Andrei Mironov (1941–1987)), as he attempts to remove it from Semen's arm. Throughout the film, the arm-in-a-cast acts as Semen's sidekick, often beating Semen on the head when he says or does something outrageously stupid. Gaidai also introduces the entire gang of smugglers through close-ups of their hands at the beginning of the film in a scene that unfolds as a rhythmic sequence of shots depicting a comic skirmish among the smugglers' greedy hands passing, counting, hiding and steeling gold coins from each other. One of Gaidai's favourite comic devices is the close-up of a body part in an unusual function (a cast arm fighting on its own with a smuggler) or in an unusual garb (an arm in a cast decorated with jewels). While most directors favour the close-up of a performer's face, Gaidai – following his favourite filmmaker Chaplin – deploys the close-up to fetishise a body part in order to produce maximal comic effect. But if in the first part of the film visual gags involve characters' arms, in the second part of the film, the gags engage the characters' lower bodies, above all, their legs, feet and – occasionally – rear ends. In the finale the protagonist appears with his leg in a cast, immobile, moving only with the assistance of a construction crane and surrounded by his family. The film's title, *The Diamond Arm*, epitomises the body part as the film's fully-fledged character competing with human characters for the role of the film's protagonist.

The gender politics of body representation in Gaidai's films deserve special attention. Because of numerous images of semi-dressed females, it is tempting to assume that Gaidai's films embrace the scopic regime of classical Hollywood cinema, with the woman serving as 'the signifier for the male other', to use Laura Mulvey's term. But as a Soviet filmmaker Gaidai remained beyond the gender politics of American cinema. In his films the female body exists not as a visualised commodity circulated within the visual market; instead, nudity is a female garb that serves to carnivalise the uniformed body characteristic of Stalinist culture. The individual body, male or female, is turned into a grotesque body when set against the militarised norm of the Soviet collective body.

While the female body turns comic when it becomes mobile and aggressive, the male body becomes comic when it loses mobility. The main cause for the paralysis of the male body is fear: when Semen is abroad, he is afraid of walking around a foreign city alone without his group of Soviet tourists; when he returns to the Soviet border, he is worried of crossing without being guided by the Soviet police, and goes through the customs twice, awaiting special instructions for his life after his trip abroad. Moreover, Semen's will and body are completely paralysed by his fear that either the smugglers will attack him or he will inadvertently do something adverse to the Soviet police's instructions.

In fact, Semen is unable to act upon his own free will. His trip abroad comes about only because his wife has decided to send him on a holiday rather than buy a fur coat. The film evokes a grotesque Gogolian relationship between man losing his animate nature and inanimate objects acquiring a (human) life of their own. The relationship between the inert, almost inanimate Semen and his wife's fur coat recalls the relationship between the human copying machine, Akakii Akakievich, and his animated overcoat in Gogol's eponymous Petersburg tale. Moreover, Semen moves only when instructed either by the smugglers or by the police. When both cops and robbers order him to do something at the same time, Semen gets confused and hears a strange, paranoid humming in his head that puts him in a state of mental and physical paralysis. Semen turns into a broken social machine, whose elasticity is impeded by contradictory social constraints imposed on him by others. His arm in a plaster cast provides a humorous synecdoche of Semen's social and psychological condition. The laughter evoked by this character originates from the viewers' sense of superiority over the protagonist's comatose body and mind, and is therefore liberating.

Semen's body is so grotesquely dehumanised that his part could only be performed by an actor with a talent for overtly physical comedy. Gaidai and his co-authors Iakov Kostiukovskii and Moris Slobodskoi wrote the screenplay with one actor in mind: the clown Iurii Nikulin (1921–1997). In his rendition of Semen Gorbunkov, Nikulin combined histrionic acting with a stone-face expression that turned out to be the most precise comic image of the 'Soviet man'. Nikulin's performance solidified the success of the character conceived by Gaidai, and Semen Semenovich has been imprinted in Russian popular consciousness as the comic icon of repressed humanity, a carnivalistic inversion of the ideal Soviet man visualised by filmmakers in the Stalin era.

The focus on physical humour also determined the remaining cast list for *The Diamond Arm*. Apart from Nikulin, Gaidai invited Andrei Mironov and Anatolii Papanov (1922–1987), both actors at the Moscow Satire Theatre led by Vsevolod Meyerhold's disciple, Valentin Pluchek. For the part of the blonde he chose an actress capable of playing a seduction scene in a comically exaggerated style, whilst rejecting in the process actresses with excessive sex appeal. The Artistic Council of Mosfil'm Studio eventually confirmed Svetlana Svetlichnaia (b. 1940) for the part, over the Estonian actress Eeve Kivi, who was deemed to be too 'Western' and erotic.

Fear and danger, followed by an escape through a comic turn, are common components of slapstick comedies. While fear paralyses the protagonist of *The Diamond Arm*, vodka liberates him. Hence, vodka as freedom agent becomes the key ingredient of the film's *mise-en-scène*. As an exemplary citizen, Semen does not drink at all before his trip abroad. When he tells the Soviet authorities how he inadvertently became involved in the smuggling scheme and offers his cooperation, they suggest that he might consider loosening up and drink at least a little bit to fight his paranoia. This therapeutic advice brings most unexpected results: every time he gets drunk Semen discovers a totally different self. Vodka liberates Semen from all his fears: he becomes agile, free and even aggressive, but only for the time of intoxication; as soon as he sobers up, Semen lapses back into his Soviet coma.

In preparing his films, Gaidai emulated the work of Charlie Chaplin. Before each new film project Gaidai would watch two Chaplin films: *City Lights* (1931) and *Modern Times* (1936). Surprisingly, Gaidai eschewed the most obvious route of social satire, which was common for Chaplin's art as well as for Soviet cinema of the time (*Daite zhalobnuiu knigu* (*Give Me a Complaints Book*, 1964), *Dobro pozhalovat', ili postoronnim vkhod vospreshchen* (*Welcome, or No Trespassing*, 1964), *Tridtsat tri* (*33*, 1965)), and preferred slapstick comedy instead. In the long run such a choice proved more destructive for the ideological foundation of Soviet film, because Gaidai's films of the 1960s deconstructed the fundamental discursive mechanisms underlying Soviet cinema as an ideological institution. For example, in *The Diamond Arm* Gaidai parodied the role of sound in Soviet comedy, which – as ideological anchor for the visual image – had remained unchanged since the advent of talkies under Stalin. The film's opening credits are accompanied by the sound of mysterious steps of invisible characters, their hard breathing, and a terrifying scream. This blood-curdling soundtrack provides a backdrop for humorous intertitles, such as, 'The film has been shot by a half-hidden camera.' Gaidai parodies the guiding role of sound in Soviet film, where the word with its ideological weight always controlled the possible ambiguity of the cinematic image. In *The Diamond Arm*, the horrific scream misleads and confuses the viewer, who is not sure what to expect next: a mystery, a comedy or a horror film. The scream also becomes a red herring, a parody of Stalinist mass song that had conveyed the meaning of the narrative to the viewer.

Audiences were even confused about some of the film's narrative turns because of the sound. For example, one of the joking intertitles thanked private citizens and state organisations for providing genuine diamonds and gold for the film's shooting. Whenever viewers met with the film crew, one of the most common requests was to say who had provided the diamonds and gold. Soviet viewers were accustomed to transparent narratives with sound providing continuity of the narrative. The written word, such as credits or intertitles, was supposed to convey the absolute, *pravda*-like, truth. Gaidai's interplay between the soundtrack and the frame, therefore, led to the viewer's utter confusion. Thus, Gaidai not only parodies the function of sound as established in Stalinist cinema, but also returns to sound as 'the element of montage' proposed by Eisenstein, Pudovkin and Aleksandrov in their famous 'Statement on Sound'.

Furthermore, Gaidai's films redefine the role of songs in Soviet film. Song had played a special role in Soviet cinema, because of its potential to convey a clear ideological message. Grigorii Aleksandrov's *Veselye rebiata* (*The Happy Guys*, 1934) established the canon of musical comedy, in which mass song provided the foundation of the ideological narrative. The musical comedies' positive heroes were in charge of such songs that were later broadcast around the country and recommended for communal singing as an indispensable aural manifestation of Soviet identity. While Gaidai also made song a key part of his comedies, he had the villains, not the positive heroes, perform these songs. Villains could sing about prohibited topics and were free to express unconventional opinions. Their songs neither controlled the images nor did they convey an ideological message, but rather served as ironic parables of Soviet life. Gaidai thus replaced the mass song with the carnivalesque song, the musical and verbal structure of which was in tune with the clownish bodies of his characters.

In *The Diamond Arm* songs underscore the most repressed aspects of Soviet life: freedom of movement, freedom from fear, and last but not least bodily and sexual freedom. Mikhail Brashinskii notes that *The Diamond Arm* set the tone for permissible dissidence against the Soviet regime in the late 1960s with its Aesopian language, its parables with political underpinnings and its absurdist humour. The film's songs played a crucial role in articulating the perception of Soviet life as 'normalised absurdity' that had replaced the Stalin-era atmosphere of total terror. The composer Aleksandr Zatsepin (b. 1926) and poet Leonid Derbenev (1931–1995) wrote three songs for *The Diamond Arm* dealing with the major taboos of Soviet paradise: mobility, individual freedom and the right to live without fear.

First is the song of the smuggler, 'The Island of Bad Luck'. It is a parody of 'The Song of the Motherland', the unofficial Soviet anthem that glorified Stalin's new Constitution of 1936 and praised the USSR as a land of free and happy people. 'The Song of the Motherland' had been composed by Isaak Dunaevskii for Aleksandrov's *Tsirk* (*The Circus*, 1936), hailing the vastness of Soviet Russia at the height of Stalin's purges, when Soviet citizens had lost all opportunity to travel abroad. 'The Island of Bad Luck' talks of a land of savages, who work hard but cannot be happy on their island where there is no calendar, so that the savages lost track of time. The place of the song in the film's diegesis reinforces the allusion to Soviet utopia: when the heroes leave the Soviet port *en route* to foreign lands, the Count offers to sing a 'topical' song. The Soviet Union, isolated behind the Iron Curtain, is portrayed in the lyrics as a dystopian island of bad luck separated from the rest of the world.

The second song, 'The Song About Hares', is performed by Semen himself. It is the centrepiece of the film and deals with hares, the most cowardly creatures of Russian folklore, who learn nevertheless to overcome their fear. The episode that culminates in this song parodies the battle-council scene from the well-known Stalin-era film about the Civil War, *Chapaev* (1934); instead of Red Army commanders, gangsters surround a ludicrously detailed map of the restaurant and its restroom, where they hope to ambush Semen and remove his precious cast. Only one thing goes according to the smugglers' plan: Semen gets drunk. As his state of inebriation increases, so does his courage and, instead of a planned visit to the restroom, Semen gets on stage and starts singing about the cowardly hares who live in a dark and dangerous forest, but who get out of their hiding places every night and sing the same refrain: 'We couldn't care less/We couldn't care less/Bolder we'll be/Than the lion, king of beasts.' While this innocent song has no direct political agenda, the rejection of fear – even by a hare in a fairytale song performed by a drunkard – could be interpreted as an act of dissidence in a country built on terror. Indeed, when the cultural authorities previewed the film's final cut, they demanded to rework the song, firstly because it was too macabre for a comedy, and secondly because the personages, even though they were animals, should not proclaim complete indifference to authority. Ironically, the paranoid censors themselves voiced the anti-Soviet interpretation of the song. The song was nearly omitted from the film, but as often happened in Soviet cultural politics, it was vodka that resolved the conflict and cleared the clouds hanging over the controversial comedy. When the then Minister of Culture, Ekaterina Furtseva, heard the song, she became incensed at the filmmaker and yelled at her minions: 'Who "couldn't care less"? The working class couldn't care less?' Only after she was assured that the song was harmless because it was performed by a drunken clown, that is to say the drunken character played by the professional clown Iurii Nikulin, the song received Furtseva's imprimatur.

The third song, 'Help Me!', is a parodic tango about love in a tropical city performed by a passionate female voice. The aggressive blonde, Anna (Svetlana Svetlichnaia), plays the song on her tape recorder before getting undressed and launching her sexual offensive on Semen. On the one hand, the woman attacks and attempts to seduce Semen; on the other hand, Semen is a good Soviet citizen who knows that under no circumstances must he get entangled in extramarital sex. Instead of playing along with Anna, Semen crawls into a corner of the hotel room, hides his face behind his cast, and crouches before the topless temptress, petrified like a rabbit in front of a snake. Similar to the screams at the film's beginning, the tango serves as a red herring: a potentially erotic scene turns into a comic episode about Semen's fears and sexual repression. The only erotic joke possible on the Soviet screen was the protagonist's failure to perform.

When the censorship committee, led by the chairman of the State Committee for Cinematography (Goskino), Aleksei Romanov, watched the final cut of the film, they suggested numerous changes: among them, to enhance the positive image of Soviet police, to improve Semen's role as an exemplary Soviet citizen and, obviously, to cut all nudity. Above all, the Committee was petrified and puzzled by film's ending, comprised of documentary footage of a nuclear explosion. When the Committee gave Gaidai their comments, he said that he would not make any changes and would understand if the film were banned.

By the late 1960s Soviet cinema was no longer a purely ideological institution; instead it had become the most profitable branch of Soviet culture industry. A ban would have hurt, above all, the Committee's annual report and the finance department at Mosfil'm, required to account for expenditure. The censors gave Gaidai three days to consider what changes he would agree to make in order for the film to get released. Gaidai answered that he would remove the documentary footage of the nuclear explosion. The Committee, relieved to achieve at least one concession, immediately released the film after cutting the 'radioactive' ending had been cut.

The circumstances of the film's approval by Goskino reflect important shifts in cultural politics during this period. Firstly, financial concerns had become as important as ideological ones. Secondly, compromise was a more acceptable cultural strategy than an inflexible ideological stance for both cultural authorities and the artist. Finally, the inclusion of multiple endings was increasingly deployed in order to negotiate with the censors: the ending that satisfied the authorities usually differed from the ending that satisfied the artist. With the 'unclear' ending, Gaidai had thrown out a red herring for the censors in order to save the rest of his film from massive changes.

Perhaps Mikhail Brashinskii found the key to Gaidai's art of comedy when he wrote that Gaidai did not create slapstick but sought its manifestations in Soviet life and transposed them onto the screen. By means of lighthearted physical comedy Gaidai explored the changing role of the individual and the collective in Soviet culture after Stalin's death, and commented indirectly on the repressive nature of the Soviet regime. Serving as one of the few safety valves in a culture based primarily on oppression, Gaidai's comedies have remained popular with post-Soviet viewers who rated his 1960s films still among as their favorites – forty years after they were released.

Alexander Prokhorov

REFERENCES

Aleksandrov, G., S. Eisenstein and L. Pudovkin (1988 [1928]) 'Statement on Sound' in R. Taylor and I. Christie (eds) *The Film Factory: Russian and Soviet Cinema in Documents 1896–1939*. London and New York: Routledge, 234–5.

Brashinskii, M. (2001) 'Leonid Gaidai', in L. Arkus (ed.) *Noveishaia istoriia otechestvennogo kino 1986–2000, vol. 1*. St. Petersburg: Seans, 233–4.

Mulvey, L. (1975) 'Visual Pleasure and Narrative Cinema', *Screen*, 16, 3, 6–18.

NRAN GUYNE THE COLOUR OF POMEGRANATES

SERGO PARAJANOV, USSR, 1969

Sergo Parajanov's *Nran guyne* (*The Colour of Pomegranates*, 1969) emerges out of a particular set of circumstances that characterised filmmaking in the Soviet Republics in the 1960s: a return to the tradition of poetic cinema; a film industry relatively independent of market forces; a government policy encouraging celebration of specific national cultures; and a coterie of filmmakers employing stylistic innovations that would astound even the post-New-Wave international art-film circuit. Most importantly, the film owes its existence to a director with an abiding love of the decorative arts who believed that cinema could be made new by taking it back in time, transforming celluloid into the pages of an illuminated manuscript or the painting of a Persian miniature. Perhaps *The Colour of Pomegranates*, even though it appeared after the post-Stalin 'Thaw' period, also drew upon that earlier, frenetic blast of creativity that came when the government's strict control of artistic activity, which marked the Stalin era, finally loosened.

The film traces the childhood perceptions, sexual awakening, unhappy love affair, initiation into monastic life, old age and death of Arutin Sayadan (1712–1795), an eighteenth-century poet writing verse in Georgian, Armenian and Azerbaidjani. As a young troubadour, he created the pseudonym Sayat-Nova, a name that could have served as the film's title, except that Parajanov's treatment of the poet's life appeared too unconventional to bear a title that might lead filmgoers to expect a biopic. According to its introductory title card, Parajanov's film 'uses the symbolism and allegories specific to the tradition of Medieval Armenian poet-troubadours' to represent the inner world of the protagonist. Through a complex play of repetition and difference among a series of densely symbolic tableaux, Parajanov translates poetic image into filmic image.

A film 'poem', *The Colour of Pomegranates*, along with such films as *Krynytsia dlia sprah-lykh* (*A Well for the Thirsty*, Yuri Illienko, Ukraine, 1965), *Vedreba* (*The Supplication*, Tengiz Abuladze, Georgia, 1968), *Natvris khe* (*The Wishing Tree*, Abuladze, Georgia, 1976) and *Belyi parakhod* (*The White Steamship*, Bolotbek Shamshiev, Kyrgyzstan, 1976), belongs to the 'poetic' or 'archaic' school in Soviet cinema of the 1960s and 1970s. With the notable exception of Andrei Tarkovskii, most directors associated with the Archaic School – including Ukrainian Leonid Osyka, Georgian Otar Ioseliani and Armenian Artavazd Peleshyan – are non-Russian, and their films accentuate the cultural specificities of the republics in which they work. Films of this school often feature the folklore, costumes, decorative arts and music of particular ethnic groups. Enabling the making of such films, the USSR actively promoted celebrations of the distinctive cultures of its diverse republics. As James Steffen demonstrates, a proposed film about the poet Sayat-Nova, whose very tri-lingualism symbolised the 'friendship of peoples' (an important theme for the Soviet empire!) would certainly receive encouragement.

The visual ethnography of the Archaic School is often realised through a poetic style, which emphasises not the accretion of narrative information, but rather the visual and metaphorical or symbolic qualities of a shot and the graphic 'rhymes' between shots. Filmmakers of this school look back to the silent films of Aleksandr Dovzhenko as models. But sound, in their own films, rivals the visual in its striking complexity. Indeed Steffen, who insists on the importance of sound to the poetic school of the 1960s and 1970s, compares Tigran Mansuryan's soundtrack for *The Colour of Pomegranates* (an 'audio-collage' of natural sounds, folk music and fragments of music and speech) to *Musique Concrète* and the work of avant-garde composers such as Karlheinz Stockhausen.

Parajanov's *Tini zabutykh predkiv* (*Shadows of Forgotten Ancestors*, 1964) inaugurated the Archaic School. This film brought Parajanov his first international recognition and, perhaps, put him in a position where he had the freedom to develop a distinctive tableau style, characterised primarily by long takes and little or no camera movement. In the context of Parajanov's individual oeuvre, *The Colour of Pomegranates* is the first completed feature-length film fully to employ this style, which also distinguishes the features *Ambavi suramis tsikhisa* (*The Legend of Suram Fortress*, 1984) and *Ashik Kerib* (1988). *Shadows of Forgotten Ancestors*, however, still bears the powerful influence, in Yuri Illienko's cinematography, of Sergei Urusevskii's dazzling camera movements in such films as *Letiat zhuravli* (*The Cranes are Flying*, 1957), and *Neotpravlennoe pis'mo* (*The Letter Never Sent*, 1959). The edited screen tests of the unfinished *Kievski freski* (*Kiev Frescoes*, 1966), a project that aimed to represent the impact of the Nazi occupation of Kiev twenty years after the fact, and *Akop Ovnatanian* (1967), a short eponymous film about a nineteenth-century Armenian portrait painter, mark Parajanov's initial experiments with a sustained tableau aesthetic. Compared to *Shadows of Forgotten Ancestors* and the films that follow, the early films Parajanov directed – *Andriesh*

(1954), *Dumka, Nataliia Uzhvii* (1957) *Zoloti Ruky* (*Golden Hands*, 1957), *Pervyi paren'* (*The Top Guy*, 1958), *Ukrainskaia rapsodia* (*Ukrainian Rhapsody*, 1961) and *Tsvetok na kamne* (*The Flower on the Stone*, 1962) – do not particularly distinguish themselves.

The 15-year gap between *The Colour of Pomegranates* and *The Legend of Suram Fortress* roughly coincides with the period of economic and political stagnation that commences at the end of the Thaw (Nikita Khrushchev, who largely shaped thaw policies, lost power in 1964, but the effects were not keenly felt in the film industry until around 1967) and extends to Mikhail Gorbachev's accession to power in1985. During this time, Parajanov was arrested twice. In 1973 he was sentenced to five years in prison on charges of 'sodomy' and 'dissemination of pornographic imagery' and released a year early due to international pressure. He was arrested again in 1982 on bribery charges and jailed for several months. Both arrests were politically motivated. In the first instance, Parajanov was a target not for his bisexuality (a mere excuse), but for signing petitions in support of arrested Ukrainian intellectuals; in the second instance, for other public challenges to Soviet authorities. Prevented from making films for nearly 15 years, his career was put on hold immediately after his stylistic breakthrough with *The Colour of Pomegranates*.

Critical and scholarly approaches to *The Colour of Pomegranates* are diverse: Kora Tsereteli's scholarly edition of Parajanov's screenplays and letters, *Ispoved'* ('Confession'), includes Parajanov's sketches and provides useful annotations to the scenario as well as a brief, but informative introductory essay. James Steffen has explored the film's production, censorship and distribution, and his doctoral dissertation on Parajanov (the most comprehensive and important English-language scholarship on the director to date) analyses the intersection between national identity and the Archaic School more broadly. Levon Grigorian and Levon Abrahamian both provide erudite explications of the film's visual metaphors (Abrahamian further argues that Parajanov occupies a unique place in the history of visual anthropology). Barthélemy Amengual situates Parajanov's aesthetic in relation to Sergei Eisenstein's theorisation and practice of montage, specifically comparing and contrasting Parajanov's collage style (or montage *within* the shot) with Eisenstein's conceptualisation of montage between shots. We might also consider *The Colour of Pomegranates* in terms of Eisenstein's insistence on the centrality of Joyce's technique of interior monologue for the cinema.

In a 1934 lecture on James Joyce at the State Institute of Cinematography (VGIK), Eisenstein drew attention to Joyce's fragmentation of phrases; unexpected and unconventional arrangements of words; and condensation of various levels of psychic signification. Such qualities resonate with aspects of Eisenstein's own montage theory, early and late. Eisenstein's emphasis, for instance, on Joyce's 'arrangement of words, the way phrases break off' resonates with his theories of the processes of breakdown and construction that constitute montage. Perhaps better than his theoretical writing, Eisenstein's *Ivan Groznii* (*Ivan the Terrible I* (1944) and *II* (1946, released 1958)), illustrates, through film practice, the power of condensing multiple layers of meaning around a single image, partly through making one image (or tableau) 'rhyme' with another. The film demonstrates the persistence of Eisenstein's interest in realising the sensual thought of the spectator – if not the interior monologue of a character.

Parajanov's *The Colour of Pomegranates*, profoundly influenced by Eisenstein's *Ivan the Terrible*, more fully realises a cinematic interior monologue. The film simultaneously mimes the inner speech or sensual thought of its central character and, through him, the spectator. To create this vision of sensual thought, the film, like *Ivan the Terrible*, demands visual memory and active association to give meaning to its 'asyntactic' (relative to the continuity editing of conventional narrative cinema) string of images. Certain objects reappear across various tableaux – the golden ball, the kamancha. The same tableau reappears, rhythmically, differentially, with a change in only one or two of its elements. Such rhyming of elements often takes place across large segments of film. Significance gradually accrues around the object, or around the slight changes in tableau. Stasis and the long take lend the shot, or the perceived object, an intensity – as in dream imagery.

Through the tableaux that make up *The Colour of Pomegranates*, the spectator can construct a story, but cannot always exactly determine such information as duration or causal logic. (Even in the highly stylised *Ivan the Terrible*, the tableaux are not as independent of causal logic as in Parajanov's film: while Eisenstein partly structures the film's discourse through the repetition of lighting patterns and graphic motifs, he also regularly uses shots to present new story information.) The style of *The Colour of Pomegranates* cannot, however, be said to interfere with spectator construction of the story out of plot information: the style *is* the plot information. As the opening title says, 'The film does not attempt to tell the life story of a poet. Rather the filmmaker has tried to recreate the poet's inner world...' The story is not a sequential narrative – it is an experience of human consciousness, which tends to collapse time and condense meaning – the same processes that define the syntagmatic distortion and syncretism of inner speech. The strictly chronological trajectory of conventional biography – parents, birth, childhood, youth, middle age, old age, death – gives way to a subjective sense of time with its condensation of past, present and future.

Thus, in some tableaux, the actor who plays the poet as child (Melkop Alekyan) occupies the same frame with one of the actors who plays the poet at a later stage in life (Poet as youth (Sofiko Chiaureli), Poet as monk (Vilen Galstyan) and Poet in Old Age (Gogi Gegechkori)). These tableaux, like self-consciousness, hold together various images of the poet's self, which changes through time.

The very notion of an inner world implies reflective consciousness. The film fore-grounds the reflective nature of its images through two metaphors, which also happen to be central metaphors for cinema: the window and the frame. In a broader analysis of Parajanov's cinema, Abrahamian also includes mirrors, in addition to windows and frames, as a central motif in what he calls Parajanov's 'collage' aesthetic. (The mirror is, of course, a third major metaphor for the film screen.) Both window frame and picture frame distance the image from visual immediacy, raising it to the plane of reflection. Window and frame are metaphors André Bazin used to distinguish theatre from cinema; he argued that film is like a window in that the edges of its frame serve a masking function. The spectator does not imagine that the diegetic world stops at the edges of the frame. Rather, the edges of the frame simply mask the continuation of that world. In theatre, however, the edges of the stage serve to frame the action. The audience knows that the world represented on stage does not continue into the wings; what is framed is all there is.

Part of the originality of *The Colour of Pomegranates* is that the edges of the film frame function more as theatrical framing than as cinematic masking: Parajanov does nothing to activate offscreen space; it does not exist. With few exceptions, the film does not construct, with such common devices as the pan or the point-of-view sequence, a diegetic world beyond the edges of the frame: indeed the film contains only a single conventional shot/reverse-shot sequence. Rather than gaze at objects outside the frame, implying the existence, or signifi-cance, of a world beyond the edge of the tableau, characters tend to gaze straight ahead, often directly at the camera or spectator. We are presented with tableaux, complete in themselves, that often, through the eyes of the characters, look back at us. Through framing and through images that gaze back at their beholder, the film presents a highly mediated world, ultimately arriving at a representation of a consciousness that frames, allegorises and symbolises, using a long, collective tradition.

The film reflects, continually, on its process of framing. Arutin crouches on a stone table. Thunder sounds. The next shot cuts back, showing Arutin in the same position, but now his parents stand behind him, poised to cover him with carpets. This second shot appears through a window frame. The scene thus progresses from relative visual immediacy (without the frame) to distancing and separation through frame within frame.

Arutin's parents do not watch what they are doing. Instead they gaze directly at the camera, along with their son, thus appearing to look at the spectator as our reflection looks back at us when we look into a mirror. Gazing at the camera, all three characters appear curiously detached from the 'action'. Indeed in some scenes, the characters merely pose, without performing the action at all: a drummer in the film never moves his hands to produce the drumming sound heard on the soundtrack, a choir of boys never move their open mouths to produce the singing we hear. (In this film, there is very little synchronous sound.) The very motionlessness of these 'characters' creates the stasis that aligns the film with far older traditions of visual art. In the art forms that the film imitates – miniature painting, manuscript illumination, icon painting – human figures often face forward, as do Parajanov's human figures within the film. Figures face the onlooker, for instance, in the illuminated books that Arutin helps to rescue from the effects of the storm's rainwater. Though the editing implies that the child Arutin gazes at these books, we do not see them from his angle, but rather from a point of view that is more abstract. The world surrounding Arutin disappears as the book illustration fills the frame, its image absorbing all attention. The soundtrack features the sound of a page turning, but the image-track does not show the turn of the page, it simply cuts to another illustration. The cut, the edit, becomes equivalent to the turn of the page. Under Parajanov's 'camera stylo', film screen and soundtrack become a condensed, abstracted visual and aural encounter with the material sensuality of the book.

As in the thunderstorm sequence, Parajanov and cinematographer Suren Shabazyan (b. 1923) frame people and objects throughout *The Colour of Pomegranates* in doorways, arches and wall niches, doubling the film frame. The film features an empty, mobile frame in the lace-making sequence (where we see the budding passion between the poet and King Irakli II's sister), and in the graveyard sequence preceding the poet's death. In the lace-making sequence, a spinning golden cherub, suspended from the ceiling, appears within a golden frame suspended in front of it. The frame swings from side to side. In many shots of the graveyard sequence, two boys, angels costumed in white, carry an empty frame (a window) among the gravestones. As they move with the frame, they randomly capture fragments of the vast landscape behind them in a framing of space that is conventionally filmic. The motion of the empty frame in both sequences recalls the mobile framing of much contemporary cinema, which Parajanov's static camera, aligning itself with older visual art forms, resolutely denies us. Contrasted with such a mobile frame, Parajanov's motionless camera, fixated on richly symbolic tableaux, suggests the heightened selection and condensed meaning of a vision and a memory refined by a highly reflective consciousness.

In one shot from the graveyard sequence, the boys pause and look through the window frame at the camera, statically framing themselves within the frame. In other shots, tombstones perform the framing function, as when, centre-frame, the boys leap toward one another, crossing paths in mid-air. Tombstones, marking the end of life, rhyme with the frame that brackets and distances artistic, reflective vision. Sayat-Nova walks from screen left toward screen right, passing behind (and seemingly through) the frame held by the boys. He pauses within the frame and takes it from them. To his right, mourners carry forward a corpse. The corpse, framed by its black stretcher, rhymes graphically with the poet, centre-frame, who holds the frame that frames him. Since the sequence addresses the poet's own old age and approaching death, his framing metaphorically suggests the frame constituted by death, which, in putting an end to life, permits others to contemplate that life as a completed whole.

In the graveyard sequence, a voice sings Sayat-Nova's most famous song, 'The world is like an open window, and I am weary of passing through it/You wound the one that looks through it'. The lines pose a riddle. Conventionally we speak of a window onto the world – not of the world itself as a window. That would place the world at the juncture of inside and outside rather than simply on one side or the other. Rather than inner world and outer world, the world of the song is a point of pure mediation. The lines name two different actions possible in regard to the space of this window-world: passing through and looking through. The actions can be directed from inside-out and from outside-in. One looks and is looked at. If the world is like an open window, it is this sill, this threshold of consciousness and self-consciousness that arises from sensing oneself as not only seeing, but as seen. The film's human figures realise this duality on a formal level by gazing directly at the camera and, through the camera, at the spectator. If the film realises in images the inner world of a man, then the images of *The Colour of Pomegranates* are images of the poetic consciousness gazing back on itself. Parajanov's film is a reflection on reflection. More specifically, it is a reflection on a self-consciousness that is at once individual and collective – a lyricism steeped in national traditions.

Levon Abrahamian observes that the Persian word translated above as 'window' means a lattice window, and that the related Sanskrit word *pañjara* means 'cage'. He interprets the word as helping to develop the image of the poet as bird trapped in a cage. What constitutes this imprisonment only partially lies in the diegetic world whose representation appears at least at a double remove, mediated both by Sayat-Nova's poetry and Parajanov's cinematic tableaux. We might associate the motif of imprisonment with the poet's social standing, which prevents the happy outcome of his love affair with the king's sister; with the seclusion of monastic life; or with the experience of suffering and dying in the Iranian invasion of Tbilisi. But Parajanov's aesthetics, with their emphasis on the processes of framing and reflecting, suggest that the sense of confinement characterises the predicament of consciousness itself as much as the romanticised experiences of the individual poet. The film shows the very mediation of consciousness, the selective framing, reflecting and ordering of memory and perception – and the projection of meaning onto the people and objects framed, reflected and ordered. In so doing, the film emphasises both the inescapability of conscious mediation, specifically aesthetic mediation – and its potential for great beauty. The bird in the cage, like the gaze of the poet through the lattice window, appears at once beautiful and delimited.

Appropriately, the film stages the scene of Sayat-Nova's death as a shot/reverse-shot structure, moving beyond reflexive tableau to create a broader diegetic space. The dying poet faces, appropriately, a man cementing a cathedral arch with resonator jars. This worker, a figure for death, orders the poet first to sing, then to die. The cementing of resonator jars into an arch in the cathedral wall has the appearance of the plugging-up of a window (through which Death issues its command to Sayat-Nova). The blocked 'window' coincides with the ending of the film: with the poet's death, then, we leave the threshold of individual consciousness with its rhyming, self-reflexive tableaux that collapse time and condense meaning. The shot/reverse-shot sequence between Sayat-Nova and the figure of death activates offscreen space and thus activates the world beyond the framing consciousness of the poet. Formally, the scene gestures toward a world beyond the mediation of the individual consciousness just as, symbolically, the resonator jars suggest a collective and ongoing song that both includes and transcends the voice of the individual poet.

Parajanov's cinematic text is at once deeply personal and fiercely national. Parajanov identified with his eighteenth-century hero: Kora Tsereteli remarks that he wrote on a page of his notes to the film, 'Sayat-Nova is me'. At the same time, what drew him to the project were the collective cultural traditions that shaped the poet's work. Parajanov's films after *Shadows of Forgotten Ancestors* and before his imprisonment often received criticism that they were too subjective, or idiosyncratic, despite the fact that their screenplays address national themes. That criticism misses the profoundly collective nature of the cultural traditions upon which these films draw: *Kiev Frescoes* was to realise the impact of World War Two on a people; in *The Colour of Pomegranates*, the representation of a trilingual poetic tradition merges with the representation of the 'inner speech' or sensual thought of the individual poet-protagonist. The criticism that these films, which focus on national experience, are overly subjective and idiosyncratic, suggests the paradoxical nature of Parajanov's aesthetic strategy. Through real-ising, with precision, the images of an individual self-consciousness, a poet's consciousness, *The Colour of Pomegranates* aims at an expression of a collective or shared consciousness.

The conscious intentionality realised through the motifs of window and frame is highly reflective: what poet and filmmaker place in the frame often functions as a mirror. Indeed window, frame and mirror collapse into one another. Mirroring takes place on multiple levels: the director, Parajanov, sees himself mirrored in his protagonist Sayat-Nova; Sofiko Chiaureli, in playing both the poet as youth as well as the role of his beloved, transforms the lovers into mirror images of one another; on a formal level, Parajanov's cinema, through the stillness and doubling of its frames, mirrors, and is mirrored by, older arts such as manu-script illumination and miniature painting. The poet's song, equating world and life with a window that is also a frame and a mirror, suggests Stephen Daedalus's description of life in the Scylla and Charibdis section of Joyce's *Ulysses* – a description of life that reveals a single subjectivity to be inextricably linked to reflection and projection in the experience of others: 'Every life is many days, day after day. We walk through ourselves meeting robbers, ghosts, giants, old men, young men, wives, widows, brothers in love, but always meeting ourselves.' Parajanov's use of multiple actors for a single character and of a single actor for multiple characters visually realises Stephen Daedalus's thought. (In addition to playing Sayat-Nova and his beloved, Chiaureli also takes on the minor roles of the Nun in White Lace, the Angel of the Resurrection and the Pantomime.) *Ulysses*, with its intensive focus on the inner life of an individual, might be seen as the opposite of Eisenstein's early insistence on a collective 'protagonist'. The originality of *The Colour of Pomegranates* lies in its resourceful solution to the problem of bridging individual consciousness and collective cultures, humanism and formalism. With this film, Parajanov achieves one possible – and unique – realisation of Eisenstein's vision of a Joycean cinema.

Karla Oeler

REFERENCES

Abrahamian, L. (2001/02) 'Toward a Poetics of Parajanov's Cinema', *Armenian Review*, 47, 3–4 and 48, 1–2, 67–91.

Amengual, B. (1987/88) 'Sur deux neveux d'Eisenstein', *Études Litteraires*, 20, 3, 123–36.

Grigorian, L. (1991) *Tri tsveta odnoi strasti: Triptikh Sergeia Paradzhanova.* Moscow: Kinotsentr.

Parajanov, S. (2001) *Ispoved': Kinostenarii. Pis'ma*, edited by K. Tsereteli. St Petersburg: Azbuka.

Steffen, J. (1995/96) 'Parajanov's Playful Poetics: On the 'director's cut' of *The Color of Pomegranates*', *Journal of Film and Video*, 47, 4, 17–33.

_____ (2001/02) 'From Sayat-Nova to *The Color of Pomegranates: Notes on the Production and Censorship of Parajanov's Film*', *Armenian Review*, 47, 3–4 and 48, 1–2, 105–47.

_____ (2005) 'A Cardiogram of the Time: Sergei Parajanov and the Politics of Nationality and Aesthetics in the Soviet Union', unpublished doctoral theis, Emory University.

Woll, J. (2000) *Real Images: Soviet Cinema and the Thaw.* London: I. B. Tauris.

ЖИЛ ПЕВЧИЙ ДРОЗД

10

IKO SHASHVI MGALOBELI LIVED ONCE A SONG-THRUSH

OTAR IOSELIANI, USSR, 1970

Iko shashvi mgalobeli (*Lived Once a Song-Thrush*, aka *Once Upon a Time There Was a Singing Blackbird*, 1970) was produced at the Georgian studio Gruzia-Fil'm and released in the Soviet Union with 320 prints, attracting 2.6 million spectators. These figures were unusually high for a film of this kind, even if it is amusing in the context of the present day: a while ago only American films like the *Matrix* trilogy or the *Lord of the Rings* trilogy could achieve such figures in Russian distribution. However, since 2004, Russian cinema can pride itself again with figures that prove its ability to outstrip Hollywood films in box office figures with national blockbusters such as *Nochnoi dozor* (*Night Watch*, 2004) or *Turetskii gambit* (*Turkish Gambit*, 2005), reaching over 15 million viewers.

Otar Ioseliani's 87-minute feature is merely a modest sketch of life in the Georgian capital, Tblisi, in the late 1960s. It contains neither mad love nor fascinating adventures, neither a fantastic set design nor well-known actors. It initially appears to have no plot, especially as it took four scriptwriters to write it. Throughout the film, people stroll around Tblisi, discussing things of little relevance. The main character, the musician Gija Agladze, is constantly late for his orchestra rehearsals and performances. One day, while hurredly crossing the road, he is hit by a car and killed.

Lived Once a Song-Thrush is thus no simple film with a clear narrative; the antithesis of what mainstream audiences appear to like. Yet the 1960s were a time when people were drawn to films that did more than tell a simple story: Mikhail Kalatozov's *Letiat zhuravli* (*The Cranes are Flying*, 1957) or Grigorii Chukhrai's *Ballada o soldate* (*Ballad of a Soldier*, 1959) provided a coherent plot, but their appeal stemmed largely from their extraordinarily powerful visual language. For example, the episode in *Ballad of a Soldier* when the tank overturns, and with it the vision of the hero, Alesha Skvortsov, interested audiences because of the camera movements. Similar developments in cinematic language occurred in Europe at the same time. In Russia, these innovations led to the emergence of an intellectual audience that craved films that we would today call 'art-house'. The popularity of such films grew rapidly in the late 1960s (we are seeing the opposite today – a decrease in the number of people who watch art-house films). A growing number of people aspired to the exotic and the unusual, instead of being drawn to the familiar, entertaining and predictable plots of the blockbusters. Cinema was the most fashionable and cultured of all leisure activities. People went to see films even if they could not entirely comprehend them, such as Andrei Tarkovskii's *Zerkalo* (*Mirror*, 1974) and *Stalker* (1979) or Federico Fellini's *8½* (1963) – films with complex structures and unconventional plots. Yet audiences longed for the aesthetic pleasure and tried to decipher the visual metaphors contained in these films. In the late 1970s, more commercial films gained prestige and ultimately put aside the success that art-house cinema had enjoyed in the 1960s.

Moreover, in the 1960s, Georgian cinema became very popular in the USSR. For Soviet critics, the republic of Georgia had always been associated with hospitality and blue skies and its people with affluence and charm. The myth of the Caucasian people and their traditions was held in high esteem. The exotic land was both attractively remote and at the same time geographically close; Georgia was a different culture and Georgians a different nation within the Soviet land. *Lived Once a Song-Thrush* is no direct representation of these qualities, but echoes the national temperament. Russians were attracted by the foreign culture, and with Georgii Daneliia's *Mimino* (1977) that attracted 24 million spectators, Georgian cinema conquered the heart of the masses.

If *Lived Once a Song-Thrush* had been made in the Stalin era, it would certainly have been banned and denounced for its trivial subject matter. Attempts to destroy the film for similar reasons were also made in 1971, but the times had changed and the allegations were refuted. The Thaw had brought back a certain respect for man's individuality and for the value of human life. The life portrayed in a film did not necessarily have to be special or heroic, as had been required in the Stalin era. The figure of the hero was transformed into a 'Hero', a concept that was entirely positive. At the same time, the concept of the anti-hero entered Soviet usage from Western cinema: the 'carefree rider' and the 'midnight cowboy' appeared alongside the term of the 'lost generation' so prominent in Western literature of the time. The tradition of the Russian classics, ranging from Onegin and Pechorin across the entire gallery of the 'superfluous men' of nineteenth-century literature, was revived; and with it, the issue of the positive or negative qualities of the hero emerged once again.

The superfluous man had been an important phenomenon in Russian literature, but it had been attributed exclusively to negative qualities in Soviet cinema, which had insisted on a 'positive' hero who made an active contribution to society. With the arrival of the Thaw the positive hero became more reflexive and more complex. Gija is an example of the 'positive hero' with attributes of the superfluous man: he is a good man, but he is superfluous. He cannot find his place in society, yet the blame for this is not put at the feet of society. Gija leads a life separate from society, but that society does not need Gija either. He has no social function, refusing to play his part and instead withdrawing into his private life. Gija's behaviour is incompatible with the conventions of society. However, in contrast to Stalinist films, society does not eliminate him, but merely marginalises him. Ultimately, Gija destroys his own life: he fails to achieve social recognition and becomes increasingly isolated. A man who withdraws from society cannot yet survive in the late 1960s.

Ioseliani's *Lived Once a Song-Thrush* was successfully embedded in the context of its time and contemporary cinematic style. Experiments with neo-realism had come to an end, as had the fascination with 'cinema vérité' and with the French and Czech 'new waves'. An entire decade had gone by while the principles of documentary were introduced to the creation of feature films, a phenomenon that extended to Soviet cinema (examples of this tendency can be found in Marlen Khutsiev's *Iul'skii dozhd* (*July Rain*, 1966) and Andrei Konchalovskii's *Asino schast'e* (*Istoriia Asi Kliachinoi, kotoraia liubila da ne vyshla zamuzh, Asya's Happiness*, 1966; released 1988).

Lived Once a Song-Thrush was considered by many critics of the time as a piece of Georgian neo-realism, continuing the tradition of the early works of the Georgian filmmakers Rezo Chkheidze (b. 1926) and Tengiz Abuladze (1924–1994). Film historians, such as Neia Zorkaia, wrote about the stream of life that bubbles like the famous Borjomi mineral water in every frame shot by Ioseliani. Although Gija perished at a precise location – the corner of Chavchavadze Street and Rustaveli Avenue – the setting of the scene did not tie the film to Georgia's capital, but served to heighten the poetic reliability. Street scenes were rare for Soviet films of the 1960s, but they gave the film an authentic, documentary quality that stood in stark contrast to the falsified and varnished reality of Stalinist cinema. Interior shots in the flat show the life of the old woman, who is a bearer of tradition and not some useless member of society (as many old people are portrayed in Soviet film). While in Russia the links with the past had been severed through revolution and war, Georgia was deemed to have preserved some of its traditions. The old woman is such a link to the past: her memories, her knowledge of times past, together with the old photographs in the apartment connect to a personal history. The film thus intensifies the myth about the continuity of Georgian tradition, its preservation of the link between past and present. Despite the local colour, the setting is still universal enough to allow for identification with the protagonist, which may account also for the film's success abroad: it was the best foreign film in Italian distribution in 1972.

At the same time, it was obvious that *Lived Once a Song-Thrush* was a parable and Ioseliani was not merely continuing already existing traditions and conventions; he belonged to the avant-garde of Georgian cinema. For the Georgian cinematic tradition, the parable had always been a key genre, but it had never been so closely connected to contemporary reality and modern rhythms. Georgian cinema was built on mythologisation, which film-makers used to indirectly express – through metaphors – their opposition to the Soviet system. Georgian films tended to refer to the 'Golden Age' of the twentieth century (the 1910s and 1920s), and touched upon a variety of subject matter, often involving pioneering individuals and portraying them as marginal characters because of their desire for progress an innovation. Ioseliani was one of the first directors who transposed these metaphors to the contemporary world and to modern man. He was not alone in doing so – El'dar Shengelaia's *Neobyknovennaia vystavka* (*Unusual Exhibition*, 1968) is another example – but Ioseliani is the most articulate. In *Lived Once a Song-Thrush* he explores a world in which a Georgian – a Soviet – man finds a different mode of existence, underlining thereby that there are people who exist separately from society without being dissidents. *Lived Once a Song-Thrush* makes a statement about inner emigration and about withdrawal from society, which leads, in the case of Gija, literally to a dead end. Ioseliani refers here also his own condition: he emigrated to France in order to continue his creative life when this had become impossible in his native Georgia.

Lived Once a Song-Thrush is a parable about time and about the transience of human life. The parable is woven together from numerous details; from everyday, concrete and yet absolutely metaphorical details. In structural terms the film is composed of changing rhythms, which transform the film into a poem. Here is the poem's first line: early on in the film, Gija makes a narrow escape from a plant pot that falls off a balcony. After a while this episode (or phrase) is rhymed with another movement: Gija fails to notice a barrier that seals off a construction site and is almost buried under a load of grit thrown onto the street. And again, a while later he almost falls into a hatch opened by a stage worker. In another sequence of the same movement Gija tries to drink poison from a test tube; a trolleybus almost runs him over. In these rhyming lines of the poem that represent Gija's narrow escapes from death, the final scene creates the final rhyme.

However, a sense of deliberateness or predetermination never arises. Far from creating the atmosphere of a thriller by dwelling on some fatal danger that constantly threatens Gija, Ioseliani adheres to another philosophy: life consists of a series of chance events, and man cannot work out the laws behind these events. Like a miniature god (and a film director is the god of the world s/he creates on the screen), Ioseliani, who is a mathematician by education, builds a chain of events that are not objectively connected with each other but that have the power to prolong the protagonist's life or shorten it, to make it more or less saturated, to give it a comic or tragic quality. Few of these events can be prevented, but the point of view from which they are witnessed can be changed. As folk wisdom has it, 'if you can't change world around you, change the world inside you'.

When *Lived Once a Song-Thrush* was released in 1971, the idealism of the 1960s, arguably the most optimistic and humane decade of the twentieth century, still pervaded both culture and everyday life. Soviet society had suffered and now took respite from the horrors of Stalinism, of world war and the ongoing Cold War. The socialist camp was even generating an ideology of consumption. People believed in technology and progress, in the merger of races and in the conquest of space. In terms of everyday life the Khrushchev era and the early years of Brezhnev's reign had given people a break from the threats of the Soviet regime: they were able to focus on their domestic affairs. Gija is largely seen in domestic settings: visiting friends, at home or roaming the streets. His appearance at his workplace (the orchestra) is rare and lasts at most a few minutes that are just sufficient for him to beat his drums, usually at the beginning and the end of each performance.

The gaze plays an important role, as Gija tries to peer through various optical devices throughout the film: through a theodolite when visiting a friend's house, whose little boy is preoccupied with new inventions; through the lens of a movie camera; and through a microscope exploring microbes in a lab where he has followed a woman friend. Gija is not simply curious and open to the world, but he is also a man of his time – the time of 'physicists and lyricists'. Space (both architectural and cosmic), micro-organisms, cinema, every possible optical device that allows man to see the world in a variety of perspectives, as well as montage of all proportions and scales were popular in the 1960s. Thus, Ioseliani moves skilfully between the close-up, the medium shot and the long shot.

But Ioseliani's film polemically engages with the 1960s generation, the so-called *shestidesiatniki*. Although the *shestidesiatniki* were fond of optical effects created by modern technology (telescope, microscope, lenses), they have nevertheless at some point lost the focus in their field of vision: they have lost sight of man, of his mysterious nature, and of the nature that surrounds him and of which he is a part. While pursuing distant mirages in cosmic space, they failed to notice that quite close-by, nature set up dangerous traps. The illusions of the *shestidesiatniki* vanished and little time went by until the world faced other terrible inventions: the 'peaceful atom' that led to the Chernobyl disaster; Brezhnev's dreadful campaign of the assimilation of the 'virgin soils' which led to an ecological crisis; the miracles of chemistry that poisoned the air and polluted the atmosphere; and the sexual revolution that speeded up the spread of AIDS. Gija Agladze has nothing to do with all of this, but indirectly his inherent qualities of far- and short-sightedness are a metaphor for the period captured in the film.

At the time of the film's release critics debated a lot about the trace that Gija Agladze left behind. In material terms he left practically nothing, except a hook, on which his watchmaker friend can hang up his cap. But Gija was no idler, who sullenly and worthlessly squandered time. Even when alone, he is far from idle: he thinks about something, he dreams, he listens attentively to the twittering of the birds, he examines the pattern of the wallpaper that he remembers from his childhood. The camera focuses on these trivial and seemingly insignificant activities, emphasising the fact that Gija is a character who is constantly in motion – if not physically, then mentally. In numerous episodes Gija's movements are accompanied by a tune: the melody that Gija tries to write down, manifesting his skill as composer. But each time it immediately drowns in the noise of the big city, and Gija never manages to fixate it on the sheet.

Ioseliani described the leitmotif of *Lived Once a Song-Thrush* in the first draft of the filmscript (the character of Gija is here called Vano):

Vano just had to cover his eyes, and before his mental eye there were – like at rehearsal, with the part in hands – the characters of a future opera; the orchestra played, the singers rehearesed a few scores, and just as everybody got ready to start, somebody grabbed Vano by the elbow and said: 'Hi', or 'What were you thinking about?', or 'Can you give me a light?' Vano shuddered a little and would not open his eyes for a while, trying to preserve the wonderful vision, but it was too late: the orchestra had stopped playing, like a record that stops when you pull the plug from the socket. The singers lowered their sheets and sighed regretfully: 'Oh-h-h-h' and the vision disappeared. Vano said: 'Hi', or 'How are you?' or gave a light to somebody, or continued an interrupted conversation. Then, for several steps, the movement did not work.

In the final version a few things have changed, but the essence of the initial plan has remained fully intact.

Gija has not composed his precious music: no trace of it is left. It is harboured in the memory and the souls of those people who knew him. He has accomplished many kind and selfless acts, which might not even deserve to be called 'acts' as they are so spontaneous and natural. He took his friend to a doctor; he pleased old Aunt Eliso with flowers and sang some songs on her birthday; he helped a stranger in the library solve a problem; he put up some surprise visitors. But everything else in his life has been useless and pointless: Gija made a necklace from paper clips; he twisted some wire to form a spiral; he dismantled an iron, but never repaired it; he sewed a suit, but did not finish it; he returned the library books without having read them. He had many girlfriends, but he did not start a family, though he has certainly made many of the girls happy.

Ultimately, the question of the value of life arises: the life of a man who did a lot of good and no harm to anyone, except to himself; who wasted his talent and did not fulfil his destiny. Maybe his talent, his destiny, were just that: to give people small pleasures? To refuse the pragmatism of the 1970s that had taken over from the romantic 1960s – was this essential not only for the Western yuppie but also for the Soviet careerist?

Ioseliani made an unforgettable film that allows the most daring and liberal interpretations. It contains a leitmotif that continually brings back the idea of the fluidity of time. The protagonist often calls on his friend in the watch repair shop: we see the wheel that sets the pendulum in motion, that counts seconds, minutes and hours. The dial features in the very end, not as a moralising reminder of time running out, but as an image in a precise context. The secret of time is incomprehensible, but man can enjoy its flow and flesh it out; he can accelerate or slow down time subjectively.

Lived Once a Song-Thrush is Ioseliani's first experience with the deformation of space. The construction of this pseudo-documentary parable became a reference point not only for the Georgian, but also for the Soviet 'new wave'. Rostislav Iuren'ev, a most conservative film critic, regarded *Lived Once a Song-Thrush* highly and supported it in the press. The film became a classic of Georgian and Soviet cinema, as opposed to Ioseliani's *Pastorali* (*Pastoral*, 1975), which was seen in a negative light both by the Goskino officials and by the press.

Ioseliani brought the melody begun in *Lived Once a Song-Thrush* to perfection in *Pastoral*, which proved to be a watershed for Ioseliani and his last film to be made in his native Georgia. His creative work had reached a point of no return, from whence he could not move forward in the USSR. *Lived Once a Song-Thrush* had been well received: Gija may be no Soviet hero, but he is a good man who tries to be kind and help people. *Pastoral*, on the other hand, was a tragedy, presenting a pessimistic view of Soviet village life. It proved difficult to move further in this direction for Ioseliani, especially working under the conditions of double censorship: any film had to pass the Georgian censorship board and the central Soviet one, the latter being the strictest of the two. Despite the support of Eduard Shevardnadze, then the Georgian Party leader, Ioseliani would ultimately leave his native land.

It is curious to trace the development of the history of *Lived Once a Song-Thrush* after its release into 'free flight'. Figures of attendance speak to some extent about the popularity of a film, but box office statistics are usually conducted only for a year after a film's release. Nobody counted the number of people who watched *Lived Once a Song-Thrush* during the three decades after its appearance, when, in fact, it had long and substantial runs at the Cinema of Repertory Film (Kinoteatr povtornogo fil'ma) in Moscow and the Moscow Museum of Cinema; it was also repeatedly shown on television. But it is not so much a matter of the number of spectators: more importantly, *Lived Once a Song-Thrush* became a cult film.

It is somewhat surprising to what extent the director resembles his own hero. Ioseliani built his life coherently and consistently, probably even rationally. Leaving his native Georgia, he found a country that matched his character and temperament well: on the one hand, France was the home of Cartesian attitudes; on the other, it burst with its liberal, Mediterranean spirit. Ioseliani became a genuine French director, even though the cityscape of Paris in his French films reminds the viewer of the Tbilisi of his childhood or of the Moscow of his student years. Essentially an anti-globalist, Ioseliani sees the world in its uniform and almost indiscernible details. At times it seems that it does not matter to him where he makes his films: he always carries his Georgia with him around the world, like Marc Chagall took the city of Vitebsk with him into French emigration.

Certainly, Ioseliani shares certain things with Gija Agladze: he too likes 'to have a drink and have a bite', to occasionally 'aimlessly' spend a day in the company of friends. But even if Ioseliani continues to make films about heroes who have broken free from their career and their bourgeois routines, he never forgets about his own career and his own creative discipline. In contrast to other émigré directors, he makes films with a great regularity. Each new film is organically integrated into the director's world and expands it. His world is one of collapsing traditions, of dying cultures and all-pervading platitudes. He may apply his approach to a Georgian or African village, to a small monastery in Tuscany, to a tiny town in Provence, to a Parisian arrondissement, or to Venice: everywhere the communication between generations fails, patriarchal and pastoral traditions die, the old class morals disappear, and onto the stage enter the *nouveau riches* (from Russian to Japanese, and including the French) and the lumpenproletariat.

Ioseliani is an aesthete and a moderate conservative; he realises that nature is passing away, he cherishes the African life untouched by civilisation (as evidenced by his later film *Et la lumière fut* (*And Then There was Light*), 1989); he approves of the patriarchal customs of a Mediterranean village (as seen in *La Chasse aux Papillons* (*Butterfly Hunt*), 1992); he senses aristocratic roots in peasants and local people in the documentary film *Un Petit Monastère en Toscane* (*A Small Monastery in Tuscany*), 1988). These people are close to him, he who is also one of a dying breed, genetically alien to the multimedia industry and belonging clearly to the thin layer of art cinema. Such a man was Gija Agladze, the first of Ioseliani's favourite heroes.

In this sense *Lived Once a Song-Thrush* is the most optimistic of Ioseliani's films, despite its sadness. Perhaps therefore the director is irritated in the company of old fans and admirers of the film, especially from among the Russian intelligentsia where it for a long time achieved cult status. It is not that Ioseliani rejects his 1970 film, but he does not identify with it either in the same way as he may have done thirty years ago. Another century has begun, and today's thrushes sing other songs.

Andrei Plakhov

Translated by Birgit Beumers

REFERENCE

Zorkaia, N., L. Kozlov and I. Shilova (1991) 'K interpretatsii fil'ma *Zhil pevchii drozd* togda iteper', *Kinovedcheskie zapiski*, 11, 129–48.

KALINA KRASNAIA RED GUELDERBUSH

VASILII SHUKSHIN, USSR, 1973

Vasilii Shukshin (1929–74) directed five films in a career that barely spanned ten years: *Zhivet takoi paren'* (*There Lives Such a Lad*, 1964), *Vash syn i brat* (*Your Son and Brother*, 1965), *Strannye liudi* (*Strange People*, 1969), *Pechki-lavochki* (*Happy-Go-Lucky*, 1972) and *Kalina krasnaia* (*Red Guelderbush*, 1973). He graduated from the State Institute of Cinematography (VGIK) in 1960, and his film acting career stretches from 1959 to 1975, in over twenty films: his last role was in Sergei Bondarchuk's *Oni srazhalis' za rodinu* (*They Fought for Their Motherland*, 1975). The five films he directed are all based on his own literary works, which he began publishing in the late 1950s.

There Lives Such a Lad focuses on the character of young Pasha Kolokol'nikov, a village driver who seems at first flippant and lacking any sense of social responsibility, but who finally reveals his maturity when he risks his life by driving a burning lorry out of danger. *Your Son and Brother* explicitly contrasts the slow, lyrical rhythms of country life with the jarring impersonality of the town. Stepka returns to his village after some time away, but we learn that he has escaped from prison, thereby adding extra years to his sentence. Nevertheless, he is content that he has at last spent some time in his native home, as he is led away by the police. *Strange People* is comprised of three stories about village life, all showing human life in harmony with the landscape and the seasons, with folk song and gentle guitar strings accompanying shots of rivers, fields and sunsets, and where the young and older genera-tions are reconciled. In *Happy Go Lucky* a couple (played by Shukshin and his wife Lidiia Fedoseeva) travel by train through Russia on their way to a holiday in the south, and their journey is an affirmation of the essential unity of the land and its people.

Red Guelderbush is by far the most successful and popular of his films and is, as John Givens comments, 'perhaps the most sensational Soviet movie of the 1970s'. It went on to win prizes at film festivals in Warsaw, Berlin and in Yugoslavia. It is also the most personal of his films, for not only did he direct it, but he also starred in the central role, and wrote the original novella on which the film is based. *Red Guelderbush* was published in the monthly journal

Nash sovremennik (*Our Contemporary*) in 1973. This was a journal which actively promoted the works of 'village prose' throughout the 1970s, and by the late 1980s had acquired a reputation for espousing a neo-nationalistic agenda bordering on aggressive chauvinism. Certainly, the subject-matter of Shukshin's story has clear affinities with the mainstream concerns of 'village prose', whose most prominent practitioners, besides Shukshin, were Vasilii Belov (b. 1932), Valentin Rasputin (b. 1937), Fedor Abramov (1920–83) and Viktor Astaf'ev (1924–2001). These writers were united by their defence of the natural environment and rural values, indulging in frequent opposition of 'town' and 'country' and the elevation of homely rural virtues into moral and spiritual absolutes.

Both Shukshin's film (the script was published in 1988) and novella not only provoked a powerful emotional response among the Soviet public, but both also had a significant sociological resonance. Geoffrey Hosking's characterisation of Shukshin's protagonists is particularly pertinent for the characters Shukshin himself portrays on screen, and especially in this film:

> They are the children of the Soviet Union's whirlwind years of social change, in which tens of millions of people were torn away from their backgrounds and homes. Shukshin's heroes are the uprooted, who have left one milieu and never quite settled in another: village lorry drivers and chauffeurs, construction workers, demobbed soldiers, taxi drivers, *shabashniki* (odd job men), all members of a raffish social stratum which is neither of the country nor of the town. Even where his characters are firmly rooted in the village, then the village itself is changing, as urban culture, habits and concepts take hold, imperfectly understood and reflected in distorted forms.

The story (published in 1973) begins in a northern prison camp ('more northern than the city of N, in places both beautiful and austere'), where prisoners perform a concert in the 'club'. Those who are about to be released the next day sing the 'Bom-bom' chorus of the evocative and sentimental song 'Vechernii zvon' ('Evening Bells'), in line with the camp's tradition. The next day, after five years of incarceration, the 40-year-old Egor Prokudin, a minor thief, is released into freedom (*volia*).

Egor waves down a passing car and hitches a ride into town, where he first goes to the house of his former girlfriend Nina. He is refused entry, and is told that Nina is no longer living there, being forced to move north 'because of the likes of you'. He then resumes his contact with the criminal gang led by Guboshlep ('Fat Lip'). Their 'den' is raided by the police, and although they escape, Egor realises that this life is not for him and he decides to make a clean break. While in prison he had corresponded with Liuba Baikalova (played by Lidiia Fedoseeva), and had told the prison officers that she had invited him to come to her village to start a new life and mend his ways. Liuba's village is called Iasnoe, and is situated not far from Egor's own home village. Egor travels to Iasnoe, where, after some initial awkwardness and suspicion, especially on the part of her parents, he is accepted into the Baikalov household, sleeping behind the partition in the same room as Liuba's parents. His unsubtle attempt at seduction that same night, as he tries to get into Liuba's bedroom, is firmly rebuffed. The next day he travels back into town in order to return to Guboshlep the money he had been lent on his release, and at the same time organise what he hopes would be a debauched party, with the help of restaurant waiter Sergei Mikhailovich. The party turns out to be a flop, as those recruited by Mikhailovich are mainly middle-aged, plain and lonely individuals. Egor gets in a taxi and returns to Iasnoe.

Egor is offered a job as driver to the director of the farm where Liuba works as a milk-maid, but soon turns it down so as not to become what he terms 'a toady' (*ugodnik*). He and Liuba travel to a nearby village to visit an old woman Kudelikha, the aunt, Egor initially maintains, of one of his co-inmates in the prison. Throughout the visit Egor wears dark glasses and refuses to talk to the old woman, insisting that Liuba ask all the questions. It turns out, however, that it is Egor's own mother, whom he has not seen for many years and whom he refuses to address even now, even though his emotions are tested. On their return to Iasnoe Liuba is visited by her former husband, who, even with two friends, is sent packing by a fearless Egor who is obviously used to violent confrontations. Then Egor is visited by one of Guboshlep's gang, who tries to bring him back into the fold, but he rejects the offer, again violently.

Egor next turns his hand to driving a tractor, thus returning to the soil and finding inner peace. It is as he ploughs a field that he sees Guboshlep and members of his gang waiting for him next to a copse of birch trees. As Egor prepares to approach them, Shukshin provides a lyrical backdrop in his film-script:

And nothing changed in the world. A clear day shone over the ploughed field, and
at the far edge of the field the copse stood in its green splendour, washed clean by
yesterday's rain ... There was a rich smell of earth, so rich and dense was the damp

earth that one's head went slightly giddy. The earth had gathered all the strength of spring, all its vital juices, and was preparing again to give birth to life. The thin blue strip of forest in the distance, the wispy white cloud over that strip, and the sun high above – everything there was life, and life pushed at the edges, did not worry about anything or fear anyone.

As life is returning to the natural world in springtime, Egor is shot by Guboshlep. Liuba and her truck-driver brother Petro find him clutching his wound, staining the birch trees with his blood, and he dies on the field which he had been working only moments before: 'And there he lay, a Russian peasant, in his native steppe, near his home … He lay with his cheek pressed to the earth, as though he was listening to something that only he could hear.' As the gang drive off, Petro overtakes them in his truck, crashes into their car at full speed and kills all inside.

The film follows these plot developments faithfully, but with one major departure. The motif of water is prominent in the film. When Egor is released from prison, the camera tracks his long walk across wooden boards leading him to dry land, and as he takes his car ride into town, there are several shots of thawing snow and spring floods, including one of a half-submerged church. The town where Guboshlep and his gang hide out is situated on a river bank. At the end, Petro's truck crashes into the car carrying Guboshlep and his gang and pushes it into the river, submerging it immediately. Only Petro emerges from the wreckage. Water here, as elsewhere in works of 'village prose' can be seen as symbolising the flow of time, and the passage of history that draws in Egor as its victim. Birch trees, an emotive symbol of Mother Russia, represent Egor's desire for purity and peace, but, at the end, show the futility of his search, and are stained by his blood.

Shukshin's own considerable presence as an actor dominates the film, his prominent cheekbones, set jaw and tightly-closed mouth reflecting the tribulations of Egor's life, and his clipped, occasionally abrupt speech suggesting a man desperately trying to overcome his past and build a new life. Shukshin's entire performance suggests pent-up energy and will, a man caged up for too long now wanting to express himself in a 'festival of the soul' (*prazdnik dushi*).

Shukshin adds certain cinematographic flourishes to emphasise his main themes. When Egor is in the village, there are several fulsome shots of a sun-blessed Russian countryside, an idyll unspoilt by the creep of urbanisation or industrial pollution. The town, by contrast, is associated with either criminality (Guboshlep's den shot in semi-darkness) and debauchery, or at least Egor's pitiful attempt at it. The town/village dichotomy is highlighted when Egor's face is filmed alternately in light and shade while he is in the town, foregrounding the pull of heaven and hell for his soul. The two times when Egor's emotions are at their most intense – his release from prison and the meeting in disguise with his mother – are accompanied by shots of white Russian churches, suggesting not so much emotional release as spiritual absolution.

Egor's isolation from the community is highlighted from the very start of the film, when he looks very uncomfortable having to sing in a chorus. When he is in the town, unsuccessfully trying to chat up girls half his age, he is accompanied by sentimental guitar and balalaika strings. His imminent death is suggested as he sits beneath a painting of the Four Horsemen of the Apocalypse, haplessly waiting for his debauch to begin. Another painting, Ivan Kramskoi's 'An Unknown Woman' ('Neizvestnaia') from 1883, features several times in the film: the first as part of Liuba's pendant, and then again at the 'debauch', where it suggests and foreshadows Egor's subconscious desire to return to Liuba and the village.

Egor's gradual integration into the community is aided by his work on the land, accompanied by patriotic balalaika chords at the end of the film. From the early scenes in the film Egor affirms his own oneness with the natural world, especially birch trees, that enduring and evocative symbol of Russian nationhood that Egor embraces and addresses as his 'girlfriends' and 'bride'. As Egor dies, at one with the earth, an angelic chorus rises on the soundtrack as the camera focuses on his lifeless face: he may be dead, but his soul has been saved. Guboshlep pronounces Egor's epitaph, when, after shooting him, he says: 'He was a peasant. There are many of them in Russia.' In the film Guboshlep uses the word *muzhik*, the colloquial word evoking work on the land and willingness to get one's hands dirty; in the novella, he uses the more neutral *krest'ianin*. more of a sociological designation, and used in contrast to the ideologically-charged 'proletariat'. In other words, Egor had both physically and symbolically come home.

Apart from the musical motifs and those taken from Russian art, there is in the film a clear nod to one of Russia's greatest and most popular twentieth-century poets, Sergei Esenin (1895–1925). In the novella, Egor partly recites Esenin's poem 'Mir tainstvennyi, mir moi drevnii' ('Mysterious world, my ancient world') as he takes his ride into town from prison. Esenin's poem, written in 1922, is a lament for the death of the village and the incursions made by the modern world, including roads and telegraphs. The 'stony arms of the roadway' have 'squeezed the village by the neck', a field 'groans' as it is 'suffocated by telegraph poles', and the slow death of the old world is likened to a wolf being caught by hunters in a trap. Both the poet and the wolf may make a 'last, fatal leap' and strike out for what they believe in, but only 'death' ultimately awaits them.

Both the poem and Egor's recital are missing in the film, although the theme of the poem has an obvious resonance with the concerns of the 'village writers' of the 1960s and 1970s. However, the film includes an important sequence towards the end that is not included in the original novella. As Egor moves towards Guboshlep and the copse of birch trees, a black-and-white memory from the camp is inserted into the diegesis. A lone singer, to guitar accompaniment, performs a melody based on Esenin's poem 'Pis'mo materi' ('A Letter to Mother', 1924). Esenin's poem is another lament, this time from a young peasant lad who has been away from the village for eight years, and although he tells his mother that he will return, begs her not to wait for him. The village remains for him a source of moral support and strength, even though he may never return to it.

Egor's fate is therefore framed by Russian music, art and literature. In particular, the Esenin connection is important. He bemoaned the coming of urban civilisation to the village, and described himself as 'the last poet of the village' in 1920 before killing himself five years later. Shukshin in his films affirms the spiritual and moral superiority of the village over the town, and in his alter ego Egor Prokudin demonstrates the lethal consequences of social change and the incursion of urban mores into a rural setting that has existed for centuries. In this, he obviously sees himself as spiritual and literary successor to Esenin, and he, too, suffered an early death (Shukshin was 45 when he died).

Both the film and the novella contain other significant symbolic motifs, not least in the use of names. The name Liuba derives from the Russian word for love, and her surname, Baikalova, is an obvious reference to Lake Baikal, the world's largest fresh water sea situated in Siberia, and a symbol of the expanse and purity of the Russian natural environment (at least, that is, before the environmental concerns highlighted by Valentin Rasputin and others in the 1980s). There is considerable play on Egor's name: he is nicknamed 'Gore' (woe, and he is unable to escape this fate), he calls himself Zhorzh and Zhorzhik, imitating half-baked urban assimilations of foreign names, and Zhora, the honest and straightforward man of the soil. The name 'Egor' is derived from Greek, meaning 'farmer' or 'man who tills the land', and 'prokuda' is a slang word for a mischievous or naughty individual (usually a child). Finally, the name of Liuba's village, Iasnoe, means 'bright' or 'clear', and it is here where everything does become clear to Egor, and how he should live the rest of his life.

The film in particular emphasises the Christian dimension of Egor's suffering. He is like the Biblical prodigal son, returning to his native parts after a profligate time away and seeking forgiveness, not from his father, but from the land itself. He seeks what he calls a 'festival of the soul'. When he first arrives in Iasnoe, he remarks, 'How much space, you have freedom here' ('Kak prostorno, u vas volia'). The word *volia* is used throughout the novella and the film to express the idea of 'freedom', not the usual Russian word *svoboda*, denoting political or civic freedom or the release from forced activity. Rather, *volia* suggests a greater sense of personal freedom together with the expanses of the Russian countryside, a transcendent release from earthly cares and a longing for some perfect spiritual harmony, as characters seek, as Geoffrey Hosking puts it, 'to break out of the here and now, the immediate and empirical, the always imperfect, into some other, imagined world, of freedom and perfection'.

Egor's spiritual journey is above all a search for a return home. He fails to establish any contact with his actual mother, but Liuba acts as his symbolic mother. In the novella we see Liuba through Egor's eyes, and he is struck by her physical beauty. In the film, however, there is little hint of sexual attraction. Liuba as played by Lidiia Fedoseeva is above all a strong, assuring presence who helps him integrate into the local community, comforts him when he cries, and holds him when he breathes his last. It is instructive to compare her with the other major female character in the film. The flighty, acid-tongued Lius'en is Guboshlep's moll, although when she greets Egor on his release from prison after five years the viewer senses her sexual desire. She dies in the car that Petro rams at the end, thus paying the penalty for her easy morals. Liuba as mother-figure corresponds to the poetics of other works of village prose, where gender relations are determined not by the rules of sexual attraction, but above all by the mother/son relationship. The mother is idealised and offers a home and a sanctuary for the returning 'prodigal' son, although in this case the 'son' must pay for his past misdemeanours.

Egor's personal tragedy also half-conceals the crisis of masculinity that the film addresses as a subtext. At the beginning of the film Egor leaves an all-male prison colony overseen by a fatherly commanding officer who shows great concern at Egor's future prospects and well-being. Egor is unable to establish any relationship with women: Nina has decamped to the north, his attempts at chatting up town girls are risible, as is his awkwardness in addressing a policewoman who visits Iasnoe. He even denies his own mother, and only in his dying moments does he achieve any closeness with Liuba.

Only with men does Egor feel at ease, whether this be with the prison commander, the driver who takes him into town, Liuba's brother, the waiter Sergei Mikhailovich and even Guboshlep. Male bonding is cemented when he and Petro drink a bottle of Remy Martin cognac in the bath-house, and it is Petro who will avenge Egor's death. On first seeing him Liuba's father refers to him as a 'Sten'ka Razin' figure, thus equating him with the seventeenth-century Cossack who led a peasant rebellion but was eventually executed. Certainly Egor is no stranger to violence, and does not back away even when the physical odds are against him. Egor can only exist in an all-male world, and according to 'masculine' values of aggressive self-assertion and violence. Once he becomes a man of the earth, promising also to start his own family, he is killed. Egor cannot be integrated within a social community, and he remains alone even at the very moment of his death.

It remains to be said that the film is much more successful as a work of art than the original novella, which at times reads awkwardly, and where the characters (apart from Egor) are not fully developed and remain essentially as types. With its multiple cultural and Christian references, the foregrounding of music and song, and the use of landscape, Shukshin's film is a multi-layered allegory of the fate of modern man in a rapidly changing social environment. It can be viewed and enjoyed simply as a tale of a reformed criminal unable to escape his past, and in this respect the film is also very significant: it was one of few films to portray the Soviet Union's criminal underworld, thereby showing how crime can grow and flourish even in conditions of 'advanced socialism', and was the first to show the inside of a prison camp, albeit briefly and in a very sanitised way. But it can also be seen as the tragedy of a lost soul, struggling to attain some meaning and substance to his life, but falling to the inescapable forces of modern history. After all, Guboshlep at the end himself speaks for a system of government that condemned a whole generation as expendable. The Stalinist metaphor of cutting down a forest for the sake of social progress rejoiced in the fact that wood chips would fly, and that individual lives for him, as for Guboshlep, had no meaning. Shukshin's film shows the tragic cost of social and historical 'progress'.

David Gillespie

REFERENCES

Esenin, S. (1961/62) *Sobranie sochinenii v piati tomakh*. Moscow: Gosudarstvennoe izdatel'stvo khudozhestvennoi literatury.

Givens, J. (1993) 'Siberia as *Volia*: Vasilii Shukshin's Search for Freedom', in G. Diment and Y. Slezkine (eds) *Between Heaven and Hell: The Myth of Siberia in Russian Culture*. New York, St. Martin's Press, 17–84.

____ (1999) 'Vasilii Shukshin and the 'Audience of Millions': *Kalina krasnaia* and the Power of Polular Cinema', *Russian Review*, 58, 268–85.

Hosking, G. (1980) *Beyond Socialist Realism: Soviet Fiction since 'Ivan Denisovich'*. London: Paul Elek and Granada.

Shukshin, V. (1973) 'Kalina krasnaia', *Nash sovremennik*, 4, 86–133.

____ (1988) *Kinopovesti*. Moscow: Iskusstvo.

SVOI SREDI CHUZHIKH, CHUZHOI SREDI SVOIKH

AT HOME AMONG STRANGERS, A STRANGER AT HOME

NIKITA MIKHALKOV, USSR, 1974

Svoi sredi chuzhikh, chuzhoi sredi svoikh (*At Home Among Strangers, A Stranger at Home*, 1974) is Nikita Mikhalkov's first feature-length film. A descendant of a family prominent in both pre-Revolutionary and Soviet Russia, Mikhalkov owes his artistic reputation as much to his heritage as to his creative versatility. The year Mikhalkov enrolled in the Shchukin Theatre School he played the role of Kol'ka in Georgii Daneliia's *Ia shagaiu po Moskve* (*I Walk Around Moscow*, 1963), which instantly made him famous. However, his budding acting career caused trouble for him: Shchukin school students were not allowed to appear in films, because the administration believed that cinema ruins an actor for the theatre. In his senior year Mikhalkov was expelled from the school, only to be accepted in the sophomore year in the directors' department at the State Institute of Cinematography (VGIK). His was the last class to study in the workshop of the legendary Soviet film director, Mikhail Romm.

After graduating in 1971, Mikhalkov joined the Mosfil'm studio and started working on his first full-length film, *At Home Among Strangers....* The script was based on the novella *Krasnoe zoloto* (*Red Gold*), co-authored by Eduard Volodarskii (b. 1941) and Nikita Mikhalkov. The project was delayed for over two years, while Mikhalkov served his draft in the Navy in the Far East. Only in 1973 did he resume work on the film.

The action of *At Home Among Strangers...* is set in the 1920s, just after the end of the Civil War in the south of Russia (the filming took place near Groznyi, the capital of the Chechen Republic). Having returned from the war, the protagonists (Sarychev, Kungurov, Shilov, Lipiagin and Zabelin) – five former Red Cavalry men – fulfil various government duties at a regional Party committee. Their positions are not specified, but the film suggests that they are members of the Cheka – the Soviet secret police. A telegram from Moscow orders them to transport gold, confiscated from class enemies and worth over 500,000 gold roubles, to help the starving. Egor Shilov (Iurii Bogatyrev (1947–1989)) is charged with accompanying the gold in a train, despite the objection that he cannot be trusted because his brother was killed while serving in the White Army. The night before the departure Shilov is found dead in his apartment, his face disfigured. While the gold is on its way to Moscow, a group of former White officers captures the gold, killing the guards (among them Lipiagin). But the train in which they are travelling is in turn robbed by a gang of marauders led by the former Cossack captain (*esaul*) Brylov.

Back at home, when Shilov shows up at the headquarters alive and unable to account for his absence, his former comrades suspect him of treason and arrest him. His fate seems to be sealed, for he was the only one who knew about the gold and no one believes his amnesia (the viewers, however, know that he had been kidnapped and drugged). Eager to find out the truth and restore his comrades' trust, Shilov escapes from his guards and joins Brylov's gang. There he meets a former White officer Lemke (Aleksandr Kaidanovskii (1946–1995)), one of those who killed the Red guards and who, in turn, is following the trail of the gold. Eventually, Shilov identifies the gang member, a Tartar Kadyrkul (Konstantin Raikin), who is hiding the gold and 're-educates' him, convincing him to give up the gold for the common good. Brylov, however, forestalls them both and escapes with the gold. Shilov, Kadyrkul and Lemke follow him. A chase and adventures in the mountains end with a shoot-out, during which Shilov kills Brylov. Meanwhile, at the Red headquarters, the atmosphere of paranoia thickens. With one friend dead and another one missing, each of the three remaining friends is under suspicion. Eventually, Sarychev (Anatolii Solonitsyn (1934–1982)) and Kungurov (Aleksandr Porokhovshchikov (b. 1939)) find and execute the real traitor, who turns out to be a member of an underground White organisation. At the film's end, Shilov, carrying both the wounded Lemke and the bag with gold, is reunited with his comrades -in-arms.

Mikhalkov's debut as a film director marked many of the features that would become staples of his work. The production team he gathered for the film remained his permanent crew: cameramen Pavel Lebeshev (1940–2003), composer Eduard Artem'ev (b. 1937), set designer Aleksandr Adabash'ian (b. 1945), as well as several actors. For many of them, the film launched successful cinematic careers.

Mikhalkov has always combined film directing with acting and scriptwriting. In *At Home Among Strangers*… Mikhalkov directed the film, co-wrote the script, and played the role of the Cossack captain Brylov, the leader of the gang that robs the train. With the exception of the Academy Award-winner *Utomlennye solntsem* (*Burnt by the Sun*, 1994), in which Mikhalkov plays the protagonist Colonel Kotov, he appears in his own films in secondary, but often significant, roles. For instance, his role of Tsar Alexander III in *Sibirskii tsiriul'nik* (*The Barber of Siberia*, 1998) gave ground to many speculations of Mikhalkov's 'royal ambitions'.

Unlike many other directors of the same generation, Mikhalkov has avoided contemporary themes. Whether it was a conscious decision to avoid ambiguities of the present, or an individual artistic choice, the director remained faithful to this trend. With a few exceptions, Mikhalkov's films, spanning three decades and a changing ideological climate, share a preference for stylised representation, a strong genre element and narratives set in the past.

On the film's release, Mikhalkov embodied the central critical debates of the time: that of 'a young filmmaker'. For cinema of the early 1970s, this term referred to a generation of directors who started making films after Nikita Khrushchev's era of relative cultural freedom (1950s–1960s). While thematic innovation and stylistic experimentation of the 'new wave' cinema continued into the 1970s, Brezhnev's rule, known as the Stagnation, witnessed the re-emergence of censorship. Aleksandr Askol'dov's *Komissar* (*The Commissar*) and Kira Muratova's *Korotkie vstrechi* (*Brief Encounters*) were completed in 1967 but not released until Mikhail Gorbachev's era of Perestroika. Films were censored because of their style as well as thematic concerns. Strong narrative, genre cinema and ideological correctness once again became the norm. Thus, starting a directing career in this context implied navigating turbulent waters between the conservatism of the Soviet film administration and public taste.

In terms of its genre, *At Home Among Strangers...* consciously and successfully uses the narrative and formal conventions of a western, or more specifically, the 'spaghetti western', one of the most popular genres of the late 1960s and early 1970s. Mikhalkov's film borrows freely from Sergio Leone's *The Good, the Bad, and the Ugly* (1966) and *Once Upon a Time in the West* (1968), as well as from George Roy Hill's *Butch Cassidy and the Sundance Kid* (1969). Among many visual quotes is the figure of Brylov (Mikhalkov), with his wide-brimmed, soft hat and a gait fashioned after Yul Brynner.

But as important as these references are, *At Home Among Strangers...* is above all a *Russian* western, or 'eastern', and as such belongs to a long tradition of Soviet adventure narratives set during the Civil War. In many respects this period of Russian history was analogous to the conquest of the Wild West, generating similar myths and narratives. The major cultural and aesthetic features of Civil War narratives were the romanticised representation of open spaces, a cult of male brotherhood, a direct confrontation of people and values and, event more importantly, an archetypal story of the forging of the community on the frontier, amid the violence of the war. In this genre, Mikhalkov's film has a long genealogy: from *Krasnye D'iavoliata* (*Little Red Imps*, 1923) and *Chapaev* (1934) to the *Neulovimye mstiteli* trilogy (*The Illusive Avengers*, 1966, 1968, 1971) and *Beloe solntse pustyni* (*White Sun of the*

Desert, 1969). In *At Home Among Strangers...* the native mythology of the Soviet adventure film came to the viewer in an attractive Western package: 'cool' characters, fast editing and plenty of stunts and special effects, including a spectacular plunge of a train-car from an unfinished bridge.

Mikhalkov's debut film was an unquestionable success with audiences (23.7 million viewers in 1974), but was met with only condescension and ambivalence by Soviet critics. Virtually everyone noted the dynamic style, energy and, above all, the young director's professionalism and his cinematic erudition. Ironically, the latter quality also provoked major objections. The film used 'too many expressive means' and was so well-crafted as to resemble a show-case of cinematic devices. To use film critic Iurii Khaniutin's apt description, 'Mikhalkov entered film directing like a dandy, entering an art exhibit ... attracting more attention to himself than to his heroes.' By the director's own admission, this formal saturation made the film, despite its claim to a popular genre, 'difficult' for viewers. The shared opinion was that the young director wanted to show everything he learned and could do, which was partly attributed to his youth, partly to a desire to separate himself from his brother, Andrei Konchalovskii, also a talented filmmaker. *At Home Among Strangers...* was, and largely still is, considered the 'first' – and the most 'Soviet' – film by a talented filmmaker who, as befits his youth, plays with historical material and the genre of the western. More than thirty years later, the film proves to be a more complex text, symptomatic of both Mikhalkov's approach to filmmaking and, more importantly, of the culture it was made in and reflective of.

At Home Among Strangers... may be Mikhalkov's 'most Soviet' film. Yet, compared to many Soviet productions, it has aged well, not least because of the director's approach both to the adventure genre and to the historical material. The representation of the conflicting 'sides' in this thriller (the 'Reds', the 'Whites' and the 'Greens', i.e. the anarchists) conforms to the conventional Soviet version of history. At the same time, both the Whites and the Greens primarily fulfil the narrative function of antagonists, vital for the construction of a strong hero during the unheroic times of the late Soviet empire.

The film was conceived and made in the early Brezhnev period, when the population was becoming disillusioned with a stagnating social and cultural life, and tired of the public rhetoric that had lost much of its Revolutionary heroic flavour. Literature and cinema turned to the past in search of lost mythology and strong heroes. In this respect, Mikhalkov's first film follows the pattern of such films as *Belorusskii vokzal* (*The Belorussia Station*, 1970) and

Ofitsery (*Officers*, 1971), juxtaposing the bleak present to the romanticised past, and *The White Sun of the Desert*, that uses the 'Wild East' setting to comment ironically on the Soviet discourse of liberation of the Central Asia's oppressed people.

More importantly (and more typically of Mikhalkov), already in his first film the director seamlessly intertwines the private with the public and ideology with genre conventions. The narrative transposes into the 1920s the realities of the Stalinist 1930s: vigilance, suspicion and the fear of treason. But the conflict between trust and betrayal, central to the film's narrative, is treated as a private dilemma rather than a matter of state security or the revolutionary cause. To suspect a friend or to be suspected of betrayal is an equally terrifying experience, for both jeopardise sacred male brotherhood. The trauma of Soviet history is thereby transformed into an individual drama. In this sense *At Home Among Strangers...* moves freely between a western, a political thriller and a *bona fide* male-oriented melodrama.

The narration alternates between the objective and the subjective modes of telling the story, and between the omniscient and restrictive modes. In the detective/adventure plot – the search for the stolen gold – the viewer's range of knowledge is superior to any of the characters' involved (with a possible exception of the yet unidentified traitor). Thus, the viewer knows of the White officers' conspiracy to steal gold before any of the chekists. After the shock of Shilov's alleged murder, the viewer learns that Shilov has been kidnapped and drugged and that he had nothing to do with the events on the train. The sequence on the train is shot using conventions of a western or action film. Like Lemke and Shilov, the viewer does not know who stole the grip-sack containing the gold; yet this missing piece of the puzzle does not prevent us from suspecting one of Brylov's gang members.

But, like the chekists, the viewer does not know the identity of the traitor, and it is this quest that is central to the film's atmosphere and that establishes juxtaposition of past and present. The first three sequences of the film establish a series of contrasts that are central to the film. In the opening black-and-white flashback sequence, a man on horseback is rushing through the steppe, shouting 'Freedom! Equality! Brotherhood! Peace!' The Civil War has ended. A rapid series of shots follow: a laughing girl, Zabelin dancing goofily around his sabre, a close-up of Shilov spread of the ground, Lipiagin playing with a white mouse. All of protagonists are young, bursting with joy of life. The five men and a girl push an old carriage down the hill, dancing a mad dance of youth and joy. Although the carriage as the symbol of the old regime ties the celebration to the political cause, the impulse of romantic idealism in the scene claims universality. Mikhalkov's mother, Natal'ia Konchalovskaia, wrote the lyrics for the theme song, a ballad about building a boat to pass on to the next generation.

The cut to the next scene is abrupt. The scene introduces Sarychev, Kungurov and Lipiagin, who are sitting in a big room at the Red Headquarters. It is narrative present, marked by the appearance of colour. But despite the colour and the size of the room, the sequence is dark and gloomy. In the light coming from the window one can see dust and smoke. For the first two minutes, as the credits roll through the frame, the protagonists are silent and motionless, as if paralysed. The oppressive interiority of this *mise-en-scène* contrasts sharply with the over-exposed, brightly-lit exterior shots of the flashback. Instead of the swaying music, the broken clock on the wall beats 67 times, until Kungurov throws a file at it. The scene is remarkably static, but the dialogue reveals a sinister atmosphere behind this silence. To Lipiagin's comment that 'the war is not over yet', Kungurov's answers: 'It is easy when you see the enemy's face; but when … It's hard, guys.' This unfinished thought signals the former friends' major anxiety: that at any moment any one of them might turn out to be the enemy.

Zabelin's introduction into the narrative in the next scene is a remarkable example of allowing the *mise-en-scène* to express the meaning of the sequence through plastic objects. First, we see a fly on the wall, its buzzing merging with the monotonous voice of an accountant. Through an opening in a pile of papers blocking the window we see an eye of a boy curiously observing the scene from the street. Finally the camera shows Zabelin, eating cherries, his eyes glassy and empty. Lazily he takes aim at the fly with a cherry stone and 'shoots'. The buzzing stops. All this is done in one long take. Next the camera cuts to the wastebasket which holds a sabre. Cut to Zabelin who yells: 'Here it is, my paper grave! They buried the Red cavalry warrior!' Grabbing his sabre Zabelin knocks down a wall of account books that blocks the door and rushes out of his office. As he runs up the stairs, in the background we see Shilov, his image unclear and out of focus.

This delayed introduction isolates Shilov from the other four friends early in the narrative. More importantly, the goal of juxtaposing Shilov to his comrades-in-arms in the plot is simplified by the fact that all of them had *already* betrayed their brotherhood and, deep inside, they know it. The former Red cavalry men got office jobs, and it is this betrayal, the betrayal of self and of the former ideals, that is the most disturbing. Mikhalkov, thus, creates a double world on-screen, the one that does not correspond to the Red vs. White opposition. The space of the Civil War, train robbery, male bonding and open confrontation is part of the desired, romanticised past. The real opponent of this space is the bureaucratic, de-heroicised present, that breeds suspicion and fragments cherished ideals.

Like the adventure plot – the disappearance of gold and its recovery – this second conflict has its own expressive system that serves, if not to counteract, at least to redefine the adventure plot. Indeed, Shilov's mission is private rather than public: he seeks not to recover the gold and help the starving, but to redeem himself in the eyes of his friends. The chekists are constructed not as a political organisation, but as a community of friends whose brotherhood is based on their Civil War experience but whose bureaucratic environment made them replace trust with vigilance. Finally, while the film pays tribute to the trope of 'us' versus 'them', it interprets it in a typically Brezhnev-era manner. As the title suggests, somewhere along the way into the bright future, goals, ideals and identity itself became confused. Like Shilov's image on the stairs, life went out of focus.

The major principle of space organisation in *At Home Among Strangers...* is its visual, plastic nature. The cameraman Pavel Lebeshev remarks that the visual stylistics of Mikhalkov and other young directors of that time were referred to in film circles as 'cheese': the film should have a distinct 'smell', that is, express their authors' emotional or conceptual attitude to the depicted world rather than just dispassionately present events to the viewer. In case of Mikhalkov, this strong sense of individual style, traceable throughout his films, is already present in *At Home Among Strangers....*

The film uses complex, conceptually sophisticated lighting schemes that read as a conscious alternative to the 'chronicle', 'documentary' principles of constructing the *mise-en-scène*, which dominated cinema during the Thaw and were still widespread in the early 1970s. Particularly striking is the long take in which, upon learning of Shilov's alleged murder and mutilation, Sarychev walks through endless dark corridors. The camera simultaneously identifies with Sarychev's grief and makes him part of the shadowy environment. Extremely long takes in the scenes at the Soviet headquarters are in stark contrast to the fast editing in action scenes, especially in the episode of the train robbery. Often Mikhalkov abandons cutting altogether, instead using long takes with the changing *mise-en-scène*. For example, after the meeting where Kungurov makes a decision to send Shilov with the gold, he walks out of the room and opens the door. But instead of stepping out into the light, he goes back to the same dark room, which now presents a different group and a different time. This transition, combined with the sound bridge – (often unclear) voices from the next scene that break into the previous one – convey a paranoid atmosphere. Lost in a maze of suspicions, the heroes follow the mad time that is metaphorically expressed by the endless chiming of the clock at the beginning of the film.

Even external spaces are imbued with an atmosphere of paranoia. For instance, the yard is crisscrossed by a formation of soldiers and clothes-lines, and it is in this yard that Kungurov begins to suspect and 'tests' his two remaining friends. The shots of the open steppe in the flashback thus function as the signs of the 'paradise lost'. Mikhalkov returns to the exploration of the 'Eurasian steppe' in many of his films, most prominently in *The Barber of Siberia* and *Urga* (1991). The intrusion of the man-made horror that gets out of control and 'disfigures' idyllic open spaces is also the major visual motif in *Burnt by the Sun*: a colossal blimp with Stalin's image rising over the field.

The car that takes Shilov to a Cheka office is another visual motif that creates the juxtaposition of the idealised past and the ominous present. First, it is opposed to the horse as the symbol of the friends' heroic cavalry past. Second, it is linked to the carriage – the symbol of the old regime and oppression – pushed down the hill in the opening sequence. In the closing sequence, we see the car slowly driving behind the cavalry detachment and followed by Zabelin on the horse, away from Shilov. When Zabelin finally sees Shilov, he gets down and runs to him, joined by Kungurov and Sarychev. The abandoned car stops, and its awkward position in the middle of the hill recalls the discarded carriage in the opening sequence. The medium shots of each of the men closing the distance to Shilov are intercut with black-and-white images of the opening sequence, with the five of the friends in one frame, fooling around in an open field. The visual and symbolic frames close. The happy re-unification of the friends seems inevitable. It is, however, positioned outside of the film's diegesis, and Shilov's last words in the film are addressed to his enemy Lemke: 'They didn't believe me. Didn't believe – *me.*'

But despite the fast action and formal complexity, *At Home Among Strangers...* is largely a verbal film and in this respect a product of its time. Ideas are enunciated clearly in the dialogue, even at the expense of slowing down the action as do, for instance, both of Shilov's 'class-minded' conversations with Kaium and with Lemke. In a striking contrast, the opening flashback is virtually silent. Here words ('Freedom! Equality! Brotherhood! Peace!') are no more than emotional markers, an externalisation of the characters' achieved dream that defies words. In the present, the characters acquire speech but lose the ability to connect. The recurring flashback thus functions also as linguistic breakdown. Every time the situation requires Kungurov to express his judgement of Shilov's alleged treason, all he is able to say is: 'And Egor ... Well, Egor', as a smile appears on his face and the music sways, carrying him back to the heroic times of the Civil War.

While individual episodes are organised rhythmically and tonally, the film in its entirety is fragmented by multiple flashbacks: the recurring shots from the opening flashback inter-cut with the main narrative and Shilov's confused memories of the circumstances of his kidnapping. Even Brylov has his own strange vision: a group of aristocratic-looking young men and women on a picnic. The narrative status of his fantasies is unclear (it might be a memory or an externalised desire for a better present). These multiple flashbacks and their ambiguous narrative status do more than fragment the narrative: they effectively displace Soviet utopia. The communist temporality of a bright future does not have a place in the film. At best, the opening sequence projects the dream into the future but it immediately proves to be a flashback. The Revolutionary dream is thus future-in-the-past, to which characters have access only through their memory. In Thaw films communist paradise is problematised, but the possibility of getting there is not questioned, whereas in Mikhalkov's film the world of the communist dream and the narrative world are separated and irreversibly fragmented. The major carrier of hope for the communist ideal in cinema during the Thaw is a child – pure and untainted by Stalinist crimes. By the 1970s, the idea of childhood as the last retreat had become obsolete. In films of the Stagnation period (for example, those of Dinara Asanova) the world of children is treated as a microcosm of adult society, infected with prob-lems and living an aftermath of utopia. On the other hand, infantile adults (typically men) are often represented as an inferior product of Soviet ideology in many 'slice-of-life' films of the 1970s.

Mikhalkov seems unfashionably idealistic in his views of men, and many of his films are populated by dreamers. It is no surprise that his *Neokonchennaia p'esa dlia mekhanicheskogo pianino* (*An Unfinished Piece for a Mechanical Piano,* 1977) offers a superb adaptation of the notoriously elusive Chekhovian atmosphere. As some critics claim, in the final analysis all Mikhalkov's films are about the loss of a 'desired world' – the ideal environment suggested by the narrative and explored through its contrast with the 'real' world. The form and specific historical incarnations of such ideal loci differ. In *Oblomov* (1979), these are the protagonist's memories. Oblomov's flashbacks of his happy, idyllic childhood do not symbolise his disa-bling passivity, as they do in Ivan Goncharov's 1859 novel. They are instead represented as organic to Oblomov's gentle, child-like nature and his daydreaming is marked as a positive alternative to the pragmatic and soulless present. Kotov's dacha in *Burnt by the Sun* fulfils the same function: the idealised family abode disrupted by the intrusion of political reality. In *Raba Liubvi* (*Slave of Love*, 1976) Mikhalkov reconstructs for the viewer the forgotten world of the Russian silent melodrama, with its theatricality, emotional excess and the over-stylised *mise-en-scène*. This world is swept by the Revolution and denounced as reactionary escapism. But like the sweeping emotion of Revolutionary brotherhood in *At Home Among Strangers...* the nostalgic power of those silent images is congenial to Mikhalkov's own politics and aesthetics.

Mikhalkov's films have been in the cultural spotlight for the last thirty years. But so have been his 'family politics', especially the spectacular career of Mikhalkov's father Sergei who mainly wrote children's poetry, but who at the height of Stalinism in 1944 authored lyrics for the Soviet national anthem. In this sense, in *At Home Among Strangers...* Mikhalkov enters into a dialogue with his father's youth. Alternatively accused of conformism and arrogance, Mikhalkov – now the President of the Russian Filmmaker's Union and the owner of the TriTe film studio – indeed seems to prosper under any regime. Perhaps Mikhalkov's key to success is, paradoxically, his unabashed traditionalism, expressed with a sure hand of a film master and a connoisseur of Hollywood style.

Elena Prokhorova

REFERENCE

Khaniutin, I. (1979) 'Rezhissura – eto professiia', in O. Zlotnik (ed.) *Kinematograf molodykh. Sbornik*. Moscow: Iskusstvo, 124–43.

SKAZKA SKAZOK TALE OF TALES **17**

IURII NORSHTEIN, USSR, 1979

Skazka skazok (*Tale of Tales*, 1979) is a animated film of substantial duration (almost 28 minutes), great complexity and even greater renown. Potential for the later legendary status of the film began to manifest itself within twelve months of its debut, when it garnered prizes at film festivals in Germany (Oberhausen), France (Lille) and Canada (Ottawa). The years passed and filmmaker Iurii Norshtein's importance as a seminal stylist became increasingly evident: *Tale of Tales* was subsequently elevated at the Los Angeles Olympics in 1984 to 'The Greatest Animated Film of All Time'. An international committee of judges held the film in almost equal regard two decades later: in the spring of 2003, another generation and another commission (this time in Japan) declared it the 'Second Greatest Animated Film'. It was pipped at the post only by an earlier Norshtein animated film *Ezhik v tumane* (*Hedgehog in the Fog*, 1975).

By no stretch of the imagination may the storyline of this work be called linear, and English-language discussions of the film shy away from attempts to clarify thematic conflicts often termed (or dismissed as) 'stream of consciousness'. Nonetheless Paul Wells in his recent monograph *Understanding Animation* makes a valiant attempt at bringing order to bear:

Tale of Tales establishes its chief motifs early in the film – an apple glistening with raindrops; a baby suckling a mother's breast observed by a wolf cub; an old house bathed in autumn light; a group of figures on a summer picnic, established as a poet, a fisherman, a mother and child, and a child skipping with a Picasso-like minotaur. The sense of tranquillity and reassurance offered by these half-remote, half-familiar images emerges out of the alchemic relation between them – the association between the elemental world and natural development; the sense of sustenance and nurture; the notion of mutual support and *shared* time, past fusing with present, recalling ancient processes. The sense of *timelessness* possesses a mystery in itself; these small scenarios, it seems, are eternal, harmonious, somehow utopian in their insistent relevance. A number of things occur, however, which disrupt this sense of harmony. A wind of change blows beneath a tablecloth, blowing it away, as a train passes. Norshtein's pastoral peasant idyll is disrupted by the onset of war, and the strange by-products of industrial progress. The old house is suddenly surrounded by cars, a wolf cub viewing himself in the mirror of a hubcap, uncertain of his own identity. The house is set ablaze, birds fly away, subject to the whim of political events, somehow surviving in a greater, more sacred, less obviously extant, chain of being.

The film arranges these elements in a 'conscious', noticeable fashion. It begins and ends with footage of the wet apple; the cub watches a baby being breast-fed, and this motif also is positioned within both opening and closing sequences. Such themes of plenitude and reproduction find reflection in several episodes involving a small boy who shares apples with birds during a heavy winter snowfall. His generosity and cordial relationship with the natural world are of no interest to his drunken father and vapid mother. The boy's charity, just as the breast-feeding, fills the cub with a sense of quiet awe. When at one point towards the end of this complex montage, the young wolf steals a sheet of paper from a sleeping, somewhat indecisive poet and flees through heavy traffic to the forest, the stationary is suddenly metamorphosed into a baby in swaddling-clothes, as if the relationship between artistic and natural creation is an intimate one, and it takes a moment of risk for either to be set in motion.

While these modern, mythical, magical and tragic plots manufacture their system of counterpoint, the music of Bach and Mozart also helps to unite them with a celebrated wartime tango, 'Utomlennoe solntse' ('The Exhausted Sun'), used recently throughout Nikita Mikhalkov's Academy Award-winning film *Utomlennye solntsem* (*Burnt by the Sun*, 1994). It is the music to which girlfriends and wives dance their final dance with lovers or family members; it is also the melody that the cub hums in the present as he bakes potatoes over an impromptu bonfire, hiding from the clamour of a local car park. 'The Exhausted Sun' concludes the film, as ghostly soldiers of the early 1940s leave once more for (yet another) battle and a train again traverses the screen, indicative of woefully repetitive processes.

One of the most straightforward explanations of these motifs, or at least of their provenance, has come from a recent interview with the screenwriter and well-known writer Liudmila Petrushevskaia (b. 1938), where she recalls being approached in March 1976 to work with Norshtein (b. 1941) on a new film about his wartime childhood. Petrushevskaia was eight months pregnant and not keen to shoulder the responsibility of a fresh, probably lengthy, project. Norshtein suggested visiting Petrushevskaia's apartment to lessen the workload and thus she consented – with the proviso that after the birth he also take the baby for walks in its pram. Consequently, much of the screenplay was created during long strolls, and the initial childhood motifs of early drafts became those of a newborn wrapped in the draft papers of a writer. 'I was full of milk and could think only about children. That's why a baby in the screenplay had to be born swaddled in one of those pages', said Petrushevskaia.

Extra inspiration came when Norshtein sent Petrushevskaia a book of translated poetry that included lines by Nâzim Hikmet (1901–1963) and then showed her albums with various drawings by Picasso. Petrushevskaia, said the artist, should somehow combine all this with a subject of homecoming troops after World War Two. The Hikmet poem would ultimately sit at the centre of the film, a tiny text also entitled 'Tale of Tales':

> We stand above the water: the sun, a cat, plane tree, me and our fate. Cool water,
> a lofty plane tree, the sun is shining and the cat dozes. I compose a poem. Thank
> Heavens that we are alive! The glare of the water shines in our face; it shines [even] at
> the sun itself, upon the cat, the plane tree, on me and our fate.

And accordingly Petrushevskaia suggested that perhaps the central human protagonist should be a poet.

The wolf comes from a famous Russian lullaby 'Baiu-baiushki-baiu', warning of 'a little grey wolf cub who'll come and grab your sides. He'll drag you off into the forest, under a brittle willow bush.' A title for the first version of the screenplay was a direct quote from this song: 'Pridet seren'kii volchok' ('The Grey Wolf Cub Will Come'). The film studio executives declared it too scary, so the Hikmet title was used instead. By the time Norshtein was suggesting lullabies, though, Petrushevskaia already had difficulty mustering similarly sentimental memories. She was seven years old in 1945, too poor to have shoes, and sometimes ate food left in the street. Because she was three years older than Norshtein, Petrushevskaia related all of *her* memories to him; the artist had been, she felt, too young to recollect anything of import. One common and concrete reminiscence they did share was the amateur music used by families and other groups in both times of grief and celebration.

Once such titular, thematic and compositional decisions had been made, life and fantasy interwove: the itinerant little wolf became in Petrushevskaia's drafts:

an eternal soul, who could visit the Golden Age [of Russian poets in the nineteenth century], a quiet seaside abode where a happy fisherman lives with his family. In their pram a chubby child lies quietly. His sister – in a ball gown and hat – skips rope with one of Picasso's minotaurs. This is where Norshtein and his wife Francesca live beneath a plane tree. The wife does laundry, and he catches fish. They always eat outdoors with their cat, Murka. They have guests – a balding poet with a lyre and a young, chance visitor who is a young man, free from material things: a pensive passer-by.

This sketch entered the film, prior to the sequence of young wartime girls bidding farewell to their loved ones. Idylls and tragic transience were slowly being juxtaposed.

The fisherman and poet also appear to have roots in the opening lines to Pushkin's narrative poem, *Ruslan i Liudmila* (1820), telling of a leisurely 'learned cat' that wanders around a green oak tree on a distant shore, reciting tales as it does so (Norshtein's cat is lazy, yet prompts the poet to start scribing his own tales). Pushkin speaks of other magical animals, including a wolf that serves a young princess. Despite these apparent textual sources, people who grew up with Norshtein have more straightforward explanations for the genesis of the plot, seeing erstwhile friends and relatives they 'recognise' on screen from the post-war Moscow suburb of Mar'ina Roshcha. The critic Larisa Maliukova has claimed that the figure of the fisherman, for example, is actually based upon sketches of Norshtein's grandfather or that the waltzing soldiers, wives and girlfriends have real-life counterparts in various Moscow families of 1945.

All these competing ideas make the film problematic; the film studio was also worried about the story's pronounced intricacy and almost forced its makers to add explanatory on-screen text; they also wanted to chop ten minutes from the running time. Nonetheless, after a five-month silence and begrudging surrender by the studio it went on to secure a Soviet state prize and become so popular that cinemas learned not to place it anywhere in an evening's line-up other than at the end – or the public would simply vacate the premises, having no time or patience for other, duller animated films.

People were charmed by what Norshtein and Petrushevskaia called in 2000, as noted by Aleksandra Vasil'kova, a 'special theme, an accordion-theme that moves apart and widens. It leads at the film's dénouement to a single, simple sound: "We're alive." That's because our childhood took place at the end of the war, and we should always remember that happiness is every peaceful day. Every single day.' The ability of the narrative to expand within (or from) what Norshtein called in the same year the 'ether field of a film still' and then spin with baroque flourish towards other significances came, said the director, from active effort expended in striving towards optimism contrary to various obstacles, be they the horrors of war or – in later years – the paradoxically negative excess of artistic 'freedom' offered by computers, something Norshtein has always shunned, preferring to work instead with his hands, since 'liberty without limits is nothing more than a muddle', as he argued ion 2001. Accordingly he worked hard with the same flat, jointed and cut-out figures Soviet animation endorsed in the early 1920s.

Casting a judicious glance over the craftwork of those first years, Russian historians even in Norshtein's youth had usually concluded that the production of true Soviet animation had indeed begun in 1922, when the first Experimental Animation Workshop was formed, part of what would later became the State Institute of Cinematography (VGIK). Artwork of the time tended to revolve around political sketches, some based upon Vladimir Maiakovskii's drawings done for agit-posters or 'satirical windows' of the Russian Telegraph Agency (ROSTA). This early tradition of painting fat, plump-lipped capitalists and waddling priests would reappear at times in Soviet animation, for example in 1968's *25oe: Pervyi den'* (*October 25: The First Day*) by Norshtein himself, dramatising the outbreak of the Revolution in Petrograd to the music of Dmitrii Shostakovich. Businessmen and clerics, drawn in a grotesquely comic style, come under attack from anonymous, red figures of revolt that move in an angular fashion suggestive of Kazimir Malevich's paintings, especially his *Red Cavalry* from 1918.

Part of this interest in minimalist 'thrusts' beyond received limits (that is, those of *byt*, of earthly existence or the similarly restraining confines of verbose, linear narrative) comes from Norshtein's own very Soviet beginnings: thirteen square meters in a communal apartment (*kommunalka*) for four family members. The artist's father was a woodworker, whose expertise with lathes was accompanied by an ability to fix anything at home whilst whistling Wagner melodies he knew by heart. Norshtein's mother was a teacher in pre-school and the faint, barely discernible luminosity of *Tale of Tales* comes from that poorly-lit *kommunalka* after school was over, when the boy would 'draw all the time'.

This emphasis on endless work, upon process over goals, makes it hard to define a single key scene. Instead it may be appropriate to speak of a key technique. The young Norshtein's doodles hid him from Soviet reality; they offered something potentially better. Likewise, the shifting states or potentials of his adult film are stressed whenever the clarity of focused, central characters is lessened; misty cells are placed both in front of and behind these cut-out heroes. The additional splicing of these hinged figures with magazine pictures (for example of cars) or quickly flickering light in real time (from a fire or passing traffic) also stops us from seeing the cub and others as too photographic. This is underlined further by the fact that wind and light move fastest of all in the film, and tend to make any bodies in focus appear subject to other, swifter or more natural processes. Dolly shots keep those heroes or objects of attention (like a falling leaf) in the centre of the frame, stressing their subjection to faster forces as we pan (awkwardly) with the increasing speed of the wind. Everything is subject to nature's rapid alterations.

The search for vaguely discernable, natural alternatives to a cruel, cramped materialism under the Soviets would endure, playing an important role even in the series of lectures that Norshtein gave in Tokyo during 1994 and were published in *Iskusstvo kino*: 'Animation is made from the secrets of consciousness and feeling that are placed on film. No intervening matter or substance [*materiia*] will stop an image reflecting our feelings ... Feelings are reflected *by* natural matter, turning that matter into fantasy ... That's the fundamental condition of animation ... Children's feelings are stronger than adult ones.' Norshtein believes that adults, with their other, supposedly more important concerns in life, often avoid or ignore emotional experience. Yet a child is sometimes unable, as the artist says, to deal with the frightening fact that 'feelings are more powerful than thought' because he or she lacks as yet the logical ability to comprehend emotion's illogicality.

Ironically, by making complex, involved films that 'steal' lots of tiny, simple details from matter and ostensible reality, Norshtein believes that one can – with effort – reach the anatomic detail of Da Vinci's drawings, making manifest 'the flows of life' or its natural processes that *defy* logic, description or quotidian awareness. Animated films, if the selection of details is successful, reach and start to comprehend a place where Norshtein sometimes glimpses symmetries between life and death, for as he says himself, 'according to Freud, a striving for one's childhood is a striving towards death'.

The admirable degree of effort in that striving across the years becomes clear when we recall that the decade which spawned *Tale of Tales* at its conclusion was marked by the so-called Stagnation of Leonid Brezhnev's period in office. Here we find the background to (and theoretical genesis of) *Tale of Tales*. Over this decade the romantic spirit we now associate with the 1960s was brought to a halt, as 'stability' replaced Khrushchev's unpredictable experiments in agriculture, education and several bureaucratic domains. Keen not to lose their jobs, Brezhnev's subordinates instituted perhaps the most uninteresting period in Soviet history. Animation, however, was painting a much livelier picture. By 1970 the socialist art form of the animated film was still confident enough in the ongoing promise of its evolution to use titles such as *The Art of Animation Yesterday, Today and Tomorrow* or *Animation: Yesterday, Today, Always*. The pages of an animator's sketchbook promised much more than the grim routine of a politician's diary.

Looking back at its origins in the 1920s, which gave Norshtein his cut-out figures, animation now declared its enterprise had never been *totally* dedicated to the Revolution or to purging the horrors of capitalism; it was actually – in the words of Norshtein himself, as cited by Semen Ginzburg – 'resolving the problems of cinematographic rhythm … in order to penetrate the genuine form of objects, which *may not* correspond to our visual perceptions of them'. Real things, said he and other artists, are often caught better in the self-negating rhythms of alteration than in the stasis of portraiture.

In terms of how static images and stagnant politics could be improved upon with a-politicism, theoretical activity among animators under Brezhnev encouraged a criss-crossing of multiple styles, albeit within a few ground rules. These included a refusal to simply 'superimpose an image upon its real-world prototype [that is, photographic naturalism or rotoscope work, as in the early 1950s … There should] instead be a gradual *reduction* of that image, in order to increase the huge power of emotional and aesthetic persuasion', as Norshtein put it, cited by Anatolii Volkov. The removal of superfluous details would conjure ascetic, metaphorical forms made temporal by associative processes that were, according to the artist, 'not open to decoding or translation into language'. Words were therefore being replaced by images, sounds and noises. Just as detailed, wordy screenplays were negated over this decade by (or reduced to) overlapping sounds, so histories of the 1970s also began to pay more attention to ways in which animated film backdrops over time had now faded to neutral tones, while soundtracks had frequently become nothing more than indicators of perspective (for example with distant echoes), all in order to circumvent both naturalistic excess and tedious realism.

Though we often associate the word 'animation' with animated drawings, these new celebrations of mobile minimalism were lauded by wooden, clay, wire and plasticine puppets more than anybody else. Puppetry by the early 1970s, even, was more than happy to claim it had always shown 'that which a living person cannot' (or – strictly speaking – that which he cannot say) by displaying less and thus 'doing' more. Perhaps one of the best examples in this regard is Norshtein's wordless cartoon *Secha pri Kerzhentse* (*Battle of Kerzhenets*, 1971), which used 2-D cut-out and hinged figures styled as iconography of the fourteenth to sixteenth centuries in order to vivify a great Christian victory with golden hues across the glaze of fractured, antique frescoes. The film, with no recourse to words, shows the yellow of golden icons becoming the yellow of a victorious harvest.

A new respect for puppetry and hinged characters amid art historians gave long-term confidence to its practitioners. Doll-makers under Brezhnev claimed audaciously that their figurines embodied and gave voice to a greater expressiveness than anybody's drawn heroes. Nonetheless they were happy to share one common goal with their colleagues working in pen and ink: as Anatolii Karanovich put it, 'the translation of linguistic metaphors into visual images'. Nobody did this more famously than Iurii Norshtein, and by the end of the 1970s, his humble medieval figures had metamorphosed into a profoundly important demonstration of everything our artists held dear.

Norshtein, in a discussion of *Tale of Tales*, tried to define the nature of that cherished wordlessness: 'There wasn't a single word of mine in it. I had instead a substantial role in the action's development and the invention of [interwoven] plots *within* the film.' He remained necessarily passive to their subsequent development, as an accepting 'romantic'. He continued to look beyond quotidian things to expand their parameters. As he stated in *Kommersant Daily*:

[In a film like *Tale of Tales*] there mustn't be a quotidian logic, but rather something interior, something musical ... like the feelings of childhood. Then everything around you will become a part of your everyday existence and no longer appear unusual. This '*everything*' will become 'everyday' and simple ... [The problem is that] we've destroyed our sense of hearing ... Before the freedom of speech you must have the freedom of hearing ... Not every person manages to sense the beautiful freedom or joy that comes from an ability to think ... He can't manage it ... he'll much sooner feel his kinship with the crowd. And he *wants* to feel it. I see that kinship from two points of view. You can communicate with the world, nature and the cosmos. That's one form of communication or complicity. The second form is that type of kinship with the crowd that comes about much more easily.

This philosophy, developed throughout the 1970s, had once battled socialist 'naturalism' and would did so again at the end of the twentieth century – as computer graphics suddenly appeared, themselves bowing deep and long before photographic realism. Computer art was acting in the interests of capital, which led Norshtein to suggest that his version of Gogol's *The Overcoat* should be given an epigraph from the Sermon on the Mount about cupidity and emotional 'kinship' on Earth: 'Lay not up for yourselves treasures upon earth, where moth and rust doth corrupt, and where thieves break through and steal ... For where your treasure is, there will your heart be also.' He spoke out loudly against a materialistic worldview. He went – more than once – as far as saying that animated films *needed* bad, poorly-funded equipment to encourage the emotional effort of successful, treasured animation. Slick, expensive and modern machines make nothing human because they remove the human. Many artists claimed that poor wages were damaging cartoons; Norshtein stubbornly maintained the opposite. He kept championing the philosophical benefits of happily 'passive' metamorphoses that lie beyond stubborn matter or grim materialism; he held with admirable tenacity to the philosophy of 'The Greatest Animated Film of All Time'.

David MacFadyen

REFERENCES

Norshtein, Iu. (1993) 'Shag sdelan iz Kieva v Odessu', *Kommersant-Daily*, 23 September.

_____ (1999) 'Sneg na trave', *Iskusstvo kino*, 9, 102–10.

_____ (2000) 'A Happy Coincidence', *Sputnik*, 23 July.

_____ (2001) 'Iurii Norshtein, genii iskusstva mul'tipliklatsii', *Mir v nashikh rukakh*, 14 February.

Ginzburg, S. (1971) 'Iskusstvo mul'tiplikatsii vchera, segodnia i zavtra', *Voprosy kino-iskusstva*, 13, 142–93.

Karanovich, A. (1971) *Moi druz'ia kukly*. Moscow: Iskusstvo.

Maliukova, L. (2001) 'Vyrashchennyi Mar'inoi roshchei', *Novaia gazeta*, 1 October.

Petrushevskaia, L. (2002) 'Pis'ma Norshteinu i chitateliu', *Domovoi*, January.

Vasil'kova, A. (2000) 'Siuzhet-garmoshka', *Kul'tura*, 13, 6–12 April.

Volkov, A. (1971) *Problemy razvitiia sovremennoi iskusstva mul'tiplikatsii*. Moscow: VGIK.

Wells, P. (1999) *Understanding Animation*. London, Routledge.

Venzher, N. (1979) *Mul'tfil'm vchera, segodnia, vsegda*. Moscow: Soiuzminformkino.

МОСКВА СЛЕЗАМ НЕ ВЕРИТ
/В ДВУХ СЕРИЯХ/

MOSKVA SLEZAM NE VERIT MOSCOW DOESN'T BELIEVE IN TEARS

VLADIMIR MEN'SHOV, USSR, 1979

The actor-director Vladimir Men'shov (b. 1939) has not been prolific, having directed half a dozen films over a quarter of a century, and his most famous films have all been romantic comedies: *Moskva slezam ne verit* (*Moscow Doesn't Believe in Tears*, 1979), *Liubov' i golubi* (*Love and Doves*, 1985), *Shirly-myrli* (*It's All So Absurd*, 1995) and, although not really a comedy as such, *Zavist' bogov* (*Envy of the Gods*, 2000). All but *Love and Doves* have starred Men'shov's wife Vera Alentova (b. 1942), who plays the doughty heroine of *Moscow Doesn't Believe in Tears*, and this remains her most famous role. Among Men'shov's films as an actor are Karen Shakhnazarov's teenage angst drama *Kur'er* (*The Courier*, 1986), as well as his surreal fantasy *Gorod zero* (*Zero City*, 1988) and Timur Bekmambetov's vampire blockbuster *Nochnoi dozor* (*Night Watch*, 2004).

Moscow Doesn't Believe in Tears was only Men'shov's second film as director, his first being *Rozygrysh* (*The Practical Joke*, 1976). It proved to be incredibly popular across the Soviet Union and earned over a million US dollars in foreign sales. It was the second most popular film in the USSR in 1980, and went on to win prizes in Portugal and Brussels, as well as the 1980 Academy Award for Best Foreign Film.

The film is divided almost equally into two parts. It begins in 1958, and concentrates on the lives and loves in Moscow of three girls recently arrived from the provinces. Ekaterina (Katia, played by Alentova) fails her entrance exams to study medicine and gets a job in a factory in order to make ends meet and to enable her to re-apply the next year. Liudmila (Liuda, played by the popular comic actress Irina Murav'eva (b. 1949)) works in a bakery, and, together with country girl Antonina (Tonia, played by Raisa Riazanova (b. 1944)), all share a room in a women's dormitory. The start of the film could therefore be seen as a parodic reference to Chekhov's play *Three Sisters* (1901), where the sisters Ol'ga, Masha and Irina live in the country and dream of going to Moscow but never manage to do so. Here the three provincials (although not blood-related) have been in Moscow for two years and are trying to make their fortune. For Liuda and Tonia, the most important thing in life is to find a husband, whereas Katia is more career-oriented.

Men'shov skilfully captures the atmosphere of Moscow in the late 1950s, the period of the post-Stalin Thaw. The cultural atmosphere is evoked through fleeting appearances by the actors Georgii Iumatov, Tat'iana Koniukhova and Innokentii Smoktunovskii, the voice of the singer Klavdiia Shul'zhenko (1906–1984) in the background as the friends relax at Tonia's dacha, and the popular comic duo Aleksandr Shurov and Nikolai Rykunin, performing their satirical *chastushki* on television. Temporal and cultural symmetry is achieved when the friends meet again at the dacha twenty years later and the same Shul'zhenko song is heard. The relative liberalisation of the post-Stalin Thaw is characterised by the mixture of Russian and foreign music played on radio sets as Katia walks past rows of houses at the very start of the film, Third World students in Moscow, and verses recited by the young poet Andrei Voznesenskii (b. 1933). French films are shown in cinemas, and the poetry of young firebrands Evgenii Evtushenko (b. 1933) and Robert Rozhdestvenskii (1932–1994) is eagerly discussed round a dinner table.

Other signifiers of the period raise a coy smile, such as the voluntary police assistants (*druzhinniki*) discouraging couples from embracing in public. Nevertheless, a key theme is the desire for material betterment among ordinary people, and how this desire is satisfied over two decades of positively-observed social progress. In 1958 Tonia's fiancé Nikolai (Kolia) already has a car, and drives the three girls to his country dacha, where Tonia is first introduced to his parents. Things to aspire and save up for, they say, include a television and a fridge: life really is becoming better and more cheerful.

One of Katia's distant relations is Professor Tikhomirov, who, with his wife and dog, lives in a spacious and prestigious apartment in central Moscow. The camera lovingly details their affluent lifestyle: a grand piano, large study and desk, and hundreds of books. When he and his wife leave for a month's vacation, Liuda and Katia agree to dog-sit, and use the apartment to entertain various eligible young men. Liuda quickly latches on to Sergei Gurin, an up-and-coming ice-hockey player, whose eye she first catches on an underground train, while Katia is immediately taken by Rudol'f, a television cameraman who impresses her with his glib talk about the future prospects of this new cultural medium. Rudol'f introduces Katia to his domineering mother, takes her on one of his filming assignments where he films her face in close-up on national television and, just before the Tikhomirovs return to their apartment, seduces her.

Three months later, at the wedding reception for Tonia and Kolia, Katia admits that she is pregnant. She is cruelly abandoned by Rudol'f, who has already discovered that far from being the daughter of a professor, she is in fact a lowly factory worker. He advises her to have an abortion, but she resolves to have the child. Katia is visited by Rudol'f's mother who tries to mollify her with money, and attacks her with insults and half-concealed mockery. Katia is left to cry herself to sleep.

The film then shifts abruptly forward two decades. Liuda has been divorced from the alcoholic and abusive Gurin for seven years now, but he still comes round begging for a few roubles with which to buy vodka. She works in a laundry, still on the lookout for eligible and affluent men, but they, sadly for her, are all spoken for. Tonia remains happily married to Kolia and they now have three children. Katia is director of the factory where she was once a manual worker, and with a pretty and precocious teenage daughter Aleksandra. We know that Katia is a strong and independent-minded worker, for early in the film she manages to repair her own machine without any help from the (male) engineers. Nevertheless, the transition from shop-floor worker to factory boss for such a disadvantaged person is contrived and smacks of artificiality.

Katia is still single, though she has a casual relationship with Volodia, an older married man (played by Oleg Tabakov (b. 1935)). They meet and go to Volodia's flat, as his wife is away for a few days. As they are about to go to bed, the doorbell rings: it is his mother-in-law. Significantly, it is Katia who provides Volodia with all possible excuses to explain later why he did not answer the door, while he is left looking abashed and lost for words. That night, she cries herself to sleep.

The friends spend a day with Kolia and Tonia at their dacha, and, as she returns home on a suburban train, Katia meets Georgii (played with unassuming charm by Aleksei Batalov (b. 1928), then over fifty years old). They fall in love, and, despite problems along the way, by the end of the film remain together, presumably to live happily ever after.

The film combines two fairytales: the first from rags to riches, the second with Prince Charming. Katia, however, is no Cinderella with a fairy godmother to look after her. What she has is all down to her own efforts. She is a determined woman who certainly deserves her success, and, in the end, her happiness. Back in 1958, at a dinner in the Tikhomirovs' flat, the factory director Kruglov had said that life begins at forty; in Katia's case, happiness comes at forty. The romantic happy end undoubtedly appealed to cinema audiences, and Katia's troubles with unfeeling men also makes the viewer root for her. The director also makes full use of background music and *mise-en-scène* for maximum emotional impact.

The film is also significant as a cultural signpost, with its many references to the 1950s and 1970s, and as a slice of officially-sponsored social history. As a chronicle of social change, it celebrates the increasing affluence and middle-class lifestyles of Muscovites over two decades, while neatly side-stepping its own misogynist subtexts.

The most important cultural signifier is the soundtrack. The film opens and closes to Iurii Vizbor's song, 'Aleksandra', sung by Sergei and Tat'iana Nikitin, with subtle differences in the lyrics whereby the opening version, sung by a lone male voice, introduces the theme of the resilience needed to realise one's dreams, whereas the final version, performed by a male/female duet, brings about closure by emphasising how all is resolved by true love and togetherness. When Georgii invites Katia and Aleksandra to a picnic with his friends and work colleagues, a male/female duet sings to guitar accompaniment about love, as Katia and Georgii stare into each other's eyes. As a sign of increasing openness to the West, the younger generation is treated to the music of Boney-M, one of the few Western pop groups officially sanctioned and promoted in Brezhnev's USSR. Through the deliberate foregrounding of popular song and culture, Men'shov's film offers a conformist picture of progressive social change, where over two decades material standards of living are seen to have inexorably risen, a single mother can become director of a factory with responsibility for 3,000 employees, Western-style supermarkets are the norm and private car ownership is an accepted fact of life.

Furthermore, social cohesion is in full view as academics and scientists, the cream of the intelligentsia, rub shoulders and socialise with the proletariat in the form of the metal-worker Georgii. A man, eventually, can become reconciled to the fact that his wife owns more than he does. As Anna Lawton maintains, the two decades on screen are 'a period depicted as a positive progression from the childish, foolish years of the cultural thaw to the consolidation of economic goals and an affluent and mature society'.

The film is much more interesting, not so much as a barometer of trouble-free social progress, but rather in what it says about male/female relations, as discussed in Lynne Attwood's study on women in Soviet cinema. Statistical background is provided when Katia visits a club for singles, to be told that there are twice as many single women as men, and for those who are forty and above, the ratio is five to one. 'There aren't enough men', she is told by the club's director. However, the odds are always stacked on the side of men: older men can be introduced to younger women, Volodia's adultery is condoned, and Katia is all too willing to allow Georgii to take over her household.

The one unsympathetic character is Rudol'f, and even he is accorded a modicum of pity at the end. In 1958 he is a hard-hearted womaniser dominated by his mother, but two decades later he is pathetic and self-pitying, twice-divorced and lonely since the death of his mother eight years before. Nevertheless, he thinks only of himself and his own needs, not those of Katia or even his daughter Aleksandra. We know nothing about any children from his two marriages. He has also changed his name from the foreign-sounding Rudol'f to the more solidly Russian Rodion. When he sees Katia again for the first time in nearly twenty years, he fails to recognise her at first, but she immediately knows who he is, even allowing herself a joke at the expense of his name change. His evident lack of self-consciousness is shown when he insists on meeting his daughter Aleksandra, even though he had disowned her all those years ago. When he and Katia meet, it is in the same park, on the same bench, and with the same old men playing chess nearby, as twenty years before. Rudol'f/Rodion eventually does get to see his daughter, and he tries to impress her with exactly the same empty words about the future prospects of television as he had with Katia when they first met.

Gurin, as a professional sportsman, initially refrains from alcohol consumption, even refusing to drink when he first meets Liuda. We first see him drink at the party to celebrate the birth of Aleksandra. It is obvious that he later succumbs to the numerous offers of fans in bars and by the 1970s is a sad wreck of a man, accepting beer and vodka from any passer-by. We last see him promising to start a new alcohol-free life, returning the money to Liuda that he had borrowed and about to leave Moscow to go back to his home town.

The figure of Gurin brings us to an interesting sub-theme in the film: the role of alcohol in the formation and development of relationships. With Gurin and Liuda, we see how alcoholism can destroy a relationship, and thoroughly debase a once upstanding model citizen. However, when Katia and Georgii argue and part (over the fact that she earns more than he does), a sullen and disoriented Georgii is tracked down by Kolia, Tonia's husband, in Georgii's cramped home in a communal apartment. Before they can even introduce themselves, Kolia is required to drink a whole tumbler of vodka in one gulp. Thereafter male bonding is accompanied by copious amounts of vodka, washed down with pickled cucumbers and dried fish. When Kolia brings Georgii back to Katia's apartment, he can barely stand, whereas Georgii shows no sign of inebriation. The vodka-drinking scene here, as in many Russian films across the decades, is a crucial comic scene, where the more helpless the drinkers become (always men), the more comically they behave. In Men'shov's film the comedy is there, but generally at Kolia's expense; the purpose of the scene is to provide the opportunity for Katia and Georgii to settle their differences.

It is the figure of Georgii, or Gosha/Goga/Iura/Zhora, as various people in the film call him, that proves the most intriguing. When he first sets eyes on Katia on the train, he guesses immediately that she does not like dirty shoes, as his are covered in mud. He also surmises just by the look in her eyes that she is not married, and that she works in a factory, perhaps in some leadership capacity. Within a few minutes in her apartment, he knows that she does not have a husband, although by now he has met her daughter. Far from being an understanding 'new man'; conscious of a woman's needs, he nevertheless does the cooking, whilst handling himself well in a fistfight with five youths threatening Aleksandra's boyfriend.

A simple manual worker, he provides the invaluable technical back-up for the research of his colleagues, all academics with higher qualifications. Indeed, they affirm that without his 'golden hands' half the work in the institute would not get done. He shuns the trappings of material affluence, living alone in one room, thereby showing his humility and utter lack of pretension. He says that he is happy with his lot, not interested in social advancement or prestige, although he is able to quote seemingly at will the Roman Emperor Diocletian. He also builds a strong rapport with Aleksandra. As Katia says at the end of the film, 'he has no shortcomings', he is 'the most perfect man in the world'. In short, he would be every woman's dream. We know that he is divorced, but it remains unclear as to why such a 'perfect' person was not in a relationship prior to meeting Katia.

Crucially, Men'shov allows Georgii to develop in one very significant area. Georgii and Katia separate when he discovers that she is, in fact, of considerably higher social status than he is and earns more. He has insisted that he is the man and master of the house, and must take all the decisions. When they are reconciled, he accepts her social position, and the fact that she earns more than he, and she accepts that he is master of the household.

Alentova successfully bridges the gap of two decades, evolving from an impressionable and malleable young girl to a tough-talking executive, managing changes of mood and in particular diction to suggest just how many knocks the world has given her. But her character never loses her innate kindness, and gives everyone – even Rudol'f/Rodion two decades later – the benefit of the doubt. Batalov plays on his established screen persona as rugged, dependable and likeable, harking back to his earlier roles as the model working-class hero in

Bol'shaia sem'ia (*The Big Family*, 1954), the decent but doomed fiancé in Mikhail Kalatozov's *Letiat zhuravli* (*The Cranes are Flying*, 1957), Chekhov's enamoured roué Gurov in Iosif Kheifits's *Dama s sobachkoi* (*Lady with the Lapdog*, 1960), and the confident scientist Gusev ('brilliant, obsessed and doomed', according to Josephine Woll), in Mikhail Romm's *Deviat' dnei odnogo goda* (*Nine Days of One Year*, 1962).

The film can be seen as simple Soviet wish fulfilment on various levels. Traditional modes of behaviour are reinforced: Tonia is the dutiful wife and mother, and lives in total contentment; Liuda, the fixer and schemer from the start, ends the film lonely and cynical; Katia, who shows her true good nature and fortitude, despite major setbacks, is ultimately rewarded with the man she has been waiting for all her life.

There are also many implausibilities in the plot: the fact that Katia's distant professor relative leaves her to run his apartment for one month; a pregnant Katia being given her own room in a hostel at the end of the 1950s, when any accommodation in Moscow was at a premium; Katia as power-dressing self-made woman and factory director in a male-oriented workplace and socio-political environment (and demonstratively bossing the men, demanding that they fulfil the plan and their 'socialist obligations'); the appearance of Georgii as the answer to Katia's dreams. Several critics have noted the similarities between this film and the contrivances and sugary happy endings of Western, in particular Hollywood, models ('this typical Hollywood melodrama', argue Andrew Horton and Michael Brashinsky), where plot contrivances and incongruities do not hinder the sentimental, audience-pleasing resolution.

The real hero, of course, is Moscow itself, as the film begins and ends with panoramic vistas of the city. In addition to featuring in the song 'Aleksandra', we see it growing and developing throughout the film, as new houses are built and whole new suburbs appear. It may not trust tears and self-pity, but it rewards honesty and integrity, and provides a rich and dynamic background for the resolution of personal dramas, and the finding of happiness.

Moscow Doesn't Believe in Tears remains, for post-Soviet Russia, an intriguing film. It can still be viewed as a simple romantic comedy with the obligatory happy ending, but with hindsight it can also now be interpreted semiotically as a desperate attempt by a dying regime to persuade its citizens of the essential benevolence of Soviet society, a society that would cease to exist a little more than a decade later. The moral that stability depends on the happy nuclear family, whereby man and woman must know their place, is a popular one not confined only to Soviet society, of course. It maintains its interest 25 years later, therefore, not so much as a cinematic event, so much as a vital socio-cultural snapshot of a society seemingly happy with itself and moving steadily forward whereas, as we now know, the exact opposite was true.

In 2000 Men'shov and Alentova revisited much the same ground in *Envy of the Gods*. It is set in Moscow in 1983, and Alentova again plays a successful career woman, Sonia, but this time with a stable family life consisting of a doting husband and 16-year-old son. Sonia works in TV, as did Rudol'f in the earlier film, and there are also many cultural and socio-political pointers to the times, such as television footage of Politburo members and the comedian Arkadii Raikin. But if the earlier film served to affirm social bonds and progress, *Envy of the Gods* does not shy away from the dangerous political context of the times: a woman denouncing her neighbours for watching a banned video of Bernardo Bertolucci's *Last Tango in Paris*, zealous civilian police helpers (*druzhinniki*) interrupting a cinema showing to ask why members of the audience are not at work (a favourite Andropov device to encourage the 'strengthening of labour discipline'), and, most ignominiously of all, the shooting down in September 1983 by a Soviet fighter plane of an American airliner that had drifted into Soviet air space in the Far East. This, and Ronald Reagan's subsequent 'empire of evil' speech, bring the curtain down on the film, and, by implication, serve as the prologue to the beginning of the end of this society.

Moscow Doesn't Believe in Tears showed a society moving inexorably forward without reference to the outside world. Here, the flaws and untruths of this society are revealed through the intrusion of the outside world, in particular the West. Sonia's happy, stable life is thrown into disarray through her passionate affair with the French journalist André (Gerard Dépardieu). Television footage reflect the increasing tensions of the Cold War, unlike the domestic harmony propagated in the film. If *Moscow Doesn't Believe in Tears* celebrated a Moscow of material affluence and contentment, *Envy of the Gods* does not shrink from showing the shortages of cheese and salami, and the bad-tempered, potentially violent queues for vodka. Sonia's husband, a hard-drinking writer, discovers that his latest novella has been rejected for not being sufficiently 'patriotic', a clear reference to the mind-numbing and rigid conformity forced on writers in the early 1980s.

But Alentova's Sonia, like Katia before her, is determined to survive, and she does. André is expelled from Moscow as a result of rising Cold War tensions, and she returns to her family, even as she dreams of a last tango in Moscow with her very own French lover. Viewed together, both films offer tantalising insights into Russian society's self-perceptions over two decades. *Moscow Doesn't Believe in Tears* offers a proud, patriotic picture of the Soviet Union moving towards the goal of Communism, and the positive role of women, in an era officially defined as 'advanced socialism'; the post-Soviet and revisionist *Envy of the Gods* exposes the false hopes and lies hidden under layers of conformity, where a Prince Charming can offer a few days of happiness, until the dream is replaced by grey, kitchen-sink reality.

David Gillespie

REFERENCES

Attwood, L. (1993) *Red Woman on the Silver Screen: Soviet Woman and Cinema from the Beginning to the End of the Communist Era*. London: Pandora Press.

Horton, A. and M. Brashinsky (1992) *The Zero Hour: Glasnost and Soviet Cinema in Transition*. Princeton: Princeton University Press.

Lawton, A. (1992) *Kinoglasnost: Soviet Cinema in Our Time*. Cambridge: Cambridge University Press.

Woll, J. (2000) *Real Images: Soviet Cinema and the Thaw*. London and New York: I. B. Tauris.

MOI DRUG IVAN LAPSHIN MY FRIEND IVAN LAPSHIN

ALEKSEI GERMAN, USSR 1984

Voted one of the ten best Soviet films of all time by Russian critics in the late 1990s, Aleksei German's *Moi drug Ivan Lapshin* (*My Friend Ivan Lapshin*, 1984) barely made it to the screen. Although he had drafted a screenplay as early as 1969, it took German ten years to secure studio backing and another four years to complete the filming and editing. Upon its completion in 1983, the film was banned by the Leningrad Film Studio (Lenfil'm) that had originally commissioned it. Finally released in 1984, *My Friend Ivan Lapshin* was hailed by critics and viewers alike as a classic. Rooted in the historical revisionism of the Khrushchev period, the film may be unique in all of post-Stalinist Russian culture for its historical accuracy, subtlety and the depth of its critique of Stalinist utopianism.

Born in 1938, the first son of the well-known Stalinist prose writer, Iurii German (1910–67), Aleksei German studied theatre direction at the Leningrad Institute of Theatre, Music and Cinematography. After graduating in 1960, German worked for several years in provincial and Leningrad theatres, before being hired in 1965 by Lenfil'm as the assistant director for a film called *Rabochii poselok* (*Workers' Settlement*, 1965). Directed by Vladimir Vengerov (b. 1920), *Workers' Settlement* was a Soviet equivalent of William Wyler's Academy Award-winner of 1946, *The Best Years of Our Lives*. *Workers' Settlement* tells the story of a blind World War Two veteran who is saved from alcoholism and despair by his war buddies who show him that, despite his disability, he can still have a fulfilling life. German's next film, co-directed with Grigorii Aronov (1923–1984), is closer in spirit to his mature films. *Sed'moi sputnik* (*The Seventh Fellow-Traveller*, 1967), tells the surprising story of a former Tsarist general held hostage by the Bolsheviks during the Red Terror. Finally released when his sympathies with the Revolution become known, the general finds himself completely alone and abandoned by all, unwilling to rejoin the enemies of the Bolsheviks and unable to find a place in the new world created by the Revolution. In its unusual subject matter and alienated tragic hero, its suggestion of historical revisionism and its avoidance of Soviet clichés, *The Seventh Fellow-Traveller* anticipates the non-conformist style and content of German's mature films.

Today, German is known as the controversial and uncompromising director of four movies that collectively represent a remarkably mature cinematic reflection on the twin twentieth-century Russian national tragedies of Stalinism and World War Two. His directorial debut, *Proverka na dorogakh* (*Trial on the Road*, 1971/1986; original title *Operatsiia 'S Novym Godom'* (*Operation 'Happy New Year'*)) picked up where *The Seventh Fellow-Traveller* ended, telling another tragic tale of an ordinary man crushed by the forces of history. Based on his father's war prose, *Trial on the Road* tells the story of Soviet Army Sergeant Aleksandr Lazarev (Vladimir Zamanskii (b. 1928)), a former POW and collaborator who, having escaped from the Germans, gives himself up to a band of partisans. The film describes his tragic attempt to prove his loyalty to the Soviet side. Although his brave actions in several 'trial' ambushes convince most of the partisans, including the commander Lokotkov (Rolan Bykov (1929–1998)) of his loyalty, the political commissar Petushkov (Anatolii Solonitsyn) remains suspicious. At the film's end, Lazarev dies a heroic death protecting the escape of the partisans after a daring raid on a Nazi supply depot.

Despite the overwhelmingly positive responses of many leading lights of Soviet literature and cinema, who saw the film in pre-release screenings, studio censors viewed the film as ideologically incorrect and dangerous. The film's central ideological 'error' was, no doubt, raising the sensitive question of Soviet treatment of returning prisoners of war. However, the film's focus on individual weakness, errors, powerlessness and paranoia in the tragic circumstances of war and its refusal to adhere to the traditional narrative of the Soviet people's heroic struggle against the fascist invaders, contributed to its being shelved for fifteen years. *Trial on the Road* was finally released in 1986 at the height of perestroika to great popular and critical acclaim.

In retrospect, the importance of German's debut feature is apparent: in moving beyond the positive heroes, single-minded patriotism and mandatory optimism of traditional Soviet representations of war, German was the first Soviet director to follow the example of Andrei Tarkovskii's deconstruction of the Soviet war film in *Ivanovo detstvo* (*Ivan's Childhood*, 1962). By depicting war with brutal realism and focusing on the experiences of ordinary people caught up in a gigantic historical tragedy, *Trial on the Road* became the prototype of a more honest and less ideological war movie, as well as a critical influence on such important later films as Larisa Shepit'ko's *Voskhozhdenie* (*The Ascent*, 1976) and Elem Klimov's *Idi i smotri* (*Come and See*, 1985).

Despite the scandalous reception of his first film, Lenfil'm immediately commissioned German to make another film about the war. Based on stories by the prominent Soviet writer Konstantin Simonov (1915–1979), German's *Dvadtsat' dnei bez voiny* (*Twenty Days Without War*, 1976) tells a low-key story of Major Lopatin (Iurii Nikulin), a middle-aged war correspondent, on a twenty-day leave from Stalingrad. On his way from the front to his home in Tashkent, we observe through Lopatin's eyes the sufferings and the courage of people whose lives have been turned upside down by the war. When he finally arrives home, his alienation from ordinary life becomes the focus of the film. He visits his ex-wife, stops by a movie set where one of his works is being turned into a typical propaganda film, and wanders the streets alone until a chance meeting with Nina (Liudmila Gurchenko) leads to a brief and unforgettable romance. At the end of his leave and the film, Lopatkin returns to Stalingrad. Avoiding all the false heroism and clichéd patriotism of traditional Soviet war films, German emphasises the personal toll of war on the lives of ordinary soldiers and civilians, men and women at the front and the rear. Although *Twenty Days Without War* was essentially a remake of Grigorii Chukhrai's classic film of the Thaw period, *Ballada o soldate* (*Ballad of a Soldier*, 1959), it is an original film that bears all the trademark signs of German's style: a refusal to aestheticise or heroicise war, surprising and risky casting (especially of the great Russian clown Nikulin as the dramatic hero), meticulously recreated and historically accurate locations and interiors based on newsreels and photographs, understated action and subtle performances, a tragic and fatalistic atmosphere, almost total avoidance of non-diegetic music, and the use of low lighting and high-contrast black-and-white footage shot with characteristic brio by German's long-time cameraman, Valerii Fedosov. Unsurprisingly, studio officials were again critical of German's insufficiently heroic depiction of the Soviet war effort and the film's release was held up for almost one year. When it was released, *Twenty Days Without War* was immediately recognised by critics and reviewers as a milestone in Soviet cinema.

German's most recent film, *Khrustalev, mashinu!* (*Khrustalyov, My Car!*, 1998), was delayed for several years by the economic crisis in post-Soviet Russia and by the loss of American financing in the early 1990s. Set during the so-called 'Doctors' Plot' of 1953, *Khrustalyov, My Car!* tells the story of Dr Klenskii, a leading Moscow surgeon who is arrested for no good reason, brutalised and then suddenly recalled to the Kremlin, where he witnesses the death of Stalin and the apparent ascension of the secret police chief Beria. German's most challenging and darkest film, *Khrustalyov, My Car!* is a nightmarish vision of the paranoia and senseless brutality of Stalinism that has been a commercial failure with both domestic and foreign audiences. Filmed in extremely low light, with a deliberately cacophonous soundtrack that often obscures the dialogue, lacking establishing shots that could elucidate the spatial dimensions of the confusing action, and including numerous characters whose identities or role in the plot are never explained, *Khrustalyov, My Car!* makes absolutely no concessions to its audience. Despite failure at the box office and a scandalous reception at the Cannes Film Festival, some critics believe it will eventually be acknowledged as German's masterpiece.

Since the late 1990s, German has been working on an adaptation of *Trudno byt' Bogom* (*Hard to be a God*, 1966), a classic Cold War fantasy by Soviet Russia's most famous science fiction writers, Boris (b. 1933) and Arkadii (1925–1991) Strugatskii. A gloss on superpower interventions in Eastern Europe and Vietnam in the 1960s, the Strugatskiis' *Hard to be a God* is the story of emissaries from an advanced civilisation sent as observers to a planet experiencing brutal civil and religious conflicts very similar to Earth's during the Middle Ages. The central conflict of the novel concerns the hero's temptation to disobey his orders and intervene in local events, thereby changing history. While some critics have suggested that Russia's on-going intervention in Chechnya may supply the key to the director's surprising decision to adapt the Strugatskiis' novel, German himself has been reluctant to discuss his film in production.

The production and reception of German's most important film, *My Friend Ivan Lapshin*, resembles that of his other features. Years of meticulous preparation and struggle culminated in a film that inspired admiration from colleagues and opposition from the authorities. Based on Iurii German's stories and novels about a charismatic Criminal Investigator in 1930s Leningrad, the film was completed in 1983, although its release was delayed by the authorities for almost two and a half years. When finally released in 1985, it became an instant hit with critics and viewers. Indeed its release was one of the first hints of the massive changes that *glasnost'* would shortly introduce into late Soviet cinema.

Framed by a prologue and epilogue set in the 1980s, the main action of *My Friend Ivan Lapshin* takes place in 1935 in the fictional provincial town of Urchinsk. Narrated by an elderly writer who, as a young child witnessed the events of the film, the film introduces us to several members of the local militia investigating a gang of murderers and black marketeers. The arrival of a touring theatrical troupe and a big-city journalist looking for material on the work of the local militia sets in motion a subplot of misdirected and unrequited love among the main characters: Ivan Lapshin (Andrei Boltnev (b. 1946)), head of the militia Criminal Investigative Unit, falls in love with the actress Natasha Adashova (Nina Ruslanova), who is in love with the journalist Khanin (Andrei Mironov), depressed by the recent death of his wife. Unhappy in love, living in grinding poverty in crowded communal apartments, the desperately unhappy private lives of the main characters contrast powerfully with the triumphant atmosphere of Stalinism that dominates the public life of the characters and the town: to the accompaniment of brass orchestras playing military marches, Khanin attempts suicide, Lapshin's sleep is disturbed by nightmares, and Adashova begs Khanin to save her by taking her away with him to Moscow. By the film's elegiac conclusion, the criminals have been arrested or killed, Khanin boards a steamship for Moscow, while Adashova and Lapshin return to their lonely private lives. The 1930s plot ends with a striking image of Lapshin looking out of his apartment window at an approaching tram bearing a portrait of Stalin and an orchestra. At this point the film returns to the frame provided by the elderly narrator last seen in the film's prologue. His apparently random closing comments, describing changes in the city since his childhood, including increased construction, worsening traffic and more tram lines, convey a profound disappointment that contemporary Russia is still so far from achieving the utopian future so confidently envisioned in the 1930s.

While atmosphere is more important than action in all of German's films, this is nowhere more true than in *My Friend Ivan Lapshin*. The film's tone of gentle nostalgia and sympathy for the characters and their faith in the radiant future is established in an elaborately-shot prologue in which the narrator, evidently an elderly writer in the 1980s, admiringly describes the communal spirit of the 1930s and calls his story 'my confession of love for those people together with whom I lived as a child, a five-minute walk from here and half a century ago'. The narrator's apparently positive attitude towards the communal spirit and idealism of the 1930s is, however, undercut by constant references to the approaching disasters of Stalinist terror and world war and by a growing awareness of the distance between the public ideals and the private reality of the period.

At the centre of *My Friend Ivan Lapshin* are remarkably realistic recreations of the look and feel of a Russian provincial town in the 1930s and of the worldview of committed Stalinists. German's characters represent a 'lost generation' of true believers, veterans of the Revolution and Civil War, who, the audience knows, will soon be destroyed by Stalin's terror and Hitler's war. Because German's approach to his characters is sympathetic and under-stated, some viewers may miss the director's total rejection of the accumulated ideological clichés and heroic myths of traditional Soviet representations of the 1930s. Singing military marches and acting out satirical political sketches amidst communal squalor and poverty, the guests at Lapshin's birthday party capture an essential contradiction of Stalinist life: boundless enthusiasm and optimism about Socialism's brilliant future despite political intolerance and positively primitive living standards in the present. By depicting the discontents of real life in the 1930s, the poverty, ubiquitous shortages of everyday necessities as sugar and firewood, lack of privacy, and callousness towards those who live outside the protection of the State, *My Friend Ivan Lapshin* reveals the dishonesty of Soviet representations of the 1930s which, in focusing on the idealism, falsified the reality. By showing us not only his characters' strengths (for example, their idealism, asceticism and willingness to sacrifice themselves for a greater cause), but also their personal and private weaknesses (Khanin's suicidal despair at the death of his wife, the desperation that Adashova hides behind a wall of cynicism and sarcastic humour, Lapshin's clumsy romancing of Adashova and his nightmares), German succeeds in humanising the 'positive heroes' of his father's propagandistic prose works.

The title character, Ivan Mikhailovich Lapshin, 'our local Pinkerton', as he is called, is a likable character, a competent policeman, and a true believer in the promise of the Revolution. Yet, scarred by his service in the Civil War, he embodies the contradictory combination of brutality and idealism of the Bolshevik Revolution and, more specifically, of Stalinism. Although ostensibly based on the militia hero of his father's stories and novels, Andrei Boltnev's Lapshin is a very different character. Where Iurii German's militia hero was depicted as much a psychologist and social worker as a detective, concerned above all else with the root causes of criminality and the possibility of rehabilitation of criminal recidivists through labour, the Lapshin of Aleksei German's film is a pitiless and violent defender of Soviet society against its enemies. Although, on occasion, Boltnev's Lapshin pays lip service to the goal of rehabilitating criminals, the central motif of Iurii German's militia stories, he is uninterested in the roots of criminality and dismissive of criminal psychology: his job is simply to eliminate criminal elements from Soviet society any way he can.

And yet his brutality is redeemed, at least in his own eyes, by the utopian promise of the Revolution, the ultimate purpose and justification of his violence. Lapshin's combination of brutality and idealism is most clearly expressed in the phrase 'We'll clean out the scum, plant a garden and live in it', spoken as he leaves the scene of a multiple murder. Hearing Lapshin's words echo through a lifeless winter landscape, the viewer, but not Lapshin, senses the difficulty, perhaps the impossibility, of such men succeeding in planting a garden in such a bleak and dismal setting. In this way, German suggests that Lapshin's tragedy, and that of his entire generation, begins with this failure to imagine the true difficulty of realising utopian dreams in this world.

German's technique in *My Friend Ivan Lapshin* is to present seemingly random episodes and images which, over time, gradually coalesce into a general critique of some of the central ideological assumptions of Stalinism. The most important examples are the belief that human nature can be improved, either by an improved environment or by a change in life-style, and that art's purpose is not to reflect reality, but to inculcate correct ideological values in its audience. These themes are explored in various registers, from comic to dramatic, over the course of the film. That the rehabilitation of lifelong criminals is the central theme of German's Lapshin stories and novels suggests that the younger German is struggling not only with essential elements of Stalinist ideology, but with his father's role as a leading proponent of Stalinist orthodoxy in Soviet literature as well.

The interrelated themes of remaking human nature and the ideological role of art are developed in several scenes associated with a theatrical group on tour in Urchinsk. In the lobby of the theatre where the actors are performing, Lapshin and Khanin come across an exhibit organised by the local Pioneer chapter: a cage in which a fox and hen appear to live amicably. Inspired by the quasi-scientific neo-Lamarckian theories of Ivan Vladimirovich Michurin (1855–1935) and Trofim Denisovich Lysenko (1898–1976), the peaceful cohabitation of a well-fed fox and hen is intended to demonstrate the material power of environment to change animal nature. In the context of the film, however, this experiment points to the Stalinist theory of the rehabilitation of criminals through labour. Later on we learn that, due to a failure to feed the fox on schedule, its predatory instincts returned and it consumed the hen. By undercutting the Stalinist confidence in the priority of environment over nature and the ability of humans armed with the correct ideology, that is, dialectical materialism, to change the laws of nature, German also provides comic counterpoint to the more serious issues raised by the touring company's performance of a classic of the Stalinist stage, Nikolai Pogodin's *Aristokraty* (*Aristocrats*, 1935).

In *Aristocrats*, Pogodin (pseudonym of Nikolai Stukalov (1900–1962)) describes, in typical Socialist Realist fashion, the successful rehabilitation of several imprisoned criminals and class enemies through the enlightened guidance of their prison wardens and the beneficent effects of forced labour on the White Sea Canal project. The first mention of the play comes early in the film, when the actress Natasha Adashova asks Lapshin to arrange a meeting with a local prostitute to help her prepare for her role. Intrigued by the vivacious and attractive actress, Lapshin obliges her and arranges a meeting at the police station with 'Katia Napoleon', who is awaiting transfer to a labour camp for prostitution and petty theft. Lapshin's instructions to 'lay off the smut and concentrate on how you plan to rehabilitate yourself', make no impression on Katia who, after listening meekly for a few moments to Adashova reading her lines, suddenly attacks her. As in the experiment with the fox and the hen, predatory instincts prove resistant to change despite the optimistic predictions of Stalinist orthodoxy.

The disastrous failure of the play, summed up by the wheelbarrow that collapses on stage under Adashova's weight, contributes to German's double critique of Stalinist culture and the literary works of his father. As both Lapshin and his colleagues agree, although the play is not at all realistic, it is ideologically correct and, therefore, necessary. As Elena Stishova argues in her review of *My Friend Ivan Lapshin,* German reveals the essentially anti-materialist and romantic attitude of Stalinist culture by showing how it privileges ideology over reality. But in depicting the priority of ideological orthodoxy over verisimilitude, German is also suggesting that while ideologically correct Stalinist art may satisfy the needs of policemen, it falls short of the demands of a general audience.

Although some Russian viewers were critical of German's de-romanticised depiction of Russian life in the 1930s, most critics responded enthusiastically to the film's critique of Stalinist utopianism and to the almost documentary-quality of German's recreation of provincial Russia in the 1930s. The tragic plight of true believers like Lapshin, decent people blind to the contradictions of Stalinist ideology and to the pervasive signs of approaching catastrophe, summed up the Stalinist betrayal of the Revolution. German's brutally honest depiction of the poverty, squalor, shortages, over-crowding, lawlessness and brutality of the 1930s was a therapeutic shock to the system of a generation brought up on Soviet representations of the Stalinist period. With the release of *My Friend Ivan Lapshin*, Aleksei German was immediately lionised as the heir to Tarkovskii's mantle as Russia's leading filmmaker and the conscience of its film industry.

Despite some confusion concerning the relevant political and historical context, most Western reviewers and critics were able to recognise *My Friend Ivan Lapshin* as an important film and its release as an critical moment in the cultural politics of Russia. The film was especially praised for its indirect and elliptical recreation of the Stalinist past, its sympathetic irony towards its heroes and their beliefs, the actors' performances, German's unorthodox *mise-en-scene* and mobile camera, and the cinematographer Valerii Fedosov's surprising use of a combination of black-and-white, colour and sepia-tinted film stock. Writing in the *Monthly Film Bulletin*, Simon Field noted the importance of the theme of the betrayal of Revolutionary idealism, while J. Hoberman recognised how the film 'puts Bolshevik idealism in context' and suggested the importance of the Oedipal theme in the son's transformation of his father's hero.

Although contemporary post-Soviet Russian cinema has moved decisively away from the aesthetic and ideological positions of German, *My Friend Ivan Lapshin* remains one of the most important Russian films of the twentieth century. By incorporating his own family's complicity in the Stalinist past into his film, German conveys the complexities of Stalinism without either romanticising or denouncing the past. German reveals the misguided ideology, naïve utopianism and combination of idealism and brutality that made Stalinism possible, and does so in a way that allows viewers to sympathise with those who sacrificed their lives for a dream that proved impossible. German's tragic and ironic portrayal of committed Stalinists of the 1930s as victims of their own idealism represents one of the highest achievements of Russian art of the twentieth century.

Anthony Anemone

REFERENCES

Field, S. (1987) '*My Friend Ivan Lapshin*', *Monthly Film Bulletin*, 11, 339.
Hoberman, J. (1987) '*My Friend Ivan Lapshin*', *Village Voice*, 31 March.
Stishova, E. (1985) 'Blizkoe proshloe', *Iskusstvo kino*, 6, 46–53.

IGLA THE NEEDLE

RASHID NUGMANOV, USSR, 1988

Kazakh film in general would make a perfect case study for one of the former Soviet Union's national cinemas; once part of Soviet imperial culture, it always had a strong film industry. Nowadays, Kazakhstan is an independent state with a relatively prosperous economy, and its film industry has settled into a good infrastructure of multiplexes in the bigger cities and a recognition of the state's need to support the industry (the formation of a national producers' centre, the establishment of a Kazakh Film School and the organisation of international film festivals in Almaty) and of the ability to offer the locations of the country for international co-productions (for example, the US project *The Nomad* (2005) was filmed in Almaty, and Sergei Bodrov's co-production of *The Mongol* (2007) is partly financed by Kazakhstan).

Historically, the film studios in Alma-Ata (as the city was called in Soviet times) had played a key role in Soviet film history. During World War Two Mosfil'm evacuated to Alma-Ata, where the Central United Film Studios (Tsentral'naia ob"edinennaia kinostudiia, TsOKS) was in charge of the production units of directors such as Sergei Eisenstein, Vsevolod Pudovkin, Dziga Vertov, Grigorii Kozintsev and Leonid Trauberg, Fridrikh Ermler, Abram Room, the Vasil'ev Brothers and Boris Barnet. The film studios in Alma-Ata had thus benefited from first-hand contact with the avant-garde of Soviet filmmakers, but it would also continue to form an integral part of Soviet cinema. After the war the Kazakh actor Shaken Aimanov (1914–1970) directed the first Kazakh feature film, *Poema o liubvi* (*A Poem About Love*, 1954). In the constant attempts of the Soviet empire to demonstrate the intrinsic and inseparable link with its republics, Kazakhfil'm played a vital role in the rewriting of early Soviet history with the production of a 'red western' trilogy with elements of a spy thriller about the local hero Chadiarov's involvement in establishing socialist rule in Central Asia and protecting Soviet interests in Mongolia and Japan. *Konets atamana* (*The End of the Ataman*, 1970), *Transsibirskii Ekspress* (*Trans-Siberian Express*, 1977) and *Mandzhurskii variant* (*The Mandzhurian Version*, 1989), scripted with participation from Nikita Mikhalkov and Andrei Konchalovskii, were most popular with Soviet audiences.

During the 1980s Kazakhfil'm served as a platform for young experimental filmmakers from Moscow, including Sergei Bodrov Sr and Sergei Solov'ev. The most important event in this period, however, occurred in 1984 when Sergei Solov'ev selected a course of Kazakh students at the State Institute of Cinematography (VGIK). The students included Rashid Nugmanov, Darejan Omirbaev and Serik Aprymov, as well as Ardak Amirkulov, Abai Karpykov and Amir Karakulov. Educated in Moscow, these filmmakers would proceed to have a decisive influence on national Kazakh cinema in the 1990s, studied by Gul'nara Abikeeva.

Sergei Solov'ev (b. 1944) had created a number of film adaptations of the Russian classics before making his groundbreaking feature *ASSA* (1988), starring figures of the Leningrad (now St Petersburg) underground movement, including the artist Afrika (Sergei Bugaev), the 'new academician' Timur Novikov (1958–2002), and the singer Irena Kuksenaite. It also featured the music of the rock stars Viktor Tsoi ((1961–1990) leader of the band Kino), Boris Grebenshchikov (leader of Aquarium) and Zhanna Aguzarova (lead singer of Bravo). Rock music offered a different, alternative lifestyle instead of being the source of destruction and unrest, as had been the case in Iuris Podnieks's seminal documentary *Legko li byt' molodym?* (*Is it Easy to be Young*, 1986), dealing with the demolition of a train after a rock concert in Oger, Latvia in July 1985 and exploring the problems of the young rock fans who lacked confidence, who were disillusioned with life, who had no place in society and who used drugs and alcohol to escape reality. *ASSA* represents a change in the perception of underground culture in general, and rock music in particular. Bananan (played by Sergei Bugaev) is a non-violent and innately good character, who stands apart from the others because of his behaviour and his appearance (he has one earring). Solov'ev juxtaposed him to the 'Soviet' official Krymov (played by the documentary filmmaker Stanislav Govorukhin (b. 1936), a representative of the establishment), who holds power over his mistress Alika (Tat'iana Drubich (b. 1959)). Krymov may have the power to have Bananan killed, but he cannot win Alika, who learns of the plot and kills Krymov. Bananan is a romantic hero, who triumphs, even if in death. The film's finale consists of a concert by Viktor Tsoi that takes place against all rules and regulations. The concluding song 'Ia khochu peremen' ('I Want Change') expressed the dissatisfaction with a world where happiness is possible only through escaping into a dream world. *ASSA* heavily influenced the first and most important film of the 1980s, made by one of Solov'ev's Kazakh students: Rashid Nugmanov's *Igla* (*The Needle*, 1988), starring Viktor Tsoi in the main part.

The Needle is clearly influenced by a number of Solov'ev typical devices, such as the fragmentation of the narrative into episodes through the use of intertitles, mostly to indicate the passing of time ('next morning', 'that evening', 'two weeks later'); the use of non-professional actors (rock stars Petr Mamonov (b. 1951) and Viktor Tsoi, and the director Aleksandr Bashirov (b. 1955) play the three male leads); the emphasis on rock music in underground culture and the preoccupation with the young generation. However, Nugmanov's film also significantly departs from the master's devices and interest; indeed, it goes much further in a number of ways that touch upon the Eurasian theme. *The Needle* was also one of the first films to openly address the issue of drugs.

The script was created by Bakhyt Kilibaev and Aleksandr Baranov, who both made important contributions to Kazakh cinema and to Russian culture in the 1990s: Baranov went on to make his own films, while Kilibaev became a famous clip-maker in Moscow, who invented the figure of Lenia Golubkov of the advertising spots for the pyramid scheme MMM in the early 1990s.

The Needle begins in Moscow and ends in Almaty. The hero Moro (Tsoi) returns to his home town in order to collect debts from Spartak (Bashirov). On the occasion of his visit he also calls in on his former girlfriend (or school friend), the nurse Dina; he finds that she is on drugs. He tries to get her clean, taking her to a deserted settlement by the dried-up Aral Sea. When Moro discovers that Dina's boss, the doctor Arthur (Mamonov), not only got her addicted but also deals with morphine and will therefore not leave Dina in peace, he prepares to leave with her. Realising the threat that Moro poses to his drug-dealing through Dina, Arthur stabs Moro on a wintry and dark path. However, heroes never die: Moro rises again to walk down the snow-covered road with his blood leaving red dots on the white snow to the tune 'Gruppa krovi' ('Blood Type'). Positive moral values and abstinence from drugs as represented by Moro are perpetuated as he continues to live – but only in a world of dream and escape. In reality, it is the drug-dealing doctor who has triumphed. Nugmanov has no illusions about reality, but instils such illusions in his viewers. In this sense he follows Solov'ev's solution offered in *ASSA*, where rock music represents a salvation from a reality that has no room for honesty and change.

Moro is a hero and a superman, who does the right thing without preaching or moralising. He almost sniffs out Spartak, although the latter tries to hide. He senses intuitively that Dina is on drugs and knows immediately that she hides them in the fireplace. He observes his surroundings carefully and acts accordingly. Moro is a fighter who can easily beat up the baddies (even if the fights are not shown on screen), who protects the feeble and weak Spartak when he is threatened in the club, and who does not prescribe his way of life. He lives not by words, but by deeds; he only claims what belongs to him – no more, no less. He beats up the guys in the club not because he sees impending danger for himself, but for Spartak; and he destroys the morphine ampoules only after Dina is through her withdrawal symptoms. Most important, though, Moro is never afraid: he is a rebel hero who has nothing to hide and nothing to fear. In a certain sense he is a predecessor of Danila Bagrov, the killer-hero of Aleksei Balabanov's *Brat* (*Brother*, 1997), with the difference that Danila is not just ready to engage in brawls, but actually does so. And as in the case of Bagrov, we know nothing about Moro: neither who he is nor what he does for a living, nor what debts he is collecting from Spartak. Similar to Sergei Bodrov Jr in *Brother*, who seems to walk straight from his part as Vania Zhilin in *Kavkazskii plennik* (*The Prisoner of the Mountains*, 1996) into the role of the killer, Tsoi marches, as it were, from the screen world of the concert in *ASSA* into the role of the rebel Moro. Moro is committed to action rather than words, and this feature made him a cult hero. Tsoi became an icon of a whole generation of Soviet rock fans. Unlike the bands Nautilus Pompilius or Aquarium, Tsoi translated the messages of his songs into action, albeit fictional; he added another dimension to the verbal and acoustic rebellions staged by underground rock groups.

Indeed, music is rather unobtrusive in *The Needle* and Kino's songs are used sparingly. Instead, Nugmanov and Tsoi chose a selection of tunes from Soviet and international classical music as well as pop and rock, ranging from Prokof'ev's piece about the warfare between the Capulets and Montagues from *Romeo and Juliet* for the first scene between Spartak and Moro, underscoring gently the conflict between them, through to an Italian love song in the café, and to Soviet Estrada music by Muslim Magomaev (b. 1942) for the scenes when Spartak's buddies linger around in the park. Kino's songs are only deployed in the beginning and the end of the film, underlining the scenes when Moro moves towards the camera in a small Moscow alleyway, and away from the camera in the snow-ridden path at the end of the film. These tunes both deal thematically with the young generation of rebels (rebels against the system, or the establishment): 'Zvezda po imeni solntse' ('A Star by the Name of Sun') tells about the world that is at war and the young warriors who rebel without worrying about their own lives; and 'Gruppa krovi' ('Blood group') that wishes these rebels luck in their fight as they follow a higher call. Both songs reflect the idealism of the 1980s and the need for change (albeit more clearly voiced in the final song of *ASSA*), which could be expressed in the *perestroika* era. From the perspective of the post-Soviet era, this need for change and the rebelliousness of that time have only historical value as they have been superseded and overtaken by such radical and extraordinary change that neither Nugmanov nor Tsoi could have imagined at the time of making *The Needle*.

While the music is used to express the underlying attitude of the hero Moro, words express very little. Indeed, Moro asks only a few questions, there are few dialogues; it appears that gestures and acts say much more. Dina has hardly any text at all; she speaks through the key ring that plays some Hollywood movie tune, and it is the failure to return the key that makes Moro return, as though he had been called by Dina. When he drops the key he lets go of (rather than abandons) Dina before his death. She only speaks when she has injected morphine and her voice is distorted; she mentions how she met Arthur and how he helped her, how she saw an empty aquarium with dead fish, and how she moved the sculptures after her father's death. Similarly, Moro defines his views most powerfully to the conductor on the train who tries to reason with him and make him return to the carriage by showing her his middle finger. With one gesture Moro is able to say more than Spartak, who uses language abundantly, but not purposefully. Words cannot express his ideas; or else, his ideas become manifestly void of content and meaning when he tries to express them. Spartak composes excuses that he (and Moro) know very well only thinly disguise the fact that he has no money; he has waited for Moro, he has no money right now, he has a face to lose before his friends.

If Moro is a hero and a superman, then Spartak is his counterpart; an anti-hero, incapable of any meaningful action or expression. But there is also a third party in Nugmanov's composition: the doctor, Arthur, with a foreign (German) name that highlights the influence and importance of German culture for Almaty; the city is not only occupied by Soviet culture, but also by other civilisations. The question of national identity stands therefore very clearly as the backdrop of this film.

The Needle is an anti-Soviet film: not obviously, but very subtly it criticises the influence of Soviet culture, especially the mass media. The Soviet centre (Moscow) had controlled all media, such as television and radio, across the USSR. Even the time was indicated everywhere as 'Moscow time', not local time. Nugmanov makes constant reference to the omnipresence of radio and television as a means of indoctrinating people. The radio plays at the beginning, telling the story of a man who went to the station to catch a train; this is what Moro does. In Almaty, he is accompanied by the local radio presenter's voice talking about the use of tenses; time has passed since Spartak borrowed money from Moro. Then the radio announces a young man (Moro meets Spartak), before a young girl is introduced by the presenter (Moro visits Dina). Moro seems to follows the instructions from the radio like prompts for his behaviour. Dina's flat is populated with technical gadgets that are mostly dysfunctional: Moro should not to answer the phone; the television reception is distorted; another television set does not work at all; the old-fashioned record player plays jazzy music of the 1960s. Instead, the action movie on television involving a helicopter turns into a vision of Moro and Dina in the desert; it is an anticipation of their trip, not a recollection of the past. Moro takes his prompt from television, which speaks for the central (Soviet) authority. When Dina returns to the flat, the tune of the Soviet news programme 'Vremia' can be heard, while the radio plays German folk music (the German service of Radio Alma Ata, catering for the large German community that was moved there during the Stalin era from southern Russia where they settled in the eighteenth century). Later, the German folk music stems from a television programme that shows a dance performance in black-and-white; or, on another occasion, Dina is glued to the screen for a children's serial. When Moro finds Arthur in the swimming pool at the hospital and pulls the plug, leaving Arthur in the empty pool, the scene is accompanied by an Italian-language radio programme, repeating the phrases 'Buongiorno, Signore, pantalone' – a prompt for Moro to give Arthur his clothes. All these media devices are false friends; they prompt people's action, making them puppets that act for an anonymous instructor, for an invisible force. It is against this background that the film's dedication to 'Soviet television' has to be set; television is no positive information resource, but as a means through which people are indoctrinated and that deprives them of the ability to think and act independently.

The character of Spartak fits into this theme of the disillusionment with Soviet achievements: Spartak belongs to a lost generation. His buddies follow him around, but he is worried about losing face, knowing well that the time for his ideas and his views is over. Moro defines Spartak's status in Soviet society well during their first meeting; he says: 'There are two categories of people in the world, some who sit on pipes and some who need money.' He talks literally about the money he has come to collect while Spartak is hiding some pipes in the basement of a building where he works as caretaker (another reference to his belonging to the late Soviet underground, 'the generation of caretakers and janitors' that figures in the title of a song by Aquarium, describing the phenomenon of underground artists who would take up jobs as caretakers in order to fulfil the formal Soviet requirement of being employed in a 'proper' job). But figuratively Moro speaks here of some people who (like Spartak) are indebted to the past, while others (like Moro) move forward. Spartak is fighting an ideology of the past and lives in the world of the Soviet 1960s, debating the question of existence.

Spartak's outmoded philosophical concerns are also echoed in his speech delivered in the derelict zoo, when he grotesquely assumes the posture of Lenin, standing on a wooden box; parodying Lenin's revolutionary speeches, Spartak appeals to an (imaginary) crowd to follow him, because as a collective they will be stronger than being alone. He continues with a disjointed and garbled text on independence, on moving forward or backward, finally dismissing the crowd. He has lost the plot and thus echoes precisely the sense of loss and confusion that began in the *perestroika* period. Spartak is a representative of those who opposed, once upon a time, Soviet ideals; his opposition to a system failed miserably and his speeches are lost in a jungle (the empty zoo with its cages as a visual reminder) of sounds (literally reduced to animal noises).

The measuring device of the clock plays another crucial role in the film: a digital clock is shown on a number of occasions to indicate the exact time: it is 12 noon at the beginning of the film; then the times 01.00, 11.15, 15.00 and 16.30 divide up Moro's first day in Almaty. The second day passes with no reference to time until the meeting with Spartak, set for 19.37 in the evening: Moro checks the time at 19.36 and is magically transposed to the meeting place within sixty seconds. This is followed by Moro's departure on the night train at 00.03, before he realises that he forgot to return Dina's keys. Moro has spent two days in Almaty before he takes Dina to the Aral Sea, where they spent two weeks without any clocks, radios or televisions. The clock re-appears when they return to Almaty at 09.09. On that day Moro is deceived by the doctor who collects the morphine and fails to pass it on to his dealer, and by Spartak who still has no money. At 18.04 Arthur's people beat him up. Having refused to collaborate with Arthur, Moro is stabbed in the park at 22.54. It is, strangely, the third day in Almaty when Moro dies (at least according to digital time, although the scenes in the city span from summer to winter): the third day is also that of his (and Christ's) resurrection, when he rises and wanders off after having been fatally wounded.

Moro is a silent hero, a sacrificial lamb, a Christ-like figure who completes his mission. He defends basic human values, while all those aspects that have to do with civilisation are rejected outright as negative. Salvation lies in the barrenness and simplicity of the desert and in the rural lifestyle; here Moro can get Dina clean from the drugs.

Neither Dina nor Moro have any roots or any relatives. Dina's father is dead, her dacha is sold. Moro lies to his family about his trip to Almaty, pretending he never left Moscow. Moro lives in Moscow and invites Dina to leave with him. Almaty offers no future for either Dina or Moro; it is a city corrupted by Soviet and other influences, by civilisation that destroyed the national identity of the native people – although neither of the actors (Tsoi and Smirnova) belong to that nationality. Only the doctor – who should save people and not kill them – survives in the city. In fact, the opposition here is less between European/Russian and Kazakh lifestyle, but between rural and urban ways of life, between civilisation and nature. Urban civilisation may mean progress, but purity lies in a return to roots. This gives the film a more universal than anti-Soviet dimension, and it also explains the beauty with which the barren land near the Aral Sea is captured in the camera (by director of photography Murat Nugmanov), with bright blue skies and glittering, white sand. Yet even here, the Soviet presence is never missing: there is always a helicopter or an aircraft in the skies, or a track laid through the desert, reminding of Soviet territorial conquests – a theme that would be fully developed in Serik Aprymov's *Tri brata* (*Three Brothers*, 1998).

Issues of space are, therefore, crucial to an understanding of the film. Nugmanov's film revealed the barrenness of the land following the Soviet irrigation plans that led to the drying-up of the Aral Sea. He uses the absence of water (a force of life) as a leitmotif for the film and as a symbol for the absence of the force of life, of a future. If there is a future at all, it lies on the snow-covered road that leads to the land of illusions and dreams on which Moro dies. The lack of water is referred to when Dina mentions a dry aquarium with dead fish; later she wants to swim and runs towards the water – only to find the dried sea. Moro tries to incapacitate Arthur by literally drying him up as he swims in a little pool filled with water. Indeed, Arthur enjoys the privilege of using the greenhouse in the hospital precinct – a space artificially supplied with enough water to keep the plants alive.

On the other hand, all these 'dried up' or derelict spaces anticipate the abandonment of the urban architecture after the collapse of the Soviet Union and before the republics were in a (financial) position to manage their cityscapes: the empty zoo, depopulated of animals in preparation for the winter, anticipating the closure of so many zoos in the early 1990s; the dry fountains and streams by the side of streets in Almaty, as the city gets ready for the winter (which anticipate the dysfunctional fountains in the late 1990s when the capital moved to Astana and water supplies were temporarily cut); the empty pool that forebodes the empty swimming pool 'Moskva' before its demolition to make way for the reconstruction of the Cathedral of Christ the Saviour.

As the themes of the film reflect the loss of values and the impending collapse of an entire ideological reference system with an extraordinary acuteness, the film's visual language is no less innovative, such as the use of intertitles, following Solovi'ev's practice, or the use of graphics for the fight (sparks rather than real fists). The spaces in the inner city are consist-ently bleak and void of light as much as water, while the sun permeates the sky in the Aral Sea sequences.

The Needle summarises some important concerns of the Kazakh New Wave and the films that were to follow. First, the concern with the dream world, placing imagination over reality; second, the superiority of Kazakh tradition over the Soviet-style city life; third, the corruption of modern life, leading to the destruction of positive values. Nugmanov thus questions the concept of national identity and points to the conflict between Kazakh tradi-tion and 'Soviet-style' progress. He anticipates not only change in the Soviet value system, but more importantly foresees the concerns of a new, national, Kazakh cinema.

Birgit Beumers

REFERENCE

Abikeeva, G. (2001) *Kino Tsentral'noi Azii 1990–2001*. Almaty: IREX.

KAVKAZSKII PLENNIK THE PRISONER OF THE MOUNTAINS

SERGEI BODROV, RUSSIA, 1996

Kavkazskii plennik (*The Prisoner of the Mountains*, 1996) is one of the first (and, sadly, one of the few) films of the post-Soviet era to attempt an honest and critical re-evaluation of Russia's imperial legacy, in both its pre-Revolutionary and Soviet variants. Winner of the Director's Award at the 1996 Cannes Film Festival, and the Best Film Award at the Sochi Festival in the same year, it is based on a Lev Tolstoi story of the same name, which centres on a fictional episode in the nineteenth-century Russian imperial campaign in the Caucasus. Indeed, the motif of the Russian prisoner captured by 'exotically barbaric' Caucasian tribesmen is a potent myth in classical Russian literature with both Pushkin and Lermontov providing their own variants, to which Tolstoi's story, the popular 1960s film comedy by Leonid Gaidai *Kavkazskaia plennitsa* (*Kidnapping Causcasian Style*, aka *Prisoner of the Caucasus*, 1964) and Bodrov's film of 1996 (the title translates literally as 'Prisoner of the Caucasus', not 'Prisoner of the Mountains', as it was released in the West) can be considered responses. The film was directed by Sergei Bodrov who, along with writer Arif Aliev (a Muslim, familiar with local Caucasian customs) and producer Boris Giller, wrote the screenplay. Bodrov was an established director responsible for films from the Soviet era including *Neprofessionaly* (*Non-Professionals*, 1985) and *SER: Svoboda eto rai* (*SER: Freedon is Paradise*, 1989). Following *The Prisoner of the Mountains*, Sergei Bodrov Sr (b. 1948) went on to direct a number of foreign-financed films such as *The Quickie* (2001) and *The Bear's Kiss* (2002); he also contributed to the scenario for Regis Wargnier's Russian-French co-production *Est-Ouest* (*East-West*, 1999), and in 2005 embarked on a major co-production entitled *The Mongol*.

The Prisoner of the Mountains featured an early lead role for Bodrov's son, Sergei Bodrov Jr (who was killed in an accident in 2002), along with the already famous Oleg Men'shikov (b. 1971) and Valentina Fedotova (b. 1960). It transposes the events of Tolstoi's tale to the latter-day Caucasus in which Russia is again waging a campaign of occupation. Although (and this, as I shall argue, is significant), the location is never specified, there can be little doubt of the intention to encourage the viewer into identifying the events with the bloody campaign in Chechnya launched in 1994.

Following Tolstoi's plot quite closely (but not precisely), the film tells of how a young, newly-recruited Private called Ivan, or Vania (played by Bodrov Jr), together with a more experienced and battle-seasoned NCO named Sasha (played by Men'shikov), is captured and held prisoner by the Caucasian tribesman, Abdul-Murat (played by the Georgian actor Djemal Sikharulidze), who wants to exchange them for his son, held by the Russians. Ankle-chained to each other, these two soldiers of very dissimilar background and life experience (Ivan, naïve, frightened and grieved for by a caring mother; Sasha, cynical, battle-hardened and with nobody in Russia concerned about his fate) gradually begin to establish a rapport, as the initially brusque and condescending Sasha begins to take Ivan under his wing.

Eventually, Sasha persuades Ivan to engineer an abortive escape aided by Abdul-Murat's young daughter (played by Susanna Mekhralieva) with whom Ivan has made friends. The escape begins with the murder of the mute jailer Hasan, whom they had befriended, and ends in Sasha's brutal death (after he has killed a shepherd in cold blood), followed by Ivan's recapture. Ivan is now held in a deep pit and, despite the visit of his mother (Fedotova) to the region to negotiate the release of both Ivan and the son of Abdul-Murat, whom she meets, events take a grim turn when the latter is shot by the Russians. Abdul-Murat decides on immediate revenge and leads Sasha out to the mountains to be shot. In a dramatic and unexpected finale, however, Ivan is released and eventually returns home to Russia with his mother.

Bodrov's film works on a number of levels. Most obviously (though also most problem-atically), it offers a critique of Russian imperial policy in the Caucasus over two centuries. This has been highlighted in previous writing on the film. Portraying the rugged beauty of the mountain terrain and the intricate traditions and rituals of the local inhabitants, which have not changed for centuries, Bodrov condemns the Russian military intervention as threat-ening an entire way of life. By basing his film on a Tolstoi story set in the nineteenth century, he establishes the continuity of Russian imperialism from the pre-revolutionary era through to the post-Soviet period. The dignified suffering of Abdul-Murat over his imprisoned son, the naïve, unprejudiced affection of his daughter for Ivan and, most importantly, Abdul-Murat's change of heart at the end of the film, establish the Caucasian tribesman as quintes-sentially human and different from the stereotypical myth of the 'cruel Chechen with the dagger between his teeth', a stance the film works against. Indeed, Julian Graffy praises the film's depiction of the Caucasian locale as 'a place of immemorial codes – about dress, about marriage, about deference to elders and, above all, about vengeance for wrongs suffered'.

But in its excessive use of local colour and its voyeuristic fascination with the 'quaint' customs and dress and impenetrable language of the local tribespeople (who are often filmed from the viewpoint of the Russian captives), *The Prisoner of the Mountains* can also be accused of indulging in an exoticised reification of its 'noble savage' subject matter typical of the imperialist mentality from which it ultimately fails to break free. As Owen Matthews argues: 'The depiction of Chechen fighters … is little more than a caricature, with clichéd "rebels" in national costume doing a high-kicking dance by a mountain waterfall, cutting off chunks of meat from a sheep roasting over a fire, swigging vodka and heartily slapping each other on the back.' Matthews further points out that this particular scene, like several others, suffers from an imperialistic attitude to ethnographic truths about life in the Caucasus; Chechen fighters are mostly teetotal Muslims. Moreover, by eschewing the need to specify the location of the action as latter-day Chechnya (the film was actually shot in neighbouring Daghestan on a budget of $1.5 million) in the interests of a humanistic protest against war and brutality in all its manifestations (whether it be that of the occupying force or that of the occupied people), the film also runs the risk of refusing to attribute blame and thus divesting the Russians of responsibility for the specific atrocities committed in Chechnya. As Bodrov points out, 'the film is set in Chechnya but it could just as easily be about Afghanistan, Bosnia, India or wherever. After all, politics gets old very quickly, like a newspaper, and it becomes unfashionable after a year. I want people to watch the film many years from now.' The comments raise the suspicion that Bodrov may ultimately have been more interested in his place in cinematic history than in forcing home an unpalatable political truth. As Matthews suggests, unlike Francis Ford Coppola (*Apocalypse Now*, 1979) and Oliver Stone (*Platoon*, 1986), Bodrov refrains from an uncompromising portrayal of the visceral brutalities of war in the Caucasus, representing the bloodshed by implication (helicopters heading in the direction of the tribal village at the end of the film) rather than directly (the mass slaughter of the tribes-people). Perhaps because of this, the film attracted a positive response from Boris Yeltsin who, following a private viewing, sent his security men back to the director with his congratulations.

However, as Bodrov points out, it is perhaps unfair to expect a mature, in-depth critique of an imperial mission that is still unfolding (in fact, he began filming *The Prisoner of the Mountains* before the outbreak of hostilities in Chechnya): 'I want to distance myself as far as possible from the theme of the current war. It is too soon to make a film specifically about this war. It took Americans ten years before they could make films about Vietnam. What saves me is that this story is centuries old. The story has been told before by Pushkin and

Tolstoi.' The Chechnya theme was, in a sense, superimposed on a film initially conceived as being about the generality of the perennial Russia/Caucasus relationship.

Further, the film's engagement with imperialism is more subtle and complex than our discussion or previous commentary on the film has allowed for, and certainly extends beyond a simplistic plea for an end to the brutality of war. In order for us to appreciate the nature of the engagement we need to examine the implicit and explicit references cited in the film.

The helicopter gunship scene at the end of *The Prisoner of the Mountains* is strikingly similar to sequences in Francis Ford Coppola's epic Vietnam-war movie, *Apocalypse Now* – also an adaptation of a nineteenth-century literary classic dealing with imperialism (Joseph Conrad's *Heart of Darkness*). The ambiguous tributes to, and attenuated dialogue with, *Apocalypse Now* indicate Bodrov's tentative exploration of what, for Russian cinema, is a new sub-genre of the war film: the post-war protest movie. The helicopter scene in Bodrov's film is accompanied by the sound of a Soviet-style military march. Thus, Russian imperialism is linked at once with both its Soviet and its tsarist predecessors, and with twentieth-century American imperialism, confounding those who would identify Bodrov either as an anti-Russian, US apologist, or an anti-Soviet, Russian nationalist, or a nostalgic advocate of the Soviet brotherhood of nations.

The Prisoner of the Mountains is as much a dialogue with the war film as it is with conceptions of imperialist warmongering. Key intertextual tropes from classic Soviet war films are also cited, such as that of the devoted mother's concern for the safe return of her soldier-son featured in *Ballada o soldate* (*Ballad of a Soldier*, 1959). But it is the references to Hollywood that best reveal the complexity of Bodrov's project. It is no accident, for example, that Sasha's nickname is 'Sly' – a reference to Sly (Sylvester) Stallone who played the lead role in the Rambo trilogy, which extolled American military heroism. By the early 1990s, Rambo had become a cult figure in Russia itself, and by portraying the character in negative fashion (Sasha is the epitome of gung-ho militarism and exhibits cynical disregard for the lives and views of his captors), Bodrov transforms his critique of Russian military imperialism into a simultaneous assault on American cultural imperialism, positing Russia as victim as well as aggressor. His film also functions as a meta-cinematic commentary on the war film genre to which it belongs.

But US internal cultural imperialism also forms part of the ideological nexus that Bodrov's film targets. It is far from coincidental that the soundtrack to *The Prisoner of the Mountains* includes the gospel song 'Let My People Go', sung in English by Louis Armstrong, whilst Ivan and Sania are in captivity. The song derives from the period of slavery and is itself an allegorical reference to the Old Testament story of Moses appealing to the Egyptians to set the Israelites free. Thus, the captivity of the Israelites, America's enslavement of its negro population, latter-day American adventurism in Vietnam and Russia's imperial mission in Chechnya is referenced through the song's appearance in the film.

The character of Sasha, and the Rambo reference he cites, bring to light a further feature of *The Prisoner of the Mountains*' ideological subtext: its linking of imperialism and ethnic intolerance with male machismo. Sasha is, in many ways, a pathetic, failed Rambo character. His bravado, the contempt he holds for his captors and his brutal slaughter of the shepherd prove to be a doom-laden strategy compared with Ivan's own strategy of befriending Abdul-Murat's daughter. Sasha's fearless machismo is portrayed in stark contrast with Ivan's more honest naiveté and fear in the early stages of his captivity and his later sympathy for the tribesman holding him prisoner. When he is required to participate in a wrestling bout with his captors (wrestling is a national tradition in the Caucasus), he emits a pathetic and terrified roar, eliciting raucous laughter from the tribesmen, whose destructive machismo is posited as the mirror image to that of Sasha and the Russian military, and equally to blame for the pointless violence of the conflict. The scene in which Ivan is paraded, naked and humiliated, along with other new soldiers in his first Russian army recruitment ritual, reveals Bodrov's awareness of the institutionalised nature of gender identity.

It is possible even to speak of a substratum of feminine values underlying *The Prisoner of the Mountains*. In his treatment of gender roles in the film, Joe Andrew argues that 'Bodrov is not so naïve as to suggest that a young woman of the Caucasus and a widowed mother will end decades of male violence, but his film does intimate that there is another way'. In many respects, this is a traditional form of femininity, as represented in Abdul-Murat's daughter's and Ivan's mother's active intercession for peace and understanding between the warring factions. But in the way in which Ivan functions as an alternative, feminised male counterpart to Sasha's destructive machismo it offers a potentially more subversive endorsement of feminist positions unusual for post-Soviet culture in any form. Ivan's handicraft skills, demonstrated when he makes a wooden bird for Abdul-Murat's daughter, are more closely associated with the realm of feminine pursuits than with the military world (in Tolstoi's original he makes her a doll – perhaps too feminine a pursuit even for Bodrov). And the decidedly non-sexual nature of Ivan's attitude to the young girl connotes feminine paradigms of friendship and cooperation rather than masculine models of sexual conquest.

The Prisoner of the Mountains is, then, a thoughtfully constructed film with a bold ideological subtext. It is also a highly effective piece of cinematography on all levels, from the breathtaking shots of the Caucasian mountain scenery with which it is punctuated, to its carefully edited musical soundtrack which combines, in addition to the military march and the negro spiritual, local Caucasian instrumental folk music, all to very deliberate effect. It is also notable for its high-quality acting. Men'shikov's characteristically robust masculine charm, edged with world-weary cynicism, is well suited to the role of Sasha, which he carries off with considerable aplomb. But the boldest and most interesting performance is that of Bodrov Jr as Vania. He plays the role in an understated, at times almost zombie-like, mono-tone for which he was criticised in some quarters but which proves peculiarly appropriate for the role of the young recruit traumatised by war and captivity and which Bodrov Jr managed to turn into a trademark.

Bodrov Jr's distinctive acting style was to find its apotheosis in Aleksei Balabanov's later films *Brat* (*Brother*, 1997) and *Brat 2* (*Brother 2*, 2000) in which his character – that of a Chechen-veteran-turned-gangster – forms an interesting intertextual counterpoint to his role in *The Prisoner of the Mountains*. In Balabanov's films, he is, at least on the surface, the embodiment of post-Soviet masculinity and, ironically, demonstrates this 'transformation' in the retribution he exacts upon the Chechen mafia running a Moscow market in the first film, thus playing to the very Russian chauvinistic nationalism that was the target of *The Prisoner of the Mountains*. But, just as this earlier film is no ordinary war movie, so the *Brother* films are themselves no ordinary gangster movies. Their tongue-in-cheek references to Soviet and Western popular cultural texts (the machine gun from the legendary 1934 *Chapaev* film is visually cited in *Brother 2*, for example), and the odd, yet calculatedly deadpan mannerisms and speech of Bodrov Jr place ironic quotation marks around the film's overt rhetoric of macho-nationalistic chauvinism. There is, after all, a meaningful link between Bodrov Jr's roles in *The Prisoner of the Mountains* and the *Brother* films. The continuity is extended if one takes into account the part of the sensitive, French-speaking swimmer, alienated by the harsh brutalities of life in Stalin's Russia played by Bodrov Jr in *East-West*.

Despite the seriousness of its intent, *The Prisoner of the Mountains* is not devoid of humour, usually played out at the expense of the Russian captives. The two prisoners per-forming a drunken dance on their captors' roof, after consuming a hidden supply of local wine, provide one such moment. Here, as elsewhere, there is an implied contrast with the noble dignity of the local tribesmen. Perhaps the most amusing and ideologically revealing event has to do with the shooting of the film, during which the head of the security team, who also played a rebel commander in the film, appeared one night to the crew and actors with a band of men armed with machine guns and threatened to take hostages unless he was paid more money. Bodrov took the event in his stride, later commenting 'It was unpleasant at the time, but we eventually bargained them down to a much more reasonable sum. It's a different century down there', as quoted by Owen Matthews. This anecdote, more than any twist, turn or contradiction in the fictional narrative itself, demonstrates the extreme difficulties involved in articulating an anti-imperialist message from a position inside imperialism.

Nonetheless, there is no doubting the power of Bodrov's film. Nowhere is this more evident than in the finale. The dénouement begins with a rapid sequence of scenes. First, Abdul-Murat's son is shot in the back trying to escape across the hills from the Russians, who have been stung into enacting the next stage in the endless spiral of revenge afflicting the region, after one of their officers is shot during an attempt to rescue the Chechen captives. Next, Ivan's mother is told to stop crying and assured by a Russian officer that her son's captors will be made to pay for their actions. Then, an ominously silent Abdul-Murat is shown returning home with his son's body, vengeance written all over his face. The swift montage juxtaposing the brutal action at the Russian army headquarters and subtle changes in the relationship between Ivan and the young girl in the village contrasts with the lingering takes leading up to the planned execution of Ivan, which simultaneously foster narrative suspense (building on fear for the fate of the Russian captive) and aesthetic wonderment at the silent beauty of the mountain landscape (invoking the romanticisation of the locale and its inhabitants).

Following news of her brother's death, Abdul-Murat's daughter seems to change her attitude to Ivan, adopting the hostility and condescension displayed by her fellow tribespeople. She approaches him in his pit and taunts him, telling him that he is to die the following day. When he pleads with her to bring him the key to his chains so that he might escape, she merely tells him that she will dig his grave and place her necklace in it as a wedding present, predicting that he will find a bride in heaven. The vague hints of incipient sexuality that have persisted in the relationship between Ivan and the girl, rise to the surface, mingled with the tones of ethnic mistrust from which it has hitherto been free. Thus, the links between gender, sexuality and ethnicity established through the treatment of Sasha's character are confirmed from a different angle. There then follows a series of three dramatic reversals that determine the outcome of the narrative.

First, in a change of heart, Abdul-Murat's daughter decides to help Ivan once again and brings him the key to his chains. Ivan swiftly frees himself and climbs out of the pit, encouraged by the girl to hurry. However, in a second reversal, he suddenly hesitates and decides that he cannot escape since it would place his friend in danger and she would never be forgiven. Abdul-Murat arrives back, seething with grief-filled rage, and approaches Ivan, shotgun in hand. He rejects his daughter's pleas not to kill Ivan, suggesting that she should be weeping for her brother not the Russian. As he marches Ivan out to the barren mountain landscape, to the sound of Caucasian folk music, a bloody and vengeful end to Ivan's life seems certain. As Ivan edges to his place of execution, we catch a brief glimpse of Abdul-Murat's daughter staring at him from a hut, with the wooden bird that Ivan made for her swinging pathetically from the ceiling – in a further indication that the reconciliation between Russian and Chechen is to come to nothing. Filmed from a distance, the lone figures of Abdul-Murat and Ivan now appear in relief against the backdrop of the savage, unforgiving beauty of the Caucasian mountains.

As the tension rises to a crescendo, Abdul-Murat halts and the camera closes in on Ivan's head, inviting the viewer to adopt the subjective position of the grief-stricken and vengeful father. The imminent death of Ivan, resembling the death of Abdul-Murat's son, provides a formal signal that the narrative is about to draw to its tragic, but inevitable close. As Abdul-Murat raises his gun to take aim, Bodrov films the remainder of the scene in slow-motion. These frozen moment express Abdul-Murat's hesitation, as he decides whether to carry out the cruel execution. These could be seen to mirror the viewer's own moral deliberation over the justification for the act of revenge. A shot rings out and echoes amongst the mountains. Even when we see Ivan still standing, we are not inclined to think that he has survived the execution. When the figure of Sasha strides across the screen in front of Ivan, asking him what the matter is and telling him to turn round, we assume either that Ivan has imagined his presence in the moment before death, or that he has now joined Sasha in the realm beyond death, adopting Sasha's cynical view of Caucasian barbarism. It is only when Ivan turns round to see Abdul-Murat walking slowly away back to his village, gun slung over shoulder, that we realise that the most dramatic reversal has taken place: Abdul-Murat has finally broken the cycle of revenge and shown pity on the people responsible for his son's bloody slaughter. Sasha's fleeting re-appearance and words of reassurance can be interpreted to mean that even he, were he alive, could not fail to be moved by such an act of self-sacrifice.

As Ivan makes his way across the mountains back to safety he hears the sound of Russian helicopter gunships making their way to the village from which he has escaped. He looks to the sky and begins waving to them, shouting 'I'm here!', but they fly onwards, apparently unaware of his presence. He gesticulates ever more frantically, now repeating 'No, don't'. The phrase is tinged with ambivalence in that it could mean both 'No, don't fly past and ignore me!' and (more likely in the context of the film's ideational structure) 'No, don't take revenge on the villagers!' In any event, his appeal is lost and the gunships fly on to the symbolically-laden sound of a Soviet-style military march, indicating that, though the cycle of revenge may have been broken on an individual level, it remains intact on the level of inter-ethnic rivalry.

Prisoner of the Mountains concludes with a series of nostalgic, sepia-toned photographic stills of Abdul-Murat, his daughter and Sasha. Speaking, word for word, the last lines of Tolstoi's original text, Ivan's voice-over recounts in matter-of-fact tones his return to Russia and his mother, but also reminds us that he will never again see the new friends he made in the Caucasus. Even the reconciliation of the filmic text with its classic literary original is ambiguous. The reassertion of the Russian literary tradition implies a commitment to the 'civilising' value of the imperial mission implicit, at least in part, in Tolstoi's view of Russia's incursion into the Caucasus. On the other hand it invokes the humanity of great Russian realist writers such as Tolstoi in support of its impassioned appeal against the conflict and mutual suspicion that imperial missions invariably bring in their wake.

Stephen Hutchings

REFERENCES

Andrew, J. (2005) '"I love you, dear captive": Gender and Narrative in Versions of *Prisoner of the Caucasus*', in S. Hutchings and A. Vernitski (eds) *Russian and Soviet Film Adaptations of Literature, 1900–2001: Screening the Word*. London: RoutledgeCurzon.

Graffy, J. (1998) 'Soldier, Soldier', *Sight and Sound*, 3, 34–5.

Matthews, O. (1996) '*Prisoner of the Caucasus*', *RUSSIAreview*, 15 July, 36.

von Busack, R. (1997) 'Pondering Prisoner: A Talk with Sergei Bodrov, Director of *Prisoner of the Mountains*', http://www.metroactive.com/papers/metro/02.06.97/prisoner-mtn-9706.htm (accessed 21 June 2004).

BRAT BROTHER

22

ALEKSEI BALABANOV, RUSSIA, 1997

Aleksei Balabanov's *Brat* (*Brother*, 1997) was, in a sense, the first genuine Russian block-buster. Released at a time when audiences had not yet returned to cinemas that were awaiting refurbishment, *Brother* was a 'blockbuster' on account of its video sales. Thus, it cannot be compared, in theatrical release figures, to later films such as Nikita Mikhalkov's *Sibirskii tsiriul'nik* (*The Barber of Siberia*, 1999), which grossed $2.6 million at the box office, but had cost $45 million to produce, or even to its sequel *Brat 2* (*Brother 2*), which was released on 11 May 2000 and, with a budget of $1.5 million, grossed $1.08 million in the CIS (Commonwealth of Independent States) territory alone.

At the time of *Brother*'s release, Russian critics were preoccupied with cinema's relation-ship between art and commerce, education and industry, and propaganda and business. In the eyes of many, cinema remained the most powerful means of expressing moral values and providing guidance, while some Russian directors and producers began to realise cinema's potential as a business that could, one day, make a profit. The dilemma of cinema appeared to lie in its place between the fetters of ideology and capital, and its dependence on an infra-structure in desperate need of repair or reconstruction. It was not until 2000 that multi-plexes opened in Moscow, and the distribution network expanded rapidly in the period that followed, making Russia's cinemas among the most modern and largest multiplexes in the world and putting the Russian distribution market into a key position for world sales.

It is important to bear this in mind, as well as the fact that Russian film production had reached an all-time low in the year preceding the release of *Brother*. Those films that did appear were concerned with crime and the bleakness of Russian life in the Yeltsin era. Filmmakers who had provided moral guidance amidst the corruption of the Soviet system found themselves in a difficult position: should filmmakers be expected to show a cleansed version of the surrounding world and create ideals for the people to believe in? Or should they openly portray the bleakness and despair of a generation whose (Soviet) ideals had been pulled away from under their feet? It may not have been pleasant or entertaining to watch Russian films of the late 1990s that refused to create a 'positive hero' and instead showed a gruesome and blackened reality (*chernukha*), but the use of cinema for the projection of a national identity in the spirit of Socialist Realist principles (*lakirovka*, or the varnishing of reality) was then, and remains today, extremely problematic.

Balabanov's film has to be placed into this context in order to fully comprehend the significance *Brother* had for the development of the national film industry on the one hand, and for the concept of the 'Russian hero' on the other.

Brother and *Brother 2* playfully engage with the action movie genre. The plot of *Brother* concerns a killer with a good heart who reinstates justice and fights evil. The cast features largely unknown or non-professional actors (with the sole exception of Viktor Sukhorukov (b. 1951)). Danila Bagrov (Sergei Bodrov Jr) returns to his provincial hometown from army service. When he gets into trouble with the police, his mother sends him to visit his elder brother, Viktor (Sukhorukov), in St Petersburg. Viktor is a killer, who enlists Danila to shoot the 'Chechen' mafia boss, whom he has been paid to kill. Carrying out the assignment Danila realises that his brother has betrayed him, and that he is not killing a 'terrorist' who is a threat to Viktor and other people. While his own brother lets Danila down, an unknown tram driver, Sveta (Svetlana Pis'michenko), helps him. They subsequently have an affair, but Sveta stays with her husband, despite the fact that he beats her. Danila carries out his assignment: he kills the 'Chechen' and bails out his brother. Danila is a professional killer; more professional than his elder brother who had hitherto been a father-figure to him. It is this explanation that Danila uses when he tells Viktor why he is helping him and before he sends Viktor home 'to look after mum'. Whilst cold-bloodedly carrying out the killing of the Chechen and of some other mafia members who have set Viktor up, Danila is also a knight who helps the poor, suppressed and underprivileged. Having conquered the criminal world of St Petersburg, he leaves for Moscow at the end of the film; it is from his arrival in Moscow that the sequel picks up Danila's story.

Brother sets out a new type of hero, who upholds no moral standards. Unlike the soldier of the 1960s Soviet war movie, Danila is modelled on the Russian fairytale figure of Ivan-the-Fool, as Susan Larsen has convincingly argued. Danila is a dumb provincial boy where contemporary culture is concerned: he does not recognise famous people; he runs into a film location without realising it; and he has no idea where to purchase the CDs he wants. He is generally good-hearted and streetwise. He helps the poor: he defends an old man – Hoffman, the German – against a racketeer; he helps the conductor collect a fine from two Caucasian 'black arses' ('*gnida chernozhopaia*'– a phrase that has outraged Russian critics Daniil Dondurei and Viktor Matizen) travelling on a tram without a ticket; he shoots at his girlfriend Sveta's violent husband in an attempt to defend her. He is ruthless to his enemies and is a man of action: Danila possesses skill, strength and courage; he knows how to use guns, is physically fit to fight, and his actions display a sense of military logistics. A killer, he is also a romantic hero, a knight who keeps his word. Larsen has drawn attention to the parodic reference to the image of the knight in Vasnetsov's painting in Sveta's room, and the fact that Danila cannot quite live up to knighthood – because in the criminal world he is a killer. He combines within himself the contradictions at the heart of the Russian idea: the right to judge and the compassion to redeem. Danila has no role in society at large: a true killer, he is a loner, an individual acting without a reason. At the same time Balabanov also rejects the *chernukha* model, which perceives man as a victim of circumstance. The new Russian hero is no victim; instead he lives on the spur of the moment and acts according to the situation.

The title of the film parodies the concept of a 'brotherhood of people' (the collective spirit of the Soviet people). Real 'brotherhood' is further mocked when Viktor, the elder brother replacing the absent father, is protected by his younger brother: Danila saves Viktor from the Mafia bosses who hired him after Danila has successfully carried out the killing for which Viktor was paid. Yet 'brotherhood' here also means the criminal brotherhood (*bratva*) which is more clearly referred to in the sequel to *Brother*, both in the thematic concern with brothers of war and real brothers, but also in the fact that the title is a homophone of *bratva*: it is pronounced *brat-dva*. The criminal brotherhood to which Viktor belongs has superseded the relation to his real brother; later Danila abandons Viktor in Chicago and instead devotes himself to the defence of his 'brothers' of war, Il'ia and Kostia. The bond with those who share Danila's personal history is ultimately stronger than family ties. Moreover, the absence of fathers to protect any of the 'children of modern Russia' – be it Il'ia, Kostia or Danila – also hints at the collapse of the family as a functional unit in modern society and at the lack of a lineage, or linearity, instead emphasising the severed link to past and future (indeed, there are no children in the films, except for an oligarch son, who plays a purely functional part).

Danila has neither a perspective in life nor a past. If he does have a history, it is the fictional biography of Bodrov Jr's previous hero, the soldier of the Chechen war, Vania Zhilin of Bodrov Sr's *The Prisoner of the Mountains*. At the beginning of *Brother* Danila claims that he spent his army service as a scribe in some office. It soon becomes clear that this is a lie: he has very good knowledge of firearms and his manoeuvres are carefully planned. It is much more likely that Danila has served in Chechnya (as is confirmed in *Brother 2*). Danila is a young man hardened to the realities of life by his experience of war. Indeed, his personality and background are like a blank page onto which any story could be written. This is reflected in the technique of black-outs after each episode which fragment the film and allow it to be reassembled in any order. Danila is deprived of any psychological depth, and the choice of a non-professional actor reflects Balabanov's need for a façade rather than a character.

Brother begins when Danila accidentally walks into the location of a clip for the rock group Nautilus Pompilius's latest album 'Kryl'ia' ('Wings'). This song describes the absence of wings, the lack of a means that would allow man not only to move, but to float above the world.

> Some time ago we used to have time, now we have things to do:
> To prove that the strong gobble up the weak, to prove that soot is white.
> We have all lost something in this senseless war,
> By the way: where are your wings which I liked so much?

The song deals with the lost dreams of a generation that lived through the Soviet era, dreaming of freedom. Now that they are free from ideological fetters, they are busy doing things that are no longer important (or as important as fighting for ideals of freedom). The romantic dreams of the underground dissident were so much more attractive than the real world, preoccupied with insignificant trivial banalities, that the wings which allowed them to fly (in their dreams) are no longer there; there is a hint at the absence of a future, of a dream to live for. The song is about disillusionment, a theme that Danila identifies with: he searches for an ideal, and all he finds are the traces of where such ideals may have been in the past. It is for this reason that he searches for the musical icons that belong not to his generation and not to his time.

Later, Danila literally marches into lead singer Viacheslav Butusov's flat; he seeks to identify with this group of people, yet fails to realise that this is a different world from his own. In both the scene of the clip and the visit to Butusov's flat, Danila crashes back to reality – at the police station, bruised and beaten, and to the murder scene in the empty flat. Nautilus's music functions as a leitmotif for Danila's journey to St Petersburg. The band is originally from Sverdlovsk (now Ekaterinburg), but moved to St Petersburg in the early 1990s; Danila too comes from provincial Russia to St Petersburg where he finally acquires a compact disc of 'Wings'. Danila plays Nautilus most of the time on his CD player. He lives in the world of the music and only partly understands the reality that surrounds him. The songs endow the film with a dream-like quality. Bagrov's movements are paced by the rhythm of the music, and thus appear as though they were performed under a spell or under the influence of drugs, but not by an individual who reflects upon the world that surrounds him. Nautilus's songs are about another world, about day-dreams, and about the crippling effect of reality; the wings that enable man to fly have been lost and all that remains are scars. Most curious is another fact: the entire soundtrack of the film is from the albums 'Atlantida' and 'Yablokitai', which, in fact, are the two albums Danila fails to acquire in the music shops. In other words, the film's spectators hear the music that Danila wishes to hear, but has actually not yet managed to acquire. The hero lives in the sound system of another world, in which he is immortal: the CD player literally saves his life when it deflects a bullet.

Brother is set in contemporary St Petersburg, a setting that features in most of Balabanov's films, and employing his favourite locations: streets, courtyards, trams, bridges and cemeteries. Danila's arrival on a train is reminiscent of Balabanov's short film 'Trofim' for *Pribytie poezda* (*Arrival of a Train*, 1996). After leaving the station Danila strolls around the city, looking at the sights: the streets, the canals, the monument of the 'Bronze Horseman', the rostrums and St Isaac's Cathedral. Again, Balabanov's (or rather Sergei Astakhov's) camera never rises above eye-level, so the viewer never sees the city's roofs or spires. Balabanov's St Petersburg is a place that lacks perspective, for both the viewer and protagonist.

The 'German', Hoffman, takes Danila to his home; the Lutheran cemetery is Hoffman's 'rodina', the place where his ancestors rest. The German work force that was drawn to St Petersburg during the reign of Peter the Great and Catherine the Great is no longer needed in the modern city; these great-great-grandchildren of German origin are orphaned, isolated, lonely and deprived of social status. It is for these uprooted people that Bagrov feels compassion, while he would not think well of Jews and certainly not of Caucasian nationals. Viktor's claim that he wants to put the street trade under Russian control is fine with Danila: he is happy to get rid of the 'Chechen', but he is quite protective of the 'German'. Danila listens attentively to Hoffman's deliberations about the city that is a 'huge force' and takes energy away from the weak (like himself), but strengthens those who are strong (like Danila).

The centre of St Petersburg is depicted as a bustling shopping centre with McDonalds, Littlewoods and other Western shops, as well as clubs. The street markets are controlled by the mafia and form a sharp contrast to the Western shopping centres. These central areas of the city are juxtaposed to the Primorskaia district with its 1970s blocks of flats on the Baltic shore. It is here that Danila rents an apartment; that the murder of a number of 'gangsters' takes place; that Danila meets Butusov; and that he himself is shot at. Numerous monuments make St Petersburg attractive for the tourist, but the city appears as an alien place to its inhabitants. The cemetery and the Primorskaia flat are the spaces that are paradoxically filled with life, but both are spaces on the outskirts of the centre. Correspondingly, Viktor's flat in the centre is a place where people die, Svetlana's centre flat is a place of violence and racketeering, and the flat where Danila rents a room to hide and prepare for the killing is inhabited by a drunkard. Life is not in the centre, but on the periphery; it is not in the apartments but on the cemetery, while it is in living spaces that people get shot.

The tram features as a means of transport when Danila collects a fine from the two Caucasians: the tram is occupied by 'illegal' users. Another tram, not an ordinary one, but an empty car which serves only to check the tracks, res-cues Danila when he is on the run after having been shot in the stomach. The tram is driven by Sveta, who first rescues and later protects Danila. Before his departure from St Petersburg Danila catches a final glimpse of the Neva bridges and watches a tram run across the bridge, offering a frame for the view on St Petersburg and St Isaac's Cathedral. This is his farewell to the city, and the end of his love affair with the tram driver. Trams run through the city with no apparent function or destination; they seem to run because the tracks are there. They provide an aperture, a window on to the city's skyline, making it an object for the viewer's gaze rather than a living organic conglomerate.

The figure of Hoffman serves as a moral testing ground for Danila. Hoffman refuses Danila's 'dirty' money, relying on his own earnings which he makes, significantly, by selling old watches – a reference to a measuring device for time which is otherwise absent in the film. Balabanov neither condemns nor rejects the amoral conduct of his protagonist, but merely shows a new type of man: a hero who sets no standards. In this consisted the main opposition to the mainstream of Russian cinema, and this characteristic made Bagrov/Bodrov a cult figure.

Brother 2 develops further the theme of brotherhood, both criminal and social. The sequel takes Danila to Moscow, where his 'brother' from the Chechen war, Kostia, is killed when he tries to help his twin brother, a hockey player in the NHL who is being exploited by the American mafia boss Mennis. Issues of national pride pervade the film more obtrusively than in the first part: the theme of fraternity resounds in the slogans 'save our brothers' and 'we don't desert ours'. Danila and Viktor (who now works for the police in his home town

– an ironic reference to the recruitment of the Russian police force) travel to Chicago to bail out Kostia's brother Mitia. On the way, Danila also 'saves' the Russian prostitute Dasha-Marilyn, makes friends with the American truck-driver Ben, sleeps with the black television presenter Lisa Jeffrey, and recovers the money from Mennis. He may behave like a superman, but his agenda plays out like a fairytale; he reaches his aim by doing a few 'good deeds' on the way rather than by stubbornly following a plan. Danila has an innate understanding of social justice and is always ready to do a good deed; he never acts to enrich himself, but to help others, be it Dasha or Mitia. All of Danila's actions serve to punish the exploiters and reha-bilitate the exploited, asserting right over wrong, and by extension Russia over America.

While Viktor holds forth about Ukrainians and 'niggers', using the same abusive language that Danila had used for the Caucasians, or beats up a Polish-speaking cop, Danila encounters nice Americans, such as Ben Johnson, Lisa Jeffrey, the New York taxi driver and the Chicago policeman. On the other hand, the Russian émigrés rip him off (the car salesman in Brooklyn). If for Viktor power lies in money, representing the American ideal, then for Danila power lies in the truth, representing the Russian ideal. They may be brothers, but they have entirely different views; therefore Viktor stays in the US while Danila returns to Russia, rejecting the power of money.

Danila's actions also reveal the falsity of the television image: the pop singer Irina Saltykova (playing herself) is a star on the screen and casts herself as a diva, but she falls for Danila because he is not her fan. Television presenter Lisa Jeffrey is concerned with her media image, trying not to attract unnecessary attention after the accident, but she worries about her victim and takes him home. The television interview with Kostia, Il'ia and Danila portrays the three as having enjoyed themselves in the war, which is far from the truth. Television and mass media create lies and varnish reality.

Mostly, Danila does not behave like a real person: he fires his gun in the club as though he is playing a game; he injures the gun dealer in a way that is unnatural and looks staged; and he overwhelms Mennis purely with his verbal skills. For Danila, shooting is like a computer game, where the enemy lurks around every corner and behind each door. Danila is playing a virtual game with a real gun. In this sense, Balabanov is taking a critical view of the American culture of video and computer games that encourage violence.

Danila lives in a world of music in the first film, and in a world of media in the sequel; both are artificial and opposed to the real world. The Nautilus songs provided Danila's action with a dreamlike quality: in *Brother* the dream of a better life expressed in the songs inspires

Danila to his actions. In *Brother 2* it transpires that Danila has no grip at all on the real world: in the same way as he once stargazed at Butusov, he now does not know who Saltykova is, how to find Kotelnicheskaia Embankment, or what the function of roaming is. His brother Viktor is made out to be an idiot: he comments on Filipp Kirkorov's Romanian background (he is Bulgarian); he beats up a Chicago policeman; he gets drunk with prostitutes; and he takes revenge on the Ukrainian mafia 'for Sevastopol' (the main port of the Soviet Black Sea Fleet that was returned to Ukraine after the collapse of the Soviet empire). The Bagrovs are sons of a common criminal who venture into the great criminal world. If Viktor is a freak, Danila is a baby-face hardened by the war. Danila overcomes the new Russians who have become wealthy by cheating on the common people: he shows loyalty to his brothers, to his family, to his people. He avenges and rescues Russians from capitalism. Danila Bagrov of *Brother 2* remains naïve and good hearted: when Mitia, having previously denied Danila money and shelter, asks about the interest on the sum that Bagrov has retrieved from Mennis, Danila tries to see in him Kostia's spit image and twin brother rather than the cold-hearted and calculating hockey player.

Many critics have accused Balabanov of nationalism, especially citing the comments on 'black arses' and 'niggers'. While Balabanov undisputedly promotes a Russian way of life, Americans and Russians are not schematised: they include both good and bad characters. Rather, public and private images of characters are split: there are stars and those who are not. Playing Bagrov in *Brother 2*, Bodrov Jr left his own stardom and cult status aside (which he had gained through *Brother* and several television shows that he presented) to play the simpleton, the naïve boy, the fool, who is content and has no aspirations to stardom: 'I am both sky and moon to myself' ('ia sam sebe i nebo i luna'). Danila demythologises the world of stars: all people are the same, and stars are just people who want attention and love (like Jeffrey and Saltykova). When he associates himself with the media stars, Danila ascertains that he is just like them: a façade, an actor.

While *Brother 2* draws on a range of contemporary Russian music, it is not the music (as in *Brother*) that refers to the fact that the hero is living in a virtual world, but the references to space and location. Is Danila really a killer or is he just playing a game? Is he in Russia, as he claims on his mobile phone. He says to Saltykova that he is in Tula when he arrives in New York; in Biriulevo when he roams the streets of Chicago; and 'running' just before he gets to the airport. Eventually he says he will book a table at the Metropol for dinner when he boards the return flight to Moscow. Igor' Mantsov has pointed out that in Soviet cultural discourse Moscow has been the centre of the world. Balabanov reasserts Moscow as the centre of the universe (a view that dominated the geopolitical ideas of the 1920s) and resurrects the concept of Moscow not as the centre of socialist ideology, but of a practical and humanist socialism which redistributes wealth and fights crime. Balabanov is, I would argue, not a nationalist and Russophile, but a political left-winger. His hero Bagrov re-establishes social order and redistributes wealth: he is a modern Raskolnikov, with one difference: he does not act out of a need to prove himself a superman. Yet whether he carries out his acts in his mind or in reality remains unresolved. All the shootings are choreographed, paced and stylised to the soundtrack of the film, to the music that intoxicates Danila and makes him aspire to the ideals that feature on the songs. If in *Brother* he walked into the virtual reality of the film clip, then in *Brother 2* he moves comfortably in the media jungle, and with his leisurely, unassuming manner demythologises the pop icons and speaks his mind – without causing offence.

Brother created a new virtual hero who lives not in reality but in a world of games that allow him to create his own rules. Russian reality of the 1990s can indeed only be comprehended in this way: as a spoof, a game, a cartoon. It is the latter approach that Balabanov has adopted in *Zhmurki* (*Dead Man's Bluff*, 2005), in which he presents the criminal world of the 1990s as a flat and two-dimensional cardboard image. There is probably no better way to come to terms with a period of such chaos and paradox as the Yeltsin era had been for Russian society.

Birgit Beumers

REFERENCES

Dondurei, D. (1998) 'Ne brat ia tebe, gnida...', *Iskusstvo kino*, 2, 64–7.

Larsen, S. (2003) 'National Identity, Cultural Authority and the Post-Soviet Blockbuster: Nikita Mikhalkov and Aleksei Balabanov', *Slavic Review*, 62, 3, 491–511.

Mantsov, I. (2000) 'Zvezdy i soldaty', *Iskusstvo kino*, 11, 60–7.

Matizen, V. (1997) 'Skromnoe ochorovanie ubiitsy', *Seans*, 16, 41.

ALEKSANDR SOKUROV, 2002

Darkness. A voice complains that although his eyes are open he sees nothing. 'I only remember there was some sort of accident.' Suddenly a swirl of excited activity engulf us. Women in furs with elegant hairstyles and men in old-fashioned military uniform. 'Where am I? Judging by the clothes this must be the 1800s.' We pass through the entrance and join an excited crowd; voices lead us up narrow stairs, into a dark corridor, then into an interior courtyard. The new arrivals disappear ahead as we encounter a series of internal windows. A mysterious man in black appears, addressing us directly, wondering where *he* is and what century this is. He is sorry it is not the Chateau de Chambord during the Directoire. Meanwhile a drama seems to be in progress behind the windows: a middle-aged man impatiently dismisses a woman then berates an older man, pushing him roughly to the floor. The voice whispers, 'I think I've just seen Peter the Great.' A dialogue ensues about Peter's cruelty as well as his reforms and the Russian love of tyrants. We rejoin the original guests on another staircase, then lose them again as we discover a strange wooden machine, being worked by servants. Actors in historical costume are preparing to go on stage and there is an orchestra in court uniform. We are witnessing the end of a classical opera, with allegorical characters including the figure of Time. A middle-aged woman, standing at the front of an elegant balcony, pronounces the performance good to her companions, before running out with the explanation that she needs to piss. We move on to enter another highly decorated gallery, painted with reliefs in imitation of Raphael's Vatican Loggias, accompanied by a dialogue on the Russians' skill at copying.

So begins the extraordinary journey that is *Russkii kovcheg* (*Russian Ark*, 2002). The Russian actor Sergei Dreiden (Dontsov (b. 1941)) plays a character modelled on the Marquis de Custine, the French author of a popular traveller's account of Russia published in 1840. His unseen interlocutor is Aleksandr Sokurov, director of some 21 documentaries and 15 feature films. And the space we are exploring in their company is the complex of palaces and galleries in St Petersburg, now known collectively as the Hermitage. It was begun in the mid-eighteenth century by the empress Catherine II – whom we have just seen enjoying one of the fruits of European culture which she introduced to Russia – with the imperial Winter Palace as its centrepiece. Having survived Revolution and siege, the ensemble now houses a collection of over three million works of art drawn from all cultures and periods.

When *Russian Ark* burst upon the world at the Cannes Film Festival in 2002 it was hailed as unique, largely on the basis of its bold use of digital technology to achieve cinema's 'first' authentic 90-minute continuous tracking shot. Sokurov has frequently insisted that this should not be considered out of context, that it is merely the technique used to achieve an artistic goal. Yet it has continued to dominate thinking about the film, separating it from the rest of his work and indeed from other contexts, such as comparisons with other recent 'time travel' narratives such as Woody Allen's *Zelig* (1983), Sally Potter's *Orlando* (1992) and Robert Zemeckis's *Forrest Gump* (1994).

Sokurov's film can also usefully be related to earlier Russian contexts, including the 'foreign visitor' genre that lay dormant throughout much of the Soviet era after Lev Kuleshov's pioneering *Neobychainye prikliucheniia Mistera Vesta v strane bol'shevikov* (*The Extraordinary Adventures of Mr West in the Land of the Bolsheviks*, 1924), Aleksandr Macheret's *Dela i liudi* (*Men and Jobs*, 1932) and Vsevolod Pudovkin's *Dezertir* (*The Deserter*, 1933). Fifty years later, during the period of perestroika in the late 1980s, when Soviet cinema threw off its long-standing enforced sobriety and invoked a hectic vein of fantasy to deal with the taboos of the Stalinist past, a number of films showed the past erupting into the present, as in Tengiz Abuladze's *Monanieba* (*Pokaianie*, *Repentance*, 1986), or preserved as a kind of museum, as in Karen Shakhnazarov's *Gorod Zero* (*Zero City*, 1988).

A decade later, *Russian Ark* would appear at a moment when Russia's image in the world had shrunk from its prominence during the era of Gorbachev and Yeltsin to an impoverished repertoire of brutal border wars and rapacious neo-capitalism. In contrast to films reflecting these themes, it offers a vision of the continuity of Russian history and culture from the time of Peter the Great to the present, focused through the prism of St Petersburg and the Hermitage. And in doing so, it radically subverts the conventions of the 'heritage film' by making its viewers constantly aware of the artifice of historical representation, while grounding them in the physical fabric of the Hermitage as historical monument by means of an avant-garde formal procedure.

This description could well be applied to Sergei Eisenstein's account of the Bolshevik Revolution in *Oktiabr'* (*October*, 1927), also set largely in and around the Hermitage buildings, and many critics saw the 'unedited' *Russian Ark* as, effectively, a rejection of Eisensteinian montage, assuming this to be intrinsically a matter of rapid editing. But after the coming of sound, Eisenstein continued to revise and develop his conception of montage, applying it to literature, painting and architecture as well as cinema. By the 1940s, his conception of montage came to focus on the issue of how the means of depiction creates an artistic image; and his interest in continuous forms of representation led him to Chinese scroll painting and to the moving camera constantly reframing scenes in his last film, *Ivan Groznyi* (*Ivan the Terrible*, 1944–46). Sokurov's moving camera is also involved in continuously reframing the 'raw material' of the Hermitage galleries and his actors to create new juxtapositions *within the frame* and hence new meanings, in a thoroughly Eisensteinian manner.

Sokurov was born in 1951 and therefore belongs to a generation of Russians that was too young to experience the exhilaration of the cultural Thaw in the late 1950s, but had to endure the Brezhnev era's stagnation and the repression that followed in the early 1980s. Growing up as the child of an army family, stationed in Poland and Turkmenistan, he then took a correspondence course in history from Gorky University while working in television, before studying at the State Institute of Cinematography (VGIK), only to have his 1978 diploma film *Odinokii golos cheloveka* (*The Lonely Human Voice*, released 1987) banned along with most of his subsequent documentaries made at the Leningrad documentary studio.

Paradoxically, the banning of his early work may have insulated Sokurov from the culture of compromise and self-censorship that afflicted many Soviet-era filmmakers. When the Filmmakers' Union was encouraged by Gorbachev to spearhead the era of reform in 1986, one of its first actions was to announce that a handful of hitherto banned filmmakers, including Sokurov, would have their work publicly promoted. Two trends also emerged in his work at this time, which can be seen to point towards the future project of *Russian Ark*. For his third feature, Sokurov adapted George Bernard Shaw's play *Heartbreak House*, which the author subtitled a 'fantasia in the Russian manner on English themes', for a fantasia of his own, *Skorbnoe beschuvstvie* (*Anaesthesia Dolorosa*, released 1987). Shaw's play was written during World War One and mingled reflections on the causes of the war with a sense of apocalyptic foreboding. Sokurov would further enlarge the fantasy of Shaw's play, introducing both documentary and grotesque elements to create an absurdist multi-layered universe, which includes footage of Shaw, who becomes a quasi-fictional character, prefiguring the Marquis de Custine's role in *Russian Ark*. The other new trend in Sokurov's work began with a film called simply *Elegia* (*Elegy*, 1985), which celebrated the visit to Russia of Fedor Chaliapin's now elderly daughters. Using ultra-slow motion cinematography to give the daughters an almost ghost-like quality, intercut with newsreel and images of the 1920s when Chaliapin went into exile, Sokurov created the first of a series of highly personal 'elegies'. Apart from their recurrent theme of reflection on the past and on mortality, it is in these poetic films of widely differing length and form that Sokurov has developed his own voice – the same voice that accompanies us throughout *Russian Ark*.

His later feature films have taken different literary sources – the Strugatskii brothers' science fiction novella *Za milliard let do kontsa sveta* (*A Billion Years Before the End of the World* aka *Definitely Maybe*, 1976) for *Dni Zatmeniia* (*Days of Eclipse*, 1988) and Flaubert's *Madame Bovary* in the case of *Spasi i sokhrani* (*Save and Protect*, 1989) – and translated them into radically incongruous settings, as if to expose the mystery lurking beneath their relatively familiar surfaces. But the key to the dramaturgy of *Russian Ark* lies in one of Sokurov's least overtly challenging, yet most innovative, previous films: *Tikhie stranitsy* (*Whispering Pages*, 1993). The pages in question are those of classic nineteenth-century Russian literature, especially Dostoevskii's *Prestuplenie i nakazanie* (*Crime and Punishment*, 1866) but supplemented by motifs drawn from works by Gogol, Gor'kii, Tolstoi and others. Working entirely within the studio, Sokurov created a claustrophobic world which is that of the soulless, oppressive city, 'imbued with spiritual darkness', as one of his Russian critics suggests. His hero is a synthesis of all those existential figures who haunt the pages of Russian literature; and the girl victim he meets is a figure compounded of German Expressionist cinema and D. W. Griffith's melodrama. The film seems to announce a new kind of 'meta-cinema', which distils past works of literature and cinema into a meditation on what they might mean for us today. Nothing is explained, and yet for those who surrender to it, the effect amounts to a reinvention of silent cinema's universal language of mime and morality – an alchemy that Sokurov would repeat in *Russian Ark*.

Between *Whispering Pages* and *Russian Ark*, Sokurov experienced his first real international success with *Mat' i syn* (*Mother and Son*, 1997), hailed as a major achievement in lyrical intensity, but almost immediately followed by general rejection of *Molokh* (*Moloch*, 1999), an intimate portrait of Hitler at home with his entourage in Berchtesgaden. Both of these belong to ongoing trilogies, but in their midst emerged the project of making a film about, and to some extent for, the Hermitage. Like all cultural institutions in post-Soviet Russia, the Hermitage has felt the need to seek wider support than the state; and the current director, Mikhail Piotrovskii has been active in developing foreign branches to show loan exhibitions, such as the Hermitage Rooms at Somerset House in London, a collaborative venture with the Guggenheim in Las Vegas and the Hermitage Amsterdam. It was apparently in a similar entrepreneurial spirit that Piotrovskii agreed to what was originally planned as a documentary becoming a full-scale production that would take over the museum for a single day's shooting on 23 December 2001. Preparation for that day and its single complete take – all that could be recorded – had taken several years, and the forces involved included over eight hundred actors, three orchestras and 22 assistant directors, with over thirty specially-lit 'studios' distributed along nearly two kilometres. The high-definition video camera, mounted on a steadicam rig, was operated by the German cameraman Tilman Büttner, already known for shooting the long takes of Tom Tykwer's *Lola Rennt* (*Run Lola Run*, 1998), and here linked to a special large capacity hard-drive which did not require the image to be 'compressed'. After some initial computer problems, the performance and its recording took place as planned, although the resulting image was not – as some critics have claimed – a simple recording. Working with the film's German producers, Sokurov was able to enhance and retouch digitally the entire image-track. And, equally important, he was able to add to the original directly recorded sound many layers of additional ambience and music, developing an approach to sound pioneered in *Whispering Pages* and *Mother and Son*, both of which use music by Gustav Mahler, with its characteristic use of perspectival 'distance' effects.

But even if neither the image nor the sound are as simple as the film's critical reception has implied, its dominant trope remains the idea of a single take. When the film was launched in competition at the Cannes, the *Hollywood Reporter* put the proposition succinctly: '*Russian Ark* has already secured its place in cinematic history. Taking the experimentation of such films as Alfred Hitchcock's *Rope* and Robert Altman's *The Player* to the extreme, Sokurov has filmed his entire historical epic in one extended 87-minute steadicam shot.' Hitchcock's *Rope* (1948) together with Robert Montgomery's *Lady in the Lake* (1947) are perhaps the two most celebrated examples of 'single shot' narrative films (*The Player* only has an extended opening scene shot in one take). Both of the earlier films were made at a time when shots could not run longer than ten minutes, which meant that the transitions had to be disguised by various devices to give an illusion of continuity. *Rope* is a murder mystery, set in a single apartment, which uses the illusion of real time and space to maximise suspense. However *Lady in the Lake*, a Raymond Chandler adaptation, makes the camera its protagonist, so that we see characters and events as if through Philip Marlowe's eyes. Clearly, *Russian Ark* is closer to *Lady in the Lake* in its use of the subjective camera; although the intermittent voice-over by Sokurov deliberately hovers between dialogue with Custine and reflective musing.

However, it would be rash to assume that Sokurov is simply speaking as himself in his voice-over. He insists that none of his films are autobiographical and the credits of *Russian Ark* list three script collaborators. Rather, he has created a teasing dialogue between two semi-fictive characters, the time-travelling Frenchman and an invisible Russian 'Author', set in a timeless present through use of his 'favourite grammatical form, the present continuous'. Similar caution should apply to interpreting the film's innovative use of digital technology. When Mike Figgis set out to explore what consumer-level digital video can now achieve, first in *Timecode* (2000), with its four continuous 90-minute takes on the same unfolding narrative, and subsequently in *Hotel* (2001), he used deliberately trivial improvised narratives, subordinate to the aim of discovering what unobtrusive digital recording makes possible. But Sokurov's theme is far from trivial, and he has been quick to deny any experimental intent in using video for *Russian Ark*, insisting that the idea of a film to be shot 'in a single breath' came to him fifteen years before the means to do so became available. And indeed his meticulous approach was the exact opposite of Figgis's improvisation.

The Marquis de Custine and the Author continue their, and hence our, progress through the Hermitage, eventually meeting Piotrovskii himself, along with two of his predecessors (his father Boris Piotrovskii and his predecessor Orbeli, both played by actors), thus locating the film outside or 'across' mere chronological time. An important passage in this central section is the encounter with a blind woman whom Custine meets as she is running her hands over a marble statue. Ignoring the Author's advice to avoid the women, he approaches her and invites her to accompany him to see the Flemish masters. She tells him that she comes regularly to admire the art of the old masters, and they stop first in front of the *Virgin with Partridges* (1629) by van Dyck. To some extent her commentary is a conventional museum guide's lecture – the picture was acquired by Catherine II; it shows Joseph protecting the Virgin, and creates a radiant aura of divine protection. The camera moves closer to the painting, allowing its details to fill the frame; we hear distant birdsong mixed into the low piano music; and Custine muses, 'Your slender fingers see all.'

Here we seem to have the familiar, even banal, idea of the blind as 'more sensitive' than the sighted through their greater reliance on other senses – perhaps even a mystical suggestion that this blind visitor can 'see' through her fingers. The birdsong and sense of communion with the world evoked by the painting also recalls the Romantic idea of 'correspondence' – as evoked in Charles Baudelaire's poem of the same title, with its famous line 'Perfumes, colours and sounds correspond'. But what happens next challenges any such easy assumptions. Entering a large salon, the Marquis de Custine assures the woman that he values her opinion on van Dyck, but when she invites him to look at Rubens' *Feast in the House of Simon the Pharisee* (1618–

20), he looks at the floor and insists it is not there. Elsewhere in the room, characters from different periods are simultaneously present, all apparently going about their own business. Some nineteenth-century officials seem to be carrying out an audit of the pictures, bickering among themselves; two modern sailors are visiting, watched suspiciously by a female attendant. The woman insists the Rubens must be there, and eventually Custine admits it is, moving close and revelling greedily in 'the smell of oil paint' – as if parodying his earlier admiration for the woman's tactile sensitivity. The sailors try to copy him but are warned off by the attendant. Finally, in what seems like a cruel trick, Custine tells the woman she is facing the painting, when it is behind her, and invites her to 'describe' it. Her account is interrupted by the sailors volunteering historical information, and by the period officials trying to move the whole group out of the salon. As Custine leaves, he engages in a mock duel with the smallest of the officials, as they blow air at each other, before retreating.

What had started as apparently a homage to the power of great art and the interplay of the senses involved in its appreciation has become vastly more complex, and baffling during this passage. The Marquis may be a trans-historical figure, but he is also mischievous and vain – 'how was my performance', he asks the unseen Author. Art is a valuable commodity, for the Tsars and Tsarinas who bought it cheaply at auction, and the museums that now house it; and sailors may be as engaged by its power and presence as connoisseurs. But even as we try to interpret and rationalise episodes such as this, the film remains mysterious: we will never know who all these characters are – rather like the actual experience of visiting a museum like the Hermitage and wondering about other visitors around us, while overhearing scraps of their conversation. And its relentless onward momentum, broken by 'folds', when the camera pivots to look back or to move close to a detail, carries us on like a search without a goal.

One repeated theme is that the great paintings and statues are sacramental relics of the foundations of European culture in Russia. One momentous threat to this heritage is evoked when, abruptly, we enter a frosty room stacked with empty frames guarded by a man in winter furs, recalling how the Hermitage survived World War Two's siege of the city. Now we turn back to imperial history, to the time of Nicholas I for a great formal state occasion when the Tsar receives Persian emissaries, before encountering the last Tsar, Nicholas II, seen intimately at table with his young family. It is 1913 and the occasion of the last Great Imperial Ball, at which hundreds of guests dance to the playing of the present-day Mariinski (formerly Kirov Opera and Ballet) Orchestra, conducted by Valerii Gergiev. As the ball ends, the guests stream slowly out of the palace, chattering complacently among themselves.

The elegiac quality of this extended final sequence, emotionally coloured by our aware-ness of what these figures do not know about the upheavals that are about to overtake all their plans and hopes, has led many to interpret the film as a conservative fable, part of post-Soviet Russia's nostalgic return to a rose-tinted imperial past. Yet this is certainly to oversimplify a much more complex meditation on time, history, art – and cinema.

An unedited continuous film meant for Sokurov the possibility of 'fitting into the flow of time' in an organic process. Such language unavoidably recalls Andrei Tarkovskii's conception of filmmaking as 'sculpting in time', whereby the filmmaker shapes the fragments of time he has extracted from the material world through shooting into a new temporal structure for the spec-tator to experience. However, Sokurov has described *Russian Ark* as trying to 'fit myself into the very flowing of time, without remaking it according to my own wishes. I wanted to try and have a natural collaboration with time.' Whatever the philosophical differences between Sokurov and Tarkovskii, with whom he has often been compared, both share an uncompromising reverence for art which now seems distinctively Russian. Even though Russia originally launched many avant-garde challenges to the status of art during the early twentieth century, what survived – or reappeared – during the later Soviet era was a commitment to art as an absolute, a realm of value or meaning that exists beyond individual artists and their works. This idea can be traced back to the Symbolists of the late nineteenth century, for whom art became a semi-mystical cult, an alternative to the world of politics and business; but it would continue to inspire later generations of Russians, from Serge Diaghilev (1872–1929) and his collaborators in the Ballets Russes, to poets such as Boris Pasternak (1890–1960) and Anna Akhmatova (1899–1966), and eventually filmmakers, who arguably found refuge from Soviet coercion in a new cult of art.

Like Tarkovskii, Sokurov has little time for modernism or for the artistic pretensions of most commercial cinema. Since he believes that classical art of the kind so abundantly gath-ered and displayed in the Hermitage stands far above cinema in its achievements, he is happy to place filmmaking at its service. The Hermitage is an 'ark', an instrument of higher purpose, which enshrines not only the values of the past but also the values needed for the future. Like St Petersburg itself, founded by Peter the Great to give Russia its 'window on the west', the museum that Catherine II created embodies the contradiction of a culture that, in Piotrovskii's words, 'loves Europe yet which is not a part of Europe'. For Sokurov, it is a labyrinth, 'the only place in Russia where such a thing exists', and his 'artistic task' is to draw us into its spell.

To do so, he has created a film in labyrinthine form, developing the intertextuality of *Whispering Pages* in his use here of scattered 'pages' from the Hermitage's history. We may arrive and leave with the guests of the Imperial Ball at a specific moment in history, but throughout most of the film we are deliberately given few definite coordinates. The conception of history that underlies the film, and indeed much of Sokurov's work, owes much to the philosopher and religious thinker Nikolai Berdiaev (1874–1948), who left Russia shortly after the Revolution to live in France, where he was eventually recognised as one of the founders of Existentialism. Berdiaev's philosophy of history was formed by the apocalyptic experience of the 1917 Russian revolutions and he would later speak of history as 'pre-eminently tragic destiny', which 'like all tragedy, must end in resolution'. Here we can find one source of Sokurov's conviction that the times of the historical characters he shows have not ended, since 'historical time cannot depart, cannot collapse'. Berdiaev rejected the Enlightenment's 'doctrine of progress', believing instead that the great 'symbolic' achievements of true culture inevitably give way to mere bourgeois 'civilisation'. For him, as for Sokurov, Russian culture has the potential to restore cultural value to a depraved West, which has lost contact with the roots of its greatness. Hence, *Russian Ark* is addressed not only – perhaps not at all? – to Russia, but to the world that needs its values.

Whether or not we accept this distinctively Russian metaphysics, the film's commitment to a philosophy of history connects it to a renewed current of interest in such issues stretching from the popular writings of Francis Fukuyama (*The End of History*, 1992) and Philip Bobbit (*The Shield of Achilles*, 2002) to the 'metahistory' of Hayden White and the philosophy of Paul Ricoeur and Hans Gadamer. And just as Alain Resnais' *L'année dernière à Marienbad* (*Last Year at Marienbad*, 1961) once ignited widespread speculation about cinema's capacity to model our subjective sense of time, so *Russian Ark* might contribute its 'Russian idea' to a new awareness of cinema's unique modality, in sharp contrast to such other time-obsessed contemporary works as *Momento* (2000), *Irreversible* (2002) and *Eternal Sunshine of the Spotless Mind* (2004).

Meanwhile, we leave the Hermitage and its guests of 1913 to look out across what seems to be a frozen lake that stretches as far as the present. The Author bids us farewell: 'The sea is all around. We are destined to sail forever, to live forever.'

Ian Christie

REFERENCE

Berdiaev, N. (1936) *The Meaning of History*, tr. G. Reavey, Geoffrey Bles: Centenary Press.
Roxborough, S. (2002) 'Sokurov's "Ark" built in one shot', *Hollywood Reporter*, 14 May.

DOM DURAKOV HOUSE OF FOOLS

ANDREI KONCHALOVSKII, RUSSIA/FRANCE, 2002

Dom durakov (*House of Fools*, 2002) was scripted and directed by Andrei Konchalovskii (b. 1937). According to an opening inter-title, it is 'based on a true story' set in 1996, in a psychiatric hospital on the Russian border of Ingushetia, during the Chechen War. Konchalovskii is well known for a diverse range of films, including literary adaptations, such as *Pervyi uchitel'* (*The First Teacher*, 1965), a controversial film made in Kyrgyzstan, *Asino schast'e* (*Asya's Happiness*, 1967), *Dvorianskoe gnezdo* (*A Nest of Gentlefolk*, 1969), *Diadia Vania* (*Uncle Vanya*, 1972), and *Siberiada* (1979). The last two films won the director international acclaim.

In 1980, he moved to the United States and over the next two decades made films in Hollywood and Europe, working in a range of styles and genres. His film work reveals an allegorical (and auteurist) penchant for portraying historical events, conflicts between tradition and modernity, a predilection for marginal figures, a critical stance toward state power and a mistrust of the nation; he has an internationalist, or as he terms it, cosmopolitan perspective, and an eclectic style that often combines naturalism and theatricality.

A French and Russian co-production, *House of Fools* is the second film directed by Konchalovskii following his return to Russian cinema (the first was *Kurochka Riaba* (*The Speckled Hen*, 1994), a sequel to *Asya's Happiness*). It involves politics with a critical, if not experimental, style that seems to owe more to contemporary European and Russian filmmaking than to a cinematic form that adheres to a retroactive and narrowly conceived conception of national cinema. The film is not a nostalgic recollection of a bygone era but a harsh portrait of a war that has persisted since the 1990s (both in the first conflict from 1994–96 and the current war which began in 1999), with virulent and unabated intensity; a war that has witnessed the deaths of many Russians and Chechens.

House of Fools is not a conventional war film or a Social Realist film, but a satiric allegory; a darkly humorous, if not polemical, dismantling of the forms of power and violence that underpin the ongoing Russian and Chechen conflict, and indicts the adventurism of the Russian state. It does not valorise heroism; it is a film that seeks to unsettle, to interrogate conceptions of national identity, war and state power. The film also questions the role of cinema as an instrument of thought; not polemical or propagandist. The unsettling mode of storytelling relies on a method that displays a disregard for realism, prevailing conceptions of historical redemption via the nation, and a conventional justification of secular law and power as promulgated by the State.

Walter Benjamin's discussion of the demise of storytelling and his projection of the role of allegory in modernity is useful for contemplating the character and effects of *House of Fools*. In *The Origins of German Tragic Drama*, Benjamin delineates a mode for understanding how historicising has functioned in the modern world. The symbol relies on resemblance between the word and the object or idea to which it refers, signifying a unity between the visible and invisible world; allegory drives a wedge between them, revealing the imperfect and sorrowful world that constitutes modernity. In allegory, history is present, but not in the sense of providing a unified conception of the past, of the ways things were; instead, fragmentary images of the past are scattered throughout the landscape and are emblematic of loss, destruction and ruin. Of allegory, Benjamin wrote:

> In the ruin history has physically merged into the setting. And in this guise history does not assume the form of the process of an eternal life so much as that of irresistible decay. Allegory declares itself to be beyond beauty. Allegories are in the realm of thoughts what ruins are in the realm of things ... The quintessence of these decaying objects is the polar opposite to the idea of transfigured nature ... But it is as something incomplete and imperfect that objects stare out from the allegorical structure.

This conception of allegory provides a guide to trace how *House of Fools* (and other Konchalovskii's films, such as *Siberiade*), address tenuous but provocative and significant connections between past and present; the uses and abuses of history, especially national history, have animated a number of Konchalovskii's films.

Destruction and decay are ubiquitous in the film's obsession with aggression and death, the horrors of war, and the somnambulistic lives of the characters. The film's mode of allegorising presents a world of ruins and decay evident in the architecture and in the interactions of the characters. The structure of the film is episodic and elliptical: the characters appear to be in a trance and the portrayal of events militates against the possibility of reason and truth. In fact, a disregard for explanation and interpretation as tools of instrumental reason is unwavering in the film's treatment of events. The initial images of train tracks and of a train foreshadow the film's interweaving of fantasy and actual events. The bluish and dark lighting of the exterior is only relieved by bright shots (like stars) of the train's lights as the locomotive speeds through the landscape on its nightly passage. Popular singer Bryan Adams (as himself) is superimposed on shots of the train, singing to various women. These opening moments anticipate the film's blurring of the boundaries between hallucination and realism and also of the importance that music will play in highlighting the desires, fantasies and fears of characters. Music also serves self-reflexively to underscore constraints on language, but not on imagination.

After this enigmatic introduction, the spectator is presented with the first of many episodes that depict a war on the part of the inmates of a psychiatric hospital in their various forms of rebellion against the hospital authorities. The setting is not original: it is a familiar convention from early cinema to the present time, evident in such films as *Das Cabinet des Doktor Caligari* (*The Cabinet of Dr Caligari*, 1919), *King of Hearts* (1966) and *One Flew Over the Cuckoo's Nest* (1975), unsettling conventional conceptions of sanity and normality. When treated allegorically as in these films, the psychiatric asylum takes on the properties of the carnivalesque; a grotesque and disorderly vision of the world turned upside down where everything is inverted and altered, but where nonsense reveals the tension between chaos and stability. This form of the carnivalesque is associated with bodily functions that refuse to accept official constraints and are identified with animality, irreverence in behaviour and action, and with forms of verbal language and gestures that disrupt reason and meaning.

At first glance, the film appears to be a version of the grotesque world of Tod Browning's *Freaks* (1932). However, as *House of Fools* develops, the world of the hospital becomes a microcosm of the Russian world, and the patients its population. The acting is highly stylised, as befits a film whose milieu is that of the mental hospital, where the inmates' seemingly outrageous behaviour appears saner than the dominant world of power and politics. The attitudes of the inmates involve outright acts of defiance, excessive authoritarianism, a refusal to speak or eat, escape into romantic dreams, preoccupation with the body, and the wanton destruction of institutional property. The style of the film clearly seems intent on adopting strategies to unsettle the audience's notion of decorum in the service of a spurious 'reality' that produces stupefaction, deprivation, death and destruction.

Angry and obsessive inmate Vika (Marina Politseimako) spits on the floor, shouting, 'War and stupidity will feed this generation of junkies and trash.' Vika is threatened with punishment by Ali (Stanislav Varkki), an inmate and poet, who has assumed the role of disciplinarian, ordering her to wipe her spit from the floor despite or perhaps because of her claim that a 1993 Soviet law protects mental patients from harsh treatment. Her defiance is expressed in terms of an exaggerated adherence to the dictates of laws that have no substance in this milieu. Ali forces her to capitulate as the other inmates witness her surrender. Among the other inmates are sex-crazed Lucie (Elena Fomina), an old man who refuses food, Mahmud (Rasmi Dzhabrailov) wearing medals that cover his jacket, a dwarf, the effemi-nate Goga (Gevorg Ovakimian) and Downs' Syndrome-afflicted Zoia. In the portrayal of the inmates, the film focuses on their thwarted psychic and bodily needs that brings to mind the writings of Michel Foucault and Giorgio Agamben on biopower, the modern role of the state in administering the biological existence of the population.

Zhanna is played by the director's wife, Iuliia Vysotskaia (b. 1973), whose acting conveys the complexity of her role as a visionary with romantic and hallucinatory fantasies centring on popular singer Bryan Adams. She is reminiscent of Federico Fellini's Gelsomina in *La strada* (1954). Like Gelsomina, she appears defective in intelligence, an inarticulate creature who moves through the hospital somnambulantly. She serves multiple capacities within the narrative: as a nurturing figure to the other inmates, as a mediator in the inmates' arguments, as a romantic believer in love and innocence, and as a childlike figure who expresses her desire for freedom through music, through her accordion playing and the intensity of her devotion to the music of Bryan Adams. She is a bridge between the disciplinary world of the hospital (the state), the war that rages outside and the spectator. More than any other char-acter in the film, she invokes questions concerning the role of art: its utopian dimension but also its ineffectuality in the light of a world that, as the film will show, is mired in forms of destruction that further contribute to making the mental institution appear as a safe haven given the devastation and ravages of brutal warfare.

Music is critical to the film, not only in connection with Bryan Adams' singing but also with Zhanna's accordion playing. It marks the film's strategy for introducing tenuous images of freedom. During heightened moments of conflict, Zhanna plays her accordion. At those times, the lighting changes from sombre to colourful and, for a brief instant, there is momentary relief, followed by renewed aggression among the inmates. In one scene, as Zhanna's music accompanies the inmate's physical exercises, Mahmud sets fire to curtains, occasioning a disciplinary response on the part of the doctor who orders that the patients be medicated and strapped to their beds. In the face of various forms of insubordination and institutional retaliation, Zhanna maintains her desire for the singer, Bryan Adams, whom she regards as her fiancé. Called up by Zhanna's fantasies, Adams walks through the corridors and sings to her, underscoring her escapism but also her fantasies of love and art as a contrast to the grim world of authoritarian power.

Zhanna, like the other patients, continues to look for the magic train's appearance, but one day it does not arrive at the scheduled time, and the radio and phone are also cut off. A train finally does arrive, not the virtual train with the Bryan Adams of Zhanna's fantasies, but a train that announces a shift in perspective from the film's claustrophobic focus on the hospital, moving the action outside. The arrival of this train is the first intimation of the Chechen war. By contrast, in a colourful fantasy sequence, Adams appears once again and treats the doctor (Vladas Bagdonas), attendants and patients to champagne, singing to Zhanna as flower petals descend on the assembled party and all dance. The doctor abandons the premises, leaving the inmates to fend for themselves, and this otherworldly moment gives way to mayhem as the patients rush to leave the building with Vika militantly shouting: 'Down with Fascism. Take to the streets.' In an image reminiscent of *Bronenosets Potemkin* (*The Battleship Potemkin*, 1925), the old man in a wheelchair rolls down the stairs as explosions follow and the inmates retreat indoors, left to fend for themselves.

The narrative now focuses on another war through the introduction of the Chechen 'bandits', their infiltration of the hospital, and Zhanna's relationship with them. The Chechen soldiers include a wounded Lithuanian woman, a sniper (Cecilie Thomsen). Zhanna's role in the film is further complicated by her role as viewer to the events. Her character takes on the added dimension described by Gilles Deleuze as an attribute of the post-World War Two cinema. She has become a kind of viewer who, in Deleuze's terms, 'records rather than reacts', 'a prey to a vision', a 'visionary, a sleepwalker'. Her role is further elaborated, if not altered, when she goes to the basement where some of the Chechens have gathered and her accordion is appropriated by one of them, who plays a tune. After retrieving the instrument, she jokes and ineptly dances for the amused men. In jest, Ahmed (Sultan Islamov), the accordion player, proposes marriage to her, anticipating the later raucous celebration of their 'engagement'.

This scene is interrupted by the arrival of Russian soldiers who have come not to fight but to bargain over the return of the body of a dead Chechen. Zhanna's dancing for the Chechens and the encounter with the Russians are both ritualistic encounters, one involving a courtship ritual, the other an epic ritual of the return of a dead warrior. However, the presentation of these rituals is not an instance of the uncontaminated survival of past cultural practices relating to an epic and monumental view of the world, but rather they are tainted by the present, by the present war and, even more, by the film's fracturing and de-mythologising of characters and events.

Economic exchange is central to the encounter between the Russian and Chechen soldiers who regard the return of the body as an opportunity to exchange ammunition for drugs. The Russian and Chechen captains meet to decide on a price for the body of the dead Chechen. A moment of commonality between the two men is introduced when the captains discover that they had both fought in the Afghanistan war, and, moreover, the Russian acknowledges that the Chechen 'saved our asses in the Chungur attack'. An accidental shooting by a drugged Russian soldier disrupts this moment of camaraderie. The Russian captain calls his men off, abandoning the bag with the agreed-upon $2,000, shouting as he leaves: 'Give it to your mullah.'

Not only is this episode another instance of male bonding that operates through individual interaction though not in collective terms, but it also confounds the motive for the war by introducing the issue of drugs, thus reinforcing Vika's comment about the existence of a generation of 'junkies'. Drugs play a multivalent role: as treatment for controlling the inmates in the hospital, and, in relation to the war, the use of drugs invites the question of what or who produced this generation of junkies who kill and destroy. Significantly, drugs are germane to the style of the film which functions often in hallucinatory fashion to confuse fantasy and the real; but they also serve to involve the spectators in the film, inviting them to question the rationale for the war, if not their own role in its perpetuation.

In contrast to the scenes that portray the brutality of the war and the inmates' entrapment, Zhanna's decision to marry Ahmed and renounce her love for Bryan Adams produces one of the most touching and carnivalesque scenes in the film, as the inmates prepare her for the wedding by giving her presents. Lucia gives her patent leather shoes and a white dress, Vika, a wide-brimmed white straw hat, another inmate a bottle of vodka, and still another beautifies her face with make-up that makes her look like a circus clown. In return, she too dispenses gifts. Once again, this moment offers a utopian image of collectivity in contrast to the violent and estranging war that wages outside. However, there is a holdout to the festivities, the inmate Ali, who remains alone in his room, and when she comes to say goodbye to him, he pleads unsuccessfully with her to stay. After saying goodbye to the bedridden patients, (she gives an apple to the old man who refuses food), she passes into the corridor where the ubiquitous TV sits. The television set has been a silent commentator. It is set off to a side but is within the spectator's view with its images of Russian politicians and barely audible sounds. This time the screen is blank. Suitcase in hand, accordion over her shoulder, she walks out of the building as the patients watch from the window and wave.

Zhanna enters a building where the Chechens are sitting around a table and announces: 'I'm here.' Despite Ahmed's initial reluctance to marry her, he succumbs to taunts and finally proposes marriage, but a fight develops. Again Zhanna plays her accordion but to no avail, until a Chechen begins to play and the men (and Zhanna) dance. Ali interrupts the festivities to bring her home, claiming that she is ill and that the hospital is her home. For the second time, she claims that she is 'healthy'. Increasingly, the film tries to blur, if not overturn, the borders between madness and sanity. Ali's speech to the contrary, the film does not seem to be prescribing a concept of health and illness in relation to the characters and to Zhanna in particular. Rather, the film maintains its unrelenting investigation of the normal and pathological, conceding only to the impossibility of establishing clear distinctions between them and to the necessity of exploring their political role as a means of containment and maintenance of power. The treatment of the characters undermines any clear melodramatic lines between innocence and guilt. Instead, the film chooses to implicate all, thus shifting to another realm of investigation that raises questions about how cinema can find a language to confront the complexity of a dire cultural and political situation that resists conventional modes of representation.

After the celebration of the proposed marriage, Zhanna informs Ahmed that she will not marry him, declaring her love for the Canadian singer and about the need for love in terms that recall Gelsomina's quest for meaning in the Fellini film: 'We're alive because someone loves us.' Ahmed, in turn, explains how he 'never thought he would be a soldier'. Only when his brothers were killed and the roof fell in on his father did he 'call for a gun', and he wonders further when he will be killed. But Zhanna assures him that he is 'special', and questions whether he looks like his father or mother. He tells her he looks 'like a bald bastard', removing his hat to reveal a balding head. They get drunk on vodka and spend the night together outdoors.

The following morning, Zhanna reverses her decision about not having a relationship with Ahmed, claiming that since she has been unfaithful to Bryan Adams, she and Ahmed should now be together always. As is increasingly the case in this film, where moments of unity are interrupted by explosions, Vika interrupts this encounter, shouting that it is a 'joy' to see the Chechens 'fighting for their freedom' and 'Down with Russian chauvinism'. Zhanna's quest for love and Vika's quest for justice are complicated: the film refuses to 'solve' personal relationships by recourse to romance or by the militant belief in a counter-war in the name of resistance. *House of Fools* seems resolutely intent, even to the point of obfuscation, on resisting a binary and melodramatic explanation and an easy solution to the conflicts it poses. In its treatment of both romance and war the film struggles to resist cinematic and cultural clichés that attach to romance and politics.

In the final episodes, the violence of the war escalates with images of a falling helicopter, more bombings, the killing of Chechens, Ali's wounding and Goga's dancing on the smoking and ravaged earth. Zhanna wants to fight along with Ahmed but he takes off on a truck without her. She returns to her room with her baggage when the Lithuanian sniper enters. As the woman aims her rifle, Zhanna takes a broken shard of glass and jabs at photos of Ahmed that she holds in her hand. Then she notices the Lithuanian woman dead in a pool of blood and her own bleeding hand. Screaming, she runs from the room. Amidst the bombing, she again has a vision of Bryan Adams, and, ominously, a guitar propped against a wall falls to the ground. Zhanna now has a conversation with the old man who did not eat the apple she had given him, maintaining his refusal to eat. But the fruit is the occasion for one of the film's several philosophical conversations.

The old man's monologue becomes one of the direct polemic moments in the film, a comment on Zhanna's optimism and a sorrowful commentary on aggression and war. In response to her view of God as forgiving, he tells her that what he sees in the apple are images of 'people who love and destroy each other fighting for generations and dying'. He cannot eat because the faces of the people he sees in the apple torment him. In a film that has challenged the persistence of clichés about both romance and war, this moment might seem gratuitous but the words are those of an anorexic old man who is, after all, an inmate in the hospital.

The doctor now finally returns to resume the role that he had earlier abdicated, and so do the Russian soldiers brandishing weapons and seeking Chechens in hiding. Once again, the issue of drugs comes to the fore, when the officer in charge of the mission approaches the doctor for a drug, protesting: 'I can't take it any more.' His psychic discomfort notwithstanding, he is adamant that 'all Chechens should be shot'. The doctor gives him the requested drug via a needle and reflects that 'in the war it's not victory, the most important thing is death', to which the Russian soldier responds soulfully by citing Tolstoi: 'Why is a man happy when he kills another?' Nonetheless, he rushes out to kill Chechens.

In the dining room where the inmates are having lunch, Ahmed enters the room and sits by Zhanna. The doctor and the soldier appear together in the dining room, requesting the inmates for help in locating a hiding Chechen. No one becomes an informer. However, other soldiers drag in the wounded and bloody Chechen captain, and the Russians leave, believing that the building has now been 'cleansed'. The doctor notices Ahmed who has been sitting at a table with the other inmates and questions his presence. Ahmed responds: 'I'm sick. I need to be treated.' The doctor does not call the Russians back to inform them about Ahmed, but asks Ahmed to visit him in his office after lunch, thus leaving this Chechen's fate uncertain. The film concludes in ambiguous fashion by returning to shots of Zhanna holding her accordion, images of Bryan Adams on the train waving goodbye, a close-up of a rose, a repeated image in the film, and of Zhanna, slowly bowing her head until the only image that remains is of her white straw hat, leaving the spectator to question what and how to think about what s/he has seen.

Thus, the film presents a grim, uncompromising and unresolved allegory of the power of the Russian State and of the psychiatric hospital, its surrogate. *House of Fools* turns the trope of madness into a dissection of Russian culture and politics. The only possible alternative to the hospital is a virtual world of love and redemption conveyed through music and perhaps of poetry, rejected by the Russians and Chechens alike. The film's treatment of the hospital with its focus on psychically and physically maimed human beings is not offered as a plea for legal and administrative correction of the physical living conditions of the hospital inmates but as it serves the allegory, introducing the issue of the relation of the state's control of the bodies and minds of the population.

The film's linking of the mental hospital to the Chechen war makes unambiguous that modern warfare is expressed on several fronts: through the disciplinary apparatus of social institutions and through formal violence by means of deadly weapons of destruction and the blind, uncomprehending pursuit of annihilation. Despite the momentary bonding between Russian and Chechen captains and despite the Russian soldiers' recognition that they need to be anaesthetised in order to continue the slaughter, the violence persists. The treatment of the inmates presents them as differentiated from each other, as not compliant, and as communicating an awareness of, even resistance to, their situation. Through various characters – Zhanna, Ali, Ahmed, the old man, the doctor, and even the officer quoting Tolstoi – the film introduces philosophic reflections on aggression and death, all of which are tenuous, if not rhetorical.

The film is also self-critical and reflexive about its status as text in its uses of music as a surrogate for filmmaking, raising questions about the role of contemporary cinema. It is not only the musical interludes that provide reflections on art (and on this film). In contrast, the television set plays a subtle and contrary role, functioning as an invisible presence for the inmates but for the film viewer as a visible commentator on the ubiquitous presence of the state with its images of politicians whose words cannot be deciphered but whose images seem ubiquitous and ominous. The film does not resolve the conflicts it portrays. It does not provide a conciliatory and comforting view of Russian national history. What is the viewer to make of Zhanna's love for Bryan Adams, and his presence in the film, and the fantasy of romance and escape aligned to it? Is the film suggesting that music is the 'food of love' and that it (like the film) is the only hope for life or is this merely a chimera?

Marcia Landy

Author's note: I wish to express my deep gratitude to Vladimir Padunov for his scholarly insights, his reading of, comments on and suggested revisions of the text of this chapter. I hope that the resulting text merits the expenditure of his time and effort.

REFERENCES

Agamben, G. (1995) *Homo Sacer: Sovereign Power and Bare Life*, trans. D. Heller-Roazen. Stanford: Stanford University Press.

Benjamin, W. (1996) *The Origin of German Tragic Drama*, trans. J. Osborne. London: Verso.

Deleuze, G. (1989) *Cinema 2: The Time-Image*, trans., H. Tomlinson and R. Galeta. Minneapolis: University of Minnesota Press.

Foucault, M. (1980) *The History of Sexuality: An Introduction*, vol. 1, trans. R. Hurley, New York: Vintage Books.

FILMOGRAPHY

ZHIZN' ZA ZHIZN' A LIFE FOR A LIFE 1916
Director: Evgenii Bauer
Production: A. Khanzhonkov & Co
Screenplay: Evgenii Bauer, George Ohnet
Photography: Boris Savel'ev (b&w)
Art direction: Aleksei Utkin
Cast: Vera Kholodnaia (Nata), Lidiia Koreneva (Musia), Vitol'd Polonskii (Prince Bartinskii), Ivan Perestiani (Zhurov), Ol'ga Rakhmanova (Mrs Khromova)
Running time: 66'

NEOBYCHAINYE PRIKLIUCHENIIA MISTERA VESTA V STRANE BOL'SHEVIKOV THE EXTRAORDINARY ADVENTURES OF MR WEST IN THE
LAND OF THE BOLSHEVIKS 1924
Director: Lev Kuleshov
Production: Goskino
Screenplay: Nikolai Aseev
Photography: Aleksandr Levitskii (b&w)
Editing: Aleksandr Levitskii
Sound: Iurii Kotov
Music: Taras Buevskii
Art direction: Vsevolod Pudovkin
Cast: Porfirii Podobed (Mr West), Boris Barnet (Jeddy), Aleksandra Khokhlova (Countess), Vsevolod Pudovkin (Zhdan), Sergei Komarov (One-Eyed Man), Leonid Obolenskii (Dandy), Valentina Lopatina (Elly)
Running time: 95'

AELITA 1924
Director: Iakov Protazanov
Production: Mezhrabpom-Rus
Screenplay: Fedor Otsep, Aleksei Tolstoi, Aleksei Faiko
Photography: Iurii Zheliabuzhskii, Egon Schuenemann (b&w)
Music: Aleksandr Almakaev
Art direction: Sergei Kozlovskii, V. Simonov, Isaak Rabinovich
Costume design: Aleksandra Ekster
Cast: Iuliia Solntseva (Aelita), Igor' Il'inskii (Kravtsov), Nikolai Tsereteli (Los, Spiridonov), Nikolai Batalov (Gusev), Vera Orlova (Masha), Vera Kuindzhi (Natasha Los), Pavel Pol' (Erlikh), Konstantin Eggert (Tuskub), Iurii Zavadskii (Gor), Aleksandra Peregonets (Ihoshka), Iosif Tolchanov (astronomer)
Running time: 104'

STACHKA THE STRIKE 1924 (restored 1969)
Director: Sergei Eisenstein
Production: Pervaia Goskinofabrika, Proletkul't (Boris Mikhin)
Screenplay: V. Pletnev, Sergei Eisenstein, Il'ia Kravchunovskii, Grigorii Aleksandrov
Photography: Eduard Tisse (b&w)
Art direction: Vasilii Rakhals
Cast: Ivan Kliukvin (Revolutionary), Aleksandr Antonov (Member of Strike Committee), Grigorii Aleksandrov

(Factory Foreman), Mikhail Gomorov (Worker), Maksim Shtraukh (Police Spy), I. Ivanov (Police Chief), Boris Iurtsev (Thief)
Running time: 83'

ZEMLIA EARTH 1930 (restored 1971)
Director: Aleksandr Dovzhenko
Production: VUFKU (Kiev)
Screenplay: Aleksandr Dovzhenko
Photography: Daniil (Danylo) Demutskii (b&w)
Editing: Aleksandr Dovzhenko
Music and Sound: Viacheslav Ovchinnikov
Art direction: Vasilii Krichevskii
Cast: Stepan Shkurat (Opanas), Semen Svashenko (Vasilii Opanas), Iuliia Solntseva (Vasilii's sister), Elena Maksimova (Natal'ia), Ivan Franko (Arkhip Whitehorse), Petr Masokha (Khoma Whitehorse), Vladimir Mikhailov (Priest), Pavel Petrik (Party Leader), P. Umanets (Chairman of Farm), E. Bondina (Farm Girl), Luka Liashenko (kulak), Nikolai Nademskii (Semen Opanas)
Running time: 89'

CHAPAEV 1934 (restored 1963)
Director: Georgii and Sergei Vasil'ev
Production: Lenfil'm (restoration Mosfil'm)
Screenplay: Georgii and Sergei Vasil'ev
Photography: Aleksandr Sigaev, Aleksandr Ksenofontov (b&w)
Music: Gavriil Popov
Art direction: Isaak Makhlis
Sound: A. Bekker
Cast: Boris Babochkin (Chapaev), Leonid Kmit (Pet'ka), Varvara Miasnikova (An'ka), Boris Blinov (Furmanov), Illarion Pevtsov (Col. Borozdin), Stepan Shkurat (Borozdin's striker), Viacheslav Volkov (Elan), Nikolai Simonov (Zhikharev), Boris Chirkov (peasant), Georgii Vasil'ev (White officer), Georgii Zhzhenov (Teresha)
Running time: 95'

VESELYE REBIATA THE HAPPY GUYS 1934 (restored 1958, 1978)
Director: Grigorii Aleksandrov
Production: Moskinokombinat (I. Zaionts)
Screenplay: Nikolai Erdman Vladimir Mass, Grigorii Aleksandrov
Photography: Vladimir Nil'sen (b&w)
Editing: Esfir Tobak
Music: Isaak Dunaevskii
Songs: Vasilii Lebedev-Kumach
Art direction: Aleksei Utkin
Sound: Nikolai Timartsev
Cast: Leonid Utesov (Kostia Potekhin), Liubov Orlova (Aniuta), Mariia Strelkova (Elena), Elena Tiapkina (Elena's mother), Fedor Kurikhin (Mortician), Emmanuil Geller, A. Arnol'd (conductor), Robert Erdman (music teacher)
Running time: 96'

KARNAVAL'NAIA NOCH' CARNIVAL NIGHT 1956
Director: El'dar Riazanov
Production: Mosfil'm

Screenplay: Boris Laskin, Vladimir Poliakov
Photography: Arkadii Kol'tsatyi (c)
Editing: Aleksandra Kamagorova
Music: Anatolii Lepin (lyrics V. Lifshits, V. Korostylev)
Art direction: Oleg Grosse, Konstantin Efimov
Sound: V. Zorin
Cast: Igor' Il'inskii (Serafim Ogurtsov), Liudmila Gurchenko (Lena Krylova), Iurii Belov (Grisha Kol'tsov), Georgii Kulikov (Serezha Usikov), Sergei Filippov (Comrade Nekadilov), Ol'ga Vlasova (Adelaida Romashkina), Andrei Tutyshkin (Fedor Mironov), Tamara Nosova (Tosia Burigina), Gennadii Iudin (conductor), Vladimir Zel'din (clown)
Running time: 78'

BALLADA O SOLDATE BALLAD OF A SOLDIER 1959
Director: Grigorii Chukhrai
Production: Mosfil'm
Screenplay: Valentin Ezhov, Grigorii Chukhrai
Photography: Vladimir Nikolaev, Era Savel'eva (b&w)
Editing Mariia Timofeeva
Music: Mikhail Ziv
Art direction: Boris Nemechek
Costume design: L Riashentseva
Sound: Veniamin Kirshenbaum
Cast: Vladimir Ivashov (Alesha Skvortsov), Zhanna Prokhorenko (Shura), Antonina Maksimova (Alesha's mother), Nikolai Kriuchkov (General), Evgenii Urbanskii (Vasia), Ella Lazhdei (Vasia's wife), Valentina Telegina (truck driver), Evgenii Evstigneev (truck driver), Lev Borisov (soldier), Aleksandr Kuznetsov (Gavrilkin), Marina Kremneva (Zoia), Vladimir Kashpur (Zoia's husband), Evgenii Teterin (Lieutenant)
Running time: 90'

IVANOVO DETSTVO IVAN'S CHILDHOOD 1962
Director: Andrei Tarkovskii
Production: Mosfil'm
Screenplay: Vladimir Bogomolov, Mikhail Papava
Photography: Vadim Iusov (b&w)
Editing: Liudmila Feiginova
Music: Viacheslav Ovchinnikov
Art direction: Evgenii Cherniaev
Sound: Inna Zelentsova
Cast: Nikolai Burliaev (Ivan), Valentin Zubkov (Capt. Kholin), Evgenii Zharikov (Lt. Gal'tsev), Valentina Maliavina (Masha), Stepan Krylov (Captain Katasonych), Nikolai Grin'ko (Col. Griaznov), Dmitrii Miliutenko (Old Man), Irma Rausch [Irina Tarkovskaia] (Ivan's Mother), Andrei Mikhalkov-Konchalovskii (soldier)
Running time: 96'

KOROTKIE VSTRECHI BRIEF ENCOUNTERS 1967
Director: Kira Muratova
Production: Odesskaia Kinostudiia
Screenplay: Kira Muratova, Leonid Zhukhovitskii
Photography: Gennadii Kariuk (b&w)
Editing: O. Kharakova
Music: Oleg Karavaichuk

Art direction: Aleksandra Konardova, Oleg Perederyi
Costume design: L. Toltsykh
Sound: E. Rudykh, Igor' Skinder
Cast: Kira Muratova (Valentina), Vladimir Vysotskii (Maksim), Nina Ruslanova (Nadia), Lidiia Bazil'skaia, Valerii
Isakov (Stepa), Ol'ga Vikland, Aleksei Glazyrin, Svetlana Nemoliaeva (hair-dresser)
Running time: 96'

BRILLIANTOVAIA RUKA THE DIAMOND ARM 1968
Director: Leonid Gaidai
Production: Mosfil'm
Screenplay: Moris Slobodskoi, Iakov Kostiukovskii, Leonid Gaidai
Photography: Igor' Chernykh (c)
Editing: Valentina Ianovskaia
Music: Aleksandr Zatsepin (song lyrics by Leonid Derbenev)
Art direction: Feliks Iasiukevich
Sound: Evgeniia Indlina
Cast: Iurii Nikulin (Semen Gorbunkov), Nina Grebeshkova (Nadezhda Gorbunkova), Andrei Mironov (Gennadii
Kozodoev), Anatolii Papanov (Lelik), Stanislav Chekan (Captain Mikhail Ivanovich), Nonna Mordiukova
(Superintendent), Svetlana Svetlichnaia (Anna), Vladimir Guliaev (Lt. Volodia), Grigorii Shpigel' (Foreign Smuggler),
Leonid Kanevskii (Foreign Smuggler), Roman Filippov (Man in Restaurant), Igor' Iasulovich (Dog owner), Aleksandr
Khvylia (Maitre d'hotel)
Running time: 100'

NRAN GUYNE THE COLOUR OF POMEGRANATES 1970
Director: Sergo Parajanov
Production: Armenfil'm
Screenplay: Sergo Parajanov
Photography: Suren Shakhbazian (c)
Editing: Sergo Parajanov, M. Ponomarenko
Music: Tigran Mansurian
Art direction: Stepan Andranikyan
Costume design: Elene Akhvlediani, I. Karalyan, Zh. Sarabyan
Sound: M. Berko, I. Saiadyan
Cast: Sofiko Chiaureli (Poet as Young Man), Melkop Alekyan (Poet as Child), Vilen Galstyan (Poet in the cloister),
Georgi Gegechkori (Poet as old man), Spartak Bagashvili (poet's father), Medeia Djaparidze (Poet's mother), Onik
and Hovhannes Minasyan (Prince)
Running time: 74'

IKO SHASHVI MGALOBELI LIVED ONCE A SONG THRUSH 1971
Director: Otar Ioseliani
Production: Gruziia Fil'm
Screenplay: Otar Ioseliani, Dmitrii Eristavi, O. Mekhrishvili, Il'ia Nusinov, S. Kakichashvili, Semen Lungin
Photography: Abesalom Maisuradze (b&w)
Editing: Julietta Bezuashvili
Music: Teimuraz Bakuradze
Art direction: Dmitrii Eristavi
Costume design: R. Quchuloria
Sound: Otar Gegechkori

Cast: Gela Kandelaki (Gija Agladze), Gogi Chkheidze, Djangus Kakhidze, Irina Djandieri, Marina Kartsivadze, I. Mdivani, Nugzar Erkomaishvili, Deia Ivanidze, Tamara Gedevanishvili, M. Makharadze, Revaz Baramidze, G. Margvelashvili, T. Mtsatsmindeli, Vakhtang Eremashvili.
Running time: 83'

KALINA KRASNAIA RED GUELDERBUSH 1973
Director: Vasilii Shukshin
Production: Mosfil'm
Screenplay: Vasilii Shukshin
Photography: Anatolii Zabolotskii
Editing: Elena Mikhailova
Music: Pavel Chekalov
Art direction: Ippolit Novoderezhkin
Costume design: A. Dokuchaeva
Sound: V. Beliarov
Cast: Vasilii Shukshin (Egor), Lidiia Fedoseeva-Shukshina (Liuba), Aleksei Vanin (Petr), Ivan Ryzhov (Father), Mariia Skvortsova (Mother), Mariia Vinogradova (Zoia), Ol'ga Bystrova (Egor's Mother), Lev Durov (Waiter), Georgii Burkov (Guboshlep)
Running time: 108'

SVOI SREDI CHUZHIK, CHUZHOI SREDI SVOIKH AT HOME AMONG STRANGERS, A STRANGER AT HOME 1974
Director: Nikita Mikhalkov
Production: Mosfil'm
Screenplay: Eduard Volodarskii, Nikita Mikhalkov
Photography: Pavel Lebeshev (c)
Editing: Liudmila El'ian
Music: Eduard Artem'ev
Song Texts: Natal'ia Konchalovskaia
Art direction: Irina Shreter, Aleksandr Adabashian
Costume design: Alina Budnikova
Sound: R. Sobinov
Cast: Iurii Bogatyrev (Egor Shilov), Anatolii Solonitsyn (Sarychev), Sergei Shakurov (Zabelin), Aleksandr Porokhovshchikov (Nikolai Kungurov), Nikolai Pastukhov (Lipiagin), Aleksandr Kaidanovskii (Lemke), Nikita Mikhalkov (Brylov), Aleksandr Kaliagin (Vaniukin), Konstantin Raikin (Kadyrkul)
Running time: 97'

SKAZKA SKAZOK TALE OF TALES 1980
Director: Iurii Norshtein
Production: Soiuzmul'tfil'm
Screenplay: Liudmila Petrushevskaia, Iurii Norshtein
Photography: Igor' Skidan-Bosin
Editing: Natalia Abramova, Nadezhda Treshcheva
Music: Mikhail Meerovich
Art direction: Francesca Iarbusova
Sound: Boris Filchikov
Text: Aleksandr Kaliagin
Running time: 29'

MOSKVA SLEZAM NE VERIT MOSCOW DOES NOT BELIEVE IN TEARS 1980
Director: Vladimir Men'shov
Production: Mosfil'm
Screenplay: Valentin Chernykh
Photography: Igor' Slabnevich (c)
Editing: Elena Mikhailova
Music: Sergei Nikitin
Songs: Dmitrii Sukharev, Iurii Vizbor, Iurii Levitanskii
Art direction: Said Menial'shchikov
Costume design: Zhanna Melkonian
Sound: M. Bronshtein
Cast: Vera Alentova (Katia), Aleksei Batalov (Gosha), Irina Murav'eva (Liudmila), Aleksandr Fatiushin (Gurin),
Raisa Riazanova (Antonina, or Tonia), Boris Smorchkov (Nikolai), Viktor Ural'skii (Nikolai's Father), Valentina
Ushakova (Nikolai's Mother), Natal'ia Vavilova (Aleksandra), Oleg Tabakov (Volodia), Iurii Vasil'ev (Rudol'f, or
Rodion, Rachkov), Evgeniia Khanaeva (Rachkov's Mother), Zoia Fedorova (Hostel Porter), Liia Akhedzhakova (Club
Manager), Innokentii Smoktunovskii
Running time: 150'

MOI DRUG IVAN LAPSHIN MY FRIEND IVAN LAPSHIN 1984
Director: Aleksei German
Production: Lenfil'm
Screenplay: Eduard Volodarskii
Photography: Valerii Fedosov (b&w, c)
Editing: Leda Semenova
Music: Arkadii Gagulashvili
Art direction: Iurii Pugach
Costume design: Galina Deeva
Sound: Nikolai Astakhov
Cast: Andrei Boltnev (Ivan Lapshin), Nina Ruslanova (Natasha Adasova), Andrei Mironov, Aleksei Zharkov
(Okoshkin), Zinaida Adamovich, Aleksandr Filippenko, Iurii Kuznetsov, Valerii Filonov, Anatolii Slivnokov, Andrei
Dudarenko, Semen Farada, Nina Usatova,
Running time: 100'

IGLA THE NEEDLE 1988
Director: Rashid Nugmanov
Production: Kazakhfil'm
Screenplay: Aleksandr Baranov, Bakhyt Kilibaev
Photography: Murat Nugmanov (c)
Editing: Khadisha Urmurzina
Music: Viktor Tsoi
Art direction: Murat Musin
Costume design: Roza Iskakova
Sound: Andrei Vlaznev
Cast: Viktor Tsoi (Moro), Marina Smirnova (Dina), Petr Mamonov (Doctor), Aleksandr Bashirov (Spartak),
Arkhimed Iskakov, Aikhan Chataeva, Vladimir Danilenko, Grigorii Epshtein
Running time: 81'

KAVKAZSKII PLENNIK THE PRISONER OF THE MOUNTAINS 1996
Director: Sergei Bodrov Sr
Production: Karavan, BG Production, with participation of Roskomkino
Screenplay: Arif Aliev, Sergei Bodrov (based on an idea by Boris Giller)
Photography: Pavel Lebeshev (c)
Editing: Ol'ga Grinshpun, Vera Kruglova, Alan Baril
Music: Leonid Desiatnikov
Art direction: Valerii Kostrin
Costume design: Vera Romanova
Sound: Ekaterina Popova-Evans
Cast: Oleg Men'shikov (Sasha Kostylin), Sergei Bodrov Jr (Vania Zhilin), Susanna Mekhralieva (Dina), Djemal Sikharulidze (Abdul-Murat), Aleksandr Bureev (Hasan), Valentina Fedotova (Zhilin's mother), Aleksei Zharkov (Maslov), Pavel Lebeshev
Running time: 100'

BRAT BROTHER 1997
Director: Aleksei Balabanov
Production: CTB (Sergei Selianov), with Goskino and Gor'kii Film Studio
Screenplay: Aleksei Balabanov
Photography: Sergei Astakhov (c)
Editing: Marina Lipartiia
Music: Viacheslav Butusov
Art direction: Vladimir Kartashov
Costume design: Nadezhda Vasil'eva
Sound: Maksim Belovolov
Cast: Sergei Bodrov Jr (Danila Bagrov), Viktor Sukhorukov (Viktor, Danila's brother), Svetlana Pis'michenko (Sveta), Mariia Zhukova (Kat), Sergei Murzin (Kruglyi), Iurii Kuznetsov (Hoffmann), Irina Rakshina (Zina), Anatolii Zhuravvlev (Bandit), Igor' Shibanov (Militiaman), Andrei Fedortsov (Stepa), Viacheslav Butusov (Butusov), Sergei Chigrakov (Chizh), and Sergei Debizhev, Nastia Poleva, Natalia Pivovarova
Running time: 96'

RUSSKII KOVCHEG RUSSIAN ARK 2002
Director: Aleksandr Sokurov
Production: Hermitage Bridge (Ermitazhnyi most), State Hermitage Museum, Ministry of Culture of the RF, Egoli Tossell Film AG, Koppfilm GmbH (Germany), Saint Petersburg Government, Kino-Partner, For a-Film M, Sergei Astakhov Agency
Screenplay: Aleksandr Sokurov, Boris Khaimskii, Anatolii Nikiforov
Photography: Tilman Buettner (c)
Choreography: Gali Abaidulov
Music: Symphony Orchestra conducted by Valerii Gergiev
Art direction: Elena Zhukova, Natal'ia Kochergina
Costume design: Lidiia Kriukova, Tamara Seferian, Mariia Grishanova
Sound: Vladimir Persov, Sergei Moshkov
Cast: Sergei Dreiden [Sergei Dontsov] (Custine), Leonid Mozgovoi (Spy), Maksim Sergeev (Peter the Great), Mariia Kuznetsova (Catherine the Great), Natal'ia Nikulenko (Catherine I), Anna Aleksakhina (Aleksandra Fedorovna), Vladimir Baranov (Nikolai II); Directors of the Hermitage: Mikhail Piotrovskii (himself), Aleksandr Chaban (Boris Piotrovskii, his father), David Giorgobiani (Orbeli); as themselves: Alla Osipenko , Tamara Kurenkova, Lev Eliseev, Oleg Khmelnitskii
Running time: 87'

DOM DURAKOV HOUSE OF FOOLS 2002

Director: Andrei Konchalovskii

Production: Persona, Luch, Hachette Premiere, Bac Films, with participation of the Ministry of Culture of the RF

Screenplay: Andrei Konchalovskii

Photography: Sergei Kozlov (c)

Editing: Ol'ga Grinshpun

Music: Eduard Artem'ev

Art direction: Liubov' Skorina

Costume design: Svetlana Vol'ter

Sound: Vladimir Orel, Evgenii Terekhovskii

Cast: Iuliia Vysotskaia (Zhanna), Bryan Adams (himself), Cecilia Thomsen (Lithianian sniper), Vladas Bagdonas (doctor), Sultan Islamov (Ahmed), Anatolii Adoskin (Fucue), Rasmi Dzhabrailov (Mahmud), Anatolii Zhuravlev (boxer), Marina Politseimako (Vika), Vladimir Fedorov (Karlusha), Elena Fomina (Lucie), Stanislav Varkki (Ali), Gevork Ovakimian (Goga), Ruslan Naurbiev (Chechen Commander Vakhid), Evgenii Mironov (officer)

Running time: 104'

BIBLIOGRAPHY

GENERAL WORKS

reference books

Arkus, L. (ed.) (2001) *Noveishaia istoriia otechestvennogo kino 1986–2000. Kinoslovar'*. 3 vols. St Petersburg: Seans.

_____ (ed.) (2002-5) *Noveishaia istoriia otechestvennogo kino 1986-2000. Kino i kontekst*. 4 vols. St Petersburg: Seans.

Dolmatovskaia, G. and I. Shilova (1978) *Who's Who in the Soviet cinema*. Moscow: Progress.

Iutkevich, S. (ed.) (1986) *Kinoslovar'*. Moskva: Sovietskaia Entsiklopediia.

Marshall, H. (1983) *Masters of the Soviet Cinema: Crippled Creative Biographies*. London: Routledge.

Miloserdova, N. (ed.) (1996) *Kino Rossii, novye imena, 1986–1995: Spravochnik*. Moscow: NII Kinoiskusstva.

Segida, M. (ed.) (1998) *Entsiklopediia Kino Kirilla i Mefodiia 1998*. CD-ROM. Moscow: Kirill i Mefodii.

_____ (1997) *Kinomaniia 97. Entsiklopediia Rossiiskogo kinoiskusstva*. CD-ROM. Moscow: Cominfo.

Taylor, R., N. Wood, J. Graffy and D. Iordanova (eds) (2000) *The BFI Companion to Eastern European and Russian Cinema*. London: British Film Institute.

Zemlianukhin, S. and M. Segida (1996) *Domashniaia sinemateka: otechestvennoe kino 1918–1996*. Moscow: Dubl' D.

_____ (2001) *Fil'my Rossii. Igrovoe kino. 1995–2000*. Moscow: Dubl' D.

_____ (2004) *Fil'my Rossii. Igrovoe kino. TV. Video. 1992–2003*. Moscow: Dubl' D.

on russian and soviet cinema

Attwood, L. (ed.) (1993) *Red Women on the Silver Screen: Soviet Women and Cinema from the Beginning to the End of the Communist Era*. London: Pandora.

Beardow, F. (1991) 'Soviet cinema, past, present and future', *Rusistika*, 3, 19–25.

_____ (1993) 'Soviet cinema: coming to terms with the past', *Rusistika*, 7, 31–6 and 8, 2–18.

_____ (1994/95) 'Soviet cinema: women – icons or individuals?', *Rusistika*, 9, 22–42 and 10, 2–13 and 11, 35–42.

_____ (1997) 'Soviet cinema – war revisited', *Rusistika*, 15, 19–34 and 16, 8–21.

Beumers, B. (2000a) 'Myth-making and myth-taking: Lost Ideals and the War in Contemporary Russian Cinema', *Canadian Slavonic Papers*, 42, 1–2, 171–89.

_____ (2000b) 'Father Frost on 31 December: Christmas and New Year in Soviet and Russian Cinema', in Mark Connelly (ed.) *Christmas in the Movies*. London: I. B. Tauris, 185–209.

_____ (2003) 'Soviet and Russian Blockbusters: A question of genre?', *Slavic Review*, 62, 3, 441–54.

_____ (ed.) (2007–) *Studies in Russian and Soviet Cinema* (journal). Bristol: Intellect.

Beumers, B. and V. Padunov (eds) *KinoKultura*, online journal at www.kinokultura.com.

Eagle, H. (ed.) (1981) *Russian Formalist Film Theory*. Ann Arbor: Michigan Slavic Publications.

Engel, C. (ed.) (1999) *Geschichte des sowjetischen und russischen Films*. Stuttgart und Weimar: Metzler.

Eikhenbaum, B. (ed.) (1927) *Poetika kino*. Moscow, Leningrad: Kinopechat'.

Fomin, V. (2001) *Pravda skazki. Kino i traditsii fol'klora*. Moscow: Materik.

Gerould, D. (1991) 'Russian Formalist Theories of Melodrama', in Marcia Landy (ed.) *Imitations of Life: A Reader on Film & Television Melodrama*. Detroit: Wayne State University Press.

Gillespie, D. (2003) *Russian Cinema*. New York: Longman.

Golovskoy, V. and J. Rimberg (1986) *Behind the Soviet Screen*. Ann Arbor: Ardis.

Horton, A. (1993) *Inside Soviet Film Satire*. Cambridge: Cambridge University Press.

Hutchings, S. and A. Vernitski (eds) (2005) *Russian and Soviet Film Adaptations of Literature, 1900–2001: Screening the Word*. London: Routledge.

Iuren'ev, R. (1964) *Sovetskaia kinokomediia*. Moscow: Nauka.

Kenez, P. (1992) *Cinema and Soviet Society, 1917–1953*. Cambridge: Cambridge University Press.

Lawton, A. (1992) *The Red Screen: Politics, Society, Art in Soviet Cinema*. London and New York: Routledge.

Leyda, J. (1960) *Kino: A History of the Russian and Soviet Film*. Princeton: Princeton University Press.

Rimberg, J. (1973) *The Motion Picture in the Soviet Union, 1918–1952: A Sociological Analysis*. New York: Arno Press.

Shlapentokh, D. and V. (1993) *Soviet Cinematography, 1918–1991*. New York: Aldine de Gruyter.

Stites, R. (1992) *Russian Popular Culture: Entertainment and Society since 1900*. Cambridge: Cambridge University Press.

Taylor, R. (1979a) *Film Propaganda: Soviet Russia and Nazi Germany*. London: Croom Helm; republished in 1998 by

I. B.Tauris.

____ (1979b) *The Politics of the Soviet Cinema, 1917–1929*. Cambridge: Cambridge University Press.

____ (ed.) (1982) *The Poetics of Cinema: Russian Poetics in Translation, 9*. Oxford: RPT Publications.

Taylor, R. and I. Christie (eds) (1988) *The Film Factory: Russian and Soviet Cinema in Documents 1896–1939*. London and New York: Routledge.

____ (eds) (1991) *Inside the Film Factory: New Approaches to Russian and Soviet Cinema*. London and New York: Routledge.

Youngblood, D. (2007) *Russian War Films: On the Cinema Front, 1914–2005*. Lawrence: University of Kansas Press.

Zorkaya, N. (1991) *The Illustrated History of the Soviet Cinema*. New York: Hippocrene Books.

soviet and russian cultural studies

Balina, M., E. Dobrenko and Iu. Murashov (eds) (2002) *Sovetskoe bogatstvo: Stat'i o kul'ture, literature i kino*. St Petersburg: Akademicheskii proekt.

Barker, A. M. (ed.) (1999) *Consuming Russia: Popular Culture, Sex, and Society since Gorbachev*. Durham: Duke University Press.

Berry, E. E. and A. Miller-Pogacar (eds) (1995) *Re-Entering the Sign: Articulating New Russian Culture*. Ann Arbor: University of Michigan Press.

Beumers, B. (2005) *Popular Culture Russia!* Santa Barbara: ABC Clio.

Boym, S. (1994) *Common Places: Mythologies of Everyday Life in Russia*. Cambridge, MA and London: Harvard University Press.

____ (2001) *The Future of Nostalgia*. New York: Basic Books.

Clark, K. (1981) *The Soviet Novel: History as Ritual*. Chicago: Chicago University Press.

Condee, N. (ed.) (1995) *Soviet Hieroglyphics: Visual Culture in Late Twentieth-Century Russia*. London: British Film Institute/Bloomington, IN: Indiana University Press.

Graffy, J. and G. Hosking (eds) (1989) *Culture and the Media in the USSR Today*. London: Macmillan.

Günther, H. and E. Dobrenko (eds) (2000) *Sotsrealisticheskii kanon*. St Petersburg: Akademicheskii proekt.

Hutchings, S. (2004) *Russian Literary Culture and the Camera Age: The Word as Image*. London: RoutledgeCurzon.

James, V. (1973) *Soviet Socialist Realism: Origins and Theory*. New York: St Martin's Press.

Kelly, C. and D. Shepherd (1998) *Russian Cultural Studies*. Oxford: Oxford University Press.

Lahusen, T. (ed.) (1997) *Socialist Realism without Shores*. Durham, NC: Duke University Press.

Lahusen, T. and G. Kuperman (eds) (1993) *Late Soviet Culture: From Perestroika to Novostroika*. Durham, NC: Duke University Press.

Miller, F. (1990) *Folklore for Stalin*. Columbia: Columbia University Press.

Robin, R. (1992) *Socialist Realism*. Stanford: Stanford University Press.

Stites, R. (1992) *Russian Popular Culture*. Cambridge: Cambridge University Press.

van Geldern, J. and R. Stites (eds) (1995) *Mass Soviet Culture in Soviet Russia*. Bloomington, IN: Indiana University Press.

CHRONOLOGICAL

pre-revolutionary cinema

Batalin, V. (2002) *Kinokhronika v Rossii, 1896–1916gg.: Opis' kinos"emok, khraniashchikhsia v RGAKFD*. Moscow: Olma-Press.

Cherchi Usai, P., L. Codelli, C. Montanaro and D. Robinson (eds) (1989) *Silent Witnesses: Russian Films, 1908–1919*. London: British Film Institute.

Ginzburg, S. (1963) *Kinematografiia dorevolutsionnoi Rossii*. Moscow: Iskusstvo.

Ivanova, V., V. Myl'nikova, S. Skovorodnikova, Iu. Tsivian and R. Iangirov (eds) (2002) *Velikii Kinemo: Katalog sokhran-ivshikhsia igrovykh fil'mov Rossii, 1908–1919*. Moscow: Novoe literaturnoe obozrenie.

Morley, R. (2003) 'Gender Relations in the Films of Evgenii Bauer', *Slavonic and East European Review*, 81, 1, 32–69.

Sobolev, R. (1961) *Liudi i fil' my russkogo dorevoliutsionnogo kino*. Moscow: Iskusstvo.

Tsivian, Yu. (1994) *Early Cinema in Russia and its Cultural Reception*. Chicago and London: University of Chicago Press.

____ (ed.) (2005) *Lines of Resistance: Dziga Vertov and the Twenties*. Pordenone: cat. [need fuller ref]

Vishnevskii, V., V Mikhailov, V. Fomin and A. Deriabin (eds) (2004) *Letopis' Rossiiskogo kino, 1863–1929*. Moscow: Materik.

Youngblood, D. (1999) *The Magic Mirror: Moviemaking in Russia, 1908–1918*. Madison, WI and London: University of Wisconsin Press.

early soviet cinema

Aumont, J. (1987) *Montage Eisenstein*. London: British Film Institute/Bloomington, IN: Indiana University Press.

Barna, Y. (1973) *Eisenstein*. London: Secker & Warburg.

Beumers, B. (2000) 'Eisenstein: *The Battleship Potemkin*', in J. Forbes and S. Street (eds) *European Cinema*. London: Palgrave, 53–64.

Bordwell, D. (1972) 'The Idea of Montage in Soviet Art and Film', *Cinema Journal*, 11, 2, 9–17.

____ (1993) *The Cinema of Eisenstein*. Cambridge, MA and London: Harvard University Press.

Brooks, Jeffrey (1991) 'Russian Cinema and Public Discourse, 1900–1930', *Historical Journal of Film, Radio and Television*, 11, 2, 141–8.

Bulgakowa, O. (2001) *Sergei Eisenstein: A Biography*. Berlin and San Francisco: Potemkin Press.

Christie, I. and R. Taylor (eds) (1993) *Eisenstein Rediscovered*. London: Routledge.

Eisenstein, S. (1947) *Film Sense*. San Diego, London: Harcourt Brace.

____ (1949) *Film Form*. San Diego, London: Harcourt Brace.

____ (1964–71) *Izbrannye proizvedeniia*, 6 vols. Moscow: Iskusstvo.

____ (1987) *Nonindifferent Nature*. Cambridge: Cambridge University Press.

Gillespie, D. (2000) *Early Soviet Cinema: Innovation, Ideology and Propaganda*. London: Wallflower Press.

Goodwin, J. (1993) *Eisenstein, Cinema & History*. Urbana and Chicago, IL: University of Illinois Press.

Graffy, J. (2001) *Bed and Sofa*. London: I. B. Tauris.

Iuren'ev, R. (1985) *Sergei Eizenshtein. Zamysli. Fil'my. Metod. Chast' pervaia: 1898–1929*. Moscow: Iskusstvo.

Kenez, P. (1985) *The Birth of the Propaganda State: Soviet Methods of Mass Mobilization, 1917–1929*. New York: Cambridge University Press.

____ (1992) *Cinema and Soviet Society, 1917–1953*. New York: Cambridge University Press.

Kepley Jr, V. (1979) 'Foreign Films on Soviet Screens, 1922–1931', *Quarterly Review of Film Studies*, 4, 4, 429–42.

____ (1983) 'The Workers' International Relief and the Cinema of the Left, 1921–1935', *Cinema Journal*, 23, 1, 7–23.

____ (1985) 'The Origins of Soviet Cinema: A Study in Industry Development', *Quarterly Review of Film Studies*, 4, 22–38.

____ (1987) 'Building a National Cinema: Soviet Film Education, 1918–1934', *WideAngle*, 9, 3, 4–20.

____ (2003) *The End of St Petersburg*. London: I. B. Tauris.

Leyda, J. and Z. Voynow (eds) (1985) *Eisenstein at Work*. London: Methuen.

Listov, V. (1991) 'Early Soviet Cinema: the spontaneous and the planned, 1917–1924', *Historical Journal of Film, Radio and Television*, 11, 2, 121–7.

____ (1995) *Rossiia. Revoliutsiia. Kinematograf: K 100-letiiu mirovogo kino*. Moscow: Materik.

Listov, V. and E. Khokhlova (eds) (1996) *Istoriia otechestvennogo kino: dokumenty, memuary, pis'ma*. vyp. 1. Moscow: Materik.

Mal'kova, L. (2002) *Sovremennost' kak istoriia: Realizatsiia mifa v dokumental'nom kino*. Moscow: Materik.

Mayne, J. (1989) *Kino and the Woman Question: Feminism and Soviet Silent Cinema*. Columbus: Ohio State University Press.

Michelson, A. (ed.) (1984) *Kino-eye: The Writings of Dziga Vertov*. Berkeley: University of California Press.

Nesbet, A. (2003) *Savage Junctures: Sergei Eisenstein and the Shape of Thinking*. London: I. B. Tauris.

Petric, V. (1987) *Constructivism in Film: The Man with the Movie Camera*. Cambridge: Cambridge University Press.

Reeder, R. (1989) 'Agit-Prop Art: Posters, Puppets, Propaganda and Eisenstein's *Strike*', *Russian Literature Triquarterly*, 22, 255–78.

Roberts, G. (1999) *Forward Soviet: History and Non Fiction Film in the USSR*. London: I. B. Tauris.

____ (2000) *The Man with the Movie Camera*. London: I. B. Tauris.

Sargeant, A. (2001) *Vsevolod Pudovkin: Classic Films of the Soviet Avant-Garde*. London: I. B. Tauris.

Seton, M. (1978) *Sergei M. Eisenstein: A Biography*. London: Dennis Dobson.

Taylor, R. (ed.) (1998) *The Eisenstein Reader*. London: British Film Institute.

____ (2000) *The Battleship Potemkin*. London: I. B. Tauris.

____ (2002) *October*. London: British Film Institute.

Yampolsky, M. (1991) 'Reality at Second Hand', *Historical Journal of Film, Radio and Television*, 11, 2, 161–71.

Yangirov, R. (1991) 'Soviet Cinema in the Twenties: National Alternatives', *Historical Journal of Film, Radio and Television*, 11, 2, 129–39.

Youngblood, D. (1991) *Soviet Cinema in the Silent Era, 1918–1935*, Austin: University of Texas Press.

____ (1992) *Movies for the Masses: Popular Cinema and Soviet Society in the 1920s*. Cambridge: Cambridge University

Press.

_____ (1991) '"History" on Film: The Historical Melodrama in Early Soviet Cinema', *Historical Journal of Film, Radio and Television*, 11, 2, 173–84.

Zorkaia, N. and A. Vartanov (eds) (1991) *Ekrannye iskusstva i literatura: nemoe kino*. Moscow: Nauka.

cinema under stalin

Aleksandrov, G. (1975) *Gody poiskov i truda*. Moscow: Biuro propagandy sovetskogo kinoiskusstva.

_____ (1976) *Epokha i kino*. Moscow: Izdatel'stvo politicheskoi literatury.

Anderson, T. (1995) 'Why Stalinist Musicals?', *Discourse*, 17, 3, 38–48.

Chernenko, M. (2001) *Krasnaia zvezda, zheltaia zvezda*. Vinnitsa: Globus Press.

Crofts, S. (1977) 'Ideology and Form: Soviet Socialist Realism and *Chapayev*', *Essays in Poetics*, 2, 1, 43–57.

Dobrenko, E. (1995) 'Muzyka vmesto sumbura: Narodnost' kak problema muzykal'noi kinokomedii stalinskoi epokhi', *Revue des Études slaves*, 67, 2–3, 407–33.

_____ (2001) 'The Russia We Acquired: Russian Classics, the Stalinist Cinema, and the Past from the Revolutionary Perspective', *Russian Studies in Literature*, 37, 4, 61–91.

Dzhulai, L. (2001) *Dokumental'nyi illiuzion: Otechestvennyi kinodokumental'izm. Opyty sotsial'nogo tvorchestva*. Moscow: Materik.

Ferro, M. (1976) 'The Fiction Film and Historical Analysis', in Paul Smith (ed.) *The Historian and Film*. Cambridge: Cambridge University Press, 80–95.

Frolov, I. (1976) *Grigorii Aleksandrov*. Moscow: Iskusstvo.

Haynes, J. (2003) *New Soviet Man: Gender and Masculinity in Stalinist Soviet Cinema*. Manchester and New York: Manchester University Press.

Hutchings, S. (2002) 'Tchapaiev: l'homme de tous les temps, l'homme de tous les medias', *La Revue Russe*, 21, 9–16.

Iuren'ev, R. (1997) *Sovetskoe kinoiskusstvo tridtsatykh godov*. Moscow: VGIK.

Kenez, P. (1995) 'Black and White: The War on Film', in R. Stites (ed.) *Culture and Entertainment in Wartime Russia*. Bloomington, IN: Indiana University Press.

_____ (1998) 'Jewish Themes in Stalinist Films', *Journal of Popular Culture*, 31, 4, 159–69.

Kepley Jr, V. (1986) '*Earth*', in *In the Service of the State: The Cinema of Alexander Dovzhenko*, Madison: University of Wisconsin Press, 75–84.

_____ (1994) 'Dovzhenko and montage: issues of style and narration in the silent films', *Journal of Ukrainian Studies*, 19, 1, 29–44.

Laurent, N. (2000) *L'oeil du Kremlin: cinema et censure en URSS sous Staline*. Toulouse: Privat.

Liber, G. (2002) *Alexander Dovzhenko: A Life in Soviet Film*. London: British Film Institute.

Mamatova, L. (1995) *Kino: politika i liudi: 30-ye gody*. Moscow: Materik.

Margolit, E. and V. Shmyrov (1995) *iz"iatoe kino*. Moscow: Dubl' D.

Mar'iamov, G. (1992) *Kremlevskii tsenzor: Stalin smotrit kino*. Moscow: Kinotsentr.

Neuberger, J. (2003) *Ivan the Terrible*. London: I. B. Tauris.

Prokhorov, A. (2002) 'Soviet Family Melodrama of the 1940s and 1950s: From *Wait for Me* to *The Cranes are Flying*', in L. McReynolds and J. Neuberger (eds) *Imitations of Life: Two Centuries of Melodrama in Russia*. Durham, NC: Duke University Press, 208–31.

Riley, J. (2005) *Dmitri Shostakovich*. London: I. B. Tauris.

Schmulevitch, É. (1996) *Réalisme socialiste et cinéma: Le cinéma stalinien (1928–1941)*. Paris: Editions L'Harmattan.

Taylor, R. (1983) 'A "Cinema for the Millions": Soviet Socialist Realism and the Problem of Film Comedy', *Journal of Contemporary History*, 18, 439–61.

_____ (2000) '"But eastward, look, the land is brighter": Towards a Topography of Utopia in the Stalinist Musical', in D. Holmes and A. Smith (eds) *100 Years of European Cinema: Entertainment or Ideology?* Manchester: Manchester University Press, 11–26.

Taylor, R. and D. Spring (eds) (1993) *Stalinism and Soviet Cinema*. London: Routledge.

Tsivian, Y. (2001) *Ivan the Terrible*. London: British Film Institute.

Widdis, E. (2003) *Visions of a New Land: Soviet Film from the Revolution to the Second World War*. New Haven: Yale University Press.

Widdis, E. (2005) *Alexander Medvedkin*. London: I. B. Tauris.

Youngblood, D. (1991) 'The Fate of Soviet Popular Cinema During the Stalin Revolution', *The Russian Review*, 50, 148–62.

post-war cinema

Anninskii, L. (1991) *Shestidesiatniki i my*. Moscow: Souiz kinematografistov SSSR and Kinotsentr.

Beumers, B. (2005) *Nikita Mikhalkov*. London: I. B. Tauris.

Binder, E. and C. Engel (eds) (2002) *Eisensteins Erben: Der sowjetische Film von Tauwetter zur Perestrojka (1953–1991)*. Innsbruck: Innsbrucker Beiträge zur Kulturwissenschaft.

Bird, R. (2004) *Andrei Rublev*. London: British Film Institute.

Braginskii, E. and E. Riazanov (2000) *Tikhie omuty*. Moscow: Vagrius.

Drobashenko, S. (ed.) (1984) *Sovetskoe kino 70-e gody*. Moscow: Iskusstvo.

Dymshits, N. and A. Troshin (eds) (1990) *Iz proshlogo v budushchee: Proverka na dorogakh*. Moscow: VNII Kinoiskusstva.

Fomin, V. (1976) *Peresechenie parallel'nykh: Lotianu, Il'enko, Ioseliani, Mansurov, Okeev, Panfilov, Shukshin*. Moscow: Iskusstvo.

____ (1992) *Polka*. Moscow: NII Kinoiskusstva.

____ (1993) *Zapreshchenye fil'my*. Moskva: NII Kinoiskusstva.

____ (1996) *Kino i vlast': sovetskoe kino, 1965–1985 gody: dokumenty, svidetel'syva, razmyshleniya*. Moscow: Materik.

____ (ed.) (1998) *Kinematograf ottepeli: Dokumenty i svidetel'stva*. Moskva: Materik.

Gillespie, D. (2003) 'The Sounds of Music: Soundtrack and Song in Soviet Film', *Slavic Review*, 62, 3, 473–90.

Goulding, D. J. (ed.) (1989) *Post New Wave Cinema in the Soviet Union and Eastern Europe*. Bloomington, IN: Indiana University Press.

Gromov, E. (1989) *Komedii i ne tol'ko komedii*. Moscow: Soiuz kinematografistov SSSR.

Hutchings, S. (2000) 'Word and Image in El'dar Riazanov's *S legkym parom* or The Irony of (Cinematic) Fate', *Essays in Poetics*, 25, 236–55.

Iskantseva, T. (1997) *Neob"iatnyi Riazanov*. Moscow: Vagrius.

Johnson, V. T. and G. Petrie (1994) *The Films of Andrei Tarkovsky: A Visual Fugue*. Bloomington: Indiana University Press.

Kats, B. (1988) *Prostye istiny kinomuzyki*. Leningrad: Sovetskii kompozitor.

Kozintsev, G. (1977) *King Lear: The Space of Tragedy – Diary of a Film Director*. London: Heinemann.

Kudriavtsev, S. (1998) *Svoe kino*. Moscow: Dubl' D.

Le Fanu, M. (1987) *The Cinema of Andrei Tarkovsky*. London: British Film Institute.

Lebedev, N. (1994) 'Fenomen 'grustnoi' komedii v otechestvennom kino', *Kinovedcheskie zapiski*, 22, 133–51.

MacFadyen, D. (2003) *The Sad Comedy of El'dar Riazanov*. Montreal and London: McGill-Queen's University Press.

Mamatova, L. (ed.) (1983) *Aktual'nye problemy sovetskogo kino nachala 80-kh godov*. Moscow: NII Kinoiskusstva.

Martin, M. (1993) *Cinéma soviétique: de Khrouchtev à Gorbatchev*. Lausanne: L'Age d'homme.

Prokhorov, A. (2003) 'Cinema of Attraction versus Narrative Cinema: Leonid Gaidai's and El'dar Riazanov's Satires of the 1960s', *Slavic Review*, 62, 3, 455–72.

Quart, B. (1988) 'Between Mysticism and Materialism: The Films of Larisa Shepitko', *Cineaste*, 16, 3, 4–11.

Riazanov, È. (1977) *Grustnoe litso komedii*. Moscow: Molodaia gvardiia.

____ (2000) *Nepodvedennye itog*. Moscow: Vagrius.

Rifkin, B. (1992) 'The Reinterpretation of History in German's Film *My Friend Ivan Lapshin*: Shifts in Center and Periphery', *Slavic Review*, 51, 3, 431–47.

Synessiou, N. (2001) *Mirror*. London: I. B. Tauris.

Tarkovskii, A. (1994) *Time Within Time: The Diaries, 1970–1986*. London: Faber.

____ (1989) *Sculpting in Time: Reflections on the Cinema*. London: Faber.

Taubman, J. (1993) 'The Cinema of Kira Muratova', *Russian Review* 52, 367–81.

____ (2005) *Kira Muratova*. London: I. B. Tauris.

Troianovskii, V. (ed.) (1996) *Kinematograf ottepeli: Kniga pervaia*. Moscow: Materik.

Turovskaya, M. (1989) *Tarkovsky: Cinema as Poetry*. London: Faber.

Vail', P. (1999) ''60-e: sovetskoe kino i stil' epokhi. Razmyshleniia i kommentarii', in A. Troshin (ed.) *Close-Up: Istoriko-teoreticheskii seminar vo VGIKe: Lektsii 1996-1998 gody*. Moscow: VGIK, 230–3.

Vlasova, M. (ed.) (1997) *Sovetskoe kino semidesiatykh – pervoi poloviny vos'midesiatykh godov: Uchebnoe posobie*. Moscow: VGIK.

Woll J. (2000) *Real Images: Soviet Cinema of the Thaw*. London: I. B. Tauris.

____ (2003) *The Cranes are Flying*. London: I. B. Tauris.

Wood, T. (2001) 'Time Unfrozen: The films of Aleksei German', *New Left Review*, 7.

Zorkaia, N. (1974) *El'dar Riazanov: Sborni*. Moscow: Iskusstvo.

____ (2001) 'Gosudarstvennyi kinematograf 1970-kh kak podsistema kul'tury: Put' fil'ma ot tvortsa k zriteliu i dalee', in N. Zorkaia (ed.) *Khudozhestvennaia zhizn' Rossii 1970-kh godov kak sistemnoe tseloe*. St Petersburg: Aleteia, 178–92.

glasnost' and perstroika

Beardow, F. (2003) *Little Vera*. London: I. B. Tauris.

Boym, S. (1995) 'Post-Soviet Cinematic Nostalgia: From 'Elite Cinema' to Soap Opera', *Discourse*, 17, 3, 75–84.

Brashinsky, M. and A. Horton (eds) (1994) *Russian Critics on the Cinema of Glasnost'*. Cambridge: Cambridge University Press.

Budiak, L. (1990–91) 'We Cannot Live This Way: Reflections on the State of Contemporary Soviet Film', *Film Quarterly*, 44, 2, 28–33.

Condee, N. (1997) 'The Dream of Well-Being', *Sight and Sound*, 12, 18–21.

Condee, N. and V. Padunov (1987) 'The Outposts of Official Art: Recharting Soviet Cultural History', *Framework*, 34, 59–107.

Eagle, H. (1989) 'Soviet Cinema Today: On the Semantic Potential of a Discredited Canon', *Michigan Quarterly Review*, 28, 4, 743–60.

Faraday, G. (2000) *Revolt of the Filmmakers: The Struggle for Artistic Autonomy and the Fall of the Soviet Film Industry*. University Park, PA: Pennsylvania State University Press.

Galichenko, N. (1991) *Glasnost: Soviet Cinema Responds*. Austin: University of Texas Press.

Graham, S. (2000) '*Chernukha* and Russian Film', *Studies in Slavic Culture*, 1, 9–27.

Horton, A. and M. Brashinsky (1992) *The Zero Hour: Glasnost and Soviet Cinema in Transition*. Princeton: Princeton University Press.

Kepley Jr, V. (ed) (1990) '*Contemporary Soviet Cinema*', *WideAngle*, 12, 4.

Larsen, S. (1999) 'In Search of an Audience: The New Russian Cinema of Reconciliation', in A. Barker (ed) *Consuming Russia: Popular Culture, Sex, and Society since Gorbachev*. Durham, NC: Duke University Press, 192–216.

_____ (2000) 'Melodramatic Masculinity, National Identity, and the Stalinist Past in Postsoviet Cinema', *Studies in 20th Century Literature*, 24, 1, 85–120.

Lawton, A. (1992) *Kinoglasnost: Soviet Cinema in Our Time*. Cambridge: Cambridge University Press.

Menashe, L. (2001) 'Moscow Believes in Tears: The Problems (and Promise?) of Russian Cinema in the Transition Period', *Cineaste*, 26, 3, 1017.

Plakhov, A. (1989) 'Soviet Cinema into the 90s', *Sight and Sound*, 58, 2, 80–5.

Ratchford, M. (1992) 'Post-*Glasnost* Shock in the Russian Film Industry: The Euphoria is Past. Now Comes the Tough Part', *New Outlook*, 3, 1–2, 102–14.

Stishova, Y. (2001) *Territoriia kino: Postsovetskoe desiatiletie*. Moscow: Pomatur.

Widdis, E. (1996/67) 'An Unmappable System: The Collapse of Public Space in Late Soviet Film', *Film Criticism*, 21, 2, 8–24.

Woll, J. and D. Youngblood (2001) *Repentance*. London: I. B. Tauris.

Zhabskii, M. (ed.) (1997) *Ispytanie konkurentsiei: Otechestvennoe kino i novoe pokolenie zritelei*. Moscow: VNII Kinoiskusstva.

post-soviet cinema

Beumers, B. (1999a) 'Cinemarket, or the Russian Film Industry in "Mission Possible"', *Europe-Asia Studies*, 51, 5, 871–96.

_____ (ed.) (1999b) *Russia on Reels: The Russian Idea in Post-Soviet Cinema*. London: I. B. Tauris.

_____ (2000a) 'Mikhalkov: The Barber of Siberia', in J. Forbes and S. Street (eds) *European Cinema*, London: Palgrave, 195–206.

_____ (2000b) *Burnt by the Sun*. London: I. B. Tauris.

_____ (2003) 'And the Ship sails on…': Sokurov's Ghostly Ark of Russia's Past, *Rossica*, 9, 56–9.

_____ (2004) 'Tarkovsky's Return or Zvyagintsev's Vozvrashchenie', *Rossica*, 14, 60–3.

Gillespie, D. (1996) 'Identity and the past in recent Russian cinema', in W. Everett (ed.) *European Identity in Cinema*. Exeter: University Press, 53–60.

_____ (2005) 'Confronting Imperialism: The Ambivalence of War in Post-Soviet Film', in S. Webber (ed.) *Military and Society in Post-Soviet Russia*. Manchester: Manchester University Press.

Gillespie, D. and N. Zhuravkina (1996a) 'Nikita Mikhalkov's Utomlennye solntsem', *Rusistika*, 13, 58–61.

_____ (1996b) 'Sergei Bodrov's *Prisoner in the Caucasus*', *Rusistika*, 14, 56–9.

Larsen, S. (2003) 'National Identity, Cultural Authority and the Post-Soviet Blockbuster: Nikita Mikhalkov and Aleksei Balabanov', *Slavic Review*, 62, 3, 491–511.

Lawton, A. (2004) *Imaging Russia: Film and Facts*. Washington: New Academia.

Prokhorova, E. (2003) 'Can the Meeting Place be Changed? Crime and Identity Discourse n Russian Television Series of the 1990s', *Slavic Review*, 62, 3, 512–24.

ANIMATION

Asenin, S. (ed.) (1983) *Mudrost' vymysla*. Moscow: Iskusstvo.

_____ (1986) *Mir mul'tfil'ma*. Moscow: Iskusstvo.

Babichenko, D. (ed.) (1972) *Mastera sovetskoi mul'tiplikatsii*. Moscow: Iskusstvo.

Bendazzi G. (1994) *Cartoons: One Hundred Years of Cinema Animation*. London: John Libbey/Bloomington, IN: Indiana University Press.

Ivanov-Vano, I. (1950) *Risovannyi fil'm*. Moscow: Goskinoizdat.

_____ (1979) *Kadr za kadrom*. Moscow: Iskusstvo.

Kitson, C. (2005) *Yuri Norstein and Tale of Tales: An Animator's Journey*. Eastleigh: John Libbey/Bloomington, IN: Indiana University Press.

Krivulia, N. (2002) *Labirinty animatsii*. Moscow: Graal'.

_____ (2006) *Ozhivshie teni volshbnogo fonaria*. Moscow: Ametist.

MacFadyen, D. (2005) *Yellow Crocodiles and Blue Oranges*. Montreal and Kingston: McGill-Queens University Press.

Norshtein, I. and F. Iarbusova (2005) *Skazka skazok*. Moscow: Krasnaia ploshchad, exhibition catalogue (Pushkin Museum 5 April–29 May).

Venzher, N. (ed.) (1990) *Sotvorenie fil'ma*. Moscow: Soiuz kinematografistov SSSR.

Wells, P. (1999) *Understanding Animation*. London: Routledge.

CENTRAL ASIAN CINEMA

Abikeeva, G. (2001) *Kino Tsentral'noi Azii*. Almaty: IREX.

_____ (2003) *The Heart of the World: Films from Central Asia*. Almaty: Tengizchevroil, Kazakhfilm, SKIF, Kino Firm.

Dömez-Colin, Gönül (1994) 'Kazakh New Wave: Post Perestroika, Post Soviet Union', *Blimp: Film Magazine*, 30, 12–15.

Lemkin, M. (1999) 'Novye fil'my iz Kazakhstana i Kirgizii', *Novoe russkoe slovo*, 26 July, 17.

Nogerbek, B. (2004) 'Demythologizing and Reconstructing National Space in the Kazakh "New Wave"', *KinoKultura* [www.kinokultura.com] 3.

Nogerbek, B. (1998) *Kino Kazakhstana*. Almaty: Natsional'nyi prodiuserskii tsentr.

Padunov, V. (2004) 'Stars Above Almaty: Kazakh Cinema Between 1998 and 2003', *KinoKultura* [www.kinokultura.com] 3.

Pruner, L. Z. (1992) 'The New Wave in Kazakh Cinema', *Slavic Review*, 51, 4, 791–801.

Radvanyi, J. (ed.) (1991) *Le cinéma d'Asie centrale sovietique*. Paris: Centre Georges Pompidou.

Smailova, T. (ed.) (2000) *Kino Kazakhstana: Kinospravochnik*. Almaty: Zhibek Zholy.

Waller, G. (1996) 'National Cinema and Film Culture in Kazakhstan', *Asian Cinema*, 8, 1, 39–49.

INDEX